C000049492

0133391428

THE BIGGIN HILL
WING – 1941

THE BIGGIN HILL WING – 1941

From Defence to Attack

Peter Caygill

WARWICKSHIRE LIBRARY & INFO SERVICE	
Bertrams	18.12.08
940.544	£19.99

Pen & Sword
AVIATION

First published in Great Britain in 2008 by
Pen & Sword Aviation
an imprint of
Pen & Sword Books Ltd
47 Church Street
Barnsley
South Yorkshire
S70 2AS

Copyright © Peter Caygill 2008

ISBN 978 1 84415 746 4

The right of Peter Caygill to be identified as Author of this Work has been
asserted by him in accordance with the Copyright,
Designs and Patents Act 1988.

A CIP catalogue record for this book is
available from the British Library

All rights reserved. No part of this book may be reproduced or transmitted in
any form or by any means, electronic or mechanical including photocopying,
recording or by any information storage and retrieval system, without
permission from the Publisher in writing.

Typeset in Sabon by
Phoenix Typesetting, Auldgirth, Dumfriesshire

Printed and bound in England by
Biddles Kings Lynn

Pen & Sword Books Ltd incorporates the Imprints of Pen & Sword Aviation,
Pen & Sword Maritime, Pen & Sword Military, Wharncliffe Local History,
Pen & Sword Select, Pen & Sword Military Classics and Leo Cooper.

For a complete list of Pen & Sword titles please contact
PEN & SWORD BOOKS LIMITED
47 Church Street, Barnsley, South Yorkshire, S70 2AS, England
E-mail: enquiries@pen-and-sword.co.uk
Website: www.pen-and-sword.co.uk

Contents

Introduction vi

Chapter One – Early Days 1

Chapter Two – A Change of Direction 7

Chapter Three – An Experienced Team 15

Chapter Four – Setting the Trend 23

Chapter Five – The Pace Quickens 35

Chapter Six – A Night Interlude 41

Chapter Seven – The Weapon is Forged 46

Chapter Eight – Ominous Skies 53

Chapter Nine – Maximum Effort 64

Chapter Ten – Battle of Attrition 85

Chapter Eleven – The Offensive Continues 105

Chapter Twelve – A New Adversary 119

Chapter Thirteen – A Change of Guard 129

Chapter Fourteen – Stalemate 139

Chapter Fifteen – The Final Reckoning 147

Envoi 161

Appendix One – Air Combat Claims of the
    Biggin Hill Wing – 1941 169

Appendix Two – Operational Aircraft Losses
    of Biggin Hill Squadrons – 1941 177

Appendix Three – Details of Selected Operations 181

Appendix Four – Escape and Evasion 183

Appendix Five – The Great Escape 189

Index 196

Introduction

In 1940 the RAF inflicted the first defeat on Germany's *Luftwaffe* during the Battle of Britain, a victory that was achieved by Churchill's 'Few' in the face of seemingly overwhelming odds. But without the defensive system that was put in place by Fighter Command's Commander-in-Chief, Air Marshal Sir Hugh Dowding, and the tactical genius of Air Vice-Marshal Keith Park, the No.11 Group commander, the outcome would have been very different. This did not stop Dowding and Park being removed from office after the battle had been won and replaced by Air Marshal Sir William Sholto Douglas and Air Vice-Marshal Trafford Leigh-Mallory who had very different ideas when it came to tactics. This change of leadership was to lead to a complete change of emphasis as the RAF looked to go onto the attack.

Flushed with the success of the previous year, 1941 saw Fighter Command move onto the offensive as it attempted to draw the fighters on the other side of the Channel into a battle of attrition. It was hoped that by putting large numbers of aircraft into the air in the form of several Wing formations the enemy would be decisively beaten and this strategy was implemented as soon as weather conditions allowed. The fighter airfields in the south of the country bore the brunt of the fighting with the squadrons based at Biggin Hill in Kent at the forefront of the air battles that raged over northern France.

During the Battle of Britain Biggin Hill had been the target of many raids and as a result it had suffered severely. Despite the damage and loss of life it had remained operational and for the public it came to epitomise the resolve that the whole country was feeling. With the daylight battles won the perfect posting for a fighter pilot was to Biggin Hill, not least because of its location close to London with its clubs and night life. Just as the best pilots seemed to be drawn there, the publicity that they attracted and their stature within society led to a constant stream of film stars attending the parties that were arranged at every opportunity.

This book looks at the activities of the Biggin Hill Wing in 1941 through the eyes of the pilots who fought high in the skies over the English Channel and northern France. At times the fighting was equally as intensive as it had been in 1940 and this was particularly true after the German invasion of the Soviet Union on 22 June when Fighter Command attempted to prevent further units being withdrawn to the Eastern Front. Although there were plenty of opportunities for pilots to make a name for themselves they were up against the cream of the *Luftwaffe* fighter force and many were to die before they could appreciate the harsh realities of the aerial war. The actions which took place are pieced together from pilots' combat reports and first-hand accounts and these paint a vivid picture of the battles that took place.

Also included is an evaluation of the political intrigue that led to the removal of Dowding and Park which shaped the events of 1941 and the concluding chapter is a detailed assessment of the strategy adopted by Sholto Douglas and Leigh-Mallory and questions its effectiveness. There are extensive appendices which list all combat claims and losses of the Biggin Hill Wing in 1941, together with the stories of Biggin Hill-based pilots who were involved in escape and evasion after being shot down over occupied Europe.

CHAPTER ONE

Early Days

The name Biggin Hill can be traced back to 1499 when it appears for the first time in a deed, although its origin is rather more obscure. It may have been derived from the name Bygge, or, more likely, it refers to its location and means 'the hill next to the farm or house'. With the coming of the 20th century Biggin Hill was home to around 500 people who lived either side of the Westerham Road where it was joined by Jail Lane, the junction of which was the location for the Black Horse Inn. The settlement was surrounded by farmland which included Biggin Hill Farm, after which it was named. The local area was made up of the villages of Cudham, Berry's Green and Aperfield. The latter is first mentioned around 1242 and was known originally as Apuldre which probably means 'the field with the apple trees.' In Tudor times it was owned by the Dacre family and subsequently by the Christys who built Aperfield Court. In 1898 this was bought as a country retreat by Frederick H. Dougal, an Irish Law Agent who lived in Wandsworth. Dougal was to have a big influence on the development of Biggin Hill.

Although he kept Aperfield Court and its associated parkland, he started to sell the local farmland as building plots and these continued to be sold after his death in 1904. Due to an almost total lack of planning restrictions, the properties that sprang up varied tremendously in their design and construction, and this development, together with similar expansion elsewhere, was to lead to the planning laws of today. Progress was relatively slow due to the lack of a railway and all building materials had to be transported from the nearest station which added considerably to the cost. Because of its location on the North Downs the provision of a railway was far from straightforward and despite two separate schemes in 1898 and 1929, no railway has ever been built to serve Biggin Hill.

By the beginning of the First World War most of the Aperfield estate had been sold for development but the land around Cudham Lodge to the north was still being farmed by John Westacott who rented it from Earl Stanhope of Chevening. This did not last for long, however, as the Royal Flying Corps was looking for a site to carry out wireless experiments and in 1916 the site that would eventually become one of the best known airfields in the country was finally chosen. It offered a wide open space, but more than that, its relatively high location, which was approximately 600 ft above sea level, kept it largely free from fog. There was also no electrical interference in the area which might cause trouble for the trials that were about to take place. Stanhope, who was himself an army officer, was more than happy to dispose of his 80 acre estate and 'Koonowla', a former childrens hospital that was close by on the Westerham to Bromley road, was requisitioned as an Officer's mess.

The erection of wooden huts, together with a canvas hangar, was completed in January 1917 and the first aircraft to arrive was an RE.7 flown by Lt Dickie who

1

was accompanied by Air Mechanic Chadwick. The rest of the personnel of the Wireless Testing Park arrived from Joyce Green near Dartford. This had proved to be a less than ideal location as the airfield was often beset by low-lying mist which made take-off and landing difficult. One pilot had even had the misfortune to end up in a nearby sewage works. There would be no such problems at Biggin Hill and the early wireless experiments, under the technical guidance of Lt J.M. Furnival, made excellent progress.

The work that went on at Biggin Hill was to lead to the development of Radio-Telephony (R/T) equipment for use in air-defence fighters by mid-1918. The first successful trials involved air-to-air communications but it was not long before ground-to-air R/T was achieved, a long-range transmitter being built in the grounds of Aperfield Court. The strategic location of Biggin Hill was not overlooked as it lay just to the south of London and was ideally placed to defend the capital against attacks from that direction. In September 1917 'D' Flight of 39 Squadron was formed at Biggin Hill and on the night of 24/25th the first fighter sortie was flown by 2nd Lt Norman Hugh Auret, who was just twenty years of age in a BE.12a. The perils of night fighting at that time were highlighted during the night of 19/20 October when the BE.12a of Lt Edgar Stockman suffered engine failure shortly after take-off and crashed on the airfield after a flight lasting all of two minutes. Happily Stockman was unhurt, although his aircraft was a write-off.

In December 1917 Biggin Hill's night-fighter detachment was taken over by 78 Squadron but it continued to fly the obsolete BE.12a, together with a few equally antiquated BE.2es. This arrangement did not last for long, however, as 141 Squadron moved in from Rochford in early February 1918, thereby becoming the first wholly resident squadron and in the process taking on several of the original pilots who had flown with the 39 and 78 Squadron detachments. At first the BE.12s continued to be used but the squadron soon re-equipped with Bristol F.2B Fighters [before doing so 141 Squadron evaluated the Sopwith Dolphin which was found to be unsuitable for night operations and the Vickers FB.26 Vampire single-seat pusher, the prototype of which was lost in a fatal spin-related accident].

The first combat success for Biggin Hill occurred on the night of 19/20 May during a raid by twenty-eight Gotha and three Giant bombers on London. The order to commence defensive patrols was received by 141 Squadron at 2255 hrs and Bristol Fighter C851, flown by twenty-one year old Lt E.E. Turner with Lt H.B. Barwise as observer, was airborne ten minutes later. It was not until 0030 hrs that contact was made with any of the raiders when a Gotha was seen near Meopham. This aircraft had already been attacked by Major Fred Sowrey, the C.O. of 143 Squadron, in an SE.5a and so its pilot was doubly unfortunate to encounter a second RAF aircraft.

Turner, who answered to the unfortunate nickname of 'Bum', was only flying on his fourth night sortie but despite his lack of night experience he manoeuvred his aircraft into the perfect position below and to the rear of the German aircraft to allow Barwise to open fire. The Gotha was hit in the port engine and began to lose height in a flat turn but Barwise was able to fire two more bursts which hit the fuselage and starboard wings before his gun jammed. Although Turner attempted to set up another attack, his engine began to misfire as he had been flying for some time with it throttled back. When it finally did pick up again, contact with the Gotha had been lost. By this time Turner was also unsure of his position, but he was eventually able to put his aircraft down at Detling after nearly 2½ hours in the air. When questioned about the night's events Turner could not say what had happened to the

Gotha but news was soon received that it had crashed between Frinsted and Harrietsham. The fuselage gunner survived with a broken arm but the captain (observer) and pilot were both killed. For their actions Turner and Barwise were among the first recipients of the Distinguished Flying Cross (DFC).

In the immediate post-war years a number of units resided at Biggin Hill for varying periods, the most famous being 56 Squadron which used the Kent base from May 1923 to October 1927. During this period it flew Sopwith Snipes, Gloster Grebes and Armstrong Whitworth Siskins and was also responsible for testing two fighter designs from Hawker, the Woodcock and Hedgehog. One of its Commanding Officers (from September 1923 to May 1925) was S/L Sir C.J.Q. Brand KBE DSO MC DFC who was to reach senior rank in the RAF and in 1940, as an Air Vice-Marshal, was to command No.10 Group, Fighter Command. Although Biggin Hill had altered very little in its first decade, all this was about to change and in 1929 a rebuilding programme got underway which was to last for three years, the last flying unit to leave being the Night Flying Flight which was equipped with the Vickers Vimy. On the northern side of the airfield a new technical site was built and new hangars, workshops, barrack blocks and administration offices were also constructed.

Biggin Hill was reopened in September 1932 and the first flying units to arrive were 23 and 32 Squadrons. The former flew Hart Fighters (soon to be named Demon) and Bulldogs, whereas 32 Squadrons was wholly equipped with Bulldogs. The following year 23 Squadron swapped its Bulldogs for Hawker Demons but 32 Squadron had to wait until 1936 before it received more modern machinery in the shape of the Gloster Gauntlet. With the departure of 23 Squadron to Northolt in December 1936, 32 Squadron became the sole fighter unit in residence for a short time, but with the RAF expansion programme in full swing, its 'B' Flight was detached to re-form 79 Squadron on 22 March 1937. Over the coming weeks this unit was built up to squadron strength, its equipment also consisting of Gauntlets. The Munich crisis in September 1938 changed the appearance of Biggin Hill drastically with the building of air raid shelters and the application of camouflage paint to buildings to make them more difficult to spot from the air. Gone also were the brightly coloured paint schemes of the Gauntlets, replaced by drab green and brown camouflage as the RAF was put on a war footing.

With the passing of the immediate threat of war the pressure was relaxed for a time, and by the end of 1938 both 32 and 79 Squadrons were in the process of working up on the first of the eight-gun monoplane fighters, the Hawker Hurricane. The day before war was declared on 3 September 1939, Blenheim If fighters of 601 Squadron moved in for a three-month stay during which it made a long-range attack on the German seaplane base at Borkum on 28 November. The first combat success of the many achieved by Biggin Hill squadrons throughout the Second World War went to 79 Squadron when F/O J.W.E. Davies and F/Sgt F.S. Brown shared in the destruction of a Dornier Do 17 which was attacked and sent down to the east of Deal on 21 November. This was also the first enemy aircraft to be shot down by No.11 Group.

At the start of the first full year of war Biggin Hill was commanded by Group Captain Richard 'Dickie' Grice who had flown with the Royal Flying Corps during the First World War and had been awarded the DFC. Grice was immensely popular with everyone on the station and his warm, even-handed approach to dealing with the airmen and WAAFs was rewarded by a devotion to duty and hard work. When the air raids were to come later in the year his calming influence was a major factor in Biggin being able to cope in extremely difficult circumstances so that it remained operational throughout.

Biggin Hill's squadrons were fully committed during the evacuation of Dunkirk (Operation Dynamo), its Hurricanes flying patrols to prevent *Luftwaffe* bombers attacking the survivors of the British Expeditionary Force on the beaches below. It would be its resilience and fortitude during the Battle of Britain however that would catapult it to prominence, to the point where it would become a symbol of Britain's defiance in the face of a seemingly invincible foe. Although the German intelligence organisation made some spectacular errors during the summer of 1940 by under-estimating the importance of radar, and by recommending attacks on airfields that had no strategic significance, it was certainly aware of the importance of Biggin Hill.

The first major raid on Biggin Hill occurred on 18 August when a high-level bombing attack was made by approximately forty-five Heinkel He 111s of KG 1. Due to an earlier attack on Kenley by Dornier Do 17s of KG 76 this formation was able to approach virtually unmolested and deposited around 500 bombs on the aerodrome. These mainly fell on the landing ground and in woods to the east, the only damage to buildings being a direct hit on the M.T. sheds. One wireless mechanic and a member of a Bofors anti-aircraft gun were killed and three airmen were wounded. Many of the bombs that had been dropped were of delayed-action type and it was vital that these were clearly marked so that they could be seen by returning aircraft. During the raid Sgt Elizabeth Mortimer WAAF remained at her post in the Armoury where she was in charge of the switchboard. Afterwards she ran out onto the landing area to mark the unexploded bombs with red flags and continued to do so even when ordered to stop by a superior who considered it to be too dangerous. Not long after a nearby bomb exploded but after getting her breath back she carried on with her work and her courage was later recognised with the award of the Military Medal.

There was a small attack on Biggin Hill on 23 August and a larger effort on the 26th but this was repulsed by 11 Group squadrons who intercepted the German bombers well forward and the raid was broken up. However on 30 August two attacks got through, the first of which began forming up over northern France in late morning. The targets once again were sector stations in 11 Group and Biggin was attacked around noon from high level. This raid was largely ineffectual, there was no damage to buildings or services and there were no casualties, however the second raid carried out around 1800 hrs caused extensive damage. Many were also to lose their lives.

In a change of tactics the attacking force comprised just nine Junkers Ju 88s but the raid was carried out from low level which allowed a much greater degree of accuracy and virtually every bomb dropped was to count. There was severe damage to the technical and domestic areas including hangars, workshops, equipment section, barrack blocks, NAAFI, the Sergeants Mess and the married quarters. In addition electricity, water and gas services, main sewage and all telephone communications were severed. The most tragic aspect of this raid was the fact that three concrete air raid shelters were hit and in one of these thirty-nine airmen were killed. Rescue parties were quickly organised and work went on through the night to recover all the victims. Despite the devastation the telephone lines and other services were repaired and the airfield remained in use.

The next day brought the now familiar routine of two raids, one around midday with a second in the late afternoon. The first was carried out from high level and although there was further damage to buildings and services, there were no further casualties. At 1800 hrs a high level attack was followed by another low level raid by Ju 88s which were accompanied on this occasion by Messerschmitt Bf 109Es which dived low over the airfield and strafed it with cannon and machine-gun fire. There was further severe damage to infrastructure including direct hits on hangars and other buildings but the most devastating blow was a direct hit on the Operations Room which wounded Group Captain Grice. Once again there were many acts of heroism and two more WAAF telephone operators, Sgt Helen Turner and Cpl Elspeth Henderson, were awarded the Military Medal for remaining at their posts until the Ops Room had to be evacuated. The temporary telephone lines and electricity cables that had been put in place after the previous day's attack were cut once again but these were soon restored so that the airfield could continue to operate. During the strafing attack four aircraft and a number of vehicles were hit and set on fire.

With salvage operations still underway on 1 September, the first signs of activity over the French coast were seen on the radar screens at 1030 hrs and once again a high level attack made for Biggin Hill at noon. The Spitfires of 610 Squadron, which had been flying out of Biggin since May, had just departed for a rest period at Acklington but the ground crews had yet to leave and were waiting on the north side of the airfield for their transport to arrive when the raid began. They quickly took cover in the woods nearby as the bombs rained down on the landing area. One 610 Squadron pilot who had been forced to stay behind while his aircraft was made serviceable could only watch from a shelter as it received a direct hit and blew up. The raid also disrupted the funeral service for those killed two days previously. Once again the airfield was a mass of bomb craters but these were filled in and the airfield was able to reopen later in the day. There was a further low level bombing and ground strafing attack at 1800 hrs which caused further damage, however the fires were quickly brought under control.

On 2 September the stables at the nearby Keston Riding School were taken over and workshop equipment that had been salvaged was transferred to the new location. This operation was completed three days later and normal workshop repairs were recommenced. Of even greater concern was the loss of the Operations Room and a replacement facility was initially set up in a shop in the village of Biggin Hill. This was only a temporary measure and a search was commenced for more suitable accommodation. The property that was eventually chosen was Towerfields, a Victorian country house about two miles from the airfield, and this was immediately requisitioned as it offered much more in the way of space. Its remote location also meant that it was unlikely to come under attack. Two more raids were made on the 3rd but by now the airfield had been hit so severely that there was hardly anything left that had not already been damaged. One sergeant was killed.

As he looked around his once immaculate airfield Group Captain Grice wondered if there was anything he could do to prevent further raids taking place. By now there was virtually nothing left standing at Biggin Hill except for part of one hangar. To give the impression that the airfield was totally destroyed, and thus out of action, he came up with the idea of blowing up the part that was still standing. Explosive charges were duly installed and at 1800 hrs on 4 September the order was given to blow up the hangar. This was the time when the *Luftwaffe* usually showed up but on this particular day they decided to give Biggin a miss which was unfortunate for Grice as he could not blame it on the enemy. He was severely reprimanded at the Court of Enquiry that was set up afterwards but everyone on the station felt that he should have been commended. By coincidence there were very few raids after

5

this drastic action was taken although it appears more likely that this was due to a change in tactics as the Germans soon switched to the bombing of London rather than 11 Group's airfields.

Sporadic attacks were carried out during the rest of the year but there was nothing on the scale of the raids of late August. Although Biggin Hill had been battered almost beyond recognition it kept going thanks to the courage and ingenuity of those who worked tirelessly to clear its cratered landing area and repair its vital communications links with the rest of the defence network. Its example came to be seen as the epitome of the never-say-die attitude that was prevalent at the time, and its record in the summer of 1940 has led to the name of Biggin Hill becoming synonymous with Britain's struggle. In 1941 its reputation was to be further enhanced as Fighter Command went onto the offensive and the exploits of its pilots would turn it into one of the most famous fighter airfields in the world.

CHAPTER TWO

A Change of Direction

Although the events of the summer of 1940 are generally regarded as being the most glorious in the RAF's long and distinguished history, the contentious issue of tactics has tended to cloud the manner of its triumph and remains controversial to this day. The removal of Air Chief Marshal Sir Hugh Dowding as AOC-in-C in November 1940 and Air Vice-Marshal Keith Park the commander of No.11 Group the following month has also led to much negative comment. They were replaced by Air Chief Marshal Sir William Sholto Douglas and Air Vice-Marshal Trafford Leigh-Mallory respectively. The removal of the architects of victory at the end of 1940, particularly the manner of their departure, soured what should have been Fighter Command's finest moment and the political in-fighting that took place during 1940 was to have a marked effect on its strategy the following year. To understand fully the complete change in emphasis it is necessary to go back to 1936, the year which saw the setting up of RAF Fighter Command.

From the mid-1930s there was a growing realisation in Britain of the danger to world peace that was posed by the Nazi dictatorship in Germany and the first of a number of expansion programmes was initiated to increase the size of its air force. One outcome of this was a complete reorganisation of air defence with the old Air Defence of Great Britain (ADGB) being replaced by five individual Commands, namely Fighter, Bomber, Coastal, Training and Maintenance. Fighter Command came into being on 14 July 1936 with Hugh Dowding as its first Commander-in-Chief. On taking up his post Dowding was fifty-four years old and his nickname of 'Stuffy' was well chosen as he came across as being rather dour and austere. He was wedded to the task in hand but his competence on the technical and organisational aspects of the job had to be set against his management of subordinates where he was later to be found wanting.

Dowding was highly qualified to be head of Fighter Command as his previous posting had been as the Air Member for Research and Development and before that he had been the commander of RAF Inland (Fighter) Area of ADGB. Over the next four years he would oversee a transformation of air defence to the point where Britain was protected by the most sophisticated system anywhere in the world. It could also send into battle high-performance eight-gun monoplane fighters in the shape of the Hawker Hurricane and Supermarine Spitfire. Dowding's work at the Air Ministry had left him with a clear understanding of the exciting possibilities offered by Radio Direction Finding (RDF – later known as radar) and this pioneering work was the catalyst for the setting up of the first command and control system in the modern sense of the term.

The development of radar in Britain began in 1934 when H.E. Wimperis, the Director of Scientific Research at the Air Ministry, set in motion a study into the so-called 'Death Ray' which had received much publicity in the press. He contacted Robert Watson-Watt at the Radio Research Station (part of the National Physical Laboratory) who in turn asked one of his staff, Arnold Wilkins, to investigate this fanciful notion to see if there was any possibility of it being a practical proposition. It did not take Wilkins long to calculate that the energy levels needed would be impossible to achieve, but as he was doing so he recalled a Post Office report he had read in which it was claimed that aircraft flying near an experimental VHF radio telephone link had caused interference to the signals and had re-radiated them. He mentioned this to Watson-Watt and the idea of aircraft detection by radio waves was born.

A trial was set up at Weedon near the BBC's powerful short-wave transmitter at Daventry in which a Handley Page Heyford bomber was successfully tracked on an oscilloscope. Further experiments were carried out at Orfordness in Suffolk and in early 1936 a second station was built at Bawdsey Manor, near Felixstowe to assess the feasibility of having overlapping stations to provide complete radar coverage of the eastern and southern approaches. Progress was rapid and by 1939 Britain was protected by a radar system known as Chain Home (CH). As this worked on a long wavelength (10–13.5m) which could not detect low flying aircraft, a further system known as Chain Home Low (CHL) operating on 1.5m was developed to fill this gap in the radar coverage. Once hostile aircraft had crossed the coast they were tracked visually by the Observer Corps.

The mass of information from radar plots and visual sightings led to the development of a complex ground organisation to assess the data and issue instructions to fighter squadrons. The heart of the system was the Operations Room at Dowding's headquarters at Bentley Priory near Stanmore in Middlesex, which by March 1940 had been transferred to a secure location underground. Situated alongside was the filter room where the information received from the radar stations and the Observer Corps was cross-checked before being transferred to the map display in the Ops Room. This showed the whole of Great Britain and was the only place where the air defence situation for the entire country was portrayed. Dowding sat on a raised-up dais together with the commanders of the anti-aircraft artillery and the Observer Corps, together with liaison officers from the other RAF commands and armed services.

As part of the overall reorganisation, Fighter Command was split up into Groups, comprising No.11 Group protecting London and the south east, No.10 Group which covered the south west and No.12 Group which was tasked with defending the Midlands and the north. Scotland was guarded by No.13 Group. Each Group was split into a number of sectors, each with its own sector airfield, plus one or more satellite airfields. Information was passed down from Bentley Priory to the Group Operations Rooms which had a similar layout and possessed a map like that at headquarters, except that it only portrayed the Group's area of activity. The final links in the control system were the Sector Operations Rooms, each with its own controller. This was a most responsible position as this officer was in control of the squadrons while they were in the air, except when they were in combat. In most cases he was an ex pilot who could thus appreciate the air situation and position the squadrons so that they were in the best position to attack the enemy. Close control of this nature, from seeing blips on a radar screen to guiding defending fighters onto incoming raids, was completely new and some within Fighter Command were unable to come to terms with the restrictions that a rigid ground-based control system imposed on pilots' traditional freedom to decide their own tactics.

The commander of No.11 Group was Air Vice-Marshal Keith Park who had previously been Senior Air Staff Officer to Dowding at Bentley Priory. He was born in Orange, near Auckland in New Zealand on 15 June 1892 and during the First World War fought at Gallipoli and on the Western Front at the time of the Battle of the Somme. On 21 October 1916 he was blown from his horse by the explosion of a German shell and was declared unfit for further service. This did not stop him joining the Royal Flying Corps and he returned to France when posted to 48 Squadron on Bristol F.2B Fighters, a unit he was to command in 1918. In the inter-war years he was an instructor and a station commander. He took over No.11 Group in April 1940 and was very close to Dowding during the Battle of Britain. No.12 Group was led by Air Vice-Marshal Trafford Leigh-Mallory, the younger brother of George Leigh-Mallory, the noted mountaineer. Like Park, Leigh-Mallory had also fought in the Army and was wounded in 1915 during the second Battle of Ypres. Transferring to the RFC he flew with 7 Squadron before commanding 8 Squadron in the Army Co-operation role. Between the wars he spent time in Iraq and, despite having very little experience of fighters, was given the command of No.12 Group in December 1937.

The relationship between Park and Leigh-Mallory was at best frosty and at its worst was decidedly antagonistic. In many respects they were poles apart. Apart from their opposing views on tactics which became increasingly apparent during 1940, Park had a sound knowledge of what needed to be done and was dedicated to the task in hand whereas Leigh-Mallory in many respects was still coming to terms with his new role. It has even been suggested that he might not have fully understood the new defensive system that had been created. He was also referred to as 'a man of driving egoism' to the point where self aggrandisement was one of his principal aims. For someone with such ambition he saw No.12 Group as an operational backwater which was unlikely to help his career prospects to any great extent. His later championing of 'Big Wing' theory, however well intentioned, had the effect of undermining Dowding and Park which suited his ambition and his desire to be at the forefront of the decision making within Fighter Command.

In contrast Park got on extremely well with the commander of No.10 Group, Air Vice-Marshal Sir Quintin Brand who had a distinguished record as a pilot during the First World War. During service with 1 Squadron he claimed a number of victories over the Western Front and subsequently commanded 112 Squadron in the night fighter role, shooting down a Gotha bomber on the night of 19/20 May 1918. Together with Pierre van Ryneveld he made the first flight to his native South Africa in 1920, a feat for which both pilots were subsequently knighted. Following time in Egypt, he spent two years as Director of Repair and Maintenance at the Air Ministry before taking over No.10 Group in 1939.

Evidence of friction within the upper echelons of Fighter Command was apparent even during the 'phoney war' period. Following a meeting in March 1940 Park later recalled Leigh-Mallory emerging from a discussion with his C-in-C and vowing that he would 'move heaven and earth to get Dowding sacked.' This simmering resentment festered into the summer and came to a head during the climax of the Battle of Britain. In June 1940 No.242 Squadron at Coltishall in 12 Group was taken over by S/L Douglas Bader who had returned to flying having lost both legs in a flying accident. Although he had first joined the RAF in 1928, his prolonged absence from the service meant that he was relatively new to the Dowding system. His maverick stance was to show that he had very little time for it as he was about to propose a different way of fighting that was diametrically opposed to what had been laid down.

While Park was throwing his squadrons in ones and twos against much larger enemy formations, Bader came up with the idea of the 'Big Wing' which would initially comprise three squadrons and ultimately five. He even went so far as to suggest that the 12 Group squadrons should be ordered off the ground as soon as raiders were seen on the radar screens so that they could engage the enemy well forward over Kent. This completely ignored the fact that 12 Group was supposed to protect the Midlands and had a secondary role as a reserve force when the air battles in the south were of such intensity that reinforcement was needed. If Bader had had his way the reserve would have been committed to battle before 11 Group's squadrons! As the whole essence of the system created by Dowding was control at all levels, Bader's ideas were completely incompatible with it and harked back to the dogfights and free-for-alls that had taken place during the First World War.

Rather than order Bader to conform to the system, Leigh-Mallory actively promoted his ideas. Having thought about the prospect of a 'Big Wing' he was convinced it would work but for him this was only part of the attraction. If large numbers of fighters could be brought to battle and be successful it would also heap more pressure on Dowding and Park which would do his career no harm at all. The degree of political manoeuvring behind the scenes went all the way to the House of Commons as the Adjutant on Bader's squadron was Peter Macdonald who was a Member of Parliament. He lobbied hard on the supposed superiority of Bader's tactics and was granted an audience with Winston Churchill at the suggestion of Harold Balfour, the Under-Secretary of State for Air. While all this was going on Dowding and Park were completely oblivious to the fact that there was a growing movement to have them ousted.

The idea of fighting force with force was certainly an attractive one, however its proponents tended to downplay the difficulties. Early warning was vital if the 12 Group squadrons were to play a meaningful part in the battle but the Germans continually tried to confuse the defences by making feints so that fighters were in the wrong place or had to land to refuel when the real raid came over. One of Park's main concerns was to intercept before a raid took place but the length of time taken for 12 Group squadrons to take off, form up and head south to the operational area meant that, even if they were able to intercept, they were unlikely to be in a position to do this. For some, notably Air Vice-Marshal Sholto Douglas, the Deputy Chief of the Air Staff, this did not matter as long as large numbers of enemy aircraft were shot down. He would rather 'shoot down fifty of the enemy when they had bombed their target than ten forward of it.' This blind adherence to the 'numbers game' would also be seen during 1941.

Towards the end of the Battle of Britain the positions of Dowding and Park were becoming increasingly isolated. Leigh-Mallory had an ally in Sholto Douglas and Air Chief Marshal Sir Charles Portal, who was shortly to become Chief of the Air Staff, was also sympathetic to his ideas. On 17 October 1940 a meeting took place at the Air Ministry to discuss 'Major Day Tactics in the Fighter Force.' It was chaired by Sholto Douglas and surprisingly included S/L Douglas Bader who reported on his experience of controlling three or more squadrons in the air. The meeting was marked by a heated exchange between Park and Leigh-Mallory and although Dowding was in attendance it appears that he did not play a significant role in any of the discussions. The outcome was not favourable for Dowding as the meeting concluded that the employment of a large mass of fighters had great advantages, although it was conceded that it was not necessarily the complete solution to the problem of interception. The AOC-in-C was forced to concede that it would be arranged for the No.12 Group Wing to participate freely in suitable operations over 11 Group's area of activity and that he would resolve any complications of control. When the minutes of the meeting were circulated Dowding, Park and Brand all objected to the wording of several sections but these were rejected.

The political shift within Fighter Command was complete by the end of the year as Sholto Douglas replaced Dowding as the C-in-C on 24 November. Park lasted a little longer but his post as the head of 11 Group was taken by Leigh-Mallory on 18 December. For many the time was right for a change. Dowding had been due to retire on 14 July but this had been deferred until the end of October so his departure was not unexpected. Park's removal was a little more controversial although he had been suffering from ill health and the stress of the last few months had taken its toll. Although changes were perhaps inevitable, the way in which Dowding and Park were removed from their posts left a lot to be desired and reflected badly on their replacements as they had actively conspired against them. After his removal Dowding was sent on a tour of the United States and retired from the service in July 1942. Park was to take command of the air defence of Malta in 1942 where his tactics were again successful in repelling German air raids. Ironically he took over as Air C-in-C, South East Asia Command in 1945 when Leigh-Mallory, who had been due to take up this appointment, was killed when his aircraft crashed en route to the Far East.

For the pilots of 11 Group who had born the brunt of the fighting in the Battle of Britain the speed in which Dowding and Park were replaced came as a shock and most felt that they had been harshly treated. Even though Dowding had remained largely aloof during the Battle, he was still held in great affection, as was Park who had at least been rather more visible, flying into various airfields in his Hurricane whenever he had time to talk with his pilots. Instantly recognisable in his immaculate white flying suit he commanded great respect for his intelligent handling of the air fighting. In his book *Wing Leader* (Chatto and Windus, 1956) G/C J.E. 'Johnnie' Johnson recalls that interceptions were made on, at best, only 50 per cent of the occasions when a squadron was scrambled. If squadrons had been grouped together into Wings the interception rate would have been very much less with the result that many more raids would have hit their targets. He also contended that it was better to have one squadron above an enemy formation than half a dozen below! Surprisingly many pilots appeared to have been aware of the political infighting that had been going on and were of the opinion that Dowding and Park had been victims of intrigue and jealousy.

The new incumbents at Fighter Command wasted no time in changing the emphasis from defence to attack, or as Sholto Douglas put it, 'leaning towards France.' This was a return to the offensive policies that had first been adopted by Trenchard over the Western Front in the First World War and over the coming weeks and months every opportunity would be taken to wrest the initiative from the Germans. Leigh-Mallory wrote to Sholto Douglas in early December to clarify the situation that Wings had now been accepted as the way ahead. The new head of Fighter Command had his concerns that casualties would be too high in relation to the likely results, but these initial doubts were swept away in a tide of optimism and he responded by saying that he was convinced of the need to get larger formations of the RAF's own fighters into combat with the opposition. Leigh-Mallory, of course, had no qualms at all about the new policy.

It was no surprise then that the first offensive missions that were flown over northern France in 1941 involved 'Big Wings' whose main purpose was to draw the German fighter force into a battle of attrition during which (it was hoped) the latter would suffer significant losses. Pure fighter sweeps were quickly replaced by operations in which a small number of bombers were included as it was thought that these would encourage *Luftwaffe* fighters to intervene as they had shown a marked reluctance to 'play the game' when faced only with fighter opposition. This type of operation came to be known as a Circus and over 100 were to be flown during 1941. The basic principles were laid down in Fighter Command's Operation Instruction No.9 which was issued on 16 February 1941 and described 11 Group's operations over France in support of bombers supplied by 2 Group, Bomber Command or 16 Group, Coastal Command. It also stated the reasoning behind the adoption of a more offensive stance and what was hoped to be achieved by the change in tactics.

Ever since its arrival in northern France in the summer of 1940 the *Luftwaffe* had been comparatively undisturbed by offensive action on the part of the RAF. This meant that the initiative was entirely on the German side as it could be active as and when it pleased. The reverse was true for Fighter Command which throughout the previous year had been forced continuously to stand on the defensive to be in a position to repel attacks which the enemy could launch at a time of its own choosing. During the Battle of Britain German losses amounted to 1,733 aircraft but despite the large number of casualties inflicted it was considered that morale had been maintained, largely as a result of pilots and aircrew being able to recuperate at their bases without having to be constantly on the alert against possible counter attack.

There were many worthwhile targets situated along the Channel coast and just inland including ports, military establishments, supply dumps and aerodromes but the main object of the exercise was to entice the German fighter force into the air to take part in a set-piece battle. As pure fighter sweeps were likely to be ignored, the use of a small number of bombers was included in the mix so that they would cause sufficient damage to make it impossible for the defending fighters to stay on the ground. Having brought the *Luftwaffe* to the fight, it was then hoped that combat would take place under conditions tactically favourable to the RAF's fighters.

On most occasons the bomber force comprised a small number of Blenheims and these met up with their escorts over North Weald, Biggin Hill or Northolt at an altitude of 15,000 ft and then set course for France at an indicated airspeed of 180 mph. By the time that the French coast was crossed the bombers should have been flying at a minimum of 17,000 ft and this height was to be maintained until the English coast was crossed on withdrawal. The immediate protection for the bombers was provided by the Close Escort squadron which was part of the Escort Wing. This was to fly 1,000 ft above and slightly behind the highest box of bombers throughout the attack and the return journey. The close escort fighters were not to leave their charges except to repel actual attacks and were required to remain in position until approaching their home base.

The remaining two squadrons of the Escort Wing were referred to as the Escort squadrons. These flew behind the bombers, one on each flank, and not more than 3,000 ft and 5,000 ft respectively above the highest box of bombers. The role of these two squadrons was to engage enemy fighters which were seen to be posing a threat to the bombers. During the withdrawal the Escort squadrons were to remain in their allotted positions until the attacking force was approximately half way back over the Channel when they were free to carry out a separate sweep to seek out and destroy enemy aircraft.

The bomber force and the Escort Wing were in turn protected by the High Cover Wing which consisted of two or three squadrons. The High Cover Wing was to fly above and behind the Escort Wing with their squadrons stepped downwards at intervals of 2–3,000 ft from not less than 30,000 ft. The leader of the High Cover Wing was to lead the lowest squadron. The Wing (with the exception of the top squadron) had the greatest freedom of action and it was permitted to reduce height to attack any enemy formations that were seen in the vicinity. The top squadron however was to act as cover for the rest of the Wing and was only to fight if forced to do so. Once the bombers were well on their way home the High Cover Wing was freed from its previous duties and was to provide top cover for the Escort Wing during its search for enemy fighters that had been stirred into action by the bombing attack.

The final element of the Circus operation was the so-called 'Mopping Up' Wing. This comprised two or three squadrons which were to fly at a height of 25–30,000 ft. By careful timing they were to arrive off the French coast in an up-sun position at the same time and place as the bombers and their close escort squadron were about to recross it on their way home. Their role was to protect the bombers and the close escorts during the return trip across the English Channel, thus freeing the Escort squadrons and High Cover Wing to enable the former to carry out its sweep along the French coast. When the bombers were safely over the south coast, the 'Mopping Up' Wing was to return (if possible) to the other side of the Channel to assist the other two Wings, particularly during their homeward journey.

Various recommendations were given as to how the formation was to conduct itself when in the air. The direction and method of approach to the target was left to the discretion of the leader of the bomber formation. Whenever practicable, he was to bomb without delay in formation and at the height ordered. An indirect course or undue circling of the target was to be avoided as this gave enemy fighters more time to climb to an altitude in which they had the tactical advantage of height and position. Similarly the turn towards the target was to be made gently as any sudden and violent turns made it difficult for the Close Escort and Escort Wing to stay in touch without straggling and loss of cohesion. In such a situation both bombers and fighters would become vulnerable to attack by enemy fighters.

The course taken on the withdrawal from the target was also at the discretion of the bomber leader who was required to maintain the speed that had been adopted during the approach and, once again, he was to avoid any excessive manoeuvring. To ensure the most efficient use of the Air/Sea Rescue services, when the attack had been made in the Dunkirk area the attacking formation was to make for the North Foreland during the withdrawal phase of the operation. If the target had been in the vicinity of Calais the aircraft were to head for Dover and when returning from Boulogne they were to make for Dungeness.

The fighter squadrons taking part in Circus operations were reminded of the need to maintain discipline at all times, not only in keeping visual contact with the bombers and other fighter formations but in being able to provide close mutual support to each other. It was emphasized that the escort fighters were to remain as flexible as possible and 'Hendon-type' formations were to be avoided as pilots would spend most of their time keeping station rather than looking out for the enemy. The whole object of a Circus operation was to destroy any German fighters that were enticed into the air using the tactical advantages of surprise, height and sun.

It was emphasized that aircraft should only leave the protection of the others if ordered to do so by the formation leader, e.g. where a particularly favourable target was sighted which could be dealt with by a section while the rest of the squadron provided cover. From experience of the first few operations over northern France, it was clear that the majority of the losses had been the result of straggling. There was a collective responsibility in that formation leaders were required to regulate their speed during manoeuvres in such a way that gave pilots at the back the best chance of keeping up, and those junior pilots at the rear had to be disciplined and aware of what was happening at all times so that they did not become detached. Unfortunately these wise words had to be repeated over and over again during 1941 as the same mistakes continued to be made with inevitable results.

After the traumatic events of the previous year Fighter Command's pilots looked forward at last to being able to take the fight to the Germans which would make a pleasant change to the interminable dreariness of defensive patrols. Although Biggin Hill had taken terrible punishment it was fully operational and was home to many pilots who were now household names as a result of their exploits during the Battle of Britain. During 1941 more of its pilots would achieve fame, but these would be outnumbered many times over by those, equally deserving, who shone only briefly before being snuffed out.

CHAPTER THREE

An Experienced Team

With the dawning of a new year Biggin Hill was home to three fighter squadrons. The pilots of these three units were the usual mix of senior and junior ranks but after the desperate struggles of 1940, nearly all were combat veterans. No.66 Squadron was commanded by S/L Athol Forbes DFC who had joined the RAF on a short service commission in 1935. Although he was to spend some time serving with the School of Army Co-operation at Old Sarum he later transferred to fighters and became a flight commander with 303 (Polish) Squadron on Hurricanes in August 1940. During the frantic air battles of the summer he was wounded three times in the space of five days in early September but succeeded in shooting down seven German aircraft in all, of which six were bombers. He was given the command of 66 Squadron on 17 October and shortly afterwards was awarded the Virtuti Militari by the Poles.

Forbes' senior pilots included F/O H.R. 'Dizzy' Allen and F/L Bobby Oxspring DFC. Allen had been with 66 Squadron since 13 April 1940 and as a result of the leadership he displayed during the Battle of Britain, was about to be made a flight commander. His most frightening experience of the war so far had been a mid-air collision on 28 November 1940 when his Spitfire was hit by that flown by Sgt P.H. Willcocks over Edenbridge in Kent. Allen was able to take to his parachute but Willcocks was trapped in his cockpit and was killed when his machine dived into the ground. During 1941 Allen was awarded a DFC and took over as commanding officer towards the end of the year. Bobby Oxspring joined 66 in December 1938 and thereby followed in his father's footsteps as he had flown with the squadron during the First World War. His first individual combat success was a Heinkel He 111 that he brought down to the east of Rye on 11 September and over the coming weeks he was credited with seven more enemy aircraft before being shot down himself on 25 October over Tonbridge. He was slightly injured in the attack but baled out successfully and was soon back with his squadron.

P/O C.A.W. 'Bogle' Bodie had made it through the Battle of Britain despite being designated as the squadron's 'weaver' on numerous occasions to guard against surprise attacks. Not only did he survive, thanks in no small part to his excellent eyesight, but he became one of the squadron's top scorers with five aircraft confirmed and five shared plus eight more credited as probably destroyed. The choice of Bodie to be the squadron's lookout was an inspired one as he was quite at ease on his own. In keeping with his desire to do his own thing in the air, Bodie's appearance was also rather unconventional, bordering on the downright scruffy and his language was described as 'foul'. Although only twenty-two years of age, P/O John Pickering from Reading in Berkshire was fortunate to be still around as he had already been shot down twice. On 30 August he was forced to bale out over the sea 20 miles east of Aldeburgh in Suffolk when attacking a Dornier Do 17 (for which he was credited with a half share) and was picked up by the crew of a nearby light-ship. His second close shave occurred in the morning of 11 October when the *Luftwaffe* launched several fighter sweeps over Kent and Sussex. During a number of sharp exchanges Pickering was shot down over Canterbury by the German ace Major Werner Molders of JG 51, sustaining slight injuries that put him in hospital for a short time.

P/O John Kendal from Chepstow in Monmouthshire, known to all as 'Durex', had also needed the attention of a hospital (in his case Preston Hall in Aylesford, Kent) after being shot down over Tenterden on 5 October by Bf 109s. This rather evened up the score as he had shot down a 109 over Merstham, near Redhill in Surrey, just three days before, a belated birthday present as he had just turned twenty on 29 September. With the confidence of youth, Kendal was noisy and brash and could perform an incredible number of sound effects from underground trains pulling out of a station to the ricocheting of a rifle bullet. Sadly he would not live to see his 21st birthday as he died on 21 May 1941 when operating from a CAM ship during convoy PQ15 which was taking supplies to the Soviet Union.

P/O Peter Olver had only recently joined 66 Squadron but had taken part in the fighting of the previous year with 611 and 603 Squadrons. It was when flying with the latter unit that he was shot down on 25 October 1940 by Bf 109s over Hastings. Despite suffering slight wounds he managed to bale out and returned to his squadron in early November when he made his first claims, a Bf 110 and Do 17 which he shared with other members of the squadron and a Ju 87 which was credited as probably destroyed. In terms of operational experience Olver was closely matched by P/O Stanley Baker who had initially been destined to fly Blenheims having trained on this type of aircraft at 5 OTU at Aston Down. Although he was posted to 600 Squadron which was equipped with Blenheim 1f night-fighters, the desperate need for pilots capable of flying Hurricanes and Spitfires meant that he was soon sent back to Aston Down where he converted onto the latter. On completion of his training he initially joined 54 Squadron but when this unit was pulled back to Catterick in mid September he was posted to 66.

No.66 Squadron also had some very experienced NCO pilots including Sgt Harry Cook who was already an 'ace' having shot down five German aircraft plus another shared. His first combat victory had been a half share in an He 111 which was brought down near West Malling [afterwards Cook landed near to the Heinkel and confiscated the pilot's binoculars!]. He went on to destroy four Bf 109Es and a Bf 110 to become the unit's top scoring Sergeant Pilot but he was lucky to come through unscathed on 13 October when his Spitfire was badly shot up and he had to make a crash-landing at Hornchurch. His aircraft never flew again as it had to be written off due to battle damage. Sgt Douglas Hunt had been with 66 Squadron since December 1939 and was unfortunate enough to become part of the Dunkirk evacuation when he was shot down over the Channel by return fire from a Ju 88 on 2 June. The rescue of the British Expeditionary Force was in its final stages but he was able to return to his squadron courtesy of a Navy destroyer. During the summer he shared in the destruction of two He 111s and a Do 17 before claiming an He 111 outright on 15 September.

Sgt Claude Parsons from Romsey in Hampshire knew more than most about the Spitfire as before the war he had worked on the Spitfire production line at Vickers-Supermarines. Having joined the RAFVR he received his call-up papers when war was declared and trained at 6 OTU in May 1940 before being posted to 610 Squadron which was flying from Biggin Hill's satellite at Gravesend [the squadron returned to Biggin in August]. Parsons made several claims during the summer including a Bf 109 on 25 July and a Do 17 on 18 August but during the latter combat he was attacked by a Bf 109 and wounded. On recovery he joined 66 Squadron as his old unit had been pulled out of the front line to recuperate at Acklington but had further success, shooting down an He 111 and a Ju 88. There was also Sgt Jimmy 'Binder' Corbin, a builder's son from Maidstone who had been posted to 66 Squadron on 28 August. Small in stature, he bore more than a passing resemblance to George Formby. His nickname referred to a habit he had of complaining about virtually anything.

No.74 'Tiger' Squadron was led by one of Fighter Command's best known pilots, S/L Adolph 'Sailor' Malan DSO DFC. A thirty year old South African, Malan was older than many of his contemporaries and brought to his role of squadron commander not only the disciplines of the air, but the regimen that had been thrashed into him (literally) during service with the merchant navy. After being accepted for a short service commission, he commenced his flying tuition in 1936 and at the end of the year was posted to 74 Squadron with whom he would serve for the next four years. His first victories came in the skies over Dunkirk but he was to shoot to prominence during the early stages of the Battle of Britain with a string of combat successes. He was given the command of 74 Squadron on 8 August 1940 and by the end of the year his score stood at eighteen enemy aircraft confirmed. Malan adopted a particularly aggressive style of flying when in the combat zone and this, together with a sound knowledge of tactics, marked him out for further advancement. The high standards that he set for himself and everyone around him meant that 74 Squadron would remain as one of Fighter Command's top-scoring units in the first part of 1941.

Although Malan was the consummate warrior in the air, when he was off duty his manner was entirely different and there was no sign of the belligerence he displayed in the cockpit of a Spitfire. He was quietly spoken and was not noted for using one word more than was necessary to get his point across. This abruptness was not delivered in a bad-mannered or discourteous way and merely reflected his uncompromising style. He expected nothing less than the best from those in his squadron but treated them with respect and would do anything for them. In turn everyone admired him for his honesty and professionalism and would go the extra mile to do his bidding. Despite the fact that he was ruthless in battle, his true character was not violent in any way, his warm smile indicating a kind-hearted nature and showing a man who would have preferred a simpler form of life to the one that had been thrust upon him.

Malan was fortunate in that he had a good team that he could rely on including F/L Johnnie Freeborn DFC a tough, no-nonsense Yorkshireman who had also been with 74 Squadron for a considerable time, having joined in October 1938. He had the misfortune to be part of the infamous 'Battle of Barking Creek' on 6 September 1939 which in modern parlance would be termed a 'blue on blue' incident. In what turned out to be a false warning of a raid, two sections of 74 Squadron, led by Malan, were scrambled to intercept. Also in the air were Hurricanes of 56 Squadron and in the confusion two of these aircraft were shot down by Freeborn and P/O V.G. 'Paddy' Byrne. Although P/O F.C. Rose managed to bale out successfully, P/O M.L. Hulton-Harrop was killed. Freeborn and Byrne were eventually exonerated of any wrongdoing but the affair inevitably led to tension within the squadron and certain personal relationships, particularly between Freeborn and Malan, were never the same again. Such differences were not apparent in the air and Freeborn went on to underline his qualities as a fighter pilot by shooting down at least ten aircraft during the Battle of Britain.

The other flight commander on 74 Squadron was F/L John Mungo-Park DFC who had been with the squadron since his arrival from the Fleet Air Arm in September 1939. Mungo-Park came from Wallasey in Cheshire and was an extremely likeable and outgoing individual who was admired by all for his charm. Together with F/L Harbourne Stephen he had shared in the destruction of a Messerschmitt 109E on 30 November 1940 which was the 600th aircraft to be shot down by aircraft operating out of Biggin Hill.

The rest of 74 Squadron was made up of pilots with varying levels of operational experience. P/O Bob Spurdle from Wanganui in New Zealand was posted to the Tigers from 7 OTU, Hawarden on 21 August 1940 and achieved his first confirmed victory on 2 November when he shot down a Bf 109E over Maidstone. Also from New Zealand, P/O Wally Churches joined 74 Squadron at the same time as his compatriot. As on any fighter squadron its composition was a complete mix of personalities and Churches came across as being rather shy and self-effacing. These traits however, certainly endeared him with the daughter of the landlord at 'The Crown' in Knockholt which was the favoured venue for 74 Squadron to drink and relax. P/O Roger Boulding was unique on the squadron in having flown Fairey Battles on operations during the German *Blitzkrieg* in May 1940 and had then transferred to fighters, joining the Tigers on 22 August 1940.

No.74 Squadron was fortunate in having some highly capable Sergeant Pilots including Tony Mould who had been associated with the unit since 1 July 1939. Mould was well liked on the squadron and even the irascible Johnnie Freeborn managed to forgive him when he accidentally put holes in the fuel tank of his Spitfire when firing at a 109. Sgt Bill Skinner was the son of an RFC pilot in the First World War and was originally from Gloucester. He joined the Volunteer Reserve while working at the Midland Bank in London and was posted to 74 Squadron shortly before the start of the war. By the end of 1940 he had shot down eight German aircraft with another three shared and was awarded the DFM at the end of the year. John Glendinning from County Durham was another VR pilot who had obtained his 'A' Licence in March 1938. He first flew Spitfires at 7 OTU at Hawarden and served with 54 Squadron for a short time before joining the Tigers on 21 October 1940. His victory tally commenced with a brace of Junkers Ju 87s shot down into the sea off Dover on 14 November and the very next day he shot down a Bf 109E near Bognor Regis.

In contrast with the hard work ethic and the high level of discipline that was the hallmark of 74 Squadron, the third of Biggin Hill's squadrons was renowned for adopting a seemingly more relaxed approach to the job and for enjoying a glamorous lifestyle whenever it got the opportunity. No.92 'East India' Squadron had arrived at Biggin in early September 1940 and had quickly established itself as one of the top-scoring units, at the same time as suffering significant losses. When not in the air the squadron had a reputation for living it up and its excursions to London and late night parties were legendary. The arrival of S/L Johnny Kent DFC AFC to take over as the Commanding Officer at the beginning of October therefore came as rather a shock to the system. Kent was a tough Canadian who had obtained his flying licence in 1930 at the age of seventeen which made him the youngest pilot in the country at that time. Having joined the RAF he flew Gloster Gauntlets with 19 Squadron prior to becoming a test pilot at Farnborough. Before joining 92 Squadron he had been a flight commander with 303 (Polish) Squadron where he flew alongside Athol Forbes.

In his book *One of the Few* (William Kimber, 1971), Kent claims that when he arrived the squadron was suffering from low morale with a lack of discipline and that he single-handedly turned it round, however this is contested by F/L Brian Kingcome, one of 92's senior pilots. In his own book *A Willingness to Die* (Tempus Publishing, 1999) Kingcome stated that Kent referred to 92 Squadron as a 'notoriously ill-controlled rabble' and that the new C.O. had also suggested that they had become a byword for indiscipline. Kingcome had been posted to 92 Squadron as a flight commander on 27 May 1940 and had served throughout the Battle of Britain until he was shot down and wounded on 15 October. He was thus well qualified to assess the character of the squadron and he felt that Kent's criticism was unjustified, although he admitted that an outsider might misinterpret their rather laid-back attitude as being a cause for concern. He was of the opinion that the wearing of silk neck-scarves and having hair a little longer than regulation length was merely a front which hid a deeper resolve, coupled with fierce loyalty and pride. Despite a difficult start Kent was eventually accepted by 92 as he had the ability to lead by example but Kingcome maintained that rather than change the squadron, the squadron changed him! Certainly during 'Dizzy' Allen's time at Biggin nothing appeared to change, in his view the squadron still lived 'like princes' due in no small part to their hiring of a London catering firm to provide all their food and wine. With barely disguised jealousy he also noted that 'gorgeous floozies' were regularly to be seen at 92 Squadron's mess, a nearby country house that had been commandeered for the duration of the war.

No.92 Squadron's favourite pub was the White Hart at Brasted which was seven miles from the airfield and situated on the Westerham to Sevenoaks road. It was run by Teddy Preston, a reserve navy officer, and his wife Kath and offered a convivial atmosphere in which the pilots could relax amid warm fires, beamed ceilings and stone-flagged floors. The pub was also famous for its blackout blind which was in the process of being covered with the signatures of Biggin Hill's pilots [it still exists and is preserved at the Shoreham Aircraft Museum at Sevenoaks in Kent]. There were other reasons to go there as the clientele usually included Moira and Sheila Macneal who were known to the pilots as the 'Belles of Biggin Hill.' The girls were identical twins, tall, elegant and beautiful and were the daughters of Sir Hector Macneal, a shipping magnate who was now working for Lord Beaverbrook at the Ministry of Aircraft Production. Both had married pilots, Moira's husband was serving in the Middle East but Sheila was already a widow as her husband, S/L Freddie Shute of 152 Squadron, was lost when his Spitfire came down in the North Sea on 29 February 1940. After closing time it was customary to continue the festivities at The Red House in Brasted which was the home of the Macneals

Although 92 Squadron had lost many pilots throughout the year of 1940 some of those that made up the squadron at the start of the war were still around to provide a continuity of spirit. These included F/L Allan Wright DFC from Teignmouth in Devon who had become 'B' flight commander on 27 September 1940. Three days later he shot down two Bf 109Es over the south coast but was shot down himself in turn during which he suffered slight wounds, his Spitfire being written off in the subsequent crash-landing near Shoreham. By the end of the year his victory tally stood at eight plus two shared. F/O Bob Holland was another long standing member of 92 Squadron having arrived in late 1939. During 1940 he destroyed four enemy aircraft plus one shared, but was shot down himself on 15 September and was forced to bale out near Ashford, injuring his knee on landing. He soon returned to active duty and was awarded a DFC on 26 November. Holland was a proficient piano player and was thus in great demand whenever 92 Squadron organised a party or had a night out in London. On such occasions he was frequently to be seen hunched over a piano with a lit cigarette in the corner of his mouth as he played the squadron's favourite number 'In the Mood' which had been made popular by Glenn Miller and his band. He was destined not to stay with 92 for much longer as he was posted to 91 Squadron at Hawkinge as a flight commander in early 1941.

P/O Tony Bartley was another of the original members of the squadron having joined 92 in November 1939 shortly after it was re-formed at Tangmere. He was the son of Sir Charles Bartley KT, an Irish barrister who had served as a Judge in the Calcutta High Court. Bartley was prominent in the actions over Dunkirk and in the summer battles over the southern counties. He was awarded a DFC on 25 October by which time his score stood at five enemy aircraft destroyed. Bartley was described by Brian Kingcome as the squadron's 'archetypal playboy' and his good looks inevitably made him a favourite with the opposite sex. He was to survive the war and married the film actress Deborah Kerr in 1947.

In terms of combat victories very few pilots on 92 Squadron could surpass the record of P/O Ronnie Fokes. From Hillingdon in Middlesex, Fokes had joined the RAFVR in April 1937 and flew Hurricanes with 151 and 87 Squadrons as a sergeant pilot before being posted to 92 Squadron in January 1940. His first confirmed victory was a Heinkel He 111 shot down on 2 June near Dunkirk and he was to add to his score on a regular basis throughout the rest of the year. His most successful day occurred on 15 October when he accounted for an He 111 and a Bf 109E during an early morning encounter over the Channel. Later the same day he shot down another Bf 109E when on patrol in the Ashford area. Fokes was awarded a DFM on 15 November for his outstanding contribution to the air actions over southern Britain and was commissioned later the same month. By the end of the year his score stood at eight confirmed destroyed plus two shared.

P/O Geoff Wellum was posted to 92 Squadron on 21 May 1940 but had to wait until 11 September for his first victory when he shot down a Heinkel He 111 near Dungeness. Known affectionately as 'Boy' because of his youthful good looks he was to remain with the squadron until 5 August 1941 when he was awarded a DFC. Wellum was a close contemporary of P/O Trevor 'Wimpy' Wade who had also joined 92 in May 1940 having been commissioned the previous month. Wade was to have a particularly dramatic few weeks in the summer of 1940 as he had to bale out of his Spitfire on 28 July on encountering bad weather during a night patrol near Exeter. Three weeks later his aircraft was hit by return fire from a Junkers Ju 88 and he was left with no choice but to crash-land near Selsey. On 27 September in a virtually identical incident he had to force-land near Lewes, his aircraft turning over. Having been in continuous action from mid-August, his score at the end of the year was officially given as four confirmed plus two shared.

Other experienced pilots on 92 Squadron included Pilot Officers Cecil Saunders and Roy Mottram. Saunders was from London and had joined the RAF on a short service commission in August 1939. After completing his training he was posted to 92 in April 1940 and was operational until 9 September when his Spitfire was hit during combat with Bf 109s. This led to a crash landing near Rye in which his aircraft was written off and he was forced to spend a period in hospital recovering from his wounds before returning to his squadron the following month. He had the misfortune to be shot down again on 1 November but on this occasion he was unhurt and his damaged aircraft was subsequently repaired. Roy Mottram had also joined 92 Squadron in April 1940 and he too was shot down at the height of the Battle of Britain. In the morning of 18 September he was patrolling over Kent near Hollingbourne when his aircraft was attacked and badly damaged by Bf 109s. Although he was able to carry out a successful crash landing he had received slight burns during the attack and was taken to hospital so that these could be treated. He was to make a speedy recovery however and on his return to 92 Squadron was able to get his revenge by shooting down a Bf 109 over the Channel near Dover on 28 November.

Among the Sergeant pilots on 92 Squadron, Don Kingaby was one of the rising stars of RAF Fighter Command. He was the son of the Reverend P.F. Kingaby, vicar at the village of Impington to the north of Cambridge, and following an education at King's School, Ely, he worked as a clerk in an insurance office during which time he joined the RAFVR. Following call-up and flight training he was posted to 266 Squadron on Spitfires at Wittering before joining 92 Squadron on 25 September 1940. Despite a slow start his score quickly began to rise and his greatest day occurred on 15 November when he shot down four Bf 109Es in the course of two sorties, an achievement that led to the immediate award of a DFM. His apparent predilection for disposing of the premier German fighter led to the press dubbing him 'the 109 specialist' and he would enhance this reputation during 1941.

Of medium build and with a pleasant easy-going manner, Kingaby was far removed from the public's image of the dashing fighter pilot however his affable manner on the ground belied his consummate skills in the air when he appeared to take on a whole new personality, becoming much more aggressive and never flying his aircraft straight and level for more than a second whenever danger existed. This was not so much the killer instinct coming to the fore, rather what one pilot later referred to as 'a highly defined sense of self-preservation'. Other pilots who did not appreciate this philosophy soon enough, or did not have the necessary ability, generally did not last very long before being shot down.

Sgt Ralph 'Tich' Havercroft was another experienced NCO who had been with 92 Squadron since March 1940. He had been born in Cornwall but following the death of his mother at an early age he moved with his father to Hull. Sadly his father was to die when Havercroft was still in his teens and he was then brought up by an aunt. He joined the Volunteer Reserve in April 1937 and began his flying training at nearby Brough. After further training in 1939 he served with 41 Squadron for a short time before being posted to 604 Squadron on Blenheims. The twin-engined Blenheim was not an easy aircraft to fly for Havercroft as he was only 5 ft 2 in tall and he found that he could not apply sufficient rudder to control the aircraft with one engine feathered. As a result he was moved onto single-engine fighters and found the Spitfire Is of 92 Squadron much more to his liking. His first combat success occurred on 23 May 1940 when he shot down a Bf 110 off Boulogne and this was followed by a Ju 88 on 14 August. During the latter combat Havercroft's Spitfire (N3285) was another to be hit by return fire and he had to carry out a crash-landing [after repair this aircraft was delivered to 66 Squadron where it was flown by P/O 'Bogle' Bodie. As already related Bodie was 66 Squadrons's 'weaver' and it is no surprise to note that N3285 suffered damage on two separate occasions in October when in combat with Bf 109Es]

Of the other NCO pilots Sgt Hugh Bowen-Morris had been with 92 Squadron since being posted in from 64 Squadron on 12 September 1940. Bowen-Morris had joined the RAFVR in June 1939 and had learnt to fly on Tiger Moths at 9 EFTS which was run by Air Service Training at Ansty in Warwickshire. He was called up two days before war was declared and passed through 3 FTS, 14 SFTS and 7 OTU before being sent to 74 Squadron. For whatever reason he was posted out again two days later and sent to join 66 Squadron but was quickly on the move again to 64 Squadron. Once again he lasted just two days before finally settling with 92. His first combat success occurred on 27 September 1940 when he was credited with a half share in the destruction of a Junkers Ju 88 off Sheerness plus a Dornier Do 17 damaged. During these attacks his Spitfire was caught in crossfire which resulted in a crash landing on his return to Biggin Hill. Later in the year he claimed a Bf 110 as a probable and by the turn of the year was one of 92 Squadron's most dependable members.

The pilots who flew from Biggin Hill did so under the watchful gaze of the station commander, G/C Frank O. 'Mongoose' Soden DFC who was well qualified to carry out the role he had been given. Born in November 1895 in Petitcodiac, New Brunswick, Soden spent the first nine years of his life in Canada before moving with his family to England. During the First World War he served in the Royal Flying Corps and flew the Nieuport 17 and SE.5a with 60 and 41 Squadrons, becoming a flight commander with the latter unit. By the end of the war he was credited with having shot down twenty-seven enemy aircraft and for this he was awarded the DFC. His service in the inter-war period included a posting to Iraq for which he was awarded a bar to his DFC. Soden was well liked by everyone at Biggin Hill for his outgoing and convivial manner. Even though he was from an earlier generation of fighters, he retained a younger man's disrespect for authority which was admired by the pilots who were half his age as much as it was treated with condemnation and suspicion by his superiors.

Over the coming year Biggin Hill's squadrons would play a crucial role in the RAF's new offensive policy and the quality of their pilots would ensure that the station remained as the top-scoring base in Fighter Command. There would however be a significant price to pay and over the course of 1941 sixty-two Biggin-based pilots would lose their lives during operations and another twenty-six would be shot down and taken prisoner. Many more would return having been wounded during combat and others would be plucked from the cold, grey waters of the English Channel by the Air/Sea Rescue organisation after baling out of their stricken Spitfires. Some pilots would come to regard Biggin Hill as their favourite station, whereas others hated the place. Don Kingaby of 92 Squadron considered it to be the luckiest airfield that he flew from during the Second World War, but Johnnie Freeborn of 74 Squadron described it as 'a loathsome place' which was frequently visited by tragedy. They were the fortunate ones as they lived long enough to be able to form an opinion, many others were to die before they had the chance.

CHAPTER FOUR

Setting the Trend

Although Fighter Command had every intention of taking the battle to the *Luftwaffe*, during the early part of 1941 the latter was more than happy to return the compliment by flying offensive sweeps over southern Britain, often with bomb-carrying Bf 109s. Compared with the heavily laden bombers that the RAF controllers had been used to during the Battle of Britain, the 109s cruised much faster and were also capable of flying at higher altitudes. This invariably meant that there was less time to assess any incoming raid and the RAF's fighters had their work cut out in climbing into an attacking position. In many cases it was necessary to resort to inefficient standing patrols if there was to be any chance of making a successful interception.

Despite their best intentions, both sides were wholly dependent on the weather and for much of January various combinations of mist, fog, low cloud, drizzle, sleet and snow meant that operational flying was a hazardous undertaking. The first interception patrol of the year was flown by Sgt Harry Cook and Sgt Maithew of 66 Squadron on 3 January but even this ended rather ignominiously when they were forced to land at Hawkinge and were then stuck there for much of the day due to deteriorating weather conditions. The New Year had been seen in by 92 Squadron with the threat of an imminent move to the forward base at Manston hanging over its head, but this had had to be temporarily postponed due to difficulties in setting up telephone communications between the two airfields. Also on the 3rd F/L Allan Wright attempted to fly to Manston to prepare the way for the transfer of personnel but was beaten back by snow storms and low cloud [he made it the following day but by road]. Due to the severe weather the Spitfires were run up at regular intervals by the ground crews so that they were ready should they be required.

Another patrol was attempted by 66 Squadron on the 4th, this time involving P/O Stanley Baker, P/O Peter Olver and Sgt Wylde. This also ended unfortunately as Sgt Wylde became lost and flew into a balloon cable at Chessington in poor visibility. Although he was uninjured, his Spitfire (P7660) was damaged. P/O 'Bogle' Bodie and P/O Baker tried their luck the following day but their patrol had to be abandoned after an hour due to snow and accumulations of ice on their aircraft. Although the weather was equally as bad in northern France it did not seem to stop the *Luftwaffe* as a lone raider dropped nine bombs on Biggin Hill on 7 January as the resident squadrons sat out another day of fog and light snow. Better weather on the 9th allowed 92 Squadron to move to Manston at last but not before it had carried out a patrol over Maidstone with 74 Squadron. The move went without a hitch and 92 Squadron was fully operational the following day for the first in a long series of Circuses over France.

At noon six Blenheims of 114 Squadron took off from Hornchurch on their way to bomb an ammunition dump in the Foret de Guines, at the same time as nine squadrons of fighters were getting airborne to fulfil various escort duties. The Hurricanes of 242 and 249 Squadrons swept ahead of the bombers which had 56 Squadron's Hurricanes as close escort. Three squadrons of Spitfires (41, 64 and 611) were stepped up as top cover, with the final element being supplied by Biggin Hill's squadrons which were required to patrol off Cap Gris Nez to protect the force on its way out. Although several combats did take place there was no real German reaction to the raid, other than one of curiosity, and Biggin's pilots flew back without having fired their guns. Sadly this operation led to the first fatality of the year as Sgt Laurence Freese of 74 Squadron was seriously injured during a forced landing at Detling having run out of fuel and died later in hospital.

After two days of glorious winter sunshine the weather clamped in once again on 11 January although this did not deter two Bf 109Es from bombing and machine-gunning Manston in the afternoon. Very little damage was inflicted although a Spitfire which was in the hangar received a bullet hole in one of its wings. The bad weather at least gave the ideal opportunity to catch up on investitures and on the 16th S/L Johnny Kent travelled to London to receive the Virtuti Militari in recognition of his service with 303 (Polish) Squadron. Although no operational flying was carried out over the next week 74 Squadron did manage some practice flying including air firing, air drill, formation flying and several engine and R/T tests. The intrepid P/O Stanley Baker of 66 Squadron took off on the 22nd for a solo patrol of the Thames estuary and Ramsgate but this was to be the only operational flight of the day, although some practice sorties were also flown.

A slight improvement in the weather on 23 January led to the first aerial combat of the year and this involved Red section of 92 Squadron led by P/O Ronnie Fokes with Sgt David Lloyd as his wingman. The two Spitfires took off from Manston at 1030 hrs on a defensive patrol and were told to position themselves over the airfield, but below the overcast. After about thirty minutes in the air they were vectored towards an unidentified contact that had appeared on the radar screens about twenty miles to the north-east. This turned out to be a Bf 110 of EGr 210 but at the time was incorrectly identified as a Dornier Do 17Z. The 110 saw the Spitfires as they turned to attack and it headed for home at a speed later estimated as being around 300–310 mph. As this was only 20–30 mph less than the top speed of a Spitfire at low level, a long stern chase developed and after ten minutes Fokes was still 500 yards behind. He decided to open fire in an attempt to slow the 110 down and saw his tracer hitting the German aircraft. As there was no more return fire from the rear gunner it was assumed that he had been killed during the attack.

Lloyd in the meantime was approaching from the quarter but was unable to do any accurate shooting at first as his windscreen was coated in oil. He eventually closed to 100 yards and used up all of his ammunition but the only hint that his fire had been affective was a faint trail of white smoke coming from the port engine. By now the pair had concerns of their own as fuel was low and the Messerschmitt had to be left to go on its way [it succeeded in getting across the Channel but crash-landed at Zuydecoote on return]. Unfortunately the next day saw the return of low clouds which, together with occasional mist and fog ruled out any operational flying for the rest of the month.

With frustration beginning to set in the weather conditions on 2 February were sufficiently good to allow the second Circus operation of the year to take place. This took six Blenheims of 139 Squadron to bomb the docks in Boulogne, Biggin Hill's involvement being to carry out a cover patrol to protect the bombers and their close escorts. The Wing was led by 'Sailor' Malan at the head of the Tigers, with 92

Squadron behind and 66 Squadron providing top cover. With everyone in their allotted positions the English coast was left at Dungeness at 1345 hrs at a height of 15,000 ft. Height was gained so that the French coast was crossed at 18,000 ft and the Spitfires swung to the south so as to approach Boulogne with the sun behind them. The Spitfires were also flying just below a thin layer of alto-stratus cloud which gave some measure of protection from above.

As the Wing swung round towards the target area they were greeted by a heavy anti-aircraft barrage and could see the bombers down below turning away and beginning to head for home. Several small groups of enemy fighters could also be seen below and Malan took the Wing down to increase speed. When he got closer he saw four Bf 109Es at around 12,000 ft and he dived with Red section to attack. Two 109s turned towards the Spitfires but with his extra speed Malan was easily able to get onto the tail of one and opened fire at 100 yards in a steep turn to port with 30 degrees of deflection. The 109 shuddered as it was hit and dived away, smoking badly. Malan followed and fired three short bursts from dead astern which again struck the 109 and resulting in his windscreen being covered in oil. As he broke off at 4,000 ft the 109 continued its dive and crashed into the outer harbour near to what appeared to be a dredger. At some point during this particular combat Malan's No.2 S/L E.J.C. Michelmore disappeared. He had recently been attached to 74 Squadron to obtain combat experience but was shot down and killed by a Bf 109E of I/LG 2.

The other members of Malan's section also saw action. During the initial attacking dive Sgt A.D. Payne (Red 4) saw a Bf 109E approaching him quarter head-on. Opening fire from 600 yards a continuous trail of blue smoke appeared behind the 109 and it fell away into a steep dive. Payne immediately half rolled and followed his victim down and continued to fire sporadic bursts down to about 1,000 ft. At such a low height he could clearly see the splashes that some of his bullets made in the sea. Having left his pullout to the very last second Payne was unable to say what had happened to the 109 but P/O Peter Chesters (Yellow 2) later confirmed that it had continued its dive and crashed into the sea. While Payne was accounting for this 109, Sgt A.H. Smith (Red 3) turned after another which passed under Red section heading north. After climbing for a time the 109 suddenly started to turn to starboard and dived steeply. This only brought it closer to Smith, however, and as he was inside the 109's turn he was able to open fire at about 200 yards and continued firing until there was a distinct risk of collision. At the last second he broke away and the 109 was last seen diving steeply towards the sea at an altitude estimated to be 1,000 ft. After landing Bob Spurdle (Yellow 3) confirmed that he had seen something hit the water in the approximate position of Smith's 109 but in the event he was only awarded it as a probable.

A snow storm the following day abated for a short time in the afternoon and allowed F/O Tony Bartley of 92 Squadron to take off from Manston as a one man section with orders to patrol base below cloud. It was not long before he was vectored towards Dover and thence to Southend where he saw an aircraft (later identified as a Heinkel He 111 of 6/KG 55) about a mile away, flying at 4,000 ft. Having released two bombs it turned away to the south but Bartley was able to approach it from behind and underneath without being seen. Closing to only 50 yards he opened fire with cannons and machine-guns and was temporarily blinded by the violent flashes and explosions as his shells struck home. The He 111 proceeded to break up in the air and Bartley had to manoeuvre sharply to avoid pieces of debris which were flung in his direction. For a time his forwards vision became nil as the whole of the nose and windscreen of his Spitfire was covered in oil from the stricken machine. Amazingly the He 111 continued to fly but following a second attack Bartley later described the Heinkel as looking like a 'skeleton on fire' and shortly after it plunged into the Thames estuary.

On 4 February 92 Squadron flew several patrols from Manston but nothing was seen. Over at Biggin Hill some of the more senior pilots of 66 Squadron including Bobby Oxspring, 'Dizzy' Allen, 'Bogle' Bodie and Stanley Baker carried out dusk landings but once again it was Sgt Wylde who provided the drama. During a formation patrol he managed to get himself lost in bad visibility, just as he had done a month previously, and his uncanny knack of picking out the balloon defences meant that he was odds on to fly into a cable, which he did. Incredibly he managed to retain control and landed safely [shortly afterwards Wylde was temporarily posted to the Ferry Pilots Pool at White Waltham. Whether this was due to his indiscretions in hitting balloon cables and damaging his aircraft is not recorded]

In the early afternoon of 5 February 'Sailor' Malan (Red 1) was patrolling Dover at 10,000 ft together with his No.2 P/O Bill Armstrong and Yellow section, comprising F/L Johnnie Freeborn and P/O Peter Chesters. They had not been there long when they were informed of an enemy aircraft approaching the south coast between Dover and Folkstone at 4,000 ft. Having descended through a cloud layer Malan saw what he thought was a Dornier Do 215, but was in fact a Do 17Z-2 of III/KG 2. Even though the German aircraft was flying just below the overcast and could easily have flown into cloud, it took no evasive action whatsoever and Malan was able to approach from behind and slightly below to fire several bursts into the engines and fuselage. During these attacks there was return fire from the rear gunner which hit Malan's Spitfire in the spinner and port wing. He then broke away and Bill Armstrong took up the attack hitting the aircraft's port engine and causing an explosion. At this point Armstrong had to break away as his vision was completely obscured by oil which was pouring from the Dornier's engine.

As Red section turned away, Johnnie Freeborn moved in to fire from the port beam with Peter Chesters attacking from the opposite side. By now the Dornier had absorbed a considerable mount of punishment and its end was signalled by the port engine which finally exploded in a sheet of flames. As it descended towards the sea Chesters continued his attacks during the last of which he became aware of one of the crew climbing out onto the top of the port wing. With his ammunition expended, he watched in fascination and no little horror as the crewman fell into the water shortly before the bomber crashed into the sea. In his combat report Malan suggested that the bomber was out to test new armour plating especially as the rear gunner appeared to be unharmed and continued to fire for most of the action. This seems rather unlikely and the amount of ammunition expended on the kill probably says more about the inadequacies of the Browning machine-gun by this stage of the war [the Do 17Z was U5+BS, Werke Nr 3386 flown by Fw Walter Gottschlich who was killed along with his crew].

On the same day 92 Squadron's Red section comprising Pilot Officers Cecil Saunders and Ronnie Fokes took off from Manston with Yellow section (Sgt Hugh Bowen-Morris and Sgt Ream) to patrol a convoy that was proceeding along the English Channel off Ramsgate. As they were doing so Fokes reported that a bomb had exploded near one of the ships and on turning towards the scene they encountered a Junkers Ju 87. Although this type of aircraft had been withdrawn from action during the Battle of Britain, it was still occasionally seen over the Channel if weather conditions were suitable. The Ju 87 was relatively slow but it was also extremely manoeuvrable and by twisting and turning it managed to evade each and every attack. The Spitfires did, however, succeed in driving it over the land and as it was turning to spoil yet another attack, Saunders approached from the beam and fired his cannons which finally caused it blow up. On landing the pilots were able to inspect the remains of the *Stuka* as it had come down on the perimeter of Manston airfield.

By lunchtime the following day Manston was covered by 6 in of snow which made flying extremely difficult and this was compounded by mist that lay close to the ground. On the 7th two Spitfires took off on a weather test but the visibility was very bad and news was soon received that one had crashed into a hill near Deal. This was R6924 flown by P/O Bill Watling who was killed. At the time of his death Watling was twenty years of age and had been with 92 Squadron since July 1940. On 9 September he had been shot down near Biggin Hill and badly burned. On his return at the end of October it was noted that there was an ersatz look about his face as a result of his burns but other than this he was completely recovered and itching to get his revenge. Unfortunately this was not to be and his death came as a shock to 92 as he was an excellent pilot [his Spitfire was subsequently rebuilt and later flew with 504 Squadron before it was written off in January 1943 with 53 OTU].

Thankfully the weather had relented by 10 February which allowed a Channel sweep by 66, 74 and 92 Squadrons as cover to Blenheims of 59 Squadron engaged on a raid on the French coast. On this occasion the trip passed off uneventfully as there was little opposition from flak or fighters. The only other event of note on this day was when P/O Sebastian Maitland-Thompson of 92 Squadron demolished the Chance light which was a type of floodlight used for night landings. Although he was unhurt, his aircraft was a write off. The next day was a disappointing one for 92 Squadron at Manston with fog preventing flying in the afternoon. The situation was rather better at Biggin Hill and 74 Squadron managed a full twelve-aircraft patrol after lunch, initially over base but later taking in Maidstone and Canterbury at 20,000 ft. No.66 Squadron was rather more adventurous and flew an offensive patrol over northern France but ran into a formation of Bf 109Es of LG 2 near Boulogne. As ever, the 109s always seemed to have height advantage and by the time that the Spitfires were able to withdraw they did so without P/O Stanley Baker (P7568) and P/O P.R. Mildren (P7520) who were both shot down and killed.

On 14 February 66 Squadron was scrambled and ordered to head out over the Channel as there were reports of enemy activity on the other side of the Channel. The Spitfires were led by F/L 'Dizzy' Allen who described the sortie in his own inimitable style in his book *Battle for Britain* (Arthur Barker, 1973)

There was a layer of alto-cumulus cloud which I estimated to be about three thousand feet thick with its base at approximately fifteen thousand feet. "Penetrate cloud on a vector of one eight zero," the controller said. "Bandits of the fighter type will be about ten miles south of you proceeding on a northerly heading when you break cloud." This was one of those armchair Napoleons all right, and I brooded over the information he had given me. I sensed it was spurious . . . but I reluctantly concluded that he must know what he was about. I was quite mistaken – he hadn't got the first idea. I told the chaps to get into close formation and climbed into the cloud; I put them into battle formation after the blinding glare of the sun hit us as we surged upwards from the grey of the cloud. Then somebody screamed over the R/T- "Break!"

We broke and there were about fifty Me 109s diving at us. "Jack it round, jack it round!" somebody said over the R/T, and I vaguely wondered who was supposed to jack it round. Then there was a very loud bang in my cockpit followed by the stink of explosives, my right arm was hurtled into the air, and my gauntleted hand hit the cockpit canopy with such force as to bruise the knuckles very severely, as I later discovered. I gave her full boost and transferred my left hand to the control column as the right arm was now hanging helplessly down at my side, and jacked her round as hard as I could turn. The Spitfire could out-turn the Me 109 at medium altitudes and I got on to his tail. He had a big yellow nose and he had two 20 mm cannon in his wings. I closed to within 250 yards range and pressed the firing button. He was a dead duck. But nothing happened. I glanced at the pneumatic pressure gauge and saw it was reading empty. He had hit my air bottle. I half rolled out and escaped into cloud. Then I set course for Biggin Hill at low level. I had thought of ramming him but wondered whether I could have baled out in time if I had taken such action. That would not have been possible, I discovered, when I attempted to open my cockpit canopy which was jammed firmly shut.

When I arrived over the airfield, I joined the circuit, switched on my navigation lights in the optimistic hope that they were still working as some indication to others that I was in trouble – my R/T set had also been blown up. Some half-witted pilot drew into formation with me on the circuit and indicated that my navigation lights were alight. I was in no position to remove my left-hand from the control column to give him a rude message. There was a squadron of Spitfires lined up on the shorter of the two runways, ready to roll for take off. I needed the longer runway and eventually touched down across their take-off path just as the leading section was about to arrive. A few seconds later and they would have cut my head off whilst on their take off run.

I had lowered the undercarriage via emergency air and she ran on down the runway but the brakes wouldn't work because the pneumatic system was smashed. I ruddered her hard when I arrived at the end of the runway to keep away from the barbed wire before giving her a burst of throttle to assist in the turning process. She bumbled over the grass heading straight for the squadron dispersal hut. Another half-witted individual, an airman this time, began to give me signals in the belief that I was making a normal, if somewhat unconventional, return to the squadron line. As I was still doing at least twenty mph he realised the error of his ways, ran like a hare and got the hell out of it.

It was by now pretty obvious that I was going to take the squadron dispersal hut down; the ground crews made the same appreciation and removed themselves. Then, fortunately, my wheels struck a filled-in bomb crater, the Spitfire banged up on her nose, thought for a moment whether she would cartwheel on to her back, decided not to, and stayed with her tail in the air. They had to get a jemmy to break open the cockpit canopy as two German bullets had hit the runners. I could never have baled out if I had rammed him. Altogether they found forty bullet holes in LZ-X and another one caused by a cannon shell.

It appeared as though 66 Squadron had broken cloud directly under a superior force of Bf 109Es, the pilots of which could not believe their luck when presented with a squadron of Spitfires in a tactically inferior position and with the element of surprise in their favour. To make their task even more straightforward the RAF fighters were also neatly silhouetted against the cloud. The 109s, which were probably from I.(Jagd)/LG 2 based at Calais-Marck, wasted no time in dropping onto their hapless victims. Three other Spitfires were badly shot up, 'Bogle' Bodie and Sgt Claude Parsons making it back to base with P/O Peter Olver putting his damaged machine down at Hornchurch. The Spitfire flown by P/O D.A. Maxwell (P7541) however was severely hit and it was last seen diving out of control towards the layer of cloud. Nothing further was heard from him. Considering the nature of the engagement it was fortunate that only one pilot was lost. After his own close call 'Dizzy' Allen spent the night in Orpington Hospital where lumps of shrapnel were carefully removed from his right arm and he returned to flying several weeks later.

The best that 66 Squadron could manage was a Bf 109E which was claimed as damaged by P/O John Pickering. F/L Bobby Oxspring fired several bursts at a 109 at close range from astern but made no claim. There was better luck for Sgt Don Kingaby of 92 Squadron who was also airborne at the time. Kingaby had taken off from Manston at 1111 hrs with orders to patrol a convoy north of Margate together with his wingman Sgt Ream who was flying N3125. He was then requested to join up with 66 Squadron off Ramsgate but unfortunately Ream had been forced to return to base with radio trouble. Kingaby soldiered on alone but was unable to make contact before 66 flew into the cloud and lost them as a result. As he came out of the cloud layer at around 12,000 ft he saw them again in the distance but before he could join up he was attacked from behind by a 109. Pulling his Spitfire round in a steep right-hand turn, Kingaby nearly blacked himself out but managed to get in a burst of fire from the beam, followed by a longer burst from the rear quarter. The 109 rolled and went into a steep dive, entering the cloud layer with the Spitfire still in hot pursuit. As the two came out of cloud at 9,000 ft Kingaby followed his adversary down and saw it crash about three miles inland from Cap Gris Nez. The pilot did not bale out.

If anyone on 66 Squadron had thoughts that their luck had deserted them they could certainly be forgiven as on 15 February during a nine-aircraft patrol over Maidstone they were jumped yet again by a superior force of Bf 109Es. Sgt Claude Parsons, whose Spitfire had been hit the previous day, was badly shot up again and he was forced to crash land at Manston. During the attack he suffered facial injuries which led to a lengthy stay in hospital before he was eventually able to return to operations.

On 20 February 92 Squadron returned to Biggin Hill from the forward base at Manston with 74 Squadron heading in the opposite direction. A few days later it was announced that the Biggin squadrons would officially be formed into a Wing and that a new post of Wing Commander Flying would be created. Although S/L Johnny Kent was more than qualified to take over this role he was informed by G/C Soden that 'Sailor' Malan had been chosen for the post and that he was to be taken off operations for a time and sent to instruct at an Operational Training Unit. It was with great regret that Kent handed over the command of 92 to S/L Jamie Rankin who arrived on 26 February and formally took over control of the squadron on 6 March.

The appointment of Rankin to such a high profile position came as a surprise to many as he had little operational experience. He had been born in Edinburgh on 7 May 1913 and had attended the Royal High School there before moving to Longridge, near Preston. He had joined the RAF in 1935 and before the war was attached to the Fleet Air Arm for a time where he flew with 825 Squadron from HMS Glorious. During the Battle of Britain he was an instructor with 5 OTU and before his posting to 92 Squadron his only experience of fighter operations was a short spell as a supernumerary with 64 Squadron. His solid frame gave him a pugnacious look which was further accentuated by obvious signs of having suffered a broken nose. He tended to wear his black hair slicked straight back from the forehead and this revealed a florid complexion. His seemingly dour features did not reflect his personality however as he was able to party as hard and as willingly as any of the other pilots at Biggin Hill. Despite his service background, Rankin would become one of the top fighter leaders and throughout the year he would lead by example, accumulating an impressive score of victories. As his tally started to rise the Press soon began to take notice and came to refer to him as 'one a day Rankin.'

The post of Wing Commander Flying (usually shortened to Wing Leader) and the formal setting up of fighter Wings, was the culmination of Leigh-Mallory's ideas that had caused such controversy during the Battle of Britain. The responsibilities of the Wing Leader were to ensure the operational efficiency of the squadrons within the Wing and he was also required to lead the Wing on offensive operations. Under the new system all administrative tasks would largely be taken over by the Station Commander which left whoever was fulfilling the new role to concentrate on the operational side. Having been promoted to Wing Commander, 'Sailor' Malan officially took over as Wing Leader at Biggin Hill on 10 March with F/L John Mungo-Park being promoted in turn to take over as C.O. of 74 Squadron.

Amidst all this upheaval, 609 (West Riding) Squadron flew in to Biggin Hill on 24 February from Warmwell to replace 66 Squadron, inheriting their Spitfire IIs in the process. Much to their disgust 66 had been ordered to take up residence at Exeter, an unpopular decision that was compounded by the fact that they had to fly there in 609's tired old Mark Is (all except one which had tipped up on landing due to boggy ground). As 609's pilots entered the Officers Mess in ones and twos they did so with a degree of trepidation. Biggin Hill was after all the most famous airfield in the whole of RAF Fighter Command and was inhabited by its most revered pilots. The strangeness of the surroundings did not help, nor did the non-arrival of baggage or the bleakness of the huts in which the officers were temporarily installed. The mood was also not improved by a comment from G/C Soden that 609 should take part in an offensive patrol over France the following day. The last time that 609 had been scrambled as a complete squadron was the previous November.

The newcomers at Biggin Hill were led by S/L Michael Robinson DFC, however the squadron had seen many of their most experienced pilots posted away to other units and having spent ten months in 10 Group were largely untried. Michael Robinson was the son of Sir Roy, later Lord Robinson, chairman of the Forestry Commission, and had joined the RAF on a short service commission in September 1935. During the Battle of Britain he had served with 601 and 238 Squadrons and had been credited with shooting down six enemy aircraft. Whenever Michael Robinson entered a room he became the immediate centre of attention as he was tall, with youthful good looks, and conducted himself with an easy confidence so that he was able to entertain and flatter any audience. When posted to 609 Squadron however he was initially treated with considerable suspicion as a result of his privileged background and his apparent foppish manner, indeed some thought him ill-equipped to command a squadron of combat veterans. Despite initial reservations his battle-hardened pilots were quickly won over by his handling of a Spitfire and as the fighting grew to be more intense he proved to be their equal in the air.

His upbringing also meant that his contacts were seemingly endless which was of inestimable value to the squadron both socially and materially.

Thankfully several other long standing pilots were still with the squadron including F/O Johnnie Curchin DFC who was shortly to take over as 'B' Flight commander. Curchin had been born in Australia but his family subsequently moved to the UK and he joined the RAF in June 1939. He had been with 609 Squadron since 11 June 1940 and was active throughout the summer battles being responsible for the destruction of seven German aircraft plus three shared. Curchin was of medium height with brown hair and hazel eyes. He had a powerful stocky frame which exuded a kind of latent energy as his manner on the ground was quite languid. In the air, like many other pilots, he was completely different as he seemed to come alive and his speed of thought was such that his aircraft was never still for a moment.

The 'A' Flight commander for much of 609's time at Biggin Hill was F/L Paul Richey who took over from F/L Charles 'Teeny' Overton. Richey was married to Michael Robinson's sister Theresa and shared a similar upbringing to his brother-in-law, being the son of Lt Col George Richey DSO who between the wars was responsible for organising the gendarmerie for King Zog of Albania. Richey spent part of his childhood in Albania and was schooled in Switzerland. Having joined the RAF and completed his flying training he was posted to 1 Squadron which moved to France in September 1939. Following the German *Blitzkrieg* on 10 May 1940 he was heavily involved in the aerial fighting until he was badly injured by return fire from a Heinkel He 111 on 19 May. His diary of this period formed the basis of the book *Fighter Pilot* which was initially published anonymously and is widely regarded as one of the classic pieces of aviation literature. Richey's presence on 609 Squadron alongside a family member was not entirely coincidental as Michael Robinson had lobbied hard for him to be sent so that his valuable combat experience could be exploited. Of course this was not the only reason as the two men enjoyed each others company enormously and coming from the same sort of background tended to move in the same social circles.

F/O John Bisdee had become an established member of 609 Squadron having arrived straight from training in December 1939. A former scholar of Marlborough and Corpus Christi College at Cambridge, he was tall, heavily-built with fair hair and was usually referred to as 'The Bish', a nickname that was short for bishop as his manner had a certain ecclesiastical air. Although only twenty-six years of age he gave the impression of being somewhat older and on meeting him for the first time Paul Richey was struck by his apparent steadfastness. In the air this led to him being one of the most dependable members of the squadron and his cool appraisal of any potential threat was especially important for 609's junior pilots who lacked operational experience. Having got to know him a little better Richey was later to describe him as a 'benevolent bloodhound'.

P/O Keith 'Skeets' Ogilvie from Ottawa in Canada had joined the West Riding squadron in August 1940 and was known for his devilish sense of humour. Previously it had appeared as though he was destined to be retained as an instructor at the Central Flying School at Upavon however a friend that he had met during training just happened to know Lord Trenchard who was able to intervene in Ogilvie's favour. Instead he was sent to 5 OTU at Aston Down before joining 609 Squadron. During the Battle of Britain he was to share in the destruction of a Dornier Do 17 which crashed near Victoria Station in London, an event that was seen by Queen Wilhelmina of the Netherlands who later conveyed her congratulations.

Most fighter squadrons could boast at least one 'character' among their pilots and on 609 this position was filled by P/O Sydney Hill who had an extremely dry sense of humour. He also had an eye that twitched so many people he had not met before left his company under the impression that he had been winking at them. Hill had joined 609 towards the end of the Battle of Britain and had shared in the destruction of the squadron's 100th kill on 21 October (a Junkers Ju 88 with F/L F.J. Howell, the Swastika marking of which was to adorn the 609 Squadron crew-room). He was great friends with F/O Johnnie Curchin but was the virtual antithesis of the man who was soon to be his flight commander. Small in stature and with black hair that was a little longer than it should have been, his boisterous nature was always likely to get him into trouble, especially as he was liable to poke fun at virtually everyone and everything. Even though their personalities were entirely different, Curchin and Hill were almost inseparable and were often referred to as 'the heavenly twins'.

Among 609's NCO pilots was Sgt J.A. 'David' Hughes-Rees who was from Newport in Monmouthshire. He had joined the squadron at the height of the Battle of Britain direct from training and had opened his account by shooting down a Bf 110 on 25 September after which he had to crash-land his Spitfire due to engine trouble. He was to double his score on 7 October when he dispatched a Bf 109E in the Portland area. When not in the air Hughes-Rees was usually to be seen reposed in a chair and because of this was referred to as 'the sleeper'. At nearly thirty-two years of age, Sgt Tommy Rigler from Poole in Dorset was a good ten years older than most other Sergeant pilots in Fighter Command. He was a newcomer to the squadron but was to make a name for himself during 1941 and would be one of 609's most successful pilots.

If everyone thought G/C Soden had been joking when he suggested that 609 Squadron should fly an offensive sweep the day after their arrival, they had rather underestimated him as they actually flew the first operational flight from Biggin just two days after moving in. Together with 74 and 92 Squadrons they were to provide top cover to twelve Blenheims of 139 Squadron attacking Calais (Circus 5). Their safe return was awaited by an apprehensive F/O Frank Ziegler (609's Intelligence Officer) but he need not have worried unduly as the squadron merely 'stooged' over Calais at 26,000 ft being shot at on occasions by flak that was not particularly accurate. The only enemy aircraft seen were three 109s high above but they made no attempt to attack and the only scare was when the oxygen system on F/L 'Teeny' Overton's Spitfire malfunctioned and he descended out of control for 10,000 ft before regaining consciousness.

Over the coming weeks 609 Squadron settled into the routine of operational flying and it was also to become the home for a number of Belgian pilots which was Michael Robinson's way of repaying a favour as he had been helped by a Belgian Air Force detachment to escape from France in 1940. Having been injured in a flying accident when serving with 87 Squadron, Robinson was in hospital when the German break-through was made but managed to stay ahead of the Axis forces, eventually arriving in Pau, near the Pyrenees. It was here that he was helped by the Belgians who gave him military clothes and transported him to Bordeaux where he was flown back to Britain. After a nervous start, the Belgian contingent soon became fully integrated into the traditions of 609 and was to play its part to the full during the hectic air battles of the summer. The West Riding squadron also lost no time in finding suitable accommodation and moved into the nearby Southwood Manor, a medium-sized Victorian house which was to be the scene of many riotous parties over the coming weeks.

Having moved to Manston to replace 92 Squadron on 20 February, 74 Squadron got off to a good start two days later during a convoy patrol over the Thames estuary. Green section, led by P/O Wally Churches with Sgt Neil Morrison as his No.2, was at 10,000 ft when the controller informed them of an incoming enemy formation. Climbing up to 20,000 ft, Churches turned west and then saw a Bf 110 below heading in the opposite direction. On being given the order to attack, Morrison moved into line astern and the two went after the 110 which put its nose down and dived to low level. Even though their indicated airspeed showed 500 mph in the dive and 340 mph on the level, the 110 managed to stay ahead and eventually Churches had to give up. As he turned for home he saw another 110 ahead and just below and fired two short bursts with a ¼ ring of deflection, securing a number of hits. He then had to break away into cloud but the attack was taken up by Morrison who reported that the 110 had gone into the sea. As Churches descended below cloud again he saw wreckage in the sea and a yellowish liquid floating in the water. The position of the crash was about thirty-five miles east of Margate. After Green section landed it was discovered that a bullet had gone through the main spar of Morrison's Spitfire and on its way had also punctured the starboard tyre.

This was to be Morrison's penultimate combat as he failed to return from a defensive patrol on 24 February in which Sgt Jan Rogowski was injured when his Spitfire was attacked. Rogowski put his aircraft down near Eastbourne and was admitted to hospital with scalp wounds. Two days later a brief period of good weather gave 74 Squadron the opportunity to participate in Circus 5 which, as already related, was the first occasion that 609 Squadron flew with the Biggin Hill Wing. Although there was a 500 ft thick layer of cloud over Kent at 4,500 ft, in the Channel and Calais area there was only 3/10 cloud at 15,000 ft with some light cloud above. Visibility was generally good. Although this operation did not produce much in the way of contact between the opposing fighter forces, its make up was typical of a Circus at this stage of the war.

The strike element of Circus 5 comprised twelve Blenheims of 139 Squadron with Nos 1, 303 and 601 Squadrons as the Escort Wing. These in turn were protected by Biggin Hill's squadrons which provided High Cover with 54 and 64 Squadrons as the 'Mopping Up' Wing. The bombers, together with the Escort and High Cover Wings made rendezvous over Biggin Hill at 15,000 ft and set course for Calais which was reached at a height of 17,000 ft at approximately 1250 hrs. On passing over Calais the formation made a wide left-hand turn along the coast towards Dunkirk before returning for the Blenheims to drop their bombs. Ten of the twelve Blenheims attacked the target dropping 42 x 250 lb and 40 x 40 lb bombs. Hits were seen on the foreshore, in the tidal harbour and its south-west corner and also on the jetty.

The close escort comprised the Hurricanes of 1 Squadron which flew 500 ft above and to the rear of the Blenheims. This unit later reported having seen around thirty enemy fighters coming up from the St Omer area but that they were too far astern to catch up with the bombers. Nos. 303 and 601 Squadrons flew at 19–22,000 ft and patrolled the French coast for a short time after the bombers had set course for home, but no fighter opposition was encountered. The Biggin Hill Wing (led by 74 Squadron) flew at 24–28,000 ft and crossed the French coast at Dunkirk before turning to the west. Over Gravelines the Wing experienced anti-aircraft fire, although it was not particularly concentrated and no aircraft were hit. Having proceeded to Calais – Cap Gris Nez, the Wing patrolled for about twenty minutes. The only fighter opposition seen were three Bf 109s but these were too far away to be attacked.

The 'Mopping Up' Wing made two offensive sweeps in the vicinity of Cap Gris Nez at 27,000 ft. No.64 Squadron saw a section of three Bf 109s in the direction of Calais, together with another section of six. An attempt was made to attack these aircraft but they were not willing to mix it and quickly dived away to the south. Two of 64 Squadron's Spitfires attacked individual 109s but the combats were inconclusive. No.54 Squadron, flying as top cover, saw rather more action and during its second sweep intercepted 15–20 Bf 109s that were travelling towards them at the same height. These aircraft were stepped up in vics of three but on sighting the Spitfires they peeled away and dived at high speed. Heavy flak was put up over Calais which was thought to have accounted for one of the 54 Squadron Spitfires, that flown by Sgt H. Squire, although it appears more likely that he was shot down by a Bf 109E of I/LG2.

Afterwards it was concluded that the operation had been successful from the point of view that the Blenheims had carried out their attack on the designated target and had been entirely unmolested throughout. However, as the main object of Circus operations was to bring the enemy fighter force to action, the day's events had been unproductive in this respect. This was particularly disappointing as there had been numerous patrols by enemy fighters over this part of the French coast during the early part of the morning, but they were conspicuous by their absence during the period of the attack. It also appeared that it was not until the bombers and their fighter escort had actually crossed the French coast that any action was taken to get defending fighters off the ground. Those that did take to the air were reluctant to fight and were only tempted to do so if they had both a numerical and height advantage.

The last few days of February produced little of note and the month ended as it had begun with heavy rain and low cloud which meant that no operational flying was possible. The bad weather did at least allow S/L Jamie Rankin to get to know his 92 Squadron pilots as S/L Johnny Kent made his own preparations to become the Chief Flying Instructor at 53 OTU at Heston. Kent had been with 92 for six months and was still of the opinion that he had changed the unit from an 'undisciplined, leaderless mob' into a 'first class fighting unit'. This view was, of course, hotly contested by Brian Kingcome and the other senior pilots who maintained that Kent had failed to understand the true spirit of 92 Squadron. Whatever the truth the East India Squadron was to remain in the front line for the rest of the fighting season and was to spend longer in the Biggin Hill sector then any other squadron.

CHAPTER FIVE

The Pace Quickens

The first day of March dawned bright and clear and the Biggin Hill squadrons were airborne at 1530 hrs for an offensive sweep over northern France with six Spitfires of 74 Squadron's 'B' Flight providing the rear guard for 92 and 609. The French coast was crossed near Cap Gris Nez with 92 and 609 at 23–24,000 ft and 74 about 3–4,000 ft higher. After sweeping around Boulogne, anti-aircraft fire was directed at the Wing but although it was accurate in terms of direction, the flak bursts were several thousand feet too low. Shortly afterwards a group of around nine Bf 109s were seen approaching from above out of the sun and Sgt John Glendinning (Yellow 1) of 74 Squadron called the Tally Ho. As 74 had been flying in line astern formation, stepped up in pairs, it appears that the Germans had not seen them as they went straight for 92 and 609 which allowed the Tigers to turn into them. Glendinning climbed to carry out a head-on attack but lost the 109s in the sun and only picked them up again as they shot past him with one lagging and attempting to catch up. He decided to go for this one and broke hard to port to deliver a beam attack which hit the 109 in the engine, setting it on fire. It then rolled slowly over and following what appeared to be an explosion in the forward section, it turned into a mass of flames and fell in a steep spin about five miles inland from Cap Gris Nez.

In the meantime P/O Bob Spurdle (Green 3) had latched onto the leading 109 to deliver a front quarter attack that developed into a full deflection broadside into its belly. The pilot made no attempt to get away and almost instantaneously his aircraft caught fire aft of the cockpit. As Spurdle had been attacking off a tight turn, he ended up pulling a little too much and his Spitfire shuddered as it entered a high-speed stall before flicking into a spin. Not wanting to recover too soon as his aircraft would initially be vulnerable in its semi-stalled state, he allowed the spin to continue for about 5,000 ft and after pulling out he climbed up again after the enemy formation which, by then, was heading north in a shallow dive. Taking up position behind the rearmost of the 109s, Spurdle got in three bursts from dead astern and below, each of roughly one second duration. The 109 turned right and half rolled, but as it did so it left an ominous stream of glycol vapour from under its starboard wing root. Unfortunately Spurdle was not able to see what happened to this aircraft as he was forced to break away from it when the other 109s turned on him.

Having managed to dive away out of trouble, Spurdle was flying back over the Channel and approaching Manston when he saw another 109 stalking a Spitfire before shooting it down [this was the aircraft flown by S/L P.A. Wood of 74 Squadron who was uninjured when his Spitfire came down on Sandwich Flats]. Afterwards the 109 proceeded to do a climbing turn to the left and Spurdle was able to move into firing range unseen to deliver a full beam deflection attack from

500 yards down to point blank range. He then turned onto its tail but broke off when he saw dense clouds of black smoke begin to stream back from the 109, together with flames from the right-hand side of the engine. This aircraft was claimed as destroyed, as was the first 109 he had attacked over France

The good weather unfortunately did not last and the following day was dull with rain, the only airborne activity consisting of weather tests and air-to-air firing. There was very little let up for the next week and the only time the enemy was seen was on the 4th when Johnnie Freeborn and Bob Poulton of 74 Squadron damaged a Dornier Do 215 near Dunkirk. The administrative changes already referred to became official on 10 March with 'Sailor' Malan taking over as Biggin Hill's Wing Leader. The gap left by his departure was filled by F/L John Mungo-Park DFC, formerly 74's 'A' Flight commander, who was promoted to Squadron Leader.

For some the choice of Mungo-Park as 74 Squadron's new C.O. came as something of a surprise as he had done a lot of his flying as a No.2 (often with F/O Harbourne Stephen before he left the squadron in January). He thus lacked experience in leading a squadron which was of prime importance in the dangerous skies over northern France. In contrast Johnnie Freeborn had led the squadron on numerous occasions but he was overlooked. There can be no doubt that 'Sailor' Malan had a considerable say in who took over his old squadron and it appears that the ill feeling that existed between himself and Johnnie Freeborn, which dated back to the 'Battle of Barking Creek' in 1939, was a factor in the decision as to who would take command. Although there were questions in some quarters regarding Mungo-Park's leadership qualities, his relaxed style and affable manner meant that he was extremely popular with his pilots, and all were genuinely pleased that he had been selected as their new boss.

Unfortunately his command got off to an inauspicious start as Sgt John Glendinning was shot down and killed on 12 March during a patrol with F/O Bill Armstrong, the pair being bounced by Bf 109Es of JG 51 near Dungeness. Glendinning was downed by Major Werner Molders who thus recorded his seventy-fifth combat victory, a total which included fourteen aircraft shot down during the Spanish Civil War. The gap left by Mungo-Park's promotion was filled on the 16th when F/L Tony Bartley was posted in from 92 Squadron to become the Tigers 'A' Flight commander.

Not long after midday on 18 March P/O Wally Churches of 74 Squadron took off from Manston at the head of Green section to patrol a convoy with P/O Bob Spurdle and P/O Smith as his Nos. 2 and 3. On receiving a report that enemy aircraft were approaching to the north of Dungeness, Churches took his section up to 29,000 ft but this was still not enough to get into an attacking position on three Bf 109Es which were cruising serenely along in a westerly direction about 2,000 ft above. Given the 109's superior altitude performance this was not an unusual situation for an RAF pilot to find himself in and the only chance Churches had was to follow and hope for an opportunity when they eventually turned for home. Even though they were an estimated fifteen miles ahead when the first aircraft half-rolled and dived, Churches was able to cut off their retreat and dived on the leader. His initial burst of fire did not have any effect but he followed the 109 as it dived towards Folkstone, closing to around 300 yards range. The evasive tactic employed by the German pilot was to dive steeply, but with plenty of right rudder applied which left Churches with little choice but to hold his fire until the 109 had levelled out. When it did so his first burst struck the German machine in the radiator under the starboard wing as a stream of glycol appeared. A further burst hit the tail and wing surfaces and the 109 nosed over into a dive which was not recovered before it hit the sea about ten miles south-east of Folkstone.

In his combat report Churches stated that the 109's colouring on its underside was the same as their Spitfires, i.e. black under one wing and white under the other. The 109 had a yellow nose but the rest of the camouflage colouring was dark brown and green [Fighter Command's aircraft were repainted with duck egg blue undersides the following month]. The day ended sadly for 74 Squadron as P/O Halahan was killed when the Miles Magister he was flying stalled on take-off and crashed, his passenger (AC2 Ingham) being seriously injured.

No.609 Squadron's first combat claim since arriving at Biggin Hill was made by P/O Keith 'Skeets' Ogilvie on 19 March during a late afternoon convoy patrol:

At 1737 hrs Red section of 609 Squadron was ordered to patrol over a convoy off Dungeness at 5,000 ft. I was Red Leader and proceeded to the patrol line. After about half an hour of patrolling in which we passed three Hurricanes on the same duty, we were at 9,000 ft. I saw an Me 109 come from above and behind us and attack the last Hurricane which caught fire and went straight into the sea. Red 2 thinks he saw a small white dot first before the 'plane hit and the pilot may have jumped at low altitude. I saw a trawler proceed to the green patch in the water. When I saw the 109 going down on the Hurricane, Red section immediately dove on it, but due to our slow initial speed were able only to give him a burst from the quarter which I believe hit his glycol tank as it immediately poured white smoke.

He dove for the French coast and was joined by a second 109. Red 2 and myself gave chase but with absolutely full power were unable to gain any distance and, if any, lost some. At the French coast we abandoned the chase as it was apparent we were getting nowhere. During the chase I fired several bursts at 2–300 yards from astern. When last seen the 109 was still streaming white smoke, whereas the second one with it was not, but was not losing speed. Due to the amazing performance of these 109s at this altitude, I am certain they must have been the new 109F type. I do not think the 109s had seen us when they attacked the Hurricanes as we were to one side and in the sun from them.

The Bf 109s were from I/LG 2 and despite Keith Ogilvie's belief that they were the new F variant, they were in fact 109Es. The Hurricane that was shot down was Z2759 flown by P/O Tony Kershaw of 1 Squadron. Although he did bale out his parachute failed to open and he was killed.

No.92 Squadron was also airborne at this time but on this occasion the enemy were the least of their worries. When in the Hastings area at 36,000 ft, S/L Jamie Rankin (X4257) found that he was unable to control his engine speed which was suffering from fluctuating rpm. Having descended to 28,000 ft in an attempt to cure the problem he sighted Bf 109Es above and climbed back up to 33,000 ft but as he did so his revs dropped to 2,400 rpm. Shortly afterwards he lost consciousness due to a defect in the oxygen system, only coming to at 12,000 ft by which time his engine was dead and oil pressure was zero. He eventually crash-landed in a field near Maidstone. Rankin was not the only one to have problems as Adj Xavier de Montbron (R6776) had to close the throttle when he was diving through an enemy formation as his engine was running roughly. He eventually crash-landed at Chatham and Sgt Jerrold Le Cheminant also made an unscheduled return to earth in R6897. When these aircraft were inspected there was evidence of ice build up on the spinner and propeller boss which suggested that the constant speed unit (CSU) of the de Havilland propellers had frozen up. Temporary modifications to cure this problem were the use of heavier counter weights in the unit and some Spitfires were fitted with Rotol propellers which did not suffer from this particular problem. Pilots were also told to work the CSU on a regular basis as it was hoped that by altering propeller pitch the unit would not seize up as readily.

Unlike the other squadrons at Biggin Hill which were still equipped with the eight-gun Spitfire IIa, 92 Squadron had begun the year flying the Mark Ib which was armed with two 20 mm Hispano cannon and four 0.303 in Browning machine-guns. The Hispano gun had a weight of fire that was eight times that of the Browning and so was much more destructive, but at first it had an abysmal stop-page rate. It had been designed to fit between the cylinder banks of the Hispano Suiza 'V' type in-line engine and did not take very kindly to being mounted in the relatively flimsy wing structure of a Spitfire. For much of the period under consideration the Hispano was fed by a sixty-round magazine and the gun had to be laid on its side so that the bulge in the wing to accommodate the magazine was not too large. With such an installation the gun often jammed when the empty cartridge case failed to eject properly. Eventually a belt-fed mechanism was used which proved to be much more reliable but in the short term stoppages would continue to occur on a fairly regular basis.

No.92 Squadron was also the first unit in Fighter Command to fly the Spitfire V. Visually there was little to distinguish the new Spitfire from earlier versions. Apart from a slightly altered nose profile, the only other identifying feature was a larger oil cooler under the port wing which was of circular instead of semi-circular section. The main improvement lay with the Rolls-Royce Merlin 45 engine, which featured revisions to the supercharger impeller and diffuser, improving its efficiency by the order of 10 per cent. The air intake ducting was also completely revised so that pressure losses were minimised, the overall effect being to raise take-off boost to +12 lb/sq.in, with maximum combat boost increased to +16 lb/sq.in, limited to a maximum of five minutes. The engine's full-throttle altitude was 19,000 ft, an improvement of 3,000 ft over the Merlin III of the Spitfire I. The first Mark Vbs had been received towards the end of February although these were rebuilt examples of the Spitfire Ib rather than new-build aircraft. A mix of Ibs and Vbs was flown by 92 Squadron until early April and although the transition was not without its problems, such as icing up of the CSU, the superior performance of the Mark V, particularly at higher altitudes, was very much welcomed.

At this stage of the war *Luftwaffe* bombers were still being seen on a regular basis over the Channel and along the south coast, often taking advantage of cloud conditions to launch surprise attacks on shipping and other targets of opportunity. On 24 March P/O Bob Spurdle of 74 Squadron was patrolling over three minesweepers off Ramsgate at 5,000 ft with his No.2 Sgt W.P. Dales when he was warned of a Dornier in the area. On leaving their beat to the east to investigate, they sighted a Ju 88 which was crossing their path about 500 ft below and heading south-west. They immediately went into the attack but as the bomber was flying at over 250 mph both pilots had to select full boost in order to catch up. Spurdle went in first, his fire hitting the port engine which soon produced clouds of white fumes followed by brownish smoke. The port wheel also started to sag. Ever observant, Spurdle noticed that the Junkers had two large bomb-rack nacelles, one under each wing between root and engine. He then fired at the starboard engine which also began to smoke but had to hand over to Dales when his ammunition ran out. Dales fired several two-second bursts and saw his bullets entering the fuselage but there was to be no dramatic coup de grace. When last seen, the Ju 88 was flying very slowly about six miles off the French coast and Spurdle was of the opinion that it was 'holding off' prior to a landing on the water. It was later claimed as a probable [this was yet another example that the standard armament of eight Browning machine guns was no longer up to the job and needed to be replaced as a matter of priority by the 20 mm Hispano cannon]

The better weather on the 24th also allowed 92 Squadron to carry out an early morning patrol off Dungeness. 'B' Flight made contact with enemy aircraft and S/L Jamie Rankin and Adj de Montbron chased what they thought was a Heinkel He 113 back to the French coast. Rankin fired at it and appeared to have secured hits as something was seen to fall off [this was actually a Bf 109E and Rankin was one of many RAF pilots to be fooled by German propaganda which suggested that the Heinkel had actually entered *Luftwaffe* service as a fighter]. P/O 'Wimpy' Wade had also been due to take part in this operation but on take off in the semi-light he hit the Chance light with his undercarriage. Happily he was uninjured in the resultant crash-landing.

Xavier de Montbron was a Free French pilot who had learnt to fly in his native country shortly before the German invasion. Keen to carry on the fight he escaped to Casablanca before boarding a ship bound for Britain and completed his flying training in the UK, joining 64 Squadron in September 1940 at the same time as his fellow countryman Maurice Choron who would later fly with 609 Squadron from Biggin Hill. He was posted to 92 Squadron on 2 October and on 1 November he shared in the destruction of a Bf 109E near Manston along with Tony Bartley and Bob Holland. Nine days later he claimed a Junkers Ju 88 over the Channel near Dungeness which he shared with Ronnie Fokes.

Although 27 March was to see another day of defensive patrols it was to end with the loss of two pilots. In the morning S/L P.A. Wood and P/O A.H. Smith of 74 Squadron were patrolling near Dungeness when they were attacked by Bf 109Es. In a brief exchange Wood damaged one of the 109s but Smith was shot down and killed. Later in the day 'B' Flight of 609 Squadron was flying in the same area at 25,000 ft when five Bf 109Es of I/LG 2 were seen above. This operation had not started well as F/O Johnnie Curchin's oxygen tube had broken and he had been forced to hand over to P/O Jimmy Baraldi. This was the first time that Baraldi had taken the lead and he was soon informed by Sgt Bob Mercer (the squadron's 'weaver') that the 109s were diving on them from up-sun. The break was called and a sharp engagement followed but the 109s retained the initiative throughout and when 609 returned they did so without Sgt P.M.A. MacSherry who was taking part in his first combat having been with the squadron for a little over a month. It was known that his R/T was not functioning properly and although he was seen to break with the others, he would have been at a considerable disadvantage thereafter. Eventually reports were received that his Spitfire had come down near Hawkinge. Observers reported that it had dived out of control after being attacked by a 109 and although MacSherry appeared to have regained some form of control when near the ground, his aircraft subsequently crashed in a field.

The rest of the month was uneventful and finished with a glorious day on the 31st which allowed flying to be carried out from dawn to dusk. No.92 Squadron was called to readiness at 0540 hrs but was released for training by 0900 hrs. Four pilots then carried out practice attacks while two Spitfires flew to the Leysdown ranges for cannon firing. P/O Geoff Wellum did an anti-mist test to 35,000 ft to assess cockpit icing at high altitude and 'B' Flight flew a patrol over Manston in the early afternoon. At 1640 hrs the squadron was ordered to patrol Mayfield at 15,000 ft but there were no interceptions. The day was rounded off by P/O 'Wimpy' Wade and P/O Ronnie Fokes who completed a dusk patrol over Maidstone at 15,000 ft but no enemy aircraft were seen.

CHAPTER SIX

A Night Interlude

Biggin Hill is best known for the record of its day fighter squadrons, but for a short period in 1941 it was also home to the Boulton Paul Defiants of 264 Squadron which were tasked with night defence of the capital. Although the defensive system that had been set up to counter daylight attacks was second to none, it was a completely different matter at night. The change of emphasis by the *Luftwaffe* in early September 1940 towards indiscriminate bombing of civilian areas by night exposed serious shortcomings in Britain's defences which relied too heavily on inefficient anti-aircraft artillery. In most cases single-engined day fighters were virtually useless at night but as airborne interception radar was still in its infancy, there was little alternative but to employ this type of aircraft as makeshift night-fighters. At this stage of the war the only dedicated night-fighter available in any number was the twin-engined Blenheim If but its performance left a lot to be desired and it struggled to overtake *Luftwaffe* bombers even if it could be vectored into an attacking position. The more capable Beaufighter If, which first entered squadron service in September 1940, held the prospect of increased success at night but it would be some time before it was in widespread use

The problems of night defence came as a reprieve for the Boulton Paul Defiant which had been designed principally as a 'bomber-destroyer' to Specification F.9/35 with a four-gun turret and no forward firing armament. The intention had been to use the Defiant mainly by day against unescorted bombers which it was assumed would be flying from their bases in Germany. The fall of France however meant that German raids were accompanied by escort fighters so for many the Defiant became more of a liability than an asset. It was used during the air battles over Dunkirk and briefly during the Battle of Britain but after initial successes when formations of Defiants were incorrectly identified as Hurricanes, heavy losses led to it being withdrawn. From the earliest stages however the Defiant had been considered for a night role and its failure by day led to this becoming its primary task.

No.264 Squadron had first come into existence in April 1918 when it flew reconnaissance flights with Short seaplanes in the Mediterranean. It was re-formed on 30 October 1939 at Sutton Bridge and later in the year moved to Martlesham Heath where it became the first unit to fly the Defiant. By the end of 1940 the squadron was based at Gravesend and was under the command of S/L Arthur Sanders an officer with considerable experience having passed out of Cranwell in December 1933. During the intervening period he had flown Hawker Hart day bombers with 57 Squadron, instructed at 11 FTS and had been a member of the RAF's Long Range Development Unit.

Other notables on 264 included P/O Desmond Hughes who was well on the way to becoming an 'ace' with three combat victories (two by day) to his name. He had commenced his flying career in 1938 at the Cambridge University Air Squadron while he was reading law at Pembroke College and received a Direct Entry Commission in the RAFVR in October 1939. On completing the course at 5 OTU, he spent a short time with 26 Squadron before joining 264 with whom he had almost immediate success, shooting down two Do 17s on 26 August 1940. His first night victory was a Heinkel He 111 of II/KG 26 on 15 October. During his service with 264 his regular gunner was Sgt Fred Gash. Although he was to go on to record a total of eighteen victories plus one shared by the end of the war, Hughes' early score was eclipsed by Sgt Ted Thorn who, together with his gunner LAC (soon to be Sergeant) Fred Barker, accounted for eight enemy aircraft shot down plus one shared during the Dunkirk campaign. For this they both received the DFM. Following more combat success in August when they shot down another four aircraft by day, Thorn and Barker were promoted to Flight Sergeant.

Other successful members of the squadron were Pilot Officers Eric Barwell and Terry Welsh. Barwell had joined 264 Squadron as they were working up on the Defiant and saw considerable action around the time of Dunkirk claiming five German aircraft destroyed. He was fortunate to survive these initial encounters with the enemy as he and his gunner (P/O Williams) were shot down on 31 May and ended up ditching in the Channel where they were picked up by a destroyer and returned to Britain. P/O Terry Welsh, together with his gunner Sgt L.H. Hayden, claimed four victories over Dunkirk plus another shared. This pairing would also account for a Ju 88 later in the summer before the Defiant was taken out of the fight by day to take up its night role.

At the turn of the year 264 Squadron moved in to Gravesend to join the Defiants of 141 Squadron. The latter unit had briefly reacquainted itself with Biggin in the late summer of 1940 when a detachment of Defiants flew from the Kent base. Rather than the normal rivalry that might have been expected between these two outfits, there was bad feeling which at times led to confrontation. This stemmed from 141 Squadron's only contribution to the Battle of Britain on 19 July 1940 when seven out of nine aircraft were either shot down or seriously damaged and ten airmen were killed. This disaster was one of the major factors in the Defiant being withdrawn from the day battle and 'relegated' to operations by night. Although 264 Squadron had also suffered severe losses, these could be balanced against significant successes and its crews were confident of their ability to operate the Defiant by day against all opposition. The fact that this was denied them was blamed on 141 and the level of animosity that was apparent led to 264 Squadron moving to Biggin Hill on 10 January.

On the day before the move the crew of Sgt P. Endersby and Sgt Chandler chalked up 264's first combat success of the New Year. The patrol line was near Beachy Head at 13,500 ft but shortly before he reached that height Endersby saw what he assumed to be an enemy aircraft heading inland. He gave chase and the aircraft (thought to be a Ju 88) was then engaged by anti-aircraft guns. This caused it to turn away to the south-east which allowed Endersby to close in rapidly to around 150 yards and as he positioned his aircraft below the bomber's starboard wing, Sgt Chandler fired three short bursts with his four Browning machine-guns, hitting the port engine. Just as he was about to fire again the aircraft put on its navigation lights which led the crew of the Defiant to think that it might, after all, be a friendly machine. To try to get a positive identification Chandler fired a Very light but this was only answered by a burst of tracer bullets which passed uncomfortably close to his turret. At the same time the aircraft extinguished all its lights and immediately dived for the sanctuary of a layer of haze which was present over the coast. Endersby was unable to follow this manoeuvre but not long after he saw a number of bombs explode on the coastline which he assumed had been discharged from the aircraft he had attacked.

The difficulties of correct identification that Endersby had encountered were typical of night fighting during the early war period. Even in the most perfect of conditions it was not a straightforward task as the need to remain unseen meant that an attacking aircraft was restricted in the way it could approach a target. The reliance on ideal weather conditions meant that the next successful interception did not occur until 12 March and involved P/O Desmond Hughes and his gunner Sgt Fred Gash. Hughes took off from Tangmere at 1945 hrs and was vectored onto an aircraft approaching Beachy Head, but no contact was made. Vectors were then given onto a second bandit that was eventually seen at a range of 800 yards and 700 ft above. The aircraft was flying on a parallel course to the Defiant on the port beam and was identified as an He 111. Hughes manoeuvred his aircraft so that it approached the Heinkel from under its starboard wing and Gash fired a series of one-second bursts from 50 yards into the starboard engine which was soon well alight. At this point his reflector gunsight packed up but the range was so close that Gash could hardly miss and he fired several more bursts into the cabin which was seen to fill with flames. The bomber then fell into a left-hand spiral dive and crashed at Oakwood Hill, south of Dorking. Two crew members baled out, but one died when his parachute failed to open.

During the same evening P/O Terry Welsh and Sgt L.H. Hayden took off from Biggin Hill at 2305 hrs to carry out a gun test over the Channel. On reaching the coast, however, the controller at Kenley ordered them to patrol ten miles west of base at 13,000 ft and it was not long before they were vectored onto a target. A series of courses between 130 and 160 degrees were given with height being reduced to 8,000 ft. By now the Defiant (call-sign Plater 17) was back over the Channel and Welsh saw something below outlined in a patch of moonlight reflecting off the sea. As he dived down he saw that it was an aircraft and with his airspeed registering 260 mph he was able to overhaul it with ease, recognising it as a Heinkel 111. Welsh carried out a standard crossover attack from underneath the bomber with Hayden pumping several short bursts into it from short range. The De Wilde ammunition could be seen bursting inside the cabin and it was later assumed that the pilot was killed during this attack as the Heinkel entered a vertical dive before plunging into the sea. After this success Welsh and Hayden were not detained any longer and returned to Biggin, landing at five minutes after midnight.

The difficulties of night interception were apparent once again the following night when Sergeants Wilkin and Crook were directed onto a target that was heading towards the south coast. It was duly seen about 300 ft above and Wilkin closed in from the starboard side to a range of only 50 yards. Shortly after Crook had fired a two-second burst the controller informed them that there was a friendly aircraft in the area and expressed some doubt as to the identity of the aircraft they were attacking. Not that Crook was able to continue the attack as his turret had temporarily ceased to function due to an electrical fuse having fallen out due to excessive vibration. As he was unsure of the aircraft he was attacking Wilkin moved away to prevent further damage. In doing so he lost sight of it but then saw a number of incendiary bombs burst about one mile inland. A cluster of searchlights lit up and he caught sight of the aircraft once again, finally identifying it as an He 111 which was now diving steeply. It was claimed as probably destroyed [during the debrief it was later established that the controller had talked about a friendly 'single-engined' aircraft but Wilkin had not heard this]

The next full moon period occurred in early April and on the 8th S/L Arthur Sanders, and his gunner P/O F.C. Sutton, departed Biggin Hill at 2020 hrs. They flew to the usual patrol line near Beachy Head and after some time were directed towards an enemy aircraft flying inland at 16,000 ft. A long chase ensued during which the aircraft (a Heinkel 111 of KG 26) was 'boxed in' by anti-aircraft fire. By the time that Sanders was able to get into a firing position the German aircraft was to the north of London and Sutton fired a two-second burst of fire into the fuselage centre section. The Heinkel commenced a series of evasive manoeuvres but as there was no return fire, Sanders was able to formate on it, allowing Sutton to fire again. After this second attack it burst into flames, before turning over and going straight down to crash near Hitchin. Sanders immediately returned to Biggin Hill where he landed with very little fuel left having been airborne for 2 hours 15 minutes.

Just before midnight Desmond Hughes and Fred Gash took off and on being transferred to Kenley control were vectored towards a bandit to the south of base. Selecting full throttle, Hughes eventually saw the aircraft about 300 ft above and directly ahead. He turned to starboard to give his gunner a suitable field of fire and Gash opened up with two bursts, each of two seconds which hit the fuselage and starboard engine. At this point a large piece of burning debris was seen to break away. A second attack was carried out from underneath and ahead with Gash firing straight back into the enemy aircraft (another He 111) from a range of 100 yards. Having jettisoned its bomb load the Heinkel turned sharply and headed for home and was lost as it crossed the coast at about 15,000 ft. As it had absorbed considerable punishment, it was later claimed as a probable.

The following night the weather was still clear above a continuous cloud layer with tops at 7,000 ft. Among the crews airborne was the experienced pairing of F/Sgt Ted Thorn and F/Sgt Fred Barker who took off from Biggin Hill in N3366 (Plater 22) at 2250 hrs. After orbiting near Beachy Head they were sent after an intruder and saw it at a range of 1,000 yards, such was the excellent visibility. The target proved to be a Heinkel 111 and closing to 100 yards on the starboard side Barker opened fire into its fuselage. Some return fire was experienced so Thorn crossed underneath so that Barker could attack from the other side and he succeeded in setting the port engine on fire. The bomber began to lose height and further attacks were carried out as it went down, the dive becoming increasingly steep as it approached the layer of cloud. As it did so clouds of white smoke were pouring from both engines and it continued down to crash near Godalming. After returning, Thorn was extremely complimentary about the level of control he had received from Kenley, the heights in particular being described as being 'amazingly accurate'.

The night of 10/11 April was a particularly productive one for 264 Squadron as the excellent conditions of bright moonlight continued. P/O Eric Barwell and his gunner Sgt Martin took off from Biggin Hill at 2015 hrs to patrol the Kenley sector between 14,000 and 18,000 ft and were eventually vectored onto an enemy aircraft. Once again the night was so bright that the target was seen at around 1,000 yards and range was closed quite easily. Martin opened fire with multiple bursts from 300 yards down to 50 yards range which raked the bomber's fuselage and engines and it then lost airspeed as it went into a climb. The Defiant nearly stalled as Barwell attempted to follow, but as he slid underneath he could clearly distinguish it as a Heinkel 111. By this time Martin had been forced to cease firing as he had been blinded by the flashes of his own ammunition. A few seconds later the Heinkel entered a vertical dive which was so steep that Barwell was unable to follow. It then disappeared from view as it entered cloud and was not seen again, but it was later confirmed that it had crashed at Seaford between Brighton and Beachy Head. As he was low on fuel, Barwell put down at Tangmere having been airborne for two hours.

After refuelling and rearming, Barwell and Martin were in the air again at 0238 hrs. Their second sortie took them along the south coast at 12,000 ft and again they were given a steer towards a target which was reported to be on its way back to France. This turned out to be another He 111 flying at 7,000 ft but in the clear conditions the Germans saw them coming and headed for the nearest cloud cover. Despite having a height advantage only slow progress was made but eventually the Defiant was in a position where Martin could open fire. Such were the levels of brightness on this particular night that a dogfight developed, with the Heinkel pilot adopting violent evasive manoeuvres in an attempt to get away. The German gunners did the best they could but were out-gunned by Martin's four Brownings and his De Wilde ammunition could be seen bursting all along the fuselage which led to a trail of debris. As with the previous combat the Heinkel went into a dive that Barwell was unable to follow and it was lost in a layer of cloud at 3,000 ft. A return was made to Biggin Hill at 0415 hrs but as the action had taken place over the sea and the Heinkel's destruction was not confirmed, it could only be claimed as a probable.

On the same night Desmond Hughes and Fred Gash added to their increasingly impressive score of victories with another He 111, although it was initially claimed as a Ju 88. Having taken off from Tangmere, height was gained whilst flying east until, when flying at 14,500 ft, they were vectored onto an enemy aircraft returning to France. This was soon sighted at a range of 400 yards and Hughes moved in underneath and on the starboard beam. Gash opened fire with four or five short bursts of up to two seconds, which raked the length of the fuselage. This prompted the German pilot to undertake some violent evasive manoeuvres which included reducing speed by climbing and carrying out stall turns. Hughes was impressed by the way his adversary was handling his aircraft and he had extreme difficulty staying in touch. Indeed the hunter then became the hunted as the Heinkel attempted a crossover attack underneath the Defiant which achieved some very near misses. It then dived steeply towards the coast and Hughes followed it down, managing to stay in close proximity as the German attempted to get home at low level. He was able to get into position to allow Gash to open up with a good long burst and although there was no immediate result, the Heinkel suddenly turned over and went into the sea where it exploded in flames. This was witnessed by F/L Sam Thomas (also of 264 Squadron) who was patrolling above.

This proved to be the last combat victory recorded by 264 Squadron during its stay at Biggin Hill as it moved to West Malling on 14 April 1941. During its time at Biggin it had shot down six enemy aircraft with another three claimed as probably destroyed. This achievement did not go unrecognised as three crew members were invited to an investiture at Buckingham Palace on 25 March. Sgt Hayden was presented with the DFM by George VI and F/Sgt Ted Thorn and F/Sgt Fred Barker each received a bar to the DFM. With the departure of the Defiants of 264 Squadron, Biggin Hill was allowed to concentrate on its day fighter activities. With the prospect of better weather it was hoped that the long-awaited offensive could at last get under way.

CHAPTER SEVEN

The Weapon is Forged

The improvement in the weather that had been hoped for unfortunately failed to materialise and the new month of April began in disappointing fashion as low cloud and rain prevented any flying. As a result the pilots were cocooned in claustrophobic Link trainers which were ground-based aids that were used for basic instrument flying instruction. Two new faces to arrive at Biggin Hill on 3 April were Pilot Officers Neville Duke and Gordon Brettell who joined 92 Squadron from 58 OTU at Grangemouth to become the first wholly wartime-trained pilots to join the squadron. Duke thus started out on a long RAF career that would later see him become the top scoring fighter ace in the Mediterranean theatre of operations. His time on 92 was very much a learning experience and as he was often nominated as No.2 to 'Sailor' Malan when he flew with the squadron, he had the best possible tutor.

At twenty-six years of age Gordon Brettell was seven years older than Duke but the two had become close friends as they had first met at Hatfield during their basic training, and the postings lottery had decreed that they should follow each other during the rest of their tuition. During his time at university Brettell had raced an Ulster-type Austin in the Inter-Varsity races and later competed at Brooklands in a lightened and modified example that had been built by the Monaco Engineering Company. He won a number of races and in 1937 joined a select band of drivers who had survived going over the top of the Brooklands banking. This happened during the BARC Whit Monday meeting on 17 May and a photograph of him emerging from the undergrowth with a broken arm appeared on the front page of The Times newspaper the following day. Shortly after his arrival at Biggin he achieved a certain amount of notoriety when he was placed on a court martial for flying his WAAF girlfriend over from Tangmere in his Spitfire for a squadron party. The unfortunate pair happened to disembark in front of G/C Soden who took an extremely dim view of the affair. Brettell was charged with endangering one of His Majesty's fighting aeroplanes, but the charge was later dropped when Tony Bartley admitted to having done exactly the same thing.

It has been suggested that this incident was the inspiration for an idea that G/C Soden came up with to prevent his Spitfires being attacked unseen from behind. The problem of seeing the enemy early enough so that a successful break could be made before attacking aircraft were in a position to open fire had been debated endlessly, the latest RAF tactic being the use of one or two aircraft as 'weavers' behind the main formation to warn of potential attacks. G/C Soden however came up with a rather more bizarre idea. He proposed that part of the armament in the wings of some aircraft should be deleted to allow space to accommodate the radio equipment that was normally installed in the rear fuselage. With the space behind the pilot now clear he suggested that a small rear-facing seat could be installed to be occupied by a Circus midget whose sole duty would be to warn of imminent attack. Not surprisingly, the idea did not find favour with the Air Ministry and thankfully for everyone involved, not least the midgets, the scheme went the way of many other wartime 'brainwaves' which seemed like a good idea in the bar, but did not stand up in the cold light of day.

The bad weather of recent days at least allowed the chance for important visitors to introduce themselves to the men who were fighting in the front line and on 5 April Sir Archibald Sinclair, the Secretary of State for Air, paid a visit to Biggin Hill. He toured each dispersal point in turn and spent a considerable time talking to the pilots. Although they endured this intrusion with apparent good humour it was a poor substitute for flying and the following day Tony Bartley and Bob Spurdle of 74 Squadron decided to do something about it. Although operations in squadron strength were out of the question, the low cloud that was prevalent over much of northern Europe at least gave the ideal opportunity to carry out a Rhubarb operation and by 1630 hrs the two were airborne from Manston.

This type of sortie could produce excellent results but success often depended on a large slice of luck, i.e. being in the right place at the right time. Rhubarbs were also highly dangerous as they were about to find out. Having crossed into occupied Europe near Gravelines, Bartley and Spurdle flew just below the cloud base at 1,500–2,000 ft in the general direction of St Omer. Their navigation was good and eventually they flew directly over the aerodrome but there were no aircraft dispersed and no anti-aircraft fire was experienced. The roads seemed devoid of traffic and the only time they were fired on from the ground was when they crossed over what appeared to be an ammunition dump which had numerous buildings separated by blast walls.

Not long after they chanced upon a Bf 109 parked in a field which appeared as though it might have force landed. Both pilots dropped down to shoot at it with machine-guns, leaving it enveloped in a cloud of brown smoke. Their efforts had not gone unnoticed, however, and as they climbed up to the cloud base to head for home they were attacked from behind by one or more enemy aircraft. Tony Bartley only knew that he was in trouble when he observed cannon shells whistling past him. He tried to turn into the attack, but was unsure as to which direction it was coming from as shells seemed to be flying past on both sides. As the cloud base was just above he pulled back on the stick and did a tight semi-loop into the overcast. This had the desired effect of losing whoever was shooting at him and when he descended once again there was no sign of his adversary, or of his No.2. Having had a very close shave he was in no mood to hang around and returned to Manston as quickly as he could.

Bob Spurdle had come under attack at the same time and fared rather worse as his aircraft was hit by two cannon shells and four machine-gun bullets. He also sought sanctuary in the clouds but by this time his Spitfire was shaking badly and its control at low speeds was poor. As his gyro instruments had toppled Spurdle was forced to descend once again to get a horizon and to let them settle down again. Shortly after flying out of a patch of low cloud he was confronted with a Bf 110 in front of him and slightly to the left, flying in the same direction at about 400 ft. Forgetting that his own aircraft may have been seriously damaged, he immediately opened fire and saw the 110 dip its port wing and crash-land in a big field. On turning back he saw the rear gunner climb out and run away so gave him a quick 'squirt' but although he fell to the ground, Spurdle was of the opinion that he had not been hit. With his aircraft still juddering in an alarming manner he flew into cloud once again and steered 280 degrees, eventually making a landfall at Dungeness. After landing at Manston it was discovered that the port aileron controls had been shot away and a cannon shell had passed through one of the propeller blades which accounted for the vibration he had experienced.

The following morning P/O John Howard (Blue 1) and Sgt Jan Rogowski (Blue 2) of 74 Squadron were engaged on a patrol near Dover when they were sent south to intercept two unidentified aircraft. These were not encountered until they were three miles from Cap Gris Nez and turned out to be Bf 109s. The German aircraft were the first to take the initiative however and both Spitfires were fired on, Rogowski pulling up into the clouds to shake one of the 109s off his tail. Howard in the meantime had pulled round in a steep turn to the right and succeeded in getting behind the No.2 Messerschmitt. He fired a short burst but the 109 immediately dived away towards the French coast. Turning his attention to the other one, it too tried to evade by going into the clouds but Howard was able to follow it until it emerged on the other side. On firing again he saw part of the port wing come off, at which point the 109 shot upwards into the cloud never to be seen again.

When he felt that the immediate danger had passed Rogowski descended out of the clouds once again and as he did so was presented with the satisfying sight of a 109 directly in front of him. As he was in its blind spot he was able to close in to 150 yards and fired two bursts which caused the 109 to roll over and dive straight into the ground. As they had become split up both Spitfires returned to Manston separately and were troubled only by sporadic anti-aircraft fire on their way home. Jan Rogowski had been a member of 74 Squadron for a little over two months having been posted in on 2 February. He was another of the many highly experienced Polish pilots who had found their way to Britain to continue the fight and had previously flown with 162 Eskadra at Lvov in Poland. He flew with 303 Squadron at the height of the Battle of Britain, was wounded in action on 6 September and as a consequence did not return to active duty until 23 October. At the end of the year he was awarded the Krzyz Walecznych (Polish Cross of Valour).

The next combat took place on 10 April and also involved 74 Squadron. Among the Spitfires airborne that day was P7854 which was being flown by P/O Peter Chesters who had been with 74 since the end of September 1940. Chesters was born in Thorpe Bay in Essex on 29 April 1919 and came from a wealthy family that had made its money in the silk industry. He had a reputation for aggressiveness in the air but this was allied to a certain amount of impetuosity and a 'devil-may-care' attitude. His first victory had come on 27 October 1940 but his penchant for making instantaneous decisions was apparent even on this occasion. After forcing down a Bf 109E near Penshurst in Kent he then landed beside his opponent and arrested the pilot before eventually taking off again with a number of trophies. During the action on the 10th he shot down Fw Friedrich Moller of II/JG 51 who was flying Bf 109F-2 Werke Nr 5670 'Black 8' which crashed at St Nicholas-at-Wade in Kent.

On his return to Manston, Chesters let his exuberance get the better of him and he attempted a victory roll over the airfield. Johnnie Freeborn was one of those on the ground who looked on in horror as it was immediately apparent that insufficient airspeed had been allowed for such a low level manoeuvre. The Spitfire stalled as it became inverted and with not enough height to recover it crashed on the station parade ground, killing its pilot instantly.

On 11 April 92 Squadron got the chance to fly an offensive mission when reports were received of a German seaplane being towed back to France by an enemy ship. Red section, comprising S/L Jamie Rankin, F/L Brian Kingcome, Sgt David Lloyd and Sgt Gaskell, took off just after midday and flew in thick haze over the Channel to within two miles of the French coast between Cap Gris Nez and Boulogne. They were aided in this task by a Spitfire of 91 Squadron that was picked up at Hawkinge and acted as a guide. The target, a Heinkel He 59, was not spotted at first but it eventually appeared out of the murk, as did a solitary Bf 109 which turned away as soon as the Spitfires were seen. Jamie Rankin was the first to attack and fired virtually all of his cannon ammunition in a long burst which surrounded the target with shell splashes. As he broke away he witnessed the attacks by Kingcome and Lloyd which finished off the seaplane and also damaged the tow ship, described by Kingcome as a 'ketch-rigged trawler'. At this time a large force of around fifteen Bf 109s of III/JG 51 appeared and Rankin ordered the other members of his section to return independently. Before leaving himself, he picked one of the 109s on the outside of the formation and fired two short bursts with machine-gun from close range and 30 degrees deflection. As the first wisps of glycol began to appear from the 109s punctured radiators, Rankin was forced to break sharply when three 109s began to threaten him but they did not chase him for long and he was able to return to Biggin having been airborne for 1 hour and 10 minutes. Only three aircraft were to make it back as Sgt Gaskell was shot down and killed in X4062.

The initial batch of Belgian pilots for 609 Squadron began to arrive at Biggin Hill in early April. First through the gates was P/O Willi Van Lierde who had flown Fairey Foxes with the Aeronautique Militaire in 1940 and subsequently flew with 87 Squadron. The next to appear was P/O Count Yvan du Monceau de Bergendael, whose imposing name was soon reduced to 'le Duc'. He was born in London on 10 December 1915 and later attended the Belgian Royal Military Academy prior to being posted to a cavalry unit in 1938 as a Lieutenant. The following year he transferred to the Air Force and was learning to fly at the time of the German invasion. He eventually arrived in the UK having travelled through France and Morocco and after completing his training flew Hurricanes with 253 Squadron before joining 609. P/O Vicki Ortmans was another to have flown the Fairey Fox but during his subsequent escape to the UK following the occupation of his own country, he was court-martialled in absentia (among others) for having used his aircraft to fly to France. Having passed through 7 OTU at Hawarden, he was posted to 229 Squadron and during the Battle of Britain shot down a Heinkel 111 and a Dornier 17 but had to make forced landings on two other occasions when his Hurricane suffered battle damage. Others to join the Belgian 'Flight' in 609 were Pilot Officers Bob Wilmet, Francois de Spirlet, Roger Malengreau and Eugene 'Strop' Seghers.

Although several operational sweeps were carried out over the next few days there was very little sign of enemy activity. On April 17 four Spitfires of 92 Squadron flown by Cecil Saunders, 'Wimpy' Wade, Roy Mottram and Allan Wright flew to West Malling for night readiness. For the pilots this was an onerous task which was a desperate attempt to bolster the night defences by using day fighters to carry out layer patrols on moonlit nights. Even in ideal conditions it was rather like looking for a needle in a haystack and very little came of it. The only advantage of these so-called 'fighter-nights' for those taking part was that they were subsequently released for much of the following day.

The Tigers lost another experienced pilot on the 19th when P/O Wally Churches was shot down and killed. Churches had been born in Auckland on 17 July 1921 and had a pleasant, easy going manner. He was also quiet and unassuming and these traits had endeared him to everyone. He had started work as a telegraph messenger and a postman in his native country before taking his initial pilot training. Having sailed to Britain he first flew single-engined fighters at 7 OTU and was posted to 74 Squadron in the late summer of 1940. Not only did he come through his baptism of fire unscathed, he went on to make several claims, however his first confirmed 'kill' was a Bf 109E shot down on 2 November. He was however fortunate to survive a mid-air collision with his squadron colleague Sgt Bill Skinner. Of the two Spitfires, Churches' machine was the least damaged and he was able to carry out a forced landing, but Skinner had to bale out. The New Zealander's luck finally ran out when he encountered Bf 109s of JG 53 over the Channel. At the time of his death he was just nineteen years of age.

A patrol the following day by 92 and 609 Squadrons produced no contacts but on their return several aircraft were despatched to Gravesend for layer patrols over London. On the 21st 609 Squadron's 'B' Flight took off for a defensive patrol but were soon redirected onto a Sphere operation from Cap Gris Nez to Calais. This was a type of high-level sweep and all aircraft returned with nothing to report, except for P/O Willi Van Lierde who ran out of fuel and had to force land. Unfortunately the field he chose to put his aircraft down in was festooned with anti-invasion obstructions including lateral wires and although he escaped injury, his Spitfire (P8094) was badly damaged.

The only action on 22 April involved a 'night attack' on London by 609 Squadron which started at Prunier where a 'defensive circle' was formed and Michael Robinson and Keith Ogilvie competed to see who could remain upside down for the longest time. The party then adjourned to the Suivi (one of 609's favourite haunts which was noted for its music and atmoshpere) but the events here were lost in an alcoholic haze, although several squadron members later remembered seeing P/O Sydney Hill attracting plenty of attention for himself outside Lyons' Corner House by shouting impossible demands in a loud voice. Fortunately he was quickly taken inside and eased into a seat before anyone took exception to his ranting. The rest of the night passed off uneventfully and a successful return to base was made in the early hours.

On 24 April two Spitfires of 92 Squadron flown by S/L Jamie Rankin and F/L Brunier took off at 0830 hrs to patrol between Dover and Dungeness. The weather was far from ideal with poor visibility and a general overcast at 1,000 ft. Rankin was warned of a Bf 109 in the vicinity and almost at once he saw it away to his right. It was flying inland and he pulled up and over his No.2 and opened fire with a large angle of deflection. The behaviour of the 109 was odd as it took no evasive action and instead waggled its wings. Thinking it might be friendly after all, Rankin closed in to identify its markings and once he was convinced it was hostile he pulled away again and attacked with several two-second bursts, machine-gun only. After these attacks the 109 was streaming glycol and appeared to be on fire. F/L Brunier then moved in but was still suspicious of the 109 as it could easily have pulled up into cloud but was not making any attempt to do so. He fired a three-second burst with cannon and machine-guns and only then did the 109 begin to climb, his tracer passing close to it as it eventually disappeared from view. The Messerschmitt did not last much longer, its pilot (Fw Gunther Struck of 2/JG 52) baling out over Broomshill Rye in Sussex to become a prisoner of war.

There was further success for 92 Squadron on 26 April during an offensive patrol by seven aircraft led by P/O Ronnie Fokes. Having taken off from Biggin at 1300 hrs and gained height over base, the Spitfires were over the Channel when the controller informed them of suspected enemy aircraft approaching from the south. The squadron's 'weaver' reported condensation trails above and to port but on altering course to intercept, it was discovered that these were Hurricanes returning home. Resuming course for the French coast they were then told of an unidentified formation to their starboard and Fokes soon saw five Bf 109s with another two above acting as top cover. Attacking immediately, Fokes fired at one from the starboard quarter and was most surprised to see its propeller stop dead as though the engine had seized. The 109 dived away but its pilot still carried out evasive manoeuvres even though his aircraft had become a rather inefficient glider. Fokes found it impossible to carry out any further attacks but he did manage to stop it getting back to the coast of France, which was the pilot's obvious intention, and it eventually came down in shallow water just offshore [the pilot, Uffz Werner Zimmer of 4/JG 53, was killed]. As his engine was beginning to run roughly Fokes wasted no time in heading back across the Channel. Of the others, Pilot Officers Sebastian Maitland-Thompson and Neville Duke shot at another 109 but without result.

On the 27th pilots of 609 Squadron were set to carry out a standing patrol with two sections of four aircraft although eight soon became seven as P/O 'Strop' Seghers failed to get off the ground as his aircraft became caught up in a camouflage net. This was the second time that he had been unable to take off at the appointed time as two days previously a NAAFI wagon had got in his way. He thought it most odd that others should be preventing him from carrying out his duty. At the end of the day's flying Sydney Hill's birthday provided the perfect excuse for another party and this was duly announced by the beating of drums. A game of snooker soon degenerated into hockey but when Hill and Frank Ziegler began to fight a battle with soda siphons, the bar emptied quicker than in any western. The celebrations then transferred to Southwood and eventually the birthday boy was found semi-conscious on the floor and was put to bed to sleep it off.

The gradual increase in activity that had been noted over the last few weeks became even more apparent on 29 April when 609 Squadron had its busiest day of the year so far. The following is from the Squadron Operations Record Book and the stark contrast between the day's events and the evening entertainment is a reminder of the peculiar life of a fighter pilot,

At 0830 hrs the squadron set out on a 'Roadstead' operation, instructions being to rendezvous with three Blenheims and a Flight of 74 Squadron at Manston, below cloud. 74 however were never sighted. The Blenheims then crossed the Channel at zero feet, 609 Squadron 500 ft above and behind. The target, four medium-sized ships, was duly sighted between Gravelines and Dunkirk and while 609 circles above at 2,000 ft, two of the Blenheims attacked. The third which apparently dropped its bombs in mid-Channel, then machine-gunned the target and it was while waiting for the completion of this that six Me 109s dived out of cloud and attacked the squadron. The latter broke up in pairs, half returning with the Blenheims, the other half engaging in a dogfight with the 109s (probably Me 109Fs on account of their rounded wings).

F/L Curchin and P/O Seghers were attacked by three enemy aircraft and took quick-turn evasive action, Curchin firing three short bursts without apparent result. Both of these aircraft were holed, especially Seghers'. Finding the enemy aircraft's speed to be superior, they then climbed into cloud and returned to base. P/O Ortmans failed to make his guns fire owing to omitting to turn the handle away from 'safe'. Flak was experienced from the ships, also from the Navy's guns at Dover, despite the use of IFF. Sgt Bennett did not return. No one saw what happened to him, though it is possible that he landed in enemy territory. He was one of the squadron's veteran Sergeants with an He 111 to his credit from last year.

At 1409 hrs 'B' Flight went to patrol Dungeness. Flying at 26,000 ft, four Me 109s were sighted to the south and slightly above. Both sides then broke up into pairs and manoeuvred for up-sun position. A dogfight ensued with two enemy aircraft attacking P/O Hill with cannon. P/O Ogilvie attacked these, firing at both (in the melee he also got a shot at Hill which amused them both in retrospect). One enemy aircraft dived vertically downwards. F/L Curchin fired a burst at another enemy aircraft while attempting to climb after it. Though no enemy casualties are claimed, the enemy aircraft retreated to France and 609 were left in charge of the situation. At 1506 hrs 'A' Flight took off and were flying on a vector of 085 degrees at 27,000 ft when three Me 109s were sighted flying north-west at slightly higher altitude. Manoeuvring took place and the leader (F/O Bisdee) got in a short burst from 500 yards. After some further circling, one enemy aircraft dived vertically downwards pursued by F/O Bisdee and P/O Du Monceau who fired two short bursts, thus being in action for the first time.

Altogether it was a good day for the visit of the Belgian Air Attache and his staff to whom it probably seemed typical. The evening saw a concert by Noel Coward, Beatrice Lillie, Caroll Gibbons and his wife followed by an excellent cold table in the Mess which was impossible to get near. Dancing ensued and by 0330 hrs three Squadron Leaders were the serving waiters from behind the bar.

Sgt G.C. Bennett had been the first NCO pilot on 609 and had joined the West Riding squadron towards the end of 1939. His service had not been continuous however as he was shot down and badly wounded on 31 May 1940 during a patrol over the Channel near Dunkirk. On recovering from his injuries he returned to the squadron only to be shot down as recounted above by a Bf 109 of JG 51. Ironically he came down in the same general area as his first brush with death the previous year. This time he was not picked up and another link with the past had gone.

The last day of April was relatively quiet with six Spitfires of 92 Squadron carrying out a patrol over Maidstone in the afternoon which proved to be uneventful. Over at Manston 74 Squadron was in the process of moving to Gravesend which would be its home for the next two months. The month had been a difficult one as weather conditions were still not suitable for Fighter Command's offensive against the *Luftwaffe* units on the other side of the Channel. Indeed Biggin Hill's squadrons had mainly been involved in defensive duties as their counterparts were not prepared to sit around and wait for the RAF to come to them and were more than willing to take the initiative. With the coming of summer it was hoped that the much-heralded non-stop offensive would at last be able to get under way after its faltering start.

CHAPTER EIGHT

Ominous Skies

By now Fighter Command was becoming increasingly impatient with the stop-start nature of its campaign but the weather did not show any signs of improving and the first two days of May were dull and wet with no flying possible at all. On the 3rd 92 Squadron was able to put up a patrol in the morning in which a Bf 109 was fired upon by F/O Roy Mottram but no claim was submitted. Several more patrols were made over the next couple of days, including a high level 'Sphere' patrol by four aircraft of 92 Squadron's 'B' Flight on the 4th. All of these passed off without incident. Having already lost seven pilots since the start of the year, 74 Squadron had another difficult day on 6 May when escorting Blenheims during a Roadstead operation aimed at shipping in the Channel. The strike was contested by the Bf 109Fs of JG 51 and during the ensuing dogfight two Spitfires were shot down, P/O John Howard being killed with Sgt A.D. Arnott taken prisoner.

During the fight Sgt A.F Wilson saw one of his comrades come under attack from below by a 109 which attempted a loop as the Spitfire turned on its back and dived. As the 109 lost speed at the top of its loop Wilson was able to close in and fired several bursts but was then forced to break sharply as he was attacked by another 109 from behind and to his left. During this combat his engine was hit and bullets also punctured his fuel tanks which caused petrol to pour into his cockpit and accumulate on the floor directly under his seat. With the prospect of being incinerated at any time, Wilson decided to try and reach Dover but on the way he was attacked by three more 109Fs which were heading towards the main fight that was still going on. Although his Spitfire was hit again it did not catch fire and he eventually managed to lose them by climbing into cloud. Resuming his dash for home, Wilson resolved not to stay with his aircraft for a moment longer than necessary and as soon as he had crossed the English coast he baled out. In the event he only just got out in time as his Spitfire caught fire before crashing in a field.

The following day White section of 74 Squadron, led by P/O Roger Boulding, was patrolling over Canterbury in the morning when it was informed of enemy aircraft over Margate. On arrival ten Bf 109s were seen in loose formation flying in a westerly direction and Boulding immediately called the Tally-Ho. He chased after one of the 109s firing a three-second burst which hit the underside of the fuselage. The German aircraft then turned away and dived for the sea, quickly drawing away until it was out of range. Having given up on this one Boulding tried his luck with three others which were on their way back to France but found he was unable to close to firing range. He then returned to Margate where, without warning, he was attacked from behind, bullets hitting his petrol tank and glycol system. By turning tightly he was able to approach his adversary head-on and fired a short burst as it also fired at him. During this attack his aircraft was hit again, this time on the windscreen. By now both aircraft were circling each other at about 500 ft and Boulding used the superior turn performance of his aircraft to get in behind the 109. He fired several bursts as it passed in and out of cloud and a thin wisp of white vapour denoted that his bullets had hit its cooling system. By now petrol was beginning to stream into the cockpit of Boulding's Spitfire and as he was also losing glycol, he was forced to break off and return to Manston. The 109 he had attacked was last seen flying with greatly reduced speed in an easterly direction and gradually losing height.

By now 609 Squadron had been at Biggin Hill for six weeks but had yet to make a name for itself. This was all about to change, however, and it found itself the centre of attention on 8 May following an action that was destined to be known as the Battle of the Dinghy. The events were recorded with obvious delight in the squadron's Operations Record Book by Frank Ziegler, 609's Intelligence Officer,

After a night at the Suivi and several convoy patrols, the squadron little thought as it took off at 1649 hrs with the usual 'stooge' instructions to patrol Maidstone at 15,000 ft that it was about to have the most successful combat any fighter squadron had endured since the Battle of Britain. Nor has any Squadron Leader celebrated his birthday quite so heartily. It all started with a little dinghy floating in mid-Channel containing a German aviator. If he was not the very important German aviator that it is suspected he was (perhaps 'ace' Molders), he must have felt very important by the time boats from both sides had competed to rescue him and by the time 609 Squadron finished battling with the *Luftwaffe* over him. Whether important or not, his joy at being eventually rescued by his own side must have been severely tempered after witnessing six, and probably eight, of his own fighters splashing into the surrounding sea, and not a single Spitfire. What happened was briefly as follows

No.609 Squadron in three sections of four, spied a rescue boat (ours) on fire with a couple of Me 109s circling over it. Leaving Blue section as top cover, the rest dived, but were too late. Blue section meanwhile was attacked and Blue 3 (Sgt Mercer) hit. Undismayed he attacked one of two enemy aircraft which shot past him, and it dived down vertically emitting smoke. Re-forming, Red and Yellow sections found a second rescue boat with more Me 109s. Yellow section now remained as cover while Red section, joined by Blue 1 and Yellow 4, dived. Red 1 (S/L Robinson) shot the nearest into the sea. Red 2 (F/L Curchin) fired at two others in quick succession and one dived into the sea, the other was finished off by Yellow 4 (Sgt Hughes-Rees). A cannon shell then hit Curchin's wing from behind and he came home with a blocked aileron and a Spitfire covered with enemy oil.

Two further enemy aircraft were shot down in quick succession by Blue 1 (Sgt Rigler) from point blank range – his first combat. Meanwhile Blue 2 (Sgt Palmer) had chased two 109s to within five miles of Calais. He then heard on the R/T "Beauty leader being fired on." S/L Robinson had pursued his second 109 also to the French coast and had just shot it down into the surf when he was attacked by nine others from all directions. He had used all his ammunition and came back at zero feet, taking superb evasive action by turning towards each enemy aircraft as it fired, and at times doing a complete circle. He emerged unscathed, helped by the loyal Sgt Palmer who saw a Spitfire with a 109 on its tail. He immediately hopped on to the tail of the 109 and gave him a two-second burst from the quarter . . . he gave him another two-second burst from point blank range. The 109's prop appeared to slow down but as he was also being dived on by others, he had no opportunity to see anything more, except that it was gliding downwards and sideways, apparently out of control.

Final praise must go to Yellow section led by F/L Richey who did good work as top cover and were themselves attacked. They also confirmed Rigler's second victim for him. There was quite a party to greet the victors and while the C.O.'s twin victory rolls seemed to confirm the news from ops, up drove the Group Captain and the Wing Commander, their shining cars contrasting strangely with the drab, battle-worn planes with gun canvasses shot away. As each pilot emerged from his plane a little procession would move towards him wearing smiles ever more surprised, while the Intelligence Officer, busy sifting claims, would ever and anon be asked "How many do you make it now?" In the end he made it S/L Robinson 2 destroyed, F/L Curchin 1½ destroyed, Sgt Rigler 2 destroyed, Sgt Hughes-Rees ½ destroyed, Sgt Palmer 1 probably destroyed, Sgt Mercer 1 probably destroyed. Our losses were one Spitfire Cat 2. Curchin's and Mercer's machines were both damaged, especially the latter's in which (among other things) a cannon shell exploded in the fuselage, splintering the perspex, one hole being an inch above Mercer's head. After a further uneventful sweep, the day terminated in due celebration. A telegram the next day said "Congratulations on a good days work, well done" – Leigh-Mallory AOC.

The German pilot who had sparked this action was not Werner Molders but Lt Karl Pones of JG 3 who had been shot down by a Hurricane of 302 Squadron. What Frank Ziegler could not have known was that there had been a degree of over-claiming by 609's pilots and in fact only three 109s had been shot down with another severely damaged. They were all Bf 109Fs from JG 3 and the pilots lost were Lt Gunther Poopel of the 1st Staffel, Lt Julius Heger of the 4th Staffel and Fw Gerhardt Grundmann of the 6th Staffel. By the time that Leigh-Mallory's congratulatory telegram was received, however, one of 609 Squadron's heroes was already dead.

On 9 May, following two early morning convoy patrols, 'B' Flight of 609 Squadron was scrambled at 1756 hrs to patrol from Maidstone to Dungeness. Two Bf 109s were encountered at 31,000 ft and Green section led by P/O Sydney Hill gave chase as they dived for France. As one seemed to continue on its way the other circled to the west which allowed Hill to get behind it and fire all of his ammunition in two long bursts. Although the 109 was hit, it did not appear unduly troubled and disappeared in a vertical dive. Afterwards it was concluded that the first 109 had also doubled back at some point and had attacked the aircraft flown by Sgt Bob Mercer who called to say that he was going down. He eventually tried to force land on the beach at St Margaret's Bay but in doing so his Spitfire blew up and burst into flames, either as a result of hitting a rock, or exploding a land mine. Sadly, Mercer was killed instantly.

No.92 Squadron was also patrolling at this time along a line from Dungeness to Ashford at 30,000 ft but it soon had problems as the squadron's designated 'weaver' passed out due to oxygen starvation and only came to at low level. His position was taken over by P/O 'Wimpy' Wade (Yellow 1) and after an hour in the air he became aware of a Bf 109 positioning itself to attack from astern. Having warned the rest of the squadron Wade took violent evasive action in an attempt to get into an attacking position. One of the problems of carrying out extreme manoeuvres at such high altitudes was that the sudden change in pressure in the cockpit often led to the canopy icing up. Unfortunately this occurred so that Wade was unable to see anything and he then went into a spiralling vertical dive during which his airspeed indicator quickly wound up to 440 mph. The 109 attempted to follow but in doing so its control surfaces broke up and the pilot was forced to bale out. Wade was able to land without further incident despite the fact that his aircraft had been hit in the starboard ammunition drum and cannon shell splinters had entered the glycol pipelines leading to a serious loss of coolant.

Sgt Hugh Bowen-Morris was flying as Red 2 when six 109s appeared above, four of which peeled off into an attacking dive. He turned into them so that they were head-on to him but when he pulled back on the stick to climb, his aircraft stalled. As soon as it did one of the 109s half rolled onto his tail and Bowen-Morris had to take evasive action which the German pilot did not anticipate and the two very nearly collided. Perhaps as a result of this the German decided to break off the engagement and head for France but Bowen-Morris followed and fired several bursts at extreme range which caused twin streams of white vapour to appear. The 109 entered a steep dive and was last seen at about 3,000 ft descending at high speed towards the sea. The 109s were from JG 5 and they also succeeded in shooting up the Spitfire of P/O Sebastian Maitland-Thompson who was injured in the process with slight wounds to his legs and face. His Spitfire (R6908) was damaged sufficiently for it to be written off.

Although several patrols were carried out on 10 May in which enemy aircraft were encountered, the combats that did take place were largely ineffectual and neither side inflicted any real damage on the other. Having taken off at 1053 hrs 609 Squadron's 'A' Flight led by F/L Paul Richey were patrolling inland from Dungeness at 28,000 ft when four Bf 109Fs appeared about 3,000 ft above. After a while these were seen to head for the French coast but one pair returned with the other pair also turning to provide cover. Several guarded circling manoeuvres then took place between the opposing sides as they weighed each other up. F/O Bisdee fired two short bursts at one of the 109s from astern and underneath but his fire drifted wide. All of 'A' Flight attacked, and in turn were attacked themselves, but the whole thing had the air of a practice combat about it and each side broke away with nothing more substantial than a better knowledge of the strengths and weaknesses of the opposition.

On landing Richey rued the lack of performance from 609 Squadron's Spitfire IIs which were outpaced and were also outperformed in the climb by the Bf 109F. This was a more advanced version of the 109E and featured rounded wing tips, a cantilever tailplane and a retractable tailwheel. The initial version was powered by a Daimler-Benz DB 601N of 1,200 hp which offered a top speed of 369 mph but it would not be long before the F-4 variant was in service powered by a DB 601E of 1,300 hp. Although it still could not compete with a Spitfire in a turning fight, the 109F was blessed with superior altitude performance and was more than a match for the Spitfire II/V when climbing or diving.

No.609 Squadron's 'A' Flight was airborne again at 1718 hrs and sighted four Bf 109s in pairs in the same area that they had been encountered in the morning. These were soon lost to view but their attention then transferred to a group of six aircraft in the Maidstone area which were behaving in a very strange manner. Richey was extremely suspicious of their antics and maintained that they were hostile despite the controller being adamant that they were in fact friendly. Once on the ground Richey would not let the matter drop and insisted that Frank Ziegler contact Group to find out if any Fighter Command squadrons actually did behave like that. Group signalled back 'Unusual tactics observed, probably friendly, probably Polish'.

On the evening of the 10th it was 74 Squadron's turn to fly to West Malling for 'fighter nights' however this generally loathsome task was, for once at least, not being looked upon quite so badly as clear conditions of bright moonlight offered an excellent chance of success, even for day fighters. One of those airborne was P/O Roger Boulding (call-sign Knockout 17) who was patrolling over London at 18,000 ft just before midnight. The omens were not good as his propeller constant speed unit was playing up and he had just decided to return to base when he saw a twin-engined aircraft about 200 yards away, heading in a south-easterly direction. Having flown underneath it he was able to identify it as a Heinkel 111 and opened fire from astern and slightly below from around 50–100 yards. His aim was good and he saw his De Wilde ammunition striking the fuselage which produced a number of bright flashes and various pieces of debris came back at him, some striking his Spitfire in the air intake and propeller.

The Heinkel immediately took evasive action, its pilot closing the throttles to reduce speed before diving steeply. Boulding continued to fire in the dive but his job was made even more difficult as the internal face of his bullet-proof windscreen began to ice up. Despite this he managed to stay in touch with the German aircraft which only pulled out of its dive at very low level. By now Boulding's windscreen had cleared but as he was forced to fly slightly higher than the Heinkel he had great difficulty in keeping it in sight as it tended to merge with the dark background. As he was silhouetted against the slightly lighter sky, the rear gunner could keep Boulding's aircraft in view, especially if it was to the right-hand side of the Heinkel as this was 'up moon'. As he had to jink from side to side to keep the bomber in sight the gunner was able to fire some accurate bursts when he was in this position. Even so, Boulding was able to fire two more short bursts before he had to break away and return to West Malling. From his vector home he estimated his position to be ten miles south-east of Maidstone. Later it was confirmed that the Heinkel had crash-landed at Kennington near Ashford at 0005 hrs [the He 111 was A1+JN of 5/KG 53 and Hptm Albert Hufenreuther and crew were taken prisoner].

News of Boulding's success spread quickly and some of 74 Squadron's pilots, including Johnnie Freeborn, drove over to the crash site to see what they could find. Freeborn was keen to see if he could obtain a Luger pistol but was ultimately to be disappointed. Not to be outdone he then turned his attention to the Heinkel's camera but as he was dismantling it he was stopped by an agitated airman from RAE Farnborough who explained in a rather shaky voice that the installation could well be booby-trapped. The dinghy that the Tigers had purloined was also taken from them which meant that they had to make do with the bomb sight instead.

For three days from 12 May the task of performing as makeshift night-fighters was given over to 609 Squadron although in their case it turned into more of a three-day holiday. As this was the first time that 609 had been required to operate at night the pilots were seen off by the ground-based members of the squadron including Frank Ziegler who was forced to watch bare-headed as his cap ended up at West Malling courtesy of P/O Sydney Hill. Instead of the usual perils of anti-aircraft fire, collisions or simply getting lost and having to bale out, it turned out that the only night flying carried out was a couple of dusk patrols. Having caught up on their sleep, a return was made to Biggin Hill each morning for breakfast followed by release for the rest of the day. Even so there were still mutterings about the sanity of those who thought it was a good idea to risk the lives of the best day fighter pilots by sending them out at night.

By the middle of May an improvement in the weather gave 'Sailor' Malan the opportunity at last to take the initiative on a more regular basis and on the 16th all three squadrons of the Biggin Hill Wing flew together as they would do for the rest of the year. The following is the day's events as recorded in the 609 Squadron ORB

W/C Malan thought it was about time the Biggin Hill Wing got together for a little practice so with himself leading, 92 and 609 took off at 1230 hrs and met 74 from Gravesend over base. The temptation to parade his monster show of strength before the Nazis was however irresistible, so they swept up and down the Channel, little pairs of 109s skipping out of the way in fright, one of them not quick enough to avoid being damaged by 92.

In the afternoon 609 had another victory and although it was pale compared with the glories of the 8th, it ended with two Me 109s destroyed and another damaged, P/O Ogilvie, Hill and Ortmans being a representative lethal media and respectively representing the countries of Canada, Great Britain and Belgium. We suffered one Spitfire Cat 2, Sgt Palmer being surprised and having to force land at Detling. The classic remarks of the C.O. "I couldn't be more sorry" on hearing one of his weavers had been shot down, deserves engraving in stone, preferably granite. This was the start of the battle. After that the squadron began circling at 22,000 ft near Dover. P/O Wilmet was then attacked but took successful evasive action.

Four Me 109s were then sighted below and flying in the opposite direction. Leaving the faithful Yellow section as top cover, the other two dived to attack. Blue 1 (P/O Ogilvie) took the leading one and after a burst from the quarter and above at short range the enemy aircraft half rolled and went down at a steep angle followed by Ogilvie, clocking over 450 mph and firing further bursts until his ammunition was spent. It was left smoking at less than 500 ft. Blue 2 (P/O Van Lierde) fired a short burst at a second 109 and Red 4 (P/O Hill) attacked a third. After diving from 20,000 ft to 1,000ft emitting black smoke, it descended into a layer of heat haze and P/O Hill himself pulled out just in time to avoid the Dover balloons. Ogilvie's 109 was seen to crash by the Dover balloon barrage, Hill's was seen burning on the water by F/L Lyle of 75 Wing, though the reconciliation of positions and time gave the I.O. a headache. Meanwhile Blue 4 (P/O Atkinson) had done a spot of freelance chasing and shooting. The two 109s concerned then had the impudence to attack Yellow section, obediently re-formed over Dover. As F/L Richey and P/O Ortmans broke away in opposite directions, the latter had a shot at one as it flew past and then chased it most of the way to France. Though white, then black smoke issued from it, Ortmans returned saying "He no go down."

The 109 that had not got out of the way quickly enough during the Wing sweep had been attacked by Don Kingaby who was 92 Squadron's designated 'weaver'. As they were heading for home, warnings were received that 'snappers' were in the area. Almost immediately Kingaby saw two condensation trails above and behind coming from the English coast and assumed these to be 109s but they turned out to be Spitfires which joined in a general melee that had developed below. Climbing

Spitfires of 610 Squadron up from Biggin Hill during the summer of 1940.

Air Vice-Marshal Keith Park, the commander of No.11 Group Fighter Command during the Battle of Britain.

F/L John Freeborn of 74 Squadron (via Bob Cossey).

Air Vice- Marshal Trafford Leigh-Mallory seen in 1944 with F/Sgt T.P Fargher of 234 Squadron.

S/L A.G. 'Sailor' Malan who was appointed as Wing Leader at Biggin Hill in March 1941.

S/L Johnnie Kent of 92 Squadron.

One of 92 Squadron's famous parties in full swing. The front row comprises Johnnie Kent, Tony Bartley, Bob Holland and 'Wimpy' Wade. Back row – Sebastian Maitland-Thompson, Tom Wiese (I.O.) and Geoff Wellum.

Sgt Ralph 'Tich' Havercroft of 92 Squadron.

F/L John Mungo-Park who became O.C. 74 Squadron when 'Sailor' Malan took over as Biggin Hill Wing Leader (via Bob Cossey).

Sgt Hugh Bowen-Morris of 92 Squadron in the cockpit of the third of ten presentation Spitfires donated by the Falkland Islands.

'Sailor' Malan shakes hands with F/L Harbourne Stephen in the company of other 74 Squadron pilots (via Bob Cossey).

F/L Brian Kingcome of 92 Squadron.

Spitfires of 92 Squadron carry out formation practice in early 1941.

Spitfire Ib R6923 was converted to Mark Vb standard in April 1941 but was shot down over the Channel on 21 June (Sgt G.W. Aston rescued).

Spitfires of 92 Squadron about to take off.

P/O Gordon Brettell of 92 Squadron.

F/L John Mungo-Park of 74 Squadron is painted by the artist Eric Kennington.

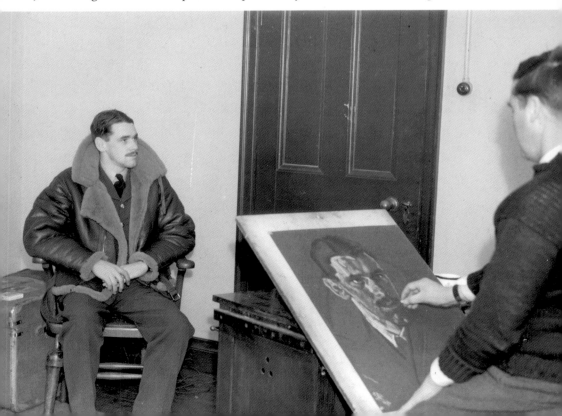

'Sailor' Malan with other 74 Squadron pilots including P/O Bob Spurdle.

Sgt Don Kingaby of 92 Squadron was dubbed 'the 109 specialist' by the press.

S/L Michael Robinson of 609 Squadron (via Norman Franks).

P/O Sydney Hill of 609 Squadron (ext right) with F/L F.J Howell.

SALVED FROM
J.U. 88.
E 100TH ENEMY AIRCRAFT
T DOWN BY 609 (F) SQUADRON
21ST OCT., 1940

F/LT. HOWELL D.F.C.
AND
P/O S.J. HILL.

A Spitfire IIa of 609 Squadron taxying at Biggin Hill (via Norman Franks).

F/L Johnnie Curchin of 609 Squadron poses in front of Spitfire IIa P8098 PR-Z, the 'Enfield Spitfire' (via Norman Franks).

92 Squadron pilots line up for the camera with Jamie Rankin at centre. From left Brettell, de Montbron, Kingcome, ?, Kingaby, Pietrasiak. Neville Duke is standing immediately in front of the Spitfire canopy with Allan Wright on his right.

Boulton Paul Defiant N3313 of 264 Squadron.

P/O F.D. Hughes of 264 Squadron (centre) with his gunner Sgt F. Gash (left) and P/O F.C. Sutton.

Sgt E.R. Thorn and Sgt F.J. Barker of 264 Squadron.

Defiant N1801 PS-B *Coimbatore II* of 264 Squadron was the aircraft flown by P/O F.D. Hughes.

A gathering on the terrace at Biggin Hill. L to R Offenberg, (US Colonel), Ogilvie, Bisdee, Rankin, MacKenzie, Malan, Robinson, ? (via Norman Franks).

to 28,000 ft in mid-Channel, Kingaby saw two 109s heading for Dungeness. As he was 500 ft above, he turned in behind them but before he could open fire he became aware of another 109 on his tail. Breaking sharply, a short dogfight ensued in which Kingaby's fire hit the 109's port wing root, prompting it to disengage by diving steeply. By now the other two 109s were above him so he broke off combat and returned to base.

Kingaby and the rest of 92 Squadron took part in the same defensive patrol as 609 Squadron which involved patrolling a line from Dungeness to Dover at 15,000 ft. During the action that followed Kingaby saw one of the 109s break off and head at full speed for the French coast and he wasted no time in following. Using full throttle and full rpm, an indicated speed of 470 mph was achieved in the dive and range was gradually reduced to 150 yards. Firing cannon and machine-gun, HE and tracer hits were observed on the starboard wing which then crumpled up and broke off. The position of the attack was about five miles off Calais at 7,000 ft. On his way back Kingaby saw another 109 going down in a steep dive with black smoke pouring from it having been attacked by other members of the squadron. This aircraft was also claimed as destroyed.

Although 'Sailor' Malan had been Wing Leader at Biggin Hill for just over two months his ideas on tactics were obviously taking some time to be accepted as witness 92 Squadron's use of 'weavers' in the operation described above. Malan had long been an advocate of his squadron flying in three sections of four aircraft in line astern formation with each individual four made up of two pairs. One of the basic faults of the vic of three was its poor lookout as the pilots of the aircraft on either side of the leader were spending all their time doing formation flying instead of scanning the sky for threats. Malan favoured the use of sections of four aircraft with Nos. 1 and 3 being the leaders, leaving the Nos. 2 and 4 as their respective wingmen. From a lookout point of view his system was an improvement in that the line astern formation was easier to fly and allowed pilots more time to search the skies around them. To maintain an acceptable level of cross-cover all aircraft had to fly a weaving course to clear the area behind them, and ended up as Mike Spick referred to it in his book *Fighter Pilot Tactics* (Patrick Stevens Ltd, 1983) 'writhing across the sky like a trio of serpents.' Naturally the effect became more pronounced towards the end of the formation so that the No.4 had to manoeuvre the most which meant that he had to use higher throttle settings, and thus more fuel, to stay in touch.

Although Malan's system was a big improvement, it was still inferior to the tactics that had been adopted by the *Luftwaffe* which placed the basic four-aircraft section in virtual line abreast. This provided excellent cross-cover as each pilot could clear the tail of the next aircraft in line and as the same throttle settings could be used throughout, no-one was in danger of running out of fuel before anyone else. Changes of direction were also easier to accomplish and there was less risk of straggling. With Malan's system if some of his aircraft were beginning to weave to the right when the Wing commenced a turn to the left (and vice versa) those on the outside of the formation were in danger of becoming detached. The tactical philosophy used by the Germans was eventually taken up by the Tangmere Wing (led by W/C Douglas Bader) in 1941 where it was known as the 'finger four' formation and after a period of time was adopted throughout Fighter Command. However, such was the degree of conservatism among the RAF's Wing Leaders that Malan's formation was still being flown by some as late as mid-1943. The degree of trial and error that went on at squadron level during 1941 can be glimpsed by the following comments of Neville Duke

When I first joined 92 Squadron in April 1941 we were still flying the basic Fighter Command vic of three formation with, or without, 'weavers'. As far as I can recall we changed to three sections of four in line astern around mid-May. For the rest of my time in the Biggin Hill Wing I cannot recall that any squadron flew any formation other than this during 1941. However I do remember some experiments with different ideas and recall very well a complete shambles when Malan tried to lead the Wing on a training flight with a formation called (for some unknown reason) 'American pairs'. This consisted of sections of two aircraft which were scattered all over the sky. It seemed like a good idea at the time and gave good area cover with a lot of freedom of action, but was quite uncontrollable as a Wing. When I left Biggin Hill and next encountered 92 Squadron out in the Western Desert (in April 1942) they were still flying with sections in line astern!

Although Malan's line astern formation was also flown by 609 Squadron, in their case a rather more fluid approach was adopted. This was introduced largely due to the recommendations of Paul Richey who had first become aware of the need for greater flexibility in fighter formations during the Battle of France. Rather than have the lead section in the middle with the other two sections to the left and right, he advocated staggering the sections vertically with that led by the squadron commander at the lowest level. These four Spitfires would also be spaced further apart and would weave from side to side. The two sections above were stepped back and manoeuvred in similar fashion but did so alternately so that when the section below commenced a turn to the right, the one above started its weave to the left. In this way virtually all of the sky above and behind was in view to at least one of the squadron members. At first Michael Robinson was not convinced, but he was a gradual convert to the system and the longer 609 went without being bounced, the more he saw its benefits. It was usually referred to as the 'Snake' and as the Spitfires could fly at higher cruising speeds, whilst still maintaining their position in relation to the bombers during Circus operations, the speed advantage of attacking fighters was reduced which allowed more time for these aircraft to be seen and for effective evasive manoeuvres to be carried out.

On 17 May 'A' Flight of 609 Squadron was patrolling Tenterden at 15,000 ft when the controller ordered the Spitfires to head for Manston as it had been reported that Bf 109s were in the area. On arrival a section of 109s was seen below and behind and a dogfight soon developed during which F/O John Bisdee, P/O Rodolphe de Grunne and P/O Vicki Ortmans all fired their guns. P/O J.A. 'Joe' Atkinson found himself in the least favourable position as he was weaving slightly below the rest of the formation and thus attracted the attention of one of the 109s. Before he could react a cannon shell slammed into his starboard wing, but the attack was not maintained which gave Atkinson the chance to dive away out of trouble. He decided to head for Rochester but as he lowered the flaps he discovered to his horror that only the port flap went down, the other having been jammed in the up position. This made the aircraft virtually uncontrollable but by keeping the speed up and with coarse use of controls, he was able to put his Spitfire (P8241) down in a ploughed field, wiping off the undercarriage in the process and bumping his head on the reflector gunsight. His troubles were not quite over however as he was viewed with considerable suspicion by the farm worker who was in the process of ploughing the field that he had arrived in. Frank Ziegler later postulated that the man may have thought another high-ranking Nazi had turned up (Rudolf Hess had flown to the UK just ten days before in a misguided attempt to broker a peace agreement) but it appears more likely that he was merely disgruntled that Atkinson had ruined some of his handiwork.

Atkinson was to become 609 Squadron's longest serving wartime member having arrived in December 1940. He had previously flown with the University Air Squadron at Oxford and after training had spent a brief period with 234 Squadron. Although he was universally known as 'Joe', his first name was actually John and he had Keith Ogilvie to thank for his nickname. On being posted to 609 at Warmwell one of Atkinson's first duties had been to organise the squadron's response to an attack by gas. Ogilvie let it be known that in Canada all gas men were called 'Joe' and the name was to stick. Atkinson remained with 609 until April 1943. He survived the war to become a senior civil servant and was awarded a knighthood.

'Joe' Atkinson's Spitfire was not the only aircraft to be written off on this day as Michael Robinson had brake failure when landing the unit's Puss Moth which was used as a general runabout and hack. Its loss was felt by many as it was a symbol of liberty and escape and had been extremely useful as a social tool in transporting pilots to wherever they needed to go, assuming that there was a suitable field located close by in which to land. Later in the day Robinson flew a dusk patrol with Keith Ogilvie who had recently been promoted to Flying Officer, but had yet to find time to attach the wider stripe to his uniform.

The next day only two patrols were possible as worsening weather set in. It was during times like this that everyone on 609 Squadron began to look towards P/O Jimmy Baraldi who had been grounded for some time with sinus trouble. Baraldi had become a kind of social manager and on this occasion he was told by Michael Robinson to head for London and not come back until he had obtained a large number of 'balls of fire' for yet another event at Southwood. He evidently succeeded magnificently as the party lasted into the small hours with more besides. Later Michael Robinson was heard to state his preference for parties at the squadron's home at Southwood stating – "When you get tired you just go to bed and send the girls back in the squadron transport." The following day only one patrol was possible but 609's pilots were kept at Readiness for most of the day as 74 Squadron was weather bound at Gravesend. Needless to say, there was considerable dissatis-faction as a result, but the mood changed on the 20th when thick fog prevented flying of any sort and everyone was released.

On 21 May the tenth Circus operation of the year was carried out when Blenheims of 21 and 110 Squadrons attacked the power station at Gosnay. Biggin Hill's involvement was to provide a cover patrol over the Channel and on this occa-sion it was 609 Squadron which saw most of the action. The squadron was orbiting in three extended sections in line astern off the North Foreland at 13,000 ft when two Bf 109s appeared out of high cloud. F/L John Bisdee (Yellow 1) manoeuvred his section so as to come in from behind the German aircraft but after firing a short burst they both dived towards France. As there was a good chance that there would be other 109s nearby, he made no attempt to follow. His reasoning was correct as four more 109s were seen above heading in the opposite direction, with another diving for home and acting as bait. Their failure thus far to lure any of 609's Spitfires out of position did not deter the German pilots, however, and soon another 109 was seen below heading south-west at 8,000 ft. This one seemed more promising and Bisdee dived down on it, firing a two-second burst from vertically above. It went down in a slow spiral from which it showed no obvious signs of pulling out.

In fact this aircraft had already been attacked higher up by P/O Vicki Ortmans but as he followed it down he had to break away as Bisdee's section cut in.

After he had stopped firing Bisdee was not able to see what happened to the 109 as tracer shot past him from behind. Looking back the air seemed to be full of gun panels and pieces of sheet metal and thinking he had been hit, he turned round sharply and pulled upwards. He also became aware of a parachute coming down behind him. As he was short of fuel and his oil temperature was also disconcertingly high he left the battle and landed at West Malling. It transpired that his aircraft had not been damaged and it was only then that he realised that the wreckage he had seen fluttering down behind him was the remains of the Spitfire flown by his No.2, P/O de Grunne. The 109 that was attacked by Ortmans and Bisdee was subsequently given as destroyed on the testimony of another squadron pilot who claimed to have seen a 109 dive into the sea.

Rodolphe de Grunne thus became the first of 609 Squadron's Belgian contingent to fall in battle. His journey to fight with the RAF had been an unusual one in that he fought in the Spanish Civil War on the side of the Nationalists where he flew the Fiat CR32 biplane fighter. During this time he destroyed ten aircraft of the Spanish Republican Air Force, mainly Polikarpov I-15s and I-16s. He had in fact flown from Biggin Hill in 1940 when serving with 32 Squadron but was shot down on 18 August by a Bf 109E of III/JG 26. Although he baled out successfully, de Grunne's Hurricane had been set on fire during the attack and he was badly burned before he was able to get out. He was to spend the next nine months recovering from his injuries. During his time with 32 Squadron de Grunne had not been the most popular of pilots due to his rather conceited attitude. As he had flown a Messerschmitt 109 in Spain there was therefore a certain amount of amusement when he was eventually shot down by one. Many pilots were superstitious to the point where they carried good luck charms with them in the air and de Grunne was no exception. Sadly the small silver horseshoe that he took with him on his last flight did not bring him good fortune. It appears that he baled out over the Goodwin Sands but his body was never found.

Throughout the rest of May the weather was not conducive to large-scale operations and the best that could be hoped for was to 'plant a little Rhubarb'. Some of 609 Squadron's Belgian pilots were keen on this type of operation, particularly P/O Vicki Ortmans who hatched a plan to beat up his old airfield at Brussels. He was eventually dissuaded from doing this on the grounds of excessive distance and had to accept a slightly less ambitious trip instead. In all ten aircraft of 609 Squadron took off in the afternoon of the 23rd with most of them refuelling at Manston or Hawkinge before setting out. All were forced to return however before crossing into occupied Europe as they found the weather to be considerably less horticultural than had been supposed.

No.74 Squadron also tried this type of operation and on 26 May F/O Henry Baker and P/O W.J. Sandman took off from Biggin Hill at 1510 hrs as Green section. After flying for about half an hour they saw a Bf 109 over the Channel but on turning to intercept, it disappeared in cloud and was not seen again. On reaching Boulogne the cloud base was too low to continue and the decision was taken to return to base. On approaching Dover another 109 was seen through the murk attacking a barrage balloon which went down in flames into the harbour. Baker immediately swung into the attack but then lost sight of the 109. As he was desperately looking around to see where it had gone it suddenly appeared on his tail and opened fire from dead astern. Throwing his aircraft into a violent turn he blacked out and on regaining consciousness found that the German machine was in front of him and slightly to the left. He opened fire with a four-second burst with slight deflection and the 109 was seen to dive into the sea about 3–4 miles south of Dover harbour.

The first Spitfire Vbs for 609 Squadron were delivered to Biggin Hill on the 27th with more arriving the following day. These had been due to arrive during the middle of April and the delay had meant the squadron had been forced to continue with their old Mark IIs for rather too long. Mickey Robinson was the first to take to the air in the new machine and pronounced it to be 'delightful to fly'. Not that 609 was able to make much use of its new aircraft as the weather continued to dominate proceedings. On the 29th Keith Ogilvie was heard to say "there's a knife outside you could cut with a mist" before turning over and going back to sleep in his chair. There was no improvement the following day and the month thus ended in disappointing fashion. It was, perhaps, best that pilots did get the chance to catch up on a little sleep as the long-awaited offensive would finally get under way in June and for most pilots of the Biggin Hill Wing it would prove to be one of the most intensive periods of operational flying of the entire war.

CHAPTER NINE

Maximum Effort

The new month of June was to see the departure of G/C Soden who was replaced as station commander by G/C Philip 'Dickie' Barwell, the elder brother of P/O Eric Barwell of 264 Squadron. Born in Knowle in Warwickshire on 2 July 1907, he entered the RAF on a short service commission in September 1925. On receiving his wings he was posted to 19 Squadron where he flew the Gloster Grebe and after being awarded a permanent commission he later served in Iraq before returning to Britain in 1934 to become an instructor at the Central Flying School at Upavon. In 1937 he was given the command of 46 Squadron flying the Gloster Gauntlet II and was still with this unit when it converted to the Hurricane in March 1939. By the time of the Battle of Britain he was a Wing Commander and was serving with HQ 12 Group but the thought of missing all the action was difficult for him to accept and he managed to fly three operational sorties with Douglas Bader's 242 Squadron. This attitude was also to manifest itself during his time at Biggin Hill as he was to be a regular addition to the Wing and often flew on offensive sweeps over France as No.2 to Michael Robinson.

As the bad weather of the previous month continued into the beginning of June little operational flying was carried out in the first few days which at least allowed pilots the opportunity to head for their favourite drinking establishments in London. The following is the entry in 609 Squadron's ORB for 2 June which shows that even this type of activity was not without its hazards

The weather is impossible and it's 609's day for release anyway. A large party accordingly moved off to town with the obvious intention of getting pickled. Dispersing in various directions, it reassembled by order of the C.O. at the Berkeley, officially at 2030, actually at 2130 and not before some members had experienced adventures. P/O de Spirlet assaulted a total stranger on the grounds that he had besmirched Belgium, a third party intervening just in time to point out that the man, so far from making insults, had been paying compliments.

P/O Hill, wandering about the streets, kept finding someone who repeatedly asked the way to the same place. This was happening for the fourth time when a car drew up and another man leapt out and asked P/O Hill if he would like a fight, forthwith aiming a heavy blow at the latter's jaw. Hill ducked, and was then surprised to see the man punching the other man's head on the ground. The assaulter, presumably satisfied, then got back into his car and drove away. Meanwhile, the Intelligence Officer sitting in the back of someone's Bentley was run into by a bus, and his minor injuries were treated at the Berkeley First Aid Post.

After the Berkeley it is needless to add that the party adjourned to the Suivi, where it was joined by S/L Mungo-Park of 74 Squadron. By about 0400 hrs tables had become entirely pooled, with people wandering about in a dream, not caring to whom they spoke, what they said, or whose drink they had. F/L Richey at last appeared and ordered the remainder of the party into the Commer [squadron transport], the C.O. having, as usual, disappeared in the Ford. Once downstairs, however, it becomes impossible to separate F/L Curchin and P/O Hill from two ladies they met in the hall, and they were left behind.

Next morning it gradually emerged that the recalcitrants had rung up a lady of title, persuaded her to dress and drive to Biggin Hill. It had then occurred to the bemused mind of F/L Curchin that as a reward it would be a good thing to take the lady for an early morning ride in the Maggy [the squadron's Miles Magister], despite 10/10 cloud at 200 ft. Thereupon ops, discovering that there were pilots at dispersal, ordered them to take off forthwith to patrol a convoy off the North Foreland. Not waiting for the arrival of Sgt Rigler, P/O Hill took off in his Spitfire and found the convoy lurking under 10/10 cloud at about 400 ft. Finding however that he was liable to plunge into the sea at any moment, he returned, somehow landed, and affected that his R/T had packed up. F/L Curchin was still sufficiently "gay" at breakfast to break a leg off the piano.

Such was the off-duty life of an officer in 609 Squadron in 1941.

Thick fog in the morning of 4 June prevented any flying before noon but conditions had improved considerably by the afternoon which allowed a Roadstead to be carried out and an evening patrol. Although these operations passed off uneventfully for 92 Squadron, it was a different matter for 609 Squadron.

At 1640 hrs 609 took off with 92 Squadron on a Roadstead. Six Blenheims were supposed to attack a couple of cargo vessels apparently stuck outside Boulogne but as far as can be made out, the Blenheims failed to release their bombs. The only opposition experienced by 609 was a barrage of heavy flak from Boulogne, but they wisely remained out of reach of this.

1926 hrs saw the beginning of a much more serious operation when the squadron took off to escort a Lysander searching off Dover for one of 54 Squadron [this was an ASR operation looking for F/L George Gribble DFC, a six-kill 'ace' who had been shot down during the earlier Roadstead]. On the way F/L Richey's section was detached with unfulfilled intention of picking up another Lysander at Hawkinge. The remaining nine aircraft were patrolling in two sections at 2,000 ft when three Me 109F were sighted directly above. S/L Robinson promptly began a steep climbing circle of them, at the same time calling on F/L Richey's section over Hawkinge to gain height and surprise the enemy aircraft from up sun. Before this could be accomplished however, one enemy aircraft by a 'brutal manoeuvre' (to quote P/O Ortmans) dived down and attacked one of our aircraft which was lagging behind and 1,000 ft below the rest. At this point we will turn to the end of the tale and watch the Intelligence Officer interview the pilots as they come in – an example of how difficult it is sometimes to reconstruct an action.

First comes P/O de Spirlet with a faulty oil gauge. He has nothing to relate. Then other pilots arrive in driblets which presuppose action. The C.O. taxies up with gun canvasses shot away, and emerges from his plane sweating. He has fought for at least ten minutes, he says, and is obviously very tired. He thinks he has got one, he saw a splash, but before that he saw a Spitfire go in. Then Sgt Rigler appears, all cock-a-hoop, he has got one – "no doubt about that" – and probably another (all very difficult, for of the three, one, says the C.O., returned to France). Next comes Ortmans. "Yes, I fire" he laughs, "but the Jerry, he go on" (thank goodness HE doesn't claim one, thinks the I.O.). Suddenly pilots stop arriving, and there are still five more missing. Everyone seems to be certain that one 109 and one Spitfire have gone into the drink. We speculate – the latter must be either Sgt Boyd or P/O Van Lierde, both No.4s. Four aircraft are reported at Hawkinge and West Malling. Momentarily there is a rumour of another one at Manston. Momentarily the C.O. smiles, for it seems that, after all, we have lost no one, and the Spitfire was another 109. Boyd and Van Lierde both come in. Then it suddenly dawns upon us, the almost unbelievable – the missing pilot is Johnnie – Johnnie Curchin.

As reconstructed afterwards, after much checking and cross-checking of times and observations made by Dover guns, balloon barrage, Air/Sea Rescue Officer etc, it appeared that the first plane to dive into the sea was not after all a Spitfire, but the 109 which broke away and dived. It attacked not Boyd or Van Lierde, but Ortmans who had been kept back by oil pressure and high temperatures. He took such effective evasive action that the enemy aircraft broke up and plunged into the sea. S/L Robinson's arduous battle was with the second 109 flown by a very experienced pilot who remained out of reach until the C.O. tried flying straight and level. Just as it was about to open fire, S/L Robinson turned sharply and throttled back, and was able to fire a long burst from astern. The 109 smoked heavily, turned on its side and dived to sea level. But the splash he saw, it was decided, was not the 109, but Curchin's Spitfire. P/O MacKenzie had seen an enemy aircraft dart between Curchin and himself, and was unable to attack it through getting into a spin. Sgt Rigler meanwhile had ascended up to 1,000 ft after a third 109 and brought it down with a full deflection shot from below. In a head-on combat with another, probably the C.O.'s, he claimed to have shot pieces off its wing.

Curchin's loss was keenly felt by the squadron as he had been a member of 609 for almost exactly a year and was one of its most popular pilots. P/O Sydney Hill was particularly affected by the loss of a close friend and his colleagues soon detected a change in him. He became much more withdrawn and the gaiety that had existed in abundance before was sadly lacking. In its place surfaced a determination to seek out the enemy as much as possible to get his revenge.

Although 92 Squadron's day had been largely uneventful it was notable due to the arrival of Sgt Adolf Pietrasiak who was about to make a name for himself in the coming weeks. Pietrasiak was born on 17 November 1916 at Kosmin, near Deblin in Poland and later joined the Polish Air Force where he was a member of 122 Eskadra. After the fall of his country he eventually arrived in Britain in June 1940 and having trained at 58 OTU, he initially flew with 303 Squadron. His arrival at Biggin Hill was the start of a dramatic period in which for a few short weeks he was one of Fighter Command's top scoring pilots, being credited with seven combat victories plus one shared (all Bf 109E/Fs). During his time on 92 Squadron he was generally referred to as 'Meaty Pete' a nickname that came about following lurid stories of his escape from occupied Europe in which he claimed to have knifed over fifty German soldiers!

A further period of bad weather meant that the next opportunity to fly an offensive mission was on the 7th when 'Sailor' Malan led a sweep of the Channel area around noon. On this occasion the invitation to the *Luftwaffe* to come up and fight was not accepted and no enemy aircraft were seen. Later in the day 609 Squadron carried out convoy patrols over the Barrow deep but all that was seen was a solitary Whitley making rather slow progress in its customary nose-down attitude. In investigating this aircraft P/O Francois de Spirlet frightened the crew to such an extent that they fired off the colours of the day assuming that he knew what they were (which he didn't). Two days later 609's 'A' Flight became fully operational on the Spitfire Vb but it would take a little longer before the whole of the squadron was able to use the new fighter.

With 92 Squadron released all day for 'fighter nights' at West Malling on 11 June, 74 and 609 Squadrons were tasked with escorting and providing top cover respectively for five Blenheims engaged on a Roadstead operation against a German tanker that had been reported in the Channel. The attack was carried out successfully, although 609 did not see it as they were patrolling in independent sections at heights from 1,000 to 8,000 ft. As the squadron turned for home two Bf 109Es appeared and attacked the second pair of Blue section comprising Keith Ogilvie and Sgt Guy Chestnut who was also from Canada. The first German aircraft was flown by Oblt Kurt Ebersberger, the leader of JG 26's 4th Staffel, who tucked in behind Chestnut's Spitfire (P8654) and raked it with cannon fire. At the time of this combat Ebersberger was a seven-kill ace having joined JG 26 before the war. He was to continue to fly with the Schlageter Geschwader until his death on 24 October 1943, by which time his score stood at twenty-eight.

Michael Robinson and John Bisdee attempted to intervene during this attack and it appeared as though one of the 109s was damaged as it flew through Bisdee's line of fire which was actually directed at the other 109. During this engagement one of Michael Robinson's cannons jammed which prompted him to turn immediately for home. As he did so he saw Chestnut's Spitfire trailing glycol and about a mile short of the Ramsgate cliffs it began to lose height. Though Robinson tried to signal Chestnut not to do so, he attempted to stretch his glide over the cliff but struck it a few feet from the top. One mainplane landed on top of the cliffs but the remainder of the airframe exploded on contact with the rock face and slithered down to rest in a mangled heap at the bottom. For a short time it was thought that Chestnut might have baled out at the last moment as coastguards reported seeing a parachute but he had in fact stayed with his aircraft and died instantly as it smashed into the cliff. He had only been with 609 for a month and this was one of his first offensive patrols.

Having carried out night flying at West Malling, 92 Squadron flew back to Biggin Hill before breakfast the following day and did not go on readiness until the afternoon. They then joined forces with 74 Squadron to escort three Blenheims in an attack on a convoy that was steaming through the Channel. On return to the English coast 92 Squadron continued to patrol at 3,000 ft off the Goodwin Sands and for a short time went to investigate a report of parachutes in the sea but found that a section of Hurricanes had got there first. As they continued to give cover to two high-speed launches, two Bf 109s appeared from hazy cloud about 2–300 ft above and started to circle. S/L Jamie Rankin climbed his section towards them and as he did so one of the 109s peeled off and dived towards him head-on.

Rankin pulled the nose of his aircraft up, expecting the 109 to break off, but it continued and opened fire at close range, hitting the Spitfire in the wing leading edge with several machine-gun bullets. At this point Rankin opened fire and continued to point blank range by which time his airspeed was extremely low. By using coarse stick and rudder he was able to flick his aircraft into a half-spin which miraculously avoided the onrushing 109. He was then set upon by another 109 which had dived below him before zooming up in a climbing turn. Rankin evaded by pulling into a steep turn towards the attack but when he rolled out there were no enemy aircraft to be seen. Although he had no idea as to the fate of the 109 that had attacked him head-on, he was later credited with its destruction on the basis of 'Y' service (wireless intercept) reports that a German aircraft had gone into the sea about two miles off Dover at the time that Rankin had been in action (1530 hrs). However, with the withdrawal of units to cover the impending invasion of the Soviet Union, the only *Luftwaffe* fighters to remain in northern France were those of JG 2 and JG 26, neither of whom lost any aircraft on this day.

After an uneventful day on the 13th, the next clash with their counterparts on the other side of the Channel occurred on 14 June during an early morning sweep in connection with Circus 12 to St Omer/Fort Rouge. The importance of maintaining flying discipline at all times was underlined during this operation and a lack of cohesion in Blue section caused a number of problems for F/L Allan Wright of 92 Squadron. During a steep turn his No.2 lost contact with him but was unable to inform him owing to R/T failure. At the same time the Nos. 3 and 4 in the section had been lagging and following Wright's manoeuvre had mistakenly identified two 109s as their comrades. Unfortunately Wright was unaware of the fact that he was now completely on his own. Looking in his mirror he saw an aircraft behind which he assumed to be his wingman but he quickly changed his mind when he saw the flashes of its guns as it began to fire at him. As he had not taken evasive action his aircraft was hit a number of times. He takes up the story

I had only been hit with seven bullets but unfortunately two had disconnected my starboard aileron from its controls and jammed it up at an angle. It took me about thirty seconds to recover control and beat it for home as fast as I could. The extraordinary aileron control also affected the fore-and-aft movements of the aircraft, causing it to climb then dive whenever I tried to ease the nose up. Luckily no other enemy aircraft attacked me and I was able to get back to the English coast using some fog patches as cover over the sea. Lympne was the first aerodrome I came to so I attempted to land there. The aircraft would not fly level at less than 145 mph but I put the wheels down intending to try the flaps. I did this well banked over against the dud aileron, but had to put the flaps up again rapidly as only one worked, rolling me over onto the opposite bank. I knew that my starboard wheel was probably punctured because of a bullet hole very close to it, so I put the wheels up again and flew the aircraft onto the ground at 140 mph. The aircraft bumped once then settled down and remained straight, although trying to tip up. From a casual inspection the engine and fuselage appeared undamaged, however, one bullet, an incendiary, had pierced one of the cannon magazines and had jammed it.

During the fight over France Sgt William Payne had also been hit and he suffered slight injuries during a forced landing at Hawkinge. The Spitfires flown by F/L Brian Kingcome and Adj Xavier de Montbron also suffered minor damage. S/L Jamie

Rankin at the head of Red section was rather more fortunate and in the early stages of the battle had moved in behind a Bf109 which was intent on attacking another Spitfire. The latter attempted to evade by half-rolling but as the 109 followed suit its pilot appeared to be oblivious to the fact that Rankin was closing in behind. When the range was down to about 150–200 yards the 109 presented a plan view to Rankin who fired a short deflection burst and let the German aircraft fly through it. One shell was seen to explode near the cockpit and the 109 went into a vertical dive which was not recovered before it entered a layer of low cloud. Even though it was not seen to crash it was credited as destroyed and on this occasion at least the claim was fully justified. Lt Robert Menge of 3/JG 26 was killed when his Bf 109E-7 Werke Nr 6490 dived into the ground following Rankin's attack [Menge had been responsible for shooting down P/O W.K Burgon of 74 Squadron just five days before during a Channel patrol].

On 16 June twelve Spitfire Vbs of 74 Squadron took off from Gravesend at 1536 hrs and fifteen minutes later joined up with 92 Squadron over Biggin Hill. Their orders were to carry out a diversionary sweep in connection with a raid by six Blenheims on Boulogne. By the time that the English coast was crossed at Beachy Head 74 Squadron was at 25,000 ft in sections of four and were in an ideal position to provide top cover for 92 Squadron which was somewhat under strength having only been able to put up seven aircraft. Shortly after crossing the French coast to the north of Le Touquet four Bf 109Fs were seen attempting to get behind 92 Squadron and S/L John Mungo-Park led 72 into the attack. As they did so a large gaggle of around sixteen 109Fs appeared on their port side at about the same level and very soon all aircraft were engaged in a hectic dogfight.

Mungo-Park fired a two-second burst of cannon and machine-gun at one enemy aircraft from 100 yards which succeeded in ripping off its tail assembly and it was last seen diving out of control. Almost immediately he found himself under attack and his Spitfire received multiple hits, including a cannon shell in the engine. He climbed as best he could but just as he was recrossing the French coast on his way home he ran into a further five 109Fs which had apparently been directed to him by red anti-aircraft flak bursts. Although his engine was still running it was extremely rough and was not delivering anywhere near full power. Ironically this proved to be an advantage as the first German aircraft to attack did so at too great a speed and overshot, providing Mungo-Park with an easy zero deflection shot. He fired the remainder of his cannon ammunition into it and had the satisfaction of seeing it burst into flames. He then managed to evade the other 109s by diving and performing aileron turns, firing the occasional burst of machine-gun to deter them from getting too close. They continued to chase him until mid-Channel when they eventually turned for home leaving Mungo-Park to nurse his crippled Spitfire the last few miles. When still just short of Folkstone at 6,000 ft his engine stopped completely and he had to glide over the coast before crash-landing near Hawkinge aerodrome.

P/O W.J. 'Sandy' Sandman from Auckland, New Zealand was flying in the Red 2 position and had followed Mungo-Park into the attack. Having briefly fired at a 109F without effect, he was forced to break into the attack by the larger formation and fired at one head-on. He then dived on a third Messerschmitt in a slight turn and fired a burst which struck it all along its fuselage. On passing overhead he felt sure that the pilot had been hit and the 109 then fell away, apparently out of control and streaming glycol. Sgt Stewart was following his section around in a wide turn to port when he noticed a lone Spitfire 500 ft below being pursued by three 109s.

He dived to attack but two of them saw him coming and turned towards him as he came down. A brief burst at one of these aircraft had no visible effect but he then following it down in a diving turn which brought the German machine and his Spitfire on a converging course. Closing in behind Stewart opened fire with cannon and machine-gun and kept firing for about four seconds. There was a bright flash near the cockpit and pieces flew off before the 109 began to pour black smoke. It then rolled over before going down and was last seen spinning slowly and still emitting thick black smoke. Sgt Yorke also fired at a 109 that was attacking another Spitfire. A two-second burst appeared to hit its engine as shortly after the propeller blades could be seen turning. It then turned on its side and went into a vertical dive.

In the meantime the pilots of 92 Squadron had also been fighting for their lives. As 74 Squadron had swung in to attack the 109s, the two sections of 92 turned in opposite directions with entirely different results. The four aircraft led by Jamie Rankin were constantly engaged for the next twenty minutes or so, whereas the other section completed the sweep without further incident. F/L Brian Kingcome was attacked continuously by swarms of 109s and fired at three but had no time to see how effective his attacks had been. Jamie Rankin, however, saw one pass straight through his colleague's tracer and turn slowly on its back before descending at an angle of 45 degrees emitting thick black smoke. Having been attacked himself, Rankin pursued a 109 to within 1,000 ft of the sea. Closing to a range of 150 yards he opened fire from astern and a large piece broke away from the Messerschmitt's wing root. He was then attacked from the rear by another 109 and thus could only claim a probable.

P/O 'Wimpy' Wade, who was Rankin's No.2, was attacked several times and as he was taking evasive action, he was informed that there was a 109 on his tail. To escape he put his aircraft into a spin and went down to 2,000 ft but then saw another homing in on Brian Kingcome. A short burst was enough to force this 109 to break off but it was soon replaced by another and as Kingcome flew in climbing turns, Wade kept him in sight and fired a number of bursts at his adversary from various angles and ranges. After his final burst at the 109 the left-hand side of the engine caught fire and it dived steeply, rolling on its back, before crashing into the sea about half a mile off Le Touquet. While he was watching the demise of this 109, another made a head-on pass at him before breaking off. Having executed a climbing turn to his left, Wade half-rolled to the right and pressed his gun button in the dive only to find that he had used all his ammunition. This was not the end of his troubles, however, as he experienced extreme difficulty in getting away from the French coast due to the numbers of enemy aircraft that were present, but eventually he was able to take advantage of some momentary inattention on the part of the Germans by diving to sea level unobserved.

The final member of the section, Sgt Hugh Bowen-Morris, fought a running battle with several more 109s during which height was gradually reduced to around 12,000 ft. Having been forced to take almost constant evasive action he was eventually presented with a relatively easy shot as he found himself directly behind one of the 109s which was climbing at relatively low airspeed. A burst of cannon removed part of the tail and then a large portion of the port wing was seen to break away. The 109 turned over and went into a slow inverted spin from a height of 3,000 ft and Bowen-Morris later saw a column of black smoke from the spot he judged it to have crashed.

Rankin's section eventually managed to disengage although each pilot returned on his own. On his way back Brian Kingcome noticed two unescorted Blenheims west of Boulogne and as there were still some 109s in the vicinity he decided to stay with them. The port engine of the rearmost Blenheim was on fire and it eventually ditched about six miles south of Folkstone. The crew were able to board their dinghy before their aircraft sank and although Kingcome climbed for an R/T fix, he was unable to get through to Biggin Hill ops as his radio had been damaged during the fight. Considering the numbers of 109s involved it was a minor miracle that all four pilots returned safely. One thing in their favour was the standard of shooting that was exhibited by the German pilots which was later described as being 'very inaccurate', but the length of the combat was of equal, if not greater, concern. If the fight had lasted just a few minutes longer, all four would have run out of fuel somewhere over the Channel. The numbers of 109s that had pounced on 92 Squadron could not be quantified, the nearest estimate Brian Kingcome could come up with for his combat report was to say that there had been 'lots and lots!'

After a relatively low-key start, Circus operations had grown in scale until they had become huge, integrated affairs with as many as 300 fighters escorting a small number of bombers. Operations on such a scale needed to be closely coordinated and could only be attempted when weather conditions were suitable. The following is the entry in the 609 Squadron ORB for the 17 June

After convoy patrols before lunch, there began the first of that long series of Circuses which were to continue for the rest of the summer. This was Circus 13, with Blenheims raiding Bethune, and 609 as part of the high cover escort at 25,000 ft, in fours. Only three Me 109s were sighted near the target area, but on approaching the French coast on the way back, several pairs were sighted coming from the north. Blue section at 20,000 ft north of Le Touquet saw a pair below at 15,000 ft and dived on them. F/L Bisdee's cannons jammed but with machine-gun only at short range he caused one of the enemy aircraft to go down 'flaming like a torch.' F/O Ogilvie using cannon and machine-gun caused the other to 'blow up with great explosion' and land in the sea in flames. Blue 3 (P/O de Spirlet) was in mid Channel at 12,000 ft when he saw a single Me 109 flying on his left on the same course. Both aircraft turned towards each other and P/O de Spirlet opened fire from the front quarter. He saw the enemy aircraft dive steeply streaming black smoke from the fuselage. S/L Robinson saw a patch of frothing water in the position. He, Sgt Hughes-Rees, P/O Atkinson, Sgt Palmer and P/O Ortmans all fired as well.

The slight injuries that Sgt William Payne of 92 Squadron had suffered just three days before did not prevent him from taking part in this operation and he was Biggin Hill's most successful pilot of the day. Before the war Payne had been a trainee auctioneer and had joined the RAFVR in August 1939. Although it looked at first as though he was destined to become an instructor he failed the course at the Central Flying School and instead passed through 57 OTU before joining 601 Squadron in February 1941. He was posted to 92 Squadron on 3 June and wasted little time in making a name for himself.

Flying as Yellow 2, Payne was nearing the French coast on the way out when he became aware of a Bf 109F coming in behind him. He turned to engage but the 109 pilot was not interested in mixing it and dived away. Shortly afterwards he saw two 109Fs 2,000 ft above him and a mile away, about to move in on a Spitfire. Climbing up underneath the rearmost 109 he fired a short burst with cannon only which raked the whole of the underside. It exploded almost at once. On returning to the French coast Payne came under fire from another 109 at about 10,000 ft between Boulogne and Le Touquet but the burst went wide of the mark. Turning to engage, the German pilot made the mistake of attempting to out-turn his opponent but in a short space of time the Spitfire was directly behind. Two short bursts of cannon and machine-gun set fire to the German aircraft and it crashed about three miles inland.

No.74 Squadron also came under attack and in the ensuing dogfight P/O H.F. Parkes and P/O Roger Boulding were shot down to become prisoners of war. The German pilots responsible were Oblt Hans-Jurgon Westphal and Lt Erdmann Neumann of III/JG 26 [the latter was to be killed in action a week later when he was shot down by Spitfires during Circus 21].

The next day brought further misery for 609 Squadron which lost another of its most popular pilots in circumstances that were difficult to determine. In the early evening 609 was patrolling in fours over the Channel along a line from Gravelines to the North Foreland, the route of Blenheims returning from France. With large numbers of friendly fighters in the area and with each section at different altitudes, P/O Sydney Hill and P/O Baudouin De Hemptinne became separated from the rest of the squadron, however, this did not deter them from going after a pair of 109s seen near Cap Gris Nez. Hill opened fire from above and astern at one of them and from R/T conversation with De Hemptinne appeared to think that it had crashed into the sea. The latter could not confirm this but only one 109 had been seen heading back to France.

After returning to Dover they proceeded to Cap Gris Nez once again and went after four more 109s but this time they were engaged by several others and the two became split up. Eventually De Hemptinne heard Hill order him to re-form and as he headed back across the Channel he saw another Spitfire away to his right and returned with it. When near Dover the other aircraft began to lose height and although De Hemptinne lost sight of it, soon after he saw a Spitfire upside down and on fire. It was later assumed that Hill had been hit during further combat over France and had been killed while attempting a force landing. However John Bisdee was of the opinion that Hill had been attempting to make it over the cliff tops as Sgt Guy Chestnut had tried to do a week before. Like his less experienced comrade, he too failed to make it. Frank Ziegler summed up Sydney Hill's qualities as follows

The loss of P/O Hill, following so soon that of F/L Curchin, was deeply felt by everyone. Wayward and mischievous as he was, he possessed a deep sense of fairness and generosity, a laugh that was spontaneous and infectious, a sense of humour that was sublime and an intelligence far greater than he would ever have admitted.

The fact that both Curchin and Hill had been lost in a matter of days was a huge blow to 609 Squadron. The mood was sombre that evening which could not be allowed to continue and as notice had just been received that P/O Jean 'Pyker' Offenberg had been awarded a DFC, Michael Robinson immediately removed the DFC ribbon from his own uniform and attached it to Offenberg's. This was the cue for the usual boisterous party and the tragedy was quickly put to the back of everyone's minds.

Offenberg was a recent arrival and had previously flown with 145 Squadron where he was a flight commander. Before that he had flown with the Belgian Air Force and on 10 May 1940 shot down a Dornier Do 17 whilst flying a Fiat CR42.

72

After the fall of his country he escaped to France and eventually made it to Britain via Algeria and Corsica. His original nickname of 'Peike' was soon anglicised to 'Pyker' and he became extremely popular with all members of the squadron, whatever their nationality, for his modesty, humour and good nature.

The following two days were relatively quiet due to a brief period of bad weather and the next combats took place on the 21st. Having been informed that they would not be called to readiness until 1300 hrs, the pilots of 92 Squadron were not particularly pleased to discover that they were required to provide a cover patrol over the Channel. This was in connection with a Circus operation (No.16) to the airfields at St Omer/Longuenesse and Fort Rouge with a take off at 1200 hrs. In the event it passed off uneventfully for the majority, although Jamie Rankin managed to shoot most of the tail off a Bf 109E over the Channel, the pilot baling out. Rankin was the only member of his squadron to fire his guns and his victim was Uffz Otto Ewald of 6/JG 26 who was flying Bf 109E-7 Werke Nr 6462. Ewald survived the ordeal but as far as he was concerned he was picked up by the wrong side and spent the rest of the war as a prisoner

In contrast to 92 Squadron several of the Tigers were engaged, particularly the members of Yellow section. F/L Don Carlson (Yellow 1) became involved with a Bf 109 which fired at him head-on, his aircraft being hit by a single bullet in the starboard wing leading edge and a cannon shell in the tailplane. The pilot of the 109 did not dive away and Carlson soon managed to turn inside the German, firing several short bursts from 150 yards. White glycol vapour eventually began to stream back and the 109 went down, apparently with its engine stopped. As he moved in again Carlson failed to take into account the 109's significantly reduced speed and he overshot before he could bring his guns to bear. Before he could set up another attack the 109 hit the water and disappeared.

As Carlson had gone into the attack another 109 had attempted to get on his tail and was engaged by his No.2, Sgt J.E. Cole. After firing a one-second deflection burst he pulled round hard to port and met the 109 head-on, firing another short burst before they passed each other. Cole then did a maximum rate turn to starboard and when he came out he saw the 109 in a climbing turn to the right. Closing to around 70 yards he fired a four-second burst with cannon and machine-guns, seeing strikes around the cockpit and wings which produced a trail of debris. The 109 began to dive towards the sea and was followed for a time by another Spitfire. As it did so it began to trail black smoke and at low altitude it appeared as though the pilot had baled out, although no parachute was seen to open. Shortly afterwards the 109 went straight into the sea. During this action P/O Tony Mould (Yellow 3) also attacked a 109 but wasted much of his ammunition when his guns continued firing when he took his thumb off the button due to a leak in the air pressure system. As the aircraft he had attacked was last seen descending with a slowly revolving propeller, he was awarded a probable.

After landing there was very little time to recuperate as a second Circus (No.17) to another *Luftwaffe* airfield, this time at Desvres, was laid on with all aircraft to be airborne by 1600 hrs. This was to lead to a number of combats and by the end of the day the Biggin Hill Wing was to submit claims for another six enemy aircraft destroyed. Flying as Target Support, 'Sailor' Malan led his Spitfires into France at Gravelines in a shallow dive from 22,000 ft so by the time that they reached Desvres the height of the three squadrons ranged from 15–18,000 ft. Malan was quick to spot a Bf 109F heading in the direction of Boulogne and closed in to 50 yards before opening fire. The 109 immediately burst into flames, coating its attacker in oil as it did so, and fell away leaving a thick trail of black smoke behind it. Malan then saw another opportunity when two 109s were encountered near Le Touquet. Again employing his penchant for getting in close, Malan moved in to 50 yards dead astern to deliver all of his aircraft's destructive power and the 109 dived into the sea just off the coast.

As Malan had been attacking the first 109 near Boulogne he had been followed by Yellow section of 74 Squadron led by F/L Don Carlson who fired at another but without effect. He then sighted four more heading towards the English coast and went for the rearmost one. As his windscreen had become coated in oil he misjudged his overtaking speed and had to overshoot after firing for only two seconds. He was compelled to break away downwards and to port but as he did so the 109 was seen to be losing glycol and even though he finished up ahead of it and below, it made no attempt to attack him.

Top cover for the Wing was provided on this occasion by 92 Squadron and on the way out Jamie Rankin attacked the last of three Bf 109Es that were seen near Boulogne. Opening up with cannon and machine-guns, several strikes were seen near the cockpit and the nose of the 109 reared up before it rolled on its back. The attack was then taken up by P/O 'Wimpy' Wade (Blue 1) who whipped round into a right-hand climbing turn before diving down onto the port quarter to fire a two-second burst to within 50 yards. A large piece of debris broke away from behind the cockpit and the 109 rolled over to the left and crashed off the coast to the south of Boulogne, but not before its pilot had baled out. Sgt G.W. Aston dispatched another 109 before being shot down himself and baling out into the Channel. He was fortunate to be picked up in quick time and soon rejoined his squadron.

Several members of 609 Squadron also had a busy time including F/O Keith Ogilvie and Sgt Bob Boyd (Yellow 1 and 2). During the turn for home Yellow section had lost position slightly with the rest of the squadron and this was enough to attract the attention of four Bf 109Fs which were first seen about 700 ft above. Boyd pulled the nose of his aircraft up to fire a short burst but in doing so lost airspeed and ended up in a semi-stalled position. A 109 immediately half-rolled onto his tail but Boyd saw him coming and closed his throttle and commenced a tight turn towards the sun. His relatively slow speed turned to his advantage when the German pilot misjudged his approach and overshot, and as he continued to dive on a straight course Boyd was able to open fire with a two-second burst of cannon and machine-guns. The 109 was badly hit and spiralled down to crash four miles north-east of Le Touquet.

When the fighters had been making their way out to the south of Boulogne they had been greeted by intense anti-aircraft fire which was accurate for height and claimed one aircraft which went down pouring glycol. After Yellow section was engaged F/O Keith Ogilvie was involved in a brief head-on fight before a general dogfight developed. Pulling round he saw a 109 slightly below and 200 yards ahead and dropped down to commence his attack. Surprisingly it took no evasive action other than to weave slightly and then turned over on its back. As it went down it entered a spin and shortly afterwards a parachute appeared. Turning for home, Ogilvie lowered the nose of his Spitfire to increase speed but he was prevented from escaping by another four 109s which were descending from further up. Due to the height advantage that the 109s had used so effectively Ogilvie had a real fight on his hands and he had to use violent evasive action to stay out of trouble. Even so two bullets hit his port wing but fortunately these did not affect his aircraft's handling.

After a desperate struggle he finally managed to shake them off but instead of making for home an error in his compass setting resulted in him ending up over the French coast once again between Le Touquet and Boulogne. Here he was engaged by the same four 109s he had just succeeded in losing and it was a case of being back to square one. By this time the fight was down to around 1,000 ft and Ogilvie was able to use some low level mist to his advantage, together with careful positioning of his aircraft in relation to the sun. He was followed to mid-Channel but here, to his unbounded relief, the 109s turned back towards France [German fighters were not normally allowed to continue their pursuit of RAF aircraft to the English side of the Channel, although in the heat of battle this rule was frequently flouted].

In the afternoon of 22 June the Biggin Hill Wing provided support to Blenheims of 139 Squadron attacking Hazebrouck. Although Frank Ziegler had plenty to record following a successful operation, the significance of the day did not go unnoticed,

Today was notable for Germany's invasion of Russia, for the shooting down of four 109s by 609 Squadron and for the successful rescue of P/O de Spirlet from the drink. Twelve Blenheims were raiding Hazebrouck yards (Circus 18) with Biggin acting as forward and withdrawal Wing. 609 were flying in three independent sections at 20/25,000 ft inland from Dunkirk when Blue Leader (F/L Bisdee) saw about nine Me 109Fs flying down the coast from Dunkirk direction. He gave the tally ho and attacked one pair which turned to port and left the pair in front unguarded. Closing to point blank range behind one of them (which took no evasive action) he fired with machine-gun continuously. Its engine caught fire and pieces of red hot metal flew off. It turned on its back and went straight down.

Blue 2 (Sgt Rigler) brought the second down from similar range (no evasive action again), then found himself alone at 8,000 ft. Seven 109s were above and two peeled off and came dead astern of him. By throttling back and turning, he caused the leader to overshoot and firing at it, saw a flash and the enemy aircraft disintegrate. Meanwhile he himself was hit in the wing by fire from another enemy aircraft and during his evasive action he was at one time inverted with a cut engine and head pressed against the perspex. "Rigler, if you ever get out if this you need never fly again," he said to himself. Calling out "Blue 2 down below in trouble," he had the impression of the aircraft diving, and one of his attackers going down in flames. Losing height to gain the cover of the haze over the sea, he found yet another 109 flying along in front at 800 ft. An unseen burst of machine-gun only was enough to send it down to crash near the sands east of Dunkirk. Owing to the behaviour of his engine and high temperature, he thought that his glycol tanks had been hit, and got ready to bale out. It wasn't necessary, however, and he landed at Manston.

P/O Offenberg (Red 2) again went off looking for trouble on his own and eventually found himself in the interesting position of firing at an Me 109E low over the sand dunes, wiping a frozen windscreen, avoiding tracer from Gravelines and watching an Me 109F that was 'floundering around a bit further inland' practically all at the same time. He damaged the 109E so successfully that glycol covered his own windscreen, and then had to avoid the attention of the 109F.

Yellow section was jumped on crossing the coast and Yellow 3 (P/O de Spirlet) was shot down, bullets also hitting P/O Ortmans who thought the enemy aircraft was his colleague. After gliding a short distance, P/O de Spirlet baled out with some difficulty from 800–1,000 ft and began inflating his Mae West on the way down. He reached the water, got into his dinghy and fell out twice, once trying to pull in the drogue and once standing up to wave. Two Spitfires of another squadron had been circling him and afterwards a Lysander appeared and dropped a smoke bomb. Two rescue boats then appeared one from the English, the other from the French coast and he feared a battle. One however turned out to be a naval boat, the other RAF; after an argument as to who should pick him up, the RAF boat won. After thirty-five minutes in the water, he was grieved to find that the crew had finished all their rum at a party the night before. After this he spent a week or two in Ramsgate Hospital having got a splinter in his leg [legend has it that he was also diagnosed as having jaundice when in hospital, but this was merely staining from the yellow marker dye that he had released in the Channel so that his position could be seen from the air!]

'Sailor' Malan continued his excellent run of form with a Bf 109F shot down near Dunkirk but on this occasion he was upstaged by his wingman, P/O W.J. 'Sandy' Sandman of 74 Squadron. Having descended to 20,000 ft in the designated patrol area near Bergues two 109s were seen 5,000 ft below and Sandman followed his leader into the attack. Although the German pilots saw them coming and dived away, the speed advantage of the Spitfires was sufficient to allow them to catch up and Sandman opened fire with a two-second burst from 250 yards at 7,000 ft. Despite the fact that he had to break away almost at once due to the proximity of other aircraft, Malan was later able to confirm that the 109 he had fired at had spun down and caught fire before hitting the ground.

By now they were just north of Gravelines at around 5,000 ft and were fired on by the coastal flak batteries but although the flak bursts were accurate for height they were well behind. At this point they were joined by another 74 Squadron Spitfire and Sandman dutifully dropped back to weave behind the other two. This was nearly his undoing as about four miles off the French coast he was set upon by six Bf 109s. By now he was at 2,000 ft and as the 109s had attacked with no height advantage he was able to use his Spitfire's superior lateral performance to spoil their efforts and set up some attacks of his own. By turning steeply all of the Germans' fire passed harmlessly behind him, as the 109s were unable to turn tightly enough to obtain the required deflection. Eventually one of the 109s filled his gunsight and he fired a two-second burst with cannon and machine-guns from astern and above at only 50 yards range. Several cannon shells hit the fuselage and several large chunks came away from it and shot past Sandman's Spitfire before the 109 rolled onto its back and dived into the sea. After a further brief engagement Sandman was able to shake off the others and made it back to land at Manston.

Although the first targets to be chosen for Circus operations were limited to those within easy reach, it was not long before deeper penetrations were being planned. Not surprisingly the pilots greeted this with a certain amount of incredulity as Don Kingaby recalls,

Most of our operations over France up to this time had been confined to sweeps around the coastal areas and very rarely did we go more than a few miles into Hunland. On 23 June we were called into the dispersal hut for briefing – 'Sailor' Malan popped his head into the hut long enough to say "Target is Bethune, look it up on the map". We looked – we looked and we looked. We were expecting a target about ten miles inside the coast and it was some time before anyone believed that that was it – fifty miles in! We had no long-range tanks then and thirty miles in meant a darn good fight and a landing at a forward base to refuel on the way home. What would it be like taking twelve bombers in fifty miles?

We were briefed for close escort and within an hour we were on our way. For the first time I saw not only the English coast disappear, but also the French coast fade from sight in the haze as we penetrated further into enemy territory. The Huns didn't catch up with our game until we had nearly reached the target and then we had a real good scrap getting home. It was in this scrap that I lost the first of my Sergeant pals (Sgt Hugh Bowen-Morris). He saw a 109 on the tail of a Spitfire and went down to get it. The Spitfire got away O.K. but 'Bowie' was left with five other 109s to deal with. After a stout fight he was badly wounded and was shot down. It was a tough break to buy it after helping an unknown comrade out of trouble.

Kingaby, who was flying as Yellow 3, was in combat himself when 109s were encountered about ten miles inland from Le Touquet on the way out. He chased one down to 5,000 ft but lost contact when he sensed that he was coming under attack himself. Not long after he came across a Bf 109E flying inland at about 500 ft and immediately dived down to deliver a beam attack. The German pilot saw him coming before Kingaby had a chance to open fire but in attempting to escape he executed a badly controlled turn and the 109 flicked into a spin before diving into the ground and exploding.

S/L Jamie Rankin at the head of Red section attacked a formation of Bf 109Es and quickly shot one down in flames from astern with no deflection. The others in the group were not particularly aggressive and merely began to weave which allowed Rankin to select a second victim quite easily. He chose one that was in a climbing turn and fired a three-second burst with cannon and machine-gun which led to the 109 turning over onto its back and diving away trailing white and black smoke. As he then came under attack himself he was forced to break away, but on looking down he saw the first 109 going down in flames and the pilot of the second attempting to bale out from his stricken machine which was also beginning to burn. Having fired again briefly at another 109E, Rankin rejoined the main formation and returned with them to Dungeness, before flying back to Biggin.

Another successful pilot during this operation was P/O Philip Archer (Blue 4) who followed a 109E down to 5,000 ft and closing in to 100 yards. The German pilot was unaware of Archer's presence and his fire caused multiple strikes on the starboard wing and tailplane. The Messerschmitt nosed over into a gentle dive which was not arrested before it hit the ground and blew up. Having climbed up again he spotted another 109 and on turning after it he fired a short burst but without result. As he was getting low on fuel Archer made for home, crossing the French coast north of Le Touquet and landing at Manston [Archer was a relatively new arrival on 92 Squadron having been posted in on 7 May. He came from Bridgetown in Barbados and had joined the RCAF before being sent overseas].

Later in the day another escort mission was laid on with the Biggin Hill Wing acting as support to six Blenheims which were to bomb the airfield at Mardyck

(Circus 20). Each of the three squadrons contributed ten aircraft and the Wing took off at 1947 hrs, crossing the French coast half an hour later at heights ranging from 25–27,000 ft. As they did so there were the customary red puffs as the marker shells burst to announce their arrival. Course was then set for St Omer, a feint manoeuvre which was intended to draw *Luftwaffe* fighters from the main 'beehive'. 'Sailor' Malan who was leading the Wing at the head of 92 Squadron saw 15–20 enemy aircraft between Boulogne and Hardelot in a large vic formation together with a number of pairs and called on 92 and 74 Squadrons to follow him into the attack. Unfortunately this was not heard by 74 as Malan's radio was not functioning properly and only 92 went with him. As he dived down he singled out a Bf 109F on the right-hand side of the formation and closed to 50 yards, firing a short burst with cannon and machine-guns with slight deflection. The 109 blew up immediately and Malan found himself flying through a shower of debris. Some of these shards of metal damaged his port wing and starboard wing root and after landing one piece was still wrapped round the pitot tube.

Seeing another 109 climbing to the right and up sun, Malan followed and again closed to 50 yards range before opening fire with a two-second burst. At such close range he could hardly miss and the 109 half rolled and dived, leaving a trail of smoke behind it. Malan followed it down to 8,000 ft firing the rest of his ammunition on the way and broke off at this height with his airspeed indicator registering 450 mph. He continued to watch it and saw it disintegrate at a height of approximately 5,000 ft, the wings breaking away and the fuselage hitting the ground ten miles south-west of Boulogne. As he had by now used up all his ammunition Malan returned to base. During these attacks he had been followed by his No.2, P/O Don Dougall, who also selected one of the 109s in the main formation and followed it as it went into a gentle turn to the left. Opening fire at 250 yards range, his first burst passed harmlessly underneath the 109, but his second hit it in the engine and tail and pieces were seen to break away. It then fell into a spin before bursting into flames. In addition to these combats 'Wimpy' Wade and Sgt Jerrold Le Cheminant each claimed 109s as probably destroyed. Despite the best efforts of the escort fighters two out of the six Blenheims which took part in this operation were shot down near Dunkirk.

Having shot down two Bf 109s a week before, Sgt William Payne did it again on 24 June thereby taking 92 Squadron's victory tally to 150. During an evening escort patrol he was flying as Red 4 at 20,000 ft about ten miles inside France near Gravelines when he saw a Spitfire about 5,000 ft below being attacked by a Bf 109E. Diving onto its tail he fired a short burst with cannon only and saw his shells strike the enemy aircraft around the cockpit area. It turned on its back and went into a spin, Payne following it down to 5,000 ft from where he saw it hit the ground and explode. On his way back to Biggin he came across another 109E around 1,000 ft above and flying parallel with the coast. As he was in the 109's blind spot he was able to climb up underneath it without being seen and fired all his guns from about 150–200 yards from astern and below. His fire entered the fuselage and the 109 belched out black smoke, before turning on its side and diving into the sea. On his way home Payne was chased by three 109Es for a time, one of which shot at him, but its fire passed underneath his Spitfire without doing any damage.

While the other squadrons had been busy over France, 609 Squadron had been performing for the press, including the unit's new mascot, William de Goat who had turned up the previous day courtesy of Vicki Ortmans. The Belgian contingent in 609 had a soft spot for a local pub called The Old Jail which was run by a lady by the name of Biddie who was a compatriot of theirs. Their fondness for her was reciprocated (Ortmans was a particular favourite) and to show her appreciation Biddie presented the young, soon to be named, William to the squadron. When not being fed milk from a baby's bottle, he was to be seen eating the newly grown grass outside the dispersal hut. He was immediately commissioned but appears to have skipped the rank of Pilot Officer completely as his first known rank was that of Flying Officer (he was to end the war as an Air Commodore).

The arrival of four press photographers had 609 Squadron pilots doing activities that they would not normally have considered taking part in including impromptu cricket matches and hay-making parties. These were hastily arranged for the cameras and a few days later appeared in the daily press and illustrated weekly papers. Not long after Tommy Rigler received his first fan mail complete with a 10/- note with which to buy cigarettes.

The pressure was maintained on 25 June with two Circus operations (Nos. 22 and 23), the first to Hazebrouck marshalling yards and the second to the airfield at St Omer/Longuenesse. 'Sailor' Malan led the Wing as top cover at 30,000 ft on the first of these and in the target area saw two Bf 109Fs about 3,000 ft below. Diving with his section he was about to open fire when he became aware of two others which were trying to move in from behind. He was too quick for them however and pulled his aircraft round in a tight turn to produce a firing opportunity with slight deflection. For once his aim was poor (apparently due to a malfunctioning reflector sight) and he missed completely, using up all his cannon ammunition in the process. Refusing to give up, he moved in to around 50 yards in which position his gunsight was hardly needed. Firing with machine-guns only, the 109 began to pour black smoke but Malan then had to turn his attention to the other Messerschmitt which had broken in the opposite direction. A brief head-on pass was the last that he saw of it. His attention was then drawn to an explosion about a mile away which he assumed had been made by the 109 he had attacked as it dived into the ground.

F/L Allan Wright of 92 Squadron was in the same section as Malan and had followed him into the attack. He continued after the leader of the first pair of 109s to be seen, firing two short bursts as it dived away. It then pulled out of the dive and began to climb vertically which allowed Wright to gain on it and fire a long burst of machine-gun down to a range of only 40 yards. The 109 began to stream glycol from the port radiator but with airspeed decaying rapidly, both aircraft spun. On recovering, Wright was able to fire once more at the 109 which stayed in a spin and was last seen by F/O Geoff Wellum at about 10,000 ft, at which point it flicked over on to its back and dived vertically.

As the Biggin Hill Wing was in the process of withdrawing P/O Neville Duke, who was flying at sea level to the west of Boulogne, looked behind him and saw six Bf 109Fs having a dogfight with two Spitfires. He immediately turned back and joined in, coming to the assistance of one of the Spitfires which had a 109F on its tail. The German pilot committed one of the cardinal sins of aerial combat by not constantly checking behind his aircraft and Duke was able to move in without being seen. He fired two bursts of cannon and machine-gun at gradually reduced range until at 50 yards he had to pull away due to turbulence caused by the 109's slipstream. It is likely that this attack killed the pilot as Duke saw him sitting quite still and not looking round. The 109 then went into a gentle dive from 2,000ft and hit the ground and blew up just to the east of Dunkirk.

During Circus 23 which was carried out in the late afternoon Sgt William Payne added to his impressive run by shooting down a Bf 109E. As he was flying along at

25,000 ft he saw a 109 down below and half-rolled and dived but was then drawn to another on his left which was going in the opposite direction. The pilot of this aircraft had similar ideas and stall turned to come back at Payne. In doing so he lost a lot of airspeed which allowed Payne to get on his tail. Closing in to around 150 yards he fired a two-second burst of cannon and the 109 immediately broke up and caught fire, the flames coming from behind the cockpit. On his way back, when about ten miles off the French coast, he came upon another 109 which appeared to be returning from the Dover area in a gradual descent through 2,000 ft. As he was lining up to take a deflection shot it suddenly turned on its back and dived into the sea. As Payne had not fired at the 109 it seems most likely that it had been damaged in a previous combat [this may have been the Bf 109F-2 flown by Fw Wolfgang Falkinger of 7/JG 2 which was reported to have come down in the sea six miles north of Calais].

On 26 June the target for Circus 24 was the power station at Comines with Biggin again providing Target Support in the area Gravelines – Dunkirk. Most of the action occurred on the way out but on this occasion it did not involve 609 Squadron which was too high to engage. 'Sailor' Malan had already attacked a Bf 109F (subsequently claimed as a probable), when many more enemy aircraft were seen approaching from the direction of St Omer. As these were reported by Jamie Rankin who was leading 92 Squadron, Malan gave instructions for him to attack with his section. On coming out of a blacked out turn, Rankin saw a 109E to his left diving towards the coast. He was able to close in rapidly and although it took evasive action, this was completely ineffective and the German pilot's efforts were later described in Rankin's combat report as 'feeble'. As he was flying directly behind the 109 when he opened fire, his Spitfire was buffeted by its slipstream but his shells found their mark and a thin trail of glycol began to pour back. The German aircraft then turned over and dived away inverted. As Rankin was intent on taking cover in some low cloud at 2,000 ft over Dunkirk, he followed it down and saw it hit the ground 10–15 miles south of Gravelines.

No.92 Squadron's Blue section led by F/L Allan Wright was flying south-south-east about twenty miles inland from Dunkirk when a formation of 12–15 Bf 109Es passed about 2,000 ft below heading in the opposite direction. Wright curved down to the right in a half-roll (partially blacking out in the process) and went for the rearmost aircraft on the starboard side. He had been seen however, and the 109s were already diving when he opened fire. Despite the 109 attempting to evade by skidding and turning, it was hit by a cannon shell in front of the cockpit and its dive became much steeper. Wright attempted to follow but found that he was unable to hold his aircraft in the dive in which his indicated airspeed exceeded 450 mph. During dives from high altitude the Spitfire initially had to be held into the dive but as speed increased it tended to become nose heavy, requiring a hefty pull on the control column. On entering the denser air at low level, however, the trim changes altered and it tended to become tail heavy resulting in a nose-up pitch which is what Wright had experienced in the latter stages of his attack. On pulling out at 5,000 ft he saw the 109 continue to dive vertically but then became aware of a Bf 109F just above the cloud layer at around 2,000 ft. He closed in to attack but was only able to fire a short burst before it escaped into the clouds. Although Wright hung around for a few minutes, no other targets presented themselves and he returned to base at zero feet.

F/Sgt 'Tich' Havercroft (Blue 3) had a similar experience to his leader as he found himself diving with a 109E which was desperately trying to reach the protection of the clouds below. A short burst of fire from the quarter and another from astern led to a plume of glycol and the 109 continued to dive at what Havercroft later considered to be a 'most excessive speed'. He followed it down in a near vertical dive and commenced his pull out at 7,000 ft but the other aircraft continued and was last seen entering the cloud layer inland from Dunkirk. As this had already been ascertained as having been at 2,000 ft, it was considered impossible that the 109 could have pulled out before hitting the ground.

Both of the 109s attacked by Wright and Havercroft were credited as having been destroyed. Although it is quite possible that these aircraft did fly straight into the ground, neither claim complied fully with Fighter Command's guidelines which stipulated that for an enemy aircraft to be confirmed as destroyed it had either to be seen to crash or to set on fire in the air, or the pilot had to be seen to bale out. As the air battles were getting bigger, so was the degree of over-claiming and as the air fighting was now taking place over occupied Europe it was not possible to count wrecks or to obtain witness statements from others not involved in the fighting to verify claims. In the fast-moving chaos of an air battle it was quite feasible for an individual aircraft to be fired on by several pilots on different occasions, each of whom, if they had seen hits, would most likely file some form of claim. Add to this a large dose of adrenaline which would still be active at debrief and the relief at having survived for another day and it is easier to see that a pilot's view of what he had been through might not necessarily correlate with what had actually happened [over-claiming also occurred on the German side, in particular JG 2 which was prone to submitting claims that bore no relation to actual RAF losses].

Although pilots could not be blamed for claiming more aircraft than had actually been shot down, the 'numbers game' could be played to everyone's advantage within Fighter Command, even if Ultra decrypts provided a more accurate picture based on German requests for replacement aircraft. At squadron level there was certainly pressure on pilots to claim absolutely everything and even when they had, they may not have heard the last of it. At least one Biggin Hill pilot was surprised to discover that a probable had been lifted to a confirmed destroyed and a damaged had been upgraded to a probable.

On 27 June the Biggin Hill squadrons took part in two offensive operations, a Roadstead and a Circus. During the former, 92 and 609 Squadrons joined up to protect three Blenheims which bombed some ships off Calais, scoring several near misses. The boats retaliated with considerable flak, some of which was of heavy calibre and sufficiently accurate that the Spitfire of Keith Ogilvie of 609 Squadron was 'lifted in the air'. The target for the Circus operation (No.25) was the steel works at Lille, most pilots being of the opinion that this was rather too far to go into France on just over 80 gallons of fuel. No.609 Squadron was subject to attacks by pairs of Bf 109s which attempted to draw some of their aircraft out of position. F/L Paul Richey's section was attacked by two which then continued their dive to safety. The Spitfires were then engaged by three more 109s from head on with Richey following one down as it spiralled towards the coast. He fired two bursts of cannon in a steep dive that produced a stream of glycol but the 109's fate went unobserved as its dive exceeded the vertical. Vicki Ortmans and 'Pyker' Offenberg were also engaged but did not put in any claims.

Although 92 and 609 Squadrons did not suffer any casualties, 74 Squadron suffered severely, the most grievous loss being that of its commanding officer, S/L John Mungo Park, who was shot down and killed in X4668. Two other Spitfires failed to return, W3210 flown by P/O 'Sandy' Sandman and W3252 flown by Sgt

C.G. Hilken, both pilots becoming prisoners of war. Clive Hilken later described his experience:

> Having twice survived being shot down, I swore that no enemy would get on my tail again without my knowledge. This resolution held good until 27 June 1941 when I flew to France as top cover, escorting a bombing sortie to the Lille district. The chap who should have been behind me had not taken off because of engine trouble, leaving me as the back man of my section. At 25,000 ft over France our squadron became separated on a weaving turn from the other squadrons of the Wing. Our C.O. applied full throttle in an attempt to regain his place in the formation but in the process the rest of us found ourselves spread over the sky up to two miles behind the main formation. Now, to weave and watch your tail meant losing the formation. The only way to catch up was to do what our C.O. had done – go full bore. We did this, then cannon shells whipped into my Spitfire. There was no warning, nothing was seen. My wireless was dead and glycol was streaming out behind. The elevator was stuck and there was a piece of metal in my ankle which was bleeding at full speed. I baled out only to find my parachute pack waving about by my side. I pulled it in and undid the snap fasteners, letting the chute out a yard or two before the wind caught it and it opened to let me down, cursing my fate yet again, to France, hospital and a POW camp.

Clive Hilken had joined 74 Squadron in August 1940 but had little in the way of combat experience before the Tigers moved to Biggin Hill two months later. He was shot down by a Bf 109E on 20 October during his first real dogfight and was forced to bale out near Tonbridge. During the attack he suffered shrapnel wounds but he was far from safe on the ground as a shotgun-armed farmer initially thought he was German until some ripe swear words convinced him otherwise. Having recovered from his injuries he rejoined 74 Squadron but was shot down again on 21 April 1941 when in combat with Bf 109Es of JG 51 during a defensive patrol. Mungo-Park was replaced as C.O. by S/L Stanley Meares who had flown with 74 Squadron from 1937–39 before becoming a fighter controller at Hornchurch. He returned to active duty in 1941 and immediately prior to joining the Tigers was a flight commander with 611 Squadron.

There was an early start the next day as the Wing provided Target Support to a relatively large force of twenty-three Blenheims drawn from 18, 21, 139 and 226 Squadrons which were to attack a power station at Comines during Circus 26. The Spitfires were airborne at 0750 hrs but only 92 Squadron was at full strength with 609 Squadron contributing nine aircraft and the Tigers, following the losses of the previous day, only six. Once again the defending *Luftwaffe* fighters were content to play a waiting game and although large numbers of Bf 109s were seen in twos and threes, no combats took place until near Gravelines on the way home. Here a number of 109s went after some Spitfires from another Wing which prompted 'Sailor' Malan (at the head of 609 Squadron) to dive after them. Leaving 74 Squadron as top cover he led 609 and 92 into the attack but the German aircraft were aware of the threat and managed to stay out of range.

Just when it appeared that the attack had been thwarted a single 109 went for another group of Spitfires below and Malan dived once again to intervene. As he did so his windscreen became iced up and by the time that it had cleared he found himself in the middle of a dogfight involving several Spitfires and 109s. A solitary

109 caught his attention and he followed it as it dived towards Calais. It was seen to attack another Spitfire but broke off as soon as Malan opened fire with machine-guns only from about 200 yards. Closing to 150 yards he fired again with his full armament in a three-second burst and the 109 began to roll to starboard and emit copious amounts of black smoke from its engine which was soon followed by flames. It then rolled slowly the opposite way and from the manner in which it manoeuvred Malan was convinced that the pilot had either been killed or badly wounded. As other 109s were in the immediate area he then wasted no time in making for the coast before diving for home.

The only other pilot to be engaged was F/L Paul Richey of 609 Squadron who was attacked by a 109 which got onto his tail. By turning as tightly as he could he managed to reverse the situation and fired several bursts of cannon as the 109 dived inland. He was not able to follow for any length of time as there were other 109s nearby, although they chose not to attack. Considerable flak was experienced from woods and sand dunes to the east of Calais, apparently aimed at the bombers. On return to Biggin Hill 609 Squadron was released in the afternoon which prompted another raid on London, this time to the Nuthouse on Regent Street. The 'appalling' atmosphere in this establishment drugged the pilots to such an extent that they did not get back until 0500 hrs the following day.

The excesses of the previous night soon caught up with 609 as 92 Squadron was released all day on the 29th and the West Riding squadron had to provide a section of Spitfires to cover a convoy in the Barrow Deep at 0930 hrs. While some pilots were lucky and continued to sleep at Dispersal, others, including Keith Ogilvie, were less than pleased to be woken up and told to take off with immediate effect. His mood improved when a DFC ribbon was pinned to his chest by Michael Robinson, the same honour being bestowed upon F/L John Bisdee. Later in the morning the squadron took off on a sweep which was recalled owing to the Hornchurch Wing being unable to supply top cover. The take off and landing did however provide entertainment for 150 Air Training Corps cadets who were being shown around Biggin Hill at the time. A sweep involving 74 and 609 Squadrons did take place in the afternoon but like many other incursions into occupied Europe without bombers, it failed to generate a response from the other side.

The last day of June got off to a slow start but by midday it became obvious that this situation would not last as details of a Circus operation (No.27), to be carried out in the evening, started to come through. The target on this occasion was a power station at Pont-a-Vendin, near Lens and the attacking force was to comprise eighteen Blenheims drawn from 18 and 139 Squadrons. Biggin's involvement was as Target Support along with the Hornchurch Wing (54, 603 and 611 Squadrons). 'Sailor' Malan's briefing decreed that 609 Squadron was to act as top cover for 74 and 92 Squadrons which meant that there was a much greater chance of 609 coming into contact with the enemy, should they decide to contest the incursion. Take off was set at 1730 hrs and when the time came 609 Squadron was able to put up a full twelve aircraft, the first time that this had happened for several days.

The Blenheims and their close escorts were on time and the Biggin Hill Wing moved into position high above them near the North Foreland before setting course for France. As soon as the coast was crossed at Gravelines numerous small forma-tions of Bf 109s (mostly the E variant) began to harass the Wing by making sharp, thrusting attacks designed to pull some of the Spitfires out of position. These were largely ignored, as there were other groups of 109s up-sun waiting for an opportu-nity to strike. The *Luftwaffe's* favourite trick of deploying small numbers of aircraft several thousands of feet below as bait was also tried but this tactic failed to entice any Spitfires to have a go at them. Having sized up their opponents the 109s became a little more confident and two made a rather more determined bid to attack 74 Squadron which prompted Michael Robinson to go down in support. He chased the two down to 5,000 ft over Merville aerodrome and then noticed another five which were trying to get into position to attack Blue section. Turning his attention to these he forced them to flee, damaging one in the process. In the confusion that had been created Sgt 'David' Hughes-Rees (Blue 4) managed to shoot down one of the 109s from below during a vertical climb.

Over the Foret de Nieppe 609 Squadron's Yellow section became involved in a fight with four Bf 109Es. F/L Richey (Yellow 1) got astern of one of them and despite some desperate evasion by the German pilot his bullets hit the engine, causing an oil leak and a fire. This aircraft was also attacked by P/O Roger Malengreau (Yellow 3) as it dived away and he followed it down to 9,000 ft when it was lost to view, its dive having gone over the vertical. In the meantime P/O Vicki Ortmans (Yellow 2) had selected another 109 and carried out numerous attacks from the rear quarter and astern during which it twisted and turned before finally 'disintegrating'. Following his initial attack F/L Paul Richey had become separated from the rest of his section and climbed to 16,000 ft to join up with some other Spitfires. Not long after he saw a gaggle of six Bf 109Es moving in behind and after a short ineffectual engagement he found himself alone again. Looking around he saw some cloud cover near the Foret de Clairmarais and sought its sanctuary but he had been seen by three more 109Es, two of which dived onto his tail, while the third attacked from his starboard quarter. Executing a violent climbing turn and side-loop he was able to get behind the latter and fired two long bursts which prompted the German pilot to disengage by diving at full speed from 1,000 ft. After eluding the other 109s and also accurate flak from St Omer, Richey flew home at tree top height taking a good look at France on his way. All of 609 Squadron's Spitfires returned safely and for once no cannon stoppages were experienced.

The second half of June had seen a significant escalation in the number of operations carried out over northern France. Continued good weather gave the opportunity for the offensive to be stepped up with one or two sweeps per day in connection with the increasing number of Circus operations. As the RAF had signalled their intentions early in the year, however, the Germans had had plenty of time to build up an extremely efficient radar-based air defence system in northern France and although the *Luftwaffe* was seriously outnumbered, the locally-based fighters were able to inflict serious losses on the British side as they usually held the tactical advantage. As the British attacks included only a small number of bombers the Germans also had the luxury of being able to decide where and when to attack, if at all. Although Fighter Command was sure of its strategy and its pilots were the equal of their opponents, the scale of the task facing the RAF could not be under-estimated.

CHAPTER TEN

Battle of Attrition

At the beginning of July Don Kingaby of 92 Squadron returned to Biggin Hill following a short period of leave. As he recalled later he then settled down to the most intensive period of operations that he was to experience, with the exception of the flying he was to do in connection with the D-Day landings in 1944. His logbook shows that he took part in twenty-three 'shows' over France in just under three weeks.

On 2 July 92 Squadron was called to readiness at 1100 hrs and were airborne fifty minutes later on a bomber escort mission. On this occasion the offensive force consisted of twelve Blenheims from 21 and 226 Squadrons and the intended target was Lille Power Station, although in the event this could not be located so the bombs were dropped on the marshalling yards at Lille and Merville aerodrome instead. Don Kingaby was flying as Yellow 3 but once in the air was asked to take over the lead of his section. The flight to the target at 17,000 ft was uneventful and it was only when the bombers did a circuit of the town that any anti-aircraft fire was experienced. Despite reports of fighters being in the vicinity as the bombers turned for home, it was not until the coast was reached that things began to liven up.

Kingaby saw two aircraft dive past him which he thought at first were Hurricanes but these turned out to be Bf 109Fs. His hesitation proved to be a blessing in disguise as soon after two more 109Fs came down in front of him, the first two having been used as bait. He wasted no time in diving after the second pair and attacked from the port quarter above. As his ammunition did not include tracer rounds he laid off about four rings of deflection and let the 109s run through a five-second burst of cannon and machine-gun. As there was a good chance that another pair of 109s might be coming down on him he pulled up hard to regain height and so did not see the effect of his fire. When he did have the opportunity to look down he saw a parachute and then two large splashes in the water where the Messerschmitts had gone in, the two aircraft having collided. This was confirmed by his No.2 Sgt Carpenter and the other members of his section.

In the same action Sgt David Lloyd dived after two 109s but had to break off as a Spitfire got in his way. He then saw a single Bf 109E away from the main formation making passes at the general melee that had developed and decided to go for this. He chose to fire a test burst to see if his deflection was correct and it evidently was as a large hole appeared underneath the cockpit, followed immediately by flames. The 109 turned over and dived vertically, hotly pursued by Lloyd who watched it all the way until it hit the ground but in doing so he left himself open to attack. Tracer shot past his starboard wing and a quick look back confirmed no less than six 109s, all of which were acting extremely aggressively. By now the other aircraft in his section were some way off and Lloyd only managed to stay out of trouble by flying his Spitfire to its limits. Although at one point he found himself flying further into France he eventually managed to shake the 109s off and returned at sea level to land and refuel at Manston.

It was during this fight that Sgt Adolf Pietrasiak opened his account with 92 Squadron, claiming the first of six 109s (plus one shared) over a nine day period. As he was passing Dunkirk he saw a Bf 109E about to launch an attack on the Blenheims and using his height advantage he quickly dived onto it and opened fire from 300 yards, initially from the rear quarter before moving into line astern. The 109 pulled up and began to half roll but in doing so slowed down significantly allowing the Pole to fire again with another four-second burst. The 109 went down out of control in a violent spin but Pietrasiak then had to break to evade another and eventually returned home with the close escort squadrons.

On the following day the objective of the Blenheims was Hazebrouck (Circus 30), with the Biggin Hill Wing as Target Support. Several small groups of 109s were encountered on approaching the target area but these declined combat and attempted to lure some of the Spitfires to the south of St Omer where it was assumed a large concentration of their comrades lay in wait. After firing briefly at a passing 109, 'Sailor' Malan turned north with his section behind him and came across a pair of 109Fs which were menacing some Spitfires below them. A series of dogfights ensued and Malan was impressed by the 109s' extreme manoeuvrability, although this was still not up to the level of a Spitfire. During these skirmishes Malan performed one turn of a spin which his No.2 (G/C Dickie Barwell) somehow managed to follow. On recovering he fired at a 109 with full deflection and as it dived away he saw its undercarriage extend, the starboard leg appearing to be fully down with the port leg waving about loosely. Closing in, he used up all of his cannon ammunition but had to break sharply to avoid collision, seeing the port under-carriage leg detach itself from the 109 as he did so. This extreme manoeuvre led to him blacking out and when he came to there was no sign of the aircraft he had been attacking.

As 74 Squadron's Spitfires were circling the target area at 16,000 ft, Yellow section was attacked by four Bf 109s which were identified as 109Es. P/O Bob Poulton (Yellow 3) called the Tally Ho and went after one of the 109s which had continued its dive and was in a gentle left-hand turn. As he was not making any impression he was left with no alternative but to fire at long range and hope for the best. Poulton could not believe his eyes when shortly after a three-second burst the port wing of the 109 broke away at the root and it spun down to crash in a small wood. It is almost certain that the pilot of this 109 was Hptm Wilhelm Balthasar, *Kommodore* of JG 2, who at the time of his death had forty-seven victories to his name including seven recorded during the Spanish Civil War. He was flying Bf 109F-4 Werke Nr 7066 when his aircraft suffered what was thought to be structural failure during a spiral dive following combat with Spitfires. The wing detached and the 109 crashed five miles north of Aire. In his combat report Bob Poulton gave the position as 'near Hazebrouck' which is approximately six miles to the east of the place where Balthasar's aircraft actually came down [Balthasar had been awarded the Ritterkreuz (Knight's Cross of the Iron Cross) on 14 June 1940 when commanding III/JG 3 and the day before his death had won the Eichenlaub (Oak Leaves). He was posthumously promoted to the rank of Major].

During the same action F/L Don Carlson (Yellow 1) went for another 109 which had climbed steeply into a semi-stall turn. After this risky manoeuvre it dived away turning gradually to port which allowed Carlson to cut across the turn until he got in range. Opening fire, he closed to about 150 yards and followed the 109 down to

5,000 ft by which time all his cannon ammunition had been expended. At this stage the German aircraft was trailing glycol and black smoke and was seen to crash in open country by Yellow 4 (Sgt Henderson).

On 4 July following a leisurely lunch, the pilots were briefed for Circus 32 to Bethune in which the Biggin Hill Wing was to act as top cover for the close escort squadrons. Take-off was at 1400 hrs and as the English coast was crossed the pilots could clearly see the wakes of the air-sea rescue launches as they set out from Dover and Ramsgate far below. Within a matter of minutes the French coast was crossed at Gravelines but the appearance of a continuous layer of low cloud led to some nervousness as the Spitfires would show up well against it. This would inevitably make it even easier for the 109s which could be seen as tiny specks climbing to get above the RAF formations, occasionally throwing off a glint of light as the sun reflected off metal or perspex.

As was often the case they only began to attack as the bombers were beginning to turn for home; diving down from around 20,000 ft and underneath the fighter cover to come up behind the Blenheims. 'Sailor' Malan saw one coming in good time and went after it, reaching it just in time to open fire and force it to break off before it could do any harm. On climbing to rejoin his formation on the port flank he saw two Bf 109Es which had lost most of their diving speed and were attempting to climb away. He attacked from one side as Sgt Adolf Petrasiak of 92 Squadron attacked from the other and it went down in flames with smoke belching from it [Pietrasiak also shot down a Bf 109F shortly after this combat]. Another 109 then appeared travelling slowly in the same direction to his left. Pushing his stick forward to lower the nose, Malan fired from 100 yards and it practically blew up, going down on its side in a mass of smoke and flames.

These attacks had led to Malan and his wingman (Dickie Barwell) becoming separated as they had flown on a reciprocal course for about a minute, in which time the main formation had drawn some way ahead. In attempting to catch up Malan and Barwell found themselves flying under a large gaggle of 20–30 Bf 109s (a mixture of Es and Fs) which were tracking the 'beehive' but were making no attempt to attack. Instead they were far more interested in the two Spitfires below them and launched a series of attacks with more and more joining in. At first it was possible to evade the attacks by turning sharply into them, but as the attacks became more frequent it was impossible to stay together and as soon as they could both dived away and headed for the cloud layer at 5,000 ft. As soon as Malan reached the cloud he began dodging various 109s by popping out of the overcast alternately above and below and also changing course by 20–30 degrees. On one occasion when he came out of the cloud he did so at the same moment as a 109E which emerged on a course at right angles to his own. A quick burst of fire scored some hits and it immediately went over onto its back and disappeared again. Emerging into clear air near St Omer Malan climbed to 10,000 ft but was attacked by a 109F near Gravelines as he was diving for home. He saw it in good time, however, and when it had got within 500 yards he broke hard towards it and completed a full circle before returning to base.

Two Biggin Hill pilots failed to return, Sgt W.G. Henderson of 74 Squadron was shot down and killed and the Spitfire flown by F/O Keith Ogilvie of 609 Squadron was badly shot up and he was forced to bale out with serious injuries to his arm and shoulder. The attack had come as the Wing had begun its retreat and was thus down sun of the German fighters. The first Ogilvie knew of his predicament was when cannon shells exploded near the cockpit of his aircraft and he was flung forwards into the instrument panel. His engine was also hit, as was the port wing which lost its aileron and had a large hole ripped through it that revealed some of the internal structure. Of more immediate concern was the large amount of blood that was splattered over the inside of the cockpit and a feeling of nausea.

At first Ogilvie thought he might be able to make it to the Channel in which case he would bale out. He jettisoned the canopy and turned his oxygen up to full to stay awake but when it became apparent that the engine had seized, as evidenced by a stationary propeller blade, and with smoke beginning to billow from under the cowling, it was obviously time to get out. Although Ogilvie was found first by some local Frenchmen he was too weak from loss of blood to be able to get away and was captured. After nine months in hospital, at first in Lille and then in Brussels, he was fit enough to be transferred to a prisoner of war camp. The German doctors did an excellent job in fixing his arm but after the war he was to joke that he could always tell when it was about to rain. During his incarceration he was to spend much of his time at Stalag Luft III and it was here that he took part in the Great Escape on the night of 24/25 March 1944 [see Appendix 5].

Although it is impossible to say who shot Ogilvie down with any degree of certainty, one of the successful German pilots on this day was Oblt Josef 'Pips' Priller, the commander of JG 26's 1st Staffel. The attack bore all the hallmarks of an 'ace' and at this stage of the war Priller had twenty-nine combat victories to his name. As Keith Ogilvie had been an extremely popular character on 609 Squadron he was missed greatly, especially his sardonic sense of humour which had defused many periods of tension. He had been due to depart on a well-earned period of leave and everyone felt that the irony would not be lost on him.

Following an uneventful bomber escort on the 5th the next operation that was contested was on 6 July during Circus 35. Prior to this mission the pilots were given a pep talk by AVM Leigh-Mallory who exhorted them to 'Keep fit, take lots of exercise and sleep'. This was greeted by several wry glances from 609 Squadron pilots, several of whom were still 'pie-eyed' after another late night at the Suivi! On this occasion 'Sailor' Malan was flying at the head of 74 Squadron and had an eventful afternoon, the events being recorded in his combat report,

> I was on the port flank of the close escort with four aircraft at 20,000 ft between Lille and St Omer when several 109Fs were seen overtaking us from behind. The rear pair, led by S/L Meares, turned to the left slightly before I did and a series of dogfights ensued. The two pairs became separated and eventually all four of us became separated. At the first opportunity I dived away in a series of half rolls and aileron turns until about 400 mph was indicated. I pulled out at 5,000 ft where I straightened up for Gravelines. I was about a mile away with my nose down when I saw a shadow cross my own flying in a down-coast direction. I immediately spotted a 109F and as I had good speed I turned onto his tail, overtaking him rapidly. He was flying at 500 ft and I closed to 400 yards and gave a four-second burst with cannon and machine-guns, closing in to about 50 yards. He was enveloped in smoke and did about four quick spins and went straight in.
>
> I then heard bullets whistling past my aircraft and I did a steep turn to my left, receiving three strikes of bullets which grazed my helmet and ricocheted off the bullet-proof windscreen into my instrument panel. During my turn I saw about six 109Fs which gave chase. I went down to 50 ft and crossed just east of Gravelines in a series of jinks and received a lot of attention from every

conceivable type of light flak from what looked like coastal batteries. I found it fairly easy to avoid by watching the streams of tracer hitting the water. I levelled out and steered a course for the English coast in the haze but was repeatedly attacked from behind by Me 109Es which forced me to turn towards them each time and making them pull up. They appeared to be very bad shots for on several occasions I was surprised, but fortunately I could see their bullets striking the water under one wing or the other, thus giving me warning. I shook them off about mid-Channel by a series of jinks, but just about the North Goodwin I was attacked by another one. I nearly got on to his tail but he used superior speed and climbed into the sun.

Although Malan had been able to escape by superb flying, some of the others in 74 Squadron were not quite so lucky. P/O Bill Skinner was shot down in W3208 to become a prisoner and Sgt L.R. Carter was shot down and killed in W3176. Sgt W.G. Lockhart (W3317), who was later credited with having destroyed two Bf 109s before also being shot down, managed to avoid being captured. He was taken in by the French and with the help of an escape organisation returned to Britain on 21 October (for the story of his evasion see Appendix 4). Of the other Biggin Hill units, Sgt C.G. Todd of 92 Squadron failed to return in W3331 and it was later reported that he had been killed.

In early July 92 Squadron was heartened by the arrival of three replacement pilots, P/O P.H. 'Hunk' Humphreys, Sgt Stan Harrison and Sgt Walter 'Johnnie' Johnston who had all arrived from 152 Squadron at Warmwell. In recent weeks 'Sailor' Malan had been having something of a battle with the Air Ministry as regards the standard of new pilots coming into the Biggin Hill Wing as those fresh from Operational Training Units were being lost at an alarming rate. Malan advocated bringing pilots in from other squadrons as they would know how to handle a Spitfire to the extremes of its performance and would also have a good grounding in tactics. This policy was backed up by the other top pilots at Biggin. Walter Johnston recalls his arrival on 92 Squadron and his first encounter with Don Kingaby

When I first saw him (Kingaby), I thought he was a line-shooter! 'Hunk' Humphreys, Stan and I had arrived from 152 in Cornwall to find the squadron away on a show. We went down to dispersal to meet the others and the ground staff and when the squadron arrived back, we three were in the crew room. The door burst open and a tousled, tired group came through with a little chap in front saying "Did you see all those *Stukas* on the deck at Calais-Marck? Hell, if they are waiting for another bash over here it'll be grand. If I don't get eight or ten on the trip, I'll be disappointed!" All were in shirt sleeves so no ranks could be seen, but this little fellow seemed as if he was one of the ringleaders. Then he noticed three new faces and at once came over to us. When we introduced ourselves as the new replacements and said we already had about eight months with 152, he nearly fell on us and kissed us, calling out to the others that at last sense had prevailed. It was only then that he put on his jacket and I saw the DFM and bar and I knew then that it wasn't conceit, just experience.

After this uncertain start, Johnston and Kingaby became good friends and eventually decided to share a room together as both had suffered the loss of room-mates before they had even had the chance to get to know them. Each respected the others flying ability and there was a feeling that if anyone was going to make it through, they would.

Having been in 11 Group since October 1940, 74 Squadron was pulled out of the front line on 8 July and left Gravesend for Acklington in Northumberland. The last opportunity to atone for some of the losses it had suffered occurred the day before during a morning Circus operation (No.37) to the Potez repair works near Albert. Yellow section, led by F/L Don Carlson, bore the brunt of the attacks which took place during the withdrawal when the sun was directly behind, thus allowing the 109s the best opportunity to approach without being seen. On being attacked Carlson pulled his Spitfire into a tight right-hand turn only to see the leading 109 pulling out of its dive and zooming up to his left. Reversing his turn he climbed after it and fired a four-second burst with cannon and machine-guns, the 109 seeming to stall before trailing glycol and black smoke. He then had to break off after being attacked by a second 109, the pilot of which appeared quite happy to turn with his Spitfire. Carlson found the 109 to be nearly as manoeuvrable as his own aircraft and as a result neither pilot was able to get into a shooting position. As the penetration had been a deep one, fuel was an important factor and Carlson broke away by spinning off his turn and diving to ground level, before returning at zero feet. After crossing the coast he throttled back to +3 lb/sq.in boost and selected weak mixture, but even so he landed at Hawkinge with only five gallons remaining.

As Carlson had been turning with the second 109, his No.2, Sgt G.F. Trott, had been right behind but was loath to open fire on the Messerschmitt as he was afraid he would also hit his leader. This was not his only problem as he in turn was being tracked by a 109 which was firing at him. As soon as he saw Carlson spin away Trott opened fire but after a few rounds, one of his cannons jammed. Undismayed he continued firing with the other until it was finished, and saw pieces fly off the fuselage and smoke pour from the engine. The 109 then seemed to quiver as though the pilot had been killed or seriously injured. It turned over and entered a spin but Trott had to take violent evasive action as he came under attack once more. His troubles were still not over as on the way home, near Crecy, two more 109Fs came down on him from above and behind. Pulling into a sharp climbing turn to the right, he blacked out completely but on coming to found that he was behind the 109s. Diving onto the nearest one he fired his machine-guns at it from a range of 100 yards which caused some damage. As fuel was also a concern he dived for home, shooting up several 'R' boats (small minesweepers) on the way before landing at Lympne.

The offensive element of this attack was made up of four Stirling bombers which had arrived six minutes late at the rendezvous so that precious fuel was wasted while the Spitfires waited for them to turn up. As it turned out this did not pose too much of a problem for the escorting fighters as the attacks had only materialised near the French coast on the way out. As they were withdrawing P/O 'Pyker' Offenberg of 609 Squadron saw a German convoy in the Channel which had two low-flying 109s for protection. These sheered off when attacked but the section was then set upon by more which arrived from the direction of Le Touquet. Offenberg chased one of these aircraft in a steep dive but had to pull up steeply to avoid hitting the water and in doing so blacked out. When he came to he noticed a large splash amongst the boats and on the basis of this was awarded with a Bf 109 as destroyed. The only known *Luftwaffe* loss that could possibly fit with these circumstances was that of Ofw Hans Tilly of JG 2, although as two Spitfires of the Biggin Hill Wing were shot down into the Channel around this time it is not inconceivable that Offenberg saw one of these as it hit the sea.

One of these aircraft was flown by Sgt G. 'Moose' Evans of 609 Squadron who had to bale out from 10,000 ft after his engine was hit. During his descent his dinghy became detached from its cover and blew away so by the time he entered the water he was reduced to his Mae West. Unfortunately he had become disorientated as he drifted down and he began swimming towards the French coast four miles away under the impression that it was the English coast. After about 1½ hours in the water he was spotted by some Spitfires and a Lysander dropped a dinghy which he had only just reached when he was picked up. The rescue launch took him to Dover where he was put in hospital with shrapnel wounds to his leg and hand. The other Spitfire shot down was that flown by Sgt C. Stuart of 74 Squadron who was picked up at about the same time.

In the afternoon Circus 38 took the Biggin Hill Wing back to the Kuhlmann works at Bethune. P/O Philip Archer was flying as Blue 2 in 92 Squadron when he saw three Bf 109Fs in loose vic formation about 3–5,000 ft below the squadron. He was given permission by Jamie Rankin to attack but on spiralling down he became aware that there were two other sections of 109s on each side of the one he had originally seen. Closing on the 109 on the right in the middle group he fired a two-second burst from dead astern at 250 yards and saw hits on the fuselage. He then turned his attention to the formation leader and fired again from directly behind. The 109 turned over on its back and emitted thick black smoke before descending in a slow spiral dive. Archer followed to about 5,000 ft but was of the opinion that it was out of control and that the pilot was probably dead. He then zoom climbed back up to 13,000 ft and joined up with the close escort squadrons before returning to base.

No.609 Squadron was not engaged however the engine of Paul Richey's Spitfire began to cut over mid-Channel due to fuel starvation and he had to glide back to Hawkinge. Although he could have made it easily, he eventually had to force land as his initial approach was blocked by several Hurricanes which cut in ahead of him. On return to Biggin Hill the pilots were honoured by a visit from Winston Churchill who was accompanied by Air Marshal Sholto Douglas. The former was rather more cheerful than on his last visit to Biggin Hill and asked the apposite question 'What would you do if these aerodromes were attacked now?' During the rest of the day the only cause for concern was the antics of William de Goat who had now shown a preference for beer instead of milk and after a hard day's drinking, was under the influence to the extent that he was unable to climb the steps to the 609 Squadron dispersal hut.

As the Tigers headed to the north-east they were replaced by 72 Squadron which moved in the opposite direction and took up residence at Gravesend on the 8th. The squadron was led by S/L Desmond Sheen DFC who had joined the Royal Australian Air Force in 1936 before transferring to the RAF shortly afterwards. After further training he was posted to 72 Squadron in June 1937 and remained with this unit apart from a brief spell as a photo-reconnaissance pilot with 212 Squadron in April/May 1940. During the Battle of Britain he had the misfortune to be shot down twice within five days; on 1 September he was forced to bale out over Kent following combat with Bf 109s and on the 5th he had to take to his parachute near Hawkinge, again after a dual with 109s. On the latter occasion his Spitfire was set on fire and he suffered slight injuries. When he returned to 72 Squadron after recovering he was made a flight commander and took over as its commanding officer in April 1941.

Of the other pilots who would feature prominently in the coming weeks Sergeant Jimmy Rosser had arrived from 7 OTU, Hawarden on 5 November 1940. He had been educated at Northampton Grammar School and was studying architecture when he was called up on 1 September 1939. A month after arriving at Biggin Hill he was given a commission and was to remain with 72 Squadron until April 1942. Sgt Cedric Stone was a recent arrival from 64 Squadron with whom he was credited with having shot down a Bf 109F over the Channel. He was commissioned in October 1941 shortly after being awarded a DFM. P/O Eric Bocock had learned to fly in 1939 during studies at Leeds University and was posted to 72 Squadron in April 1941 from 58 OTU at Grangemouth.

Due to the changeover taking place at Gravesend the Biggin Hill Wing's involvement in an early morning Circus operation (No.39) on 8 July was limited to 92 and 609 Squadrons. The target was Lens which was to be attacked by three Stirlings of 7 Squadron which had taken off from their base at Oakington shortly before 0500 hrs. This early start was far from ideal for the escort squadrons as Don Kingaby recalls,

We took off at first light to take three Stirlings in to Lens. When we arrived over the French coast the sun was still just above the horizon on our port bow. I realised that when we had reached the target and turned for home we would be in a very sticky position as the 109s would be able to come in straight and level behind us and we would not be able to see them on account of the sun. We crossed the French coast and had got about ten miles in when a 109 came in at me out of the sun and almost head-on. I only saw him at the last moment and didn't have time to fire at him. He flashed past me and fired off a Very cartridge. From that time on until we crossed out again all hell seemed to let loose. The 109s poured in from all directions and we were so busy dealing with them that it just wasn't possible to see what happened to anything we fired at. Then the Hun flak joined in with great gusto and winged one of the Stirlings. A thin stream of smoke began to pour from his outboard port engine, but he carried on and at last we reached the target which was obliterated in clouds of smoke and dust.

The bombers turned for home and then we had the sun right up our tails. Things got even hotter than before as the 109s steamed in out of the sun whilst we were blinded. The Stirling that had been hit by flak before had received another nasty knock from flak over the target and a fire now began in the outboard engine. Gradually the fire spread along the wing towards the cockpit and then she keeled over like a stricken ship and went plunging to her doom. Only three of the crew baled out and, flaming like a torch, she screamed down and plunged into the middle of a factory in a small town about ten miles from the target. We forced on and eventually reached the coast without further loss. I had fired all my ammunition but couldn't even claim a damaged because I had been too busy to see what happened when I fired.

After crossing the coast the attacks faded out and I throttled back to conserve my petrol which was getting pretty low. I landed at a forward airfield to refuel and just after two more Spitties taxied in. The show that morning had been laid on at very short notice and no-one had had time to eat anything – a very bad thing to fly on an empty stomach. I wasn't feeling too good myself, but when the occupants of the other two Spitfires got out of their cockpits I couldn't restrain a grin. They were as green as the sea they had just flown over and both hurriedly disappeared from sight behind the nearest building!

No.609 Squadron also had a difficult time and as they were flying at only 12,000 ft one of their Spitfires was nearly hit by flak. Near the target Paul Richey's Spitfire developed engine trouble and he was forced to descend below the level of the bombers, however, he was protected by the rest of his section while he nursed his engine all the way back to Hawkinge where he landed with only half a gallon of oil left. After the loss of the Stirling John Bisdee took up escort duties on another which had become detached and fired at a 109 which crossed in front of him near Gravelines. Michael Robinson also fired at a 109 which dived across the formation but the most hectic time was had by Sgt Hughes-Rees. Over the target he saw two 109s about 500 ft below and attacked one of them from astern causing it to flick onto its back and disintegrate before hitting the ground. He then experienced heavy fire from the other 109 during which his oil pressure dropped to zero. His adversary climbed above him but Hughes-Rees pulled back on the stick and fired a long burst which produced a bright flash on the starboard wing of the 109 which went into a spin and was lost to view. The engine of his Spitfire seized when at 9,000 ft over the French coast and he then attempted to glide home, making for the South Goodwin Sands. Having finally run out of height, he made a successful flapless landing on the water but as his aircraft sank he became aware that his dinghy had been punctured. He was therefore fortunate to be picked up two hours later by a boat, by which time he was unconscious. As he had also been wounded during the attack Hughes-Rees was taken to hospital, only returning to the squadron after four months recuperation

The following day 92 Squadron had one of its most successful days for some time during Circus 41, an attack by three Stirlings on Bethune. The Biggin Hill Wing (comprising 92 and 609 Squadrons) was airborne at 1300 hrs with Jamie Rankin leading and the bombers were picked up as they crossed the English coast. Rankin guided the Wing into France between Cap Gris Nez and Boulogne at 30,000 ft and when the main force was approximately 5–10 miles off Hardelot two small enemy formations were seen but these were not attacked as to do so would have meant straying from the prescribed route. The Wing gradually drew ahead of the bombers and lost height so that it arrived in the target area at 26,000 ft. As the Spitfires orbited Bethune a formation of nine Bf 109Fs was seen moving into position and Rankin ordered 92's Red and Yellow sections to follow him into the attack. The German aircraft saw them coming and split up and each section went for the nearest. Rankin singled out what he thought was the leader and followed him in a steep dive. Even though his aim was unsteady owing to excessive speed he achieved a couple of HE strikes and the 109 began to trail black smoke, at the same time as diving vertically in a quick, tight spiral.

Having ordered everyone to climb, Rankin made it back to 23,000 ft by which time the main force was on its way home and was two miles ahead. The Spitfires were continually harassed as they withdrew but the 109s did not press home their attacks. By the time that Hardelot was reached Yellow section had caught up again and with the security of increased numbers Rankin attempted to attack one of several small enemy formations but they quickly dived away. He did however manage to catch another 109F pilot unawares and closed in to 100 yards before opening fire. Rankin had intended to use his cannons but had mistakenly selected machine-guns only. In the event it made little difference as a two-second burst caused the 109 to burst into flames. Having become separated from his section, he joined the main bomber force and returned to base.

During the initial attack over the target Sgt Adolf Pietrasiak had selected a 109 which had broken away from the main bunch in a steep dive and a three-second burst of cannon and machine-gun was enough to send it crashing to the ground in flames. By now Pietrasiak was on his own and about fifteen miles from Bethune but a second opportunity arose when he saw two more 109Fs below him. He carried out a rear quarter attack on the leader and his determination was such that he followed him down a full 12,000 ft using up the rest of his ammunition. During its descent the 109 left a thick trail of black smoke and the hood was seen to come off before it crashed about twenty miles north of Bethune. By now Pietrasiak was at 7,000 ft and he too chased after the bombers and came home with them.

Although Blue section had been ordered to provide cover as Red and Yellow sections went into the attack, they were soon engaged themselves. P/O Geoff Wellum gave the order to attack a second German formation which was attempting to get behind Red Section and fired at one of the 109s from 300 yards. One of his cannon shells burst just in front of the cockpit and the Messerschmitt was last seen at a height of 6,000 ft in a slow spin with flames coming from the engine. P/O Philip Archer (Blue 3) chose a 109 on the left of the formation and was about to open fire when he saw tracer entering his starboard wing. Pulling into a steep turn to the left he found that the aircraft that had fired at him had turned in the same direction and was now slightly above him. By tightening his turn Archer was able to get behind the 109 and fired a three-second burst with no deflection at 150 yards range. It began to pour smoke and shed various pieces before entering a steep spin, apparently out of control. By now Archer was in a precarious position as he was completely alone and was attacked by the remaining 109s. Bit by bit he managed to edge his way back to the coast but another four 109s joined in midway between Bethune and Le Touquet. These aircraft took it in turns to attack in pairs from alternate directions but all turned for home as soon as the coast was reached.

It was often the case that squadrons that were lacking recent operational experience made an inauspicious start when recalled to the front line, and so it was with 72 Squadron. Having performed a number of ASR patrols on the 9th, a Wing sweep was carried out the following day routing Hardelot – Fruges – St Omer as part of Circus 42, an attack by three Stirlings on Chocques. Shortly after take-off reports were received of an incoming raid and 72 Squadron was asked to investigate. This turned out to be friendly aircraft returning from France but rather than abort the mission the squadron continued and crossed over the Channel. Haze prevented any link up with the rest of the Biggin Hill Wing and so 72 flew a rough semi-circle over northern France. Given the level of the opposition this was a hazardous undertaking even for a formation of twelve Spitfires. As the squadron withdrew it did so without three of its number which had been picked off by marauding Bf 109s. The pilots that did not return were F/O J.M. Godlewski (W3411), Sgt A.J. Casey ((P8600) and Sgt C.L. Harrison (P8604), all of whom were killed.

The battle-hardened veterans of 92 Squadron fared a little better but still returned minus one of their number. Sgt C.G. Waldern disappeared when the squadron was on its way home but none of the other pilots had any idea as to what had happened to him. To try to get some answers an air-sea rescue mission was launched and one of the pilots involved was Don Kingaby

I was sure that he had been with us when we crossed out from the French coast between Calais and Dunkirk so I went off with David Lloyd to escort an air-sea rescue Lysander on a search. We patrolled low down on the water, flying at slow speed and with our hoods open, straining our eyes for signs of a dinghy against the scintillating reflections thrown up from the sea by the sun. After two hours we sighted him, lolling in his dinghy, and drew the Lysander's attention to him. The Lissie dropped him additional rations and first aid equipment then rumbled off to guide a rescue launch to the spot while we returned to Manston for fuel. Waldern was back with us the next day none the worse for his ducking. He had apparently broken away from the squadron to attack a 109 on his own and had been bounced and shot down himself instead. Ten days later the same thing happened, but this time we heard no more of him [Waldern was shot down and killed by a Bf 109 of JG 2 on 19 July when flying W3326].

The next day Biggin Hill was visited in the morning by the Rt Hon Peter Fraser, the New Zealand Prime Minister, but in the afternoon it was business as usual with another Circus operation. No.609 Squadron had one of its more hectic days with only one pilot returning without having fired his guns:

Circus 44 ensued in the afternoon and was about 609's most successful day since 8 May. A special feature was the electrical machinations of an IFF Blenheim to deceive the enemy prior to the entry of the bombers and connected with a diversionary sweep in which Biggin took part. 609 in the lead at 27,000 ft, crossed the coast seven miles east of Dunkirk and turning towards Cassel sighted 30–40 Me 109Fs climbing up through cumulus cloud, perhaps in answer to the Blenheim's ethereal vibrations. Convinced that their plan was to gain height and catch our formation from up-sun as it exited via Gravelines, S/L Robinson turned the Wing right and flew parallel with the coast about fifteen miles inland, gradually converging on the enemy with a height advantage of 1,000 ft. The enemy aircraft were in three squadrons, line astern.

The first was allowed to go unmolested then Yellow section (led by F/L Richey) attacked the second squadron and Red section (S/L Robinson) the last. The C.O. shot one down from dead astern and the pilot baled out. He followed another in a steep dive from 27,000 ft to 10,000 ft firing with machine-gun all the way. Just as he was despairing running out of ammunition, his No.2 (the Station Commander G/C Barwell) who had stuck with him all the way, leapt into the breach and firing cannon and machine-gun turned the 109 into a ball of fire; this pilot also appearing to bale out. Previous to this, the G/C without losing touch with S/L Robinson had fired at what must have been the third of the same formation of three and caused it to emit black smoke. Meanwhile Red 3 (P/O Seghers) had followed another enemy aircraft which broke to the right and dived on a Spitfire. P/O Seghers attacked and it rolled on its back, smoking. He was then surprised to see a parachute open.

Meanwhile Yellow section had been doing some fine team work, the leader using his R/T to give orders and warnings with such good effect that the section stuck together during three consecutive engagements. During the first F/L Richey used all his cannon shells at close range on an enemy aircraft which went down pouring black smoke after making an attempt to climb and is claimed as probably destroyed. The section then dived on other enemy aircraft only to find these were already being pursued by other Spitfires (probably Blue section). They therefore broke off this attack and using the speed of their dive, climbed up to four other 109s. Leaving the nearer pair to his section, F/L Richey attacked and damaged both the others with frontal and rear quarter attacks respectively. During these and other attacks Yellow 2 (Sgt Boyd) destroyed one and damaged another, shattering the top of the cockpit and killing the pilot of the first. Yellow 3 (P/O Du Monceau) probably destroyed another which turned on its back and fell sideways out of control. Yellow 4 (Sgt Bramble) damaged another. It was a proper 'bounce'!

The pilots were still landing when a most well-timed visit was made to Dispersal by Lord Trenchard, Marshal of the RAF, a man with as many rings on his sleeve as rows of ribands on his chest. As he shook hands with the pilots there were few who could not boast that they had inflicted at least some damage on the enemy.

Dickie Barwell was certainly one of the more active station commanders that the RAF possessed. On this occasion he followed Michael Robinson into the attack and fired at the other 109 in the pair that his leader had selected. Although he achieved hits he was forced to break off to maintain his position, Robinson having continued his dive after another 109 below. This aircraft did not take any evasive action other than to dive on a straight course but as Robinson had used up all of his cannon ammunition he was reduced to using machine-guns only. Predictably these had little effect and Barwell quickly moved in when his leader broke away to the left. Closing in to about 200 yards he fired a three-second burst of cannon and machine-gun, black smoke and sparks immediately appearing from the port wing root. Robinson was later able to report that this aircraft burst into flames after Barwell's attack and eventually both wings folded before it hit the ground.

The only pilot of the Biggin Hill Wing to be shot down on this day was P/O Don Dougall of 92 Squadron, however, the circumstances of his loss showed a high degree of courage and a selfless devotion to duty on his part. Dougall had been flying as Blue 4 but had been forced to return early with his leader (Sgt David Lloyd) due to R/T failure on Lloyd's aircraft. As the pair crossed the French coast on the way home Dougall saw three 109s closing in rapidly from behind but was unable to warn his leader of the danger. Despite coming under attack himself he flew on and gradually overtook Lloyd, waggling his wings to attract his attention. By this time Dougall's Spitfire had been hit a number of times and was on fire. Due to the heroic actions of his wingman Lloyd was able to make good his escape and landed unscathed at Biggin Hill but as he had not seen Dougall bale out, everyone assumed that he had been killed. Eventually news was received that he was in fact a prisoner but that he had been badly wounded. He was to spend a year in hospital and during this period a leg had to be amputated. He was repatriated in October 1943 as part of a prisoner exchange programme. On 9 November 1943 he was awarded the DFC, the citation mentioning his total disregard for personal safety, and the following week he returned to his native Canada where he married his fiancee, Patricia Sellers from Heston in Middlesex.

Circus 47 which was carried out on 12 July was virtually a repeat of the previous day with the Biggin Hill Wing being part of the escort to a single Blenheim of 75 Wing, which was to create a diversion ahead of an attack by Stirlings on St Omer. Michael Robinson at the head of 609 Squadron was to make it a hat trick of victories with his third Messerschmitt in three days. Rendezvous should have been made at Southend with the Kenley and Northolt Wings but there was no sign of them at the appointed time so the Biggin squadrons set out alone, crossing the

French coast at 27,000 ft at Gravelines where they broke into sections of four, stepped up. After about twenty minutes 92 Squadron dived on unidentified aircraft but these proved to be Spitfires. As they did so two Bf 109Fs went after them and Robinson followed with his section, firing at long range. The lead 109 quickly sheared away but his wingman continued in a steepening dive.

Knowing that if he followed the German's manoeuvre his engine would cut, Robinson performed a slow roll and fired again from an inverted position. The 109 began to emit smoke and then appeared to imitate Robinson by carrying out a complete roll. This allowed him to close quickly and despite a frosted windscreen he fired again from 50 yards and saw various pieces of debris fly past his aircraft. These were followed by the cockpit hood and shortly afterwards by the pilot himself, the latter with his parachute just opening. In fact the German sped past so close that Robinson involuntarily ducked as he went by. As by now he had become separated from the rest of his section he continued his dive into a large thunder cloud below and returned to base [Robinson's victim was probably Uffz Erich Frohner of 7/JG 2 who baled out of his Bf 109F-2 with severe wounds].

Following a day of thunderstorms which brought a welcome end to the heatwave of the last few days, the next offensive operation was Circus 48 on 14 July, a raid by six Blenheims of 21 Squadron on Hazebrouck marshalling yards. The Biggin squadrons were airborne at 0926 hrs and as he led the Wing with 609 Squadron, Michael Robinson was left in no doubt that the *Luftwaffe* were up in force as a large number of condensation trails were seen high above when the RAF fighters were still over the Channel. Shortly after crossing the French coast at 27,000 ft a large formation of Bf 109Fs was seen flying north at the same altitude but as Robinson began to manoeuvre the Wing in behind them, an even bigger formation was seen above and up sun, the two groups amounting to at least fifty aircraft, split up into twos and fours.

Warning the rest of the Wing about the 109s that were at a higher level, Robinson proceeded to attack a pair in the first group, missing one with a deflection shot and firing a long range burst at the other. The latter entered a steep dive which was maintained from 26,000 ft down to 2,000 ft but Robinson stuck to the task and fired several more bursts which produced a trail of debris and increasing amounts of black smoke from the engine. The fate of this aircraft could not be confirmed with certainty due to the proximity of other 109s, although as its dive had gone beyond the vertical it was later claimed as destroyed. During this high speed dive Robinson's No.2, Sgt 'Goldie' Palmer, had followed closely behind, so close in fact that his aircraft was hit by some of the pieces breaking away from the Messerschmitt. The speed built up in the dive carried them back up to 17,000 ft together with the Bf 109Fs that had harassed them at low level and Sgt Palmer fired at one of these, as did Roger Malengreau, but without result. Malengreau also made the mistake of joining up with a formation of 109s but realised his error in time and managed to get away before they noticed him. Following his dive and climb to height, Robinson was of the opinion that the climb performance of the Bf 109F was superior to their Spitfire Vbs above 25,000 ft, about equal below 15,000 ft, and slightly inferior in an all-out dive.

Robinson's warning of the 109s up-sun did not prevent Sgt W. Lamberton of 72 Squadron from being shot down in R7219. Flying as top cover, 72 Squadron had been distracted by a group of 109s below them and had then witnessed an attack on another squadron close by. This gave Oblt 'Pips' Priller all the opportunity he needed and he launched a head-on attack which left Lamberton's aircraft going down in flames. Although wounded, he survived to become a PoW.

A second Circus operation that should have taken place later in the day was cancelled after all the pilots had been told to assemble at the Intelligence Office by tannoy. As everyone was in one place with nothing better to do, the opportunity was taken to discuss various points, Dickie Barwell being particularly keen on this. A frequent complaint of his was the poor standard of the pilots' R/T procedures. This could have a serious impact on operational effectiveness and was a separate issue to the use of foul language, a habit which had already earned a stern letter from the AOC in the interests of listening WAAFs in the control rooms. The day was also notable for a large influx of pilots who arrived to join 609 Squadron. The reinforcements were most welcome, especially as none needed any further training and were ready for operations. They comprised Pilot Officers D.A. Barnham and D.L Cropper, together with Sergeants M.C. Folkard, P. Nash, E.W. Pollard and J.E. Van Schaick

Low clouds which brought the threat of heavy rain on the 16th meant that Rhubarb operations were the only type of offensive flying that could be contemplated. F/L John Bisdee and Lt Maurice Choron of 609 Squadron formed a pair but turned back before the French coast was reached as the weather was considered to be unsuitable. The Belgian pairing of Vicki Ortmans and P/O Baudouin de Hemptinne was rather more adventurous and the two did a low-level reconnaissance over their homeland which took in the route Nieuport – Ypres – de Haan. No suitable targets were seen until they were back over the water when they encountered some minesweepers on the way home. Unfortunately they were prevented from attacking these due to intense anti-aircraft fire which was directed at them from the shore. They were flying so low that these shells were being fired at them horizontally.

During the day Michael Robinson and Dickie Barwell took advantage of the poor weather to fly over to Farnborough where they inspected a Bf 109F which had recently force landed in the UK. This was the Bf 109F-2 Werke Nr 12764 of Hptm Rolf Pingel the *Gruppenkommandeur* of I/JG 26 who had rashly followed a Stirling bomber back across the Channel during Circus 42 on 10 July. As he attempted to shoot it down his aircraft was hit by return fire and it was then further damaged in combat with a Spitfire of 306 Squadron flown by Sgt Jan Smigielski. Pingel made a successful force-landing in a field near the main road from Dover to Deal and thus presented the RAF with its first example of the 109F. It was quickly repaired and put back into the air as ES906 but was written off in a crash on 20 October 1941 which killed F/O M. Skalski of the Air Fighting Development Unit.

Although there was an improvement in the weather the following day there was rather too much cloud which ruined an attempted sweep by the Biggin Hill Wing in the morning. The intended route was Gravelines – St Omer – Hardelot but several cloud layers, culminating in a solid overcast at 23,000 ft, meant that the Wing had to fly on vectors with considerable risk of collision. Such was the degree of difficulty that the sweep was called off before the French coast had been crossed. A second attempt was made later in the day with rather more success, but P/O L.B. Fordham of 72 Squadron was hit by flak and was forced to bale out over the Channel. By the time that the rescue services got to him, however, he had drowned.

No large scale operations were possible on the 18th due to the weather so John Bisdee and 'Pyker' Offenberg of 609 Squadron took off for a Rhubarb over occupied Europe. They were recalled when still over the Channel but Offenberg did not hear the order and continued on his way to cross the Belgian coast at Nieuport. Bisdee returned to join the rest of his squadron which had been allocated as escort to three Blenheims of 21 Squadron which were to attack shipping off Calais. In the event they were unable to locate them and the Blenheims went into the attack with only a single squadron of Spitfires to support them. Two of the bombers were shot down by flak and the third was so badly damaged that when it returned to Manston it never flew again.

On 19 July there was an improvement in the weather and Circus 51 took place. This was an attack by Stirlings on Lille and on this occasion the Biggin Hill squadrons were to act independently with two flying via Gravelines to Gheluwe in Belgium and the third heading to St Omer via St Inglevert, all at 25,000 ft. If no combats had taken place by this stage in the operation all squadrons were to converge on the target. That at least was the intention, but the bombers turned up five minutes early so that 609 Squadron (with the exception of Blue section) accompanied them to the target area and all the way back. Michael Robinson later reported that there were a number of determined attacks on the Stirlings by pairs of 109s which dived from either flank and behind, in some cases right through the formation. Several of his pilots had combats but most of the 109s dived away into thick cloud and 609's only claim was for a damaged awarded to 'Pyker' Offenberg. A large formation of 20–30 Bf 109s kept a watching brief waiting for stragglers and a Stirling was seen to go down in flames having been hit by flak near Dunkirk [this was N6018 of 15 Squadron – of the eight man crew only two survived]

The other two Biggin Hill squadrons had a disappointing day with the only other claim being a probable awarded to Sgt J.C. Carpenter of 92 Squadron. The East India Squadron lost Sgt C.G. Waldern who was shot down and killed in W3326 by a Bf 109 of JG 2. On their way back over the Channel 72 Squadron's Spitfires were followed by the Bf 109Fs of I/JG 26 again led by Oblt 'Pips' Priller. The latter was to account for another 72 Squadron pilot when he shot down Sgt R.F. Lewis in W3181. Sgt G.F. Breckon was also badly shot up and was fortunate to survive when he crash landed on Ramsgate beach as he came down in the middle of a minefield.

The following day was a frustrating one as there was a return of bad weather to the point that the 'Jim Crows' of 91 Squadron at Hawkinge were grounded. 'Pyker' Offenberg took off from Biggin at 0820 hrs on a weather reconnaissance and dived over Hawkinge to prove the point that flying was not totally out of the question. On his return though he reported masses of cloud at various levels but this did not deter those in command who gave the go ahead to Circus 52 which was to head for the now familiar marshalling yards at Hazebrouck. Predictably the operation ended in a complete shambles and all participating aircraft were ordered to return to base. It was later calculated that around 10,000 gallons of fuel had been wasted which prompted one pilot to comment ' . . . and I can't get two gallons to drive to London.'

Even more fuel was used in the evening when 609 Squadron was ordered to patrol Horsham at 15,000 ft. This was in response to radar activity over the French coast and after returning, 92 and 609 were scrambled again at 2200 hrs which was almost unprecedented. The respective Intelligence Officers rushed to the Operations Room to see what was happening only to be told that the 20+ enemy aircraft that had been circling Le Touquet for the last hour had just landed. By now 92 and 609 Squadrons were over the Channel and were less than pleased to be told to return as the Germans appeared to have been playing an elaborate game of cat and mouse. The Wing finally landed at 2300 hrs.

On 21 July Biggin Hill formed the Escort Cover Wing to Circus 54 in which three Stirlings bombed Lille. Top cover was provided by 609 Squadron which did well to put up twelve aircraft as Michael Robinson and all but one of the Belgians were not able to take part as they were about to leave for London for an investiture. Take off was at 0744 hrs and 609 flew in six pairs, half on either flank, at 23,000 ft which was 1,000 ft lower than briefed to avoid leaving condensation trails. A number of enemy aircraft were seen and one of these accounted for Sgt K.W. Bramble who was picked off when he lost position with the rest of the squadron.

Shortly after leaving the target area Sgt John Van Schaick was attacked by two Bf 109Fs from up-sun and felt his aircraft being hit in the tail. Breaking away downwards he turned for home and only levelled out at about 3,000 ft near Calais. He was just considering attacking a gunpost on the beach when he saw tracer coming from astern and saw two 109s which he assumed were the same two that had fired at him previously. All three began to circle one another at 500 ft low over the house tops before Van Schaick made a break for the Channel. The 109s followed and this time his aircraft was hit in the starboard mainplane. A steep turn brought him behind one of the German aircraft and a burst of cannon fire caused it to shed a wing tip which was sufficient incentive for its pilot to head for home. The other 109 attempted a head-on attack which developed into another turning competition in which there was likely to be only one winner. After a short time the Spitfire was in position for another cannon attack and the second 109 soon departed streaming oil and glycol. As he had previously put out a Mayday call, Van Schaick contacted control to say that he thought he could now make it back and eventually landed at Manston. Another Circus (No.55) was flown to Mazingarbe in the evening but this passed off uneventfully.

The next major engagement for the Biggin Hill Wing occurred on 23 July. The day's work started shortly after lunch with Circus 59 to the Foret D'Eperlecques in which 'Sailor' Malan, S/L Desmond Sheen and Red section of 72 Squadron attacked two small vessels to the west of Dunkirk. In the evening there was yet another trip to Mazingarbe (Circus 60) which was to be hotly contested. Many 109s were seen and a general melee took place over Le Touquet but the hazy conditions made contact difficult. Sgt Jaroslav Sika of 72 Squadron was flying in the Yellow 2 position when he was attacked by two Bf 109Fs. As he pulled around sharply to the left, the first 109 passed in front and a little above. Allowing a quarter ring of deflection he opened fire with two short bursts from 150 yards. The first burst produced black smoke from the engine and the second hit the rudder which pitched the 109 into a slow spin. As it went down the spin became faster and Sika followed it down to 4,000 ft. By this time the smoke had thickened considerably and the pilot appeared to have lost control. Having evaded the second 109 Sika returned to Biggin where it was found that his Spitfire had been damaged by cannon fire in the port wing with further bullet holes in the starboard wing and tail.

Although 609 Squadron started with a full complement of twelve aircraft it was soon down to only five. Two pilots returned early with oxygen trouble and another joined another formation having had undercarriage problems. Shortly afterwards Dickie Barwell who was leading Yellow section had R/T trouble and signalled that he too was returning but the rest of his section misunderstood and followed him back. This left Paul Richey who was leading the squadron with just four other aircraft for company. Even then his problems were far from over as his radio was also playing up and he was unable to maintain contact with the leading squadrons.

Whilst orbiting south-east of the Foret de Nieppe five 109s dived down from astern but their attack was foiled by a quick turn into them and they soon climbed for the protection of a thin layer of cloud. Richey then led his section in a climb into the sun when two Bf 109Es appeared out of high cloud and passed in front of them.

When attacked they made the mistake of turning away which gave Richey the opportunity to swing in from behind and open fire with a deflection shot. Several short bursts produced a stream of oil and bits of debris were seen to fall away. This aircraft then inverted itself in a flick manoeuvre that would have been impossible to achieve if it had been under control due to its high speed which was later estimated to be in excess of 300 mph. This dogfight was also witnessed by 'Sailor' Malan and a member of 72 Squadron who confirmed that the pilot baled out. Sgt 'Goldie' Palmer (Red 2) fired his guns at the second 109 which shed some small pieces in its dive.

In the morning of 24 July everyone at Biggin had begun to prepare themselves for Circus 61, an attack on the marshalling yards at Hazebrouck, but this operation was postponed at short notice and replaced by a Roadstead mission to Fecamp. This at least offered some variety as the target was a large merchantman that was travelling up the Channel escorted by several flak ships. It also made a change to escort Bristol Beauforts instead of the usual Blenheims. As these proceeded to launch their torpedoes, some of 609 Squadron's Spitfires shot up the flak ships but only Tommy Rigler claimed to have caused any damage. As it turned out the Beauforts fared little better as all their torpedoes missed the intended target. Paul Richey became involved with a *Schwarm* of four 109s in the target area and a number of other pilots reported having seen a Spitfire dive into the sea. Happily for 609 no pilots were missing and the splash was assumed to have been made by one of the 109s. It was later credited to Brian Kingcome of 92 Squadron who was the only pilot from the Wing to have shot at one. Kingcome was Garrick leader on this occasion and as the ship was reached he saw about twenty 109s just inland, six of which left the main formation to circle the Wing about 2,000 ft above. One pilot decided to dive on the Beauforts and Kingcome followed him down firing a short burst from astern. As he was wary of being attacked himself from behind he zoom climbed back up to the safety of his squadron and was unaware of the 109's fate until informed by 609. On the way back the Wing was followed by a number of 109s but they stayed well out of range and made no further attempts to attack.

As the pilots landed back at Biggin at 1310 hrs they were dismayed to learn that Circus 61 was back on again and that lunch would consist of a few dried up sandwiches. They were also informed that they were to be in the air again within the hour and to make matters worse the beer even failed to arrive. Having taken off again at 1400 hrs the Biggin Hill Wing flew as High Cover to nine Blenheims and not for the first time, the raiding force flew directly over the flak hotspot at Dunkirk instead of the intended route which lay five miles to the east. This was not all they had to contend with as long before the French coast was reached large formations of 109s were seen moving into position. Once the coast had been crossed 'Sailor' Malan decided to take the initiative and ordered his squadrons to separate and go into the attack, 609 Squadron being given the main enemy formation. A number of dogfights broke out but most of these were inconclusive as the 109s, on this occasion at least, did not appear willing to get into a fight. After damaging one of a pair, Michael Robinson went after another and used up all of his ammunition, prising various pieces from it, both large and small. The last he saw of it the 109 was 'spinning like a top.' Tommy Rigler fired at another and was more than surprised when an object that had detached itself from the 109 opened out into a parachute.

No.92 Squadron was also engaged. When about five miles inland and flying at 24,000 ft Sgt C.H. Howard (Yellow 4) became aware of a Bf 109F on his tail and immediately yanked his control column over to the right-hand corner of the cockpit, sending his aircraft into a tight climbing turn to the right. This violent manoeuvre succeeded in throwing off the 109 but it also led to Howard losing contact with his comrades. Seeing a section of four aircraft above and to his right that appeared to be Spitfires he climbed to join up with them but his recognition skills clearly left a lot to be desired as they turned out to be 109s. Luckily for him they had not seen him coming and he was able to move in behind the last in line and deliver a four-second burst from close range. The 109 nosed over into a near vertical dive and soon began to trail thick black smoke behind it. Due to the proximity of the others Howard was not able to follow but he was able to snatch a quick look a few second later, by which time the 109 had dived about 10,000 ft and had turned on its back.

Sgt Walter 'Johnnie' Johnston was another to have become separated from the rest of his section and when flying to the south of Dunkirk at 23,000 ft he saw two Bf 109Fs above and to his left. The German aircraft circled behind him and attacked, one from each quarter so that he was covered from either direction. Johnston turned to the left but immediately half rolled to the right and on pulling out found that one of the 109s had followed him down but had pulled out too soon and had dived straight over him. He fired a three-second burst which caused the 109 to spout black smoke before dropping its port wing and going into a spiral dive. About five minutes later Johnston spotted three more 109s above him in line astern formation. The No.3 peeled off to attack but opened fire well out of range. Johnston throttled back and allowed it to cross his path at a range of around 150 yards, opening fire with a large angle of deflection and continuing until it had passed right through his burst. The wings of the 109 appeared to wobble violently and like his previous victim its port wing went down and it descended in a tight spiral to the left. Not long after smoke began to pour from the machine and it was last seen at about 1,500 ft still diving and trailing smoke.

The final member of 92 Squadron to put in a claim was F/L J.A. Thomson. Whilst following Brian Kingcome approximately twenty miles to the south-west of Dunkirk he saw a 109 away to his right and was able to manoeuvre into position directly behind at very close range. As he fired all of his cannon ammunition in two equal bursts, the German pilot took evasive action but his aircraft was hit and appeared to quiver. Thomson continued to fire with his machine-guns and as he did so the 109 turned over but did not dive. After checking that he was not being followed Thomson looked for his victim once more but all he saw in the position he had last seen it was a parachute. In his combat report he also noted that a blob of liquid appeared on his windscreen resembling blood

Towards the end of July it was 609 Squadron's turn to operate from Gravesend with 72 Squadron taking their place at Biggin. After two days of bad weather which prevented the move, they finally made it on the 28th. Gravesend had opened as a civilian aerodrome in October 1932 when a school of flying was formed which offered pilot instruction up to commercial standard. It had been the first home of Percival Aircraft Ltd which produced the successful Gull three-seat tourer there before moving to Luton. With the cessation of civil flying at the outbreak of the Second World War, Gravesend was requisitioned by the Air Ministry to become a satellite of Biggin Hill. During the Battle of Britain it was the home of 501 and 66 Squadrons, the former unit including Sgt J.H. 'Ginger' Lacey who was the RAF's top scoring NCO pilot.

The Officers were accommodated in the splendid surroundings of Cobham Hall which dated back to Tudor times and belonged to the Earl of Darnley who retained a wing for his own use. In their use of the Hall they were treading in the footsteps of many English monarchs from Elizabeth I to Edward VIII. Another illustrious figure in its history was Charles Dickens who regularly walked through the grounds from his house in Higham to the Leather Bottle pub in Cobham village. Among the amenities was oak furniture and floral lavatory basins and the pilots could also sit in the anteroom among massive classical columns and gaze at 'not so masterly' Old Masters in the picture gallery.

In complete contrast to their day job, the extensive gardens, which featured well-manicured 16th Century lawns, offered a wonderfully tranquil atmosphere, although this was often disturbed by shotgun blasts as some of the Belgian pilots went after rabbits in the nearby park. There was even evidence of past triumphs as the Ashes had been brought home to Cobham Hall when the Honourable Ivo Bligh, later the 8th Earl of Darnley, led the victorious English cricket team against the Australians in 1883 [Cobham Hall is now an independent boarding school for girls and was used during the BBC production of Dickens' Bleak House which was tele-vised in the autumn of 2005].

The next day 609 Squadron had a new commanding officer as Michael Robinson left to become Biggin Hill's Wing Leader in place of 'Sailor' Malan. The command of 609 was taken up by S/L G.K. 'Sheep' Gilroy, described by Frank Ziegler as a slightly dour but kindly Scotsman. Gilroy was born in Edinburgh on 1 June 1914 and his nickname referred to time spent as a sheep farmer in Scotland. He had joined 603 Squadron of the Auxiliary Air Force in 1938 and had been one of the first fighter pilots to see action when he intercepted German bombers seeking naval targets in the Firth of Forth in October 1939. During the Battle of Britain his score steadily increased but he was shot down on 1 September and had to bale out. As it turned out his problems were far from over as he was nearly lynched by an angry mob who assumed that he was German and he was only rescued by the timely inter-vention of the Home Guard. Having suffered slight wounds during this episode he was injured more seriously in December when his Spitfire was hit by another which was attempting a crash-landing. After recovering he was made a flight commander and took part in many of the early sweeps and Circus operations from Hornchurch. It was soon to become apparent that Gilroy was blessed with excellent eyesight as he invariably saw enemy fighters before anyone else. This was a major factor not only in his longevity but was beneficial to all members of 609 which had the lowest loss rates in the Biggin Hill Wing.

Having settled in at their new home 609 Squadron flew its first operation on the 31st which was described thus in the ORB:

With both other squadrons of the Wing released, 609 was called upon to attack some alleged 'E' boats ten miles south-east of Dover. The others were already revving up their engines when the C.O. in his office with the Adjutant heard about the matter and dashed out to lead the squadron for the first time. The target was duly located but whether the vessels consisted of fifteen 'E' or 'R' boats, or five minesweepers each with two paravanes was a matter about which the pilots could never be brought to agree. Attacks were made from 3,000 ft down to zero feet after which the formation made speedily for France. One of them attacked three times by P/O de Hemptinne was seen to stop and another returned, presumably to take off the crew. Another attacked by P/O Barnham weaved drunkenly as if the helmsman had been rendered u/s.

A number of bursts of light flak were experienced at about 3,000 ft before our aircraft attacked and nearly all pilots reported machine-gun tracer during their dive down to 200 ft. It was probably the latter which hit Sgt Boyd. After breaking away he was heard muttering that he had better bale out and presently, after an unsuccessful attempt to reach the English coast, did so. P/O MacKenzie circled him in the water and after five minutes he was picked up by a naval launch. He returned to Gravesend the same evening, clad in the uniform of an AC2, in the pocket of which was a little souvenir of the Navy in the shape of a half bottle of rum. His chief concern was lest he had offended a female correspondent of the Toronto Star aboard the rescue launch by shouting 'Hurry up, it's f . . . . g cold!' And then on reaching shore, bystanders had the cheek to ask him whether he had baled out for a newspaper stunt.

At the end of July 609 Squadron said goodbye to John Bisdee, its longest serving member, when he was posted out to be an instructor at 61 OTU. He had joined the squadron back in December 1939 and had been given the command of 'B' Flight after the death of Johnny Curchin. Just two weeks before his departure he was awarded the DFC, his combat score standing at six destroyed plus two shared at this time. The following year he was to command 601 Squadron in Malta where he used the same tactics that were employed by 609 over France and he ended the war as a Group Captain having also commanded 323 Wing in Italy. With the departure of Bisdee, 609's 'B' Flight was taken over by 'Pyker' Offenberg who was promoted to Flight Lieutenant.

Although July ended in disappointing fashion thanks once again to the weather, the early part of the month had seen some of the biggest air battles of the war but despite the fact that the Fighter Command hierarchy was getting exactly what it wanted, there was controversy over the effectiveness of the policy of taking the fight to the Germans in northern France. As already noted small numbers of four-engined Stirling heavy bombers had been used on several Circus operations instead of Blenheims but the Commander-in-Chief of Bomber Command, Air Marshal Sir Richard Peirse, was sceptical and considered that these huge combined operations were not really worth the effort. After frank discussions Peirse decided to withdraw his Stirlings so that they could be used for night attacks on Germany. Sholto Douglas remained convinced that his fighters would eventually get the upper hand but the whole strategy was based on there being an offensive element to lure the *Luftwaffe* into the air. This meant that 2 Group's Blenheims would continue to form the bombing element for the foreseeable future.

CHAPTER ELEVEN

The Offensive Continues

The first few days of August were characterised by further bad weather and although Fighter Command did its best to carry on with the offensive, many operations were rendered abortive and contact with the enemy was much reduced. On 2 August conditions were only suitable for Rhubarbs and six pilots of 609 Squadron flew over to Occupied Europe on the lookout for targets of opportunity. Lt Maurice Choron knocked some pieces off a tugboat near Boulogne harbour, P/O Du Monceau had a brief skirmish with a Bf 109 before attacking two army vehicles and 'Sheep' Gilroy fired at a train. Although this type of operation was certainly exhilarating as it was carried out at low level, it was often fraught with danger. On this occasion 'Pyker' Offenberg was fortunate not to be hit as he stumbled upon an airfield and was subject to the full weight of its anti-aircraft defences as he flew over and P/O J. Muller, another of 609's Belgians, ran out of fuel and force landed near Chatham.

There was very little activity until the 7th, a brief hiatus that left both sides spoiling for a fight. There was thus a high degree of probability that Circus 67, an attack by six Blenheims of 107 Squadron on St Omer, would be hotly contested, especially as the target happened to be one of the main *Luftwaffe* aerodromes in northern France. The Biggin Hill Wing took off at 1030 hrs and joined up with the Blenheims and their close escort at Manston before setting course for the French coast at a height of 16,000 ft. They were forming part of the Escort Cover Wing and the first signs of enemy activity came shortly after passing over Gravelines when two 109s were seen below. Blue section of 92 Squadron led by Don Kingaby dived to attack while the remaining aircraft kept a wary eye on the skies above them as it was possible that the 109s were acting as bait. Using his height advantage to close on the pair, Kingaby chose the right-hand 109 and fired a three-second burst from a range of 500 yards which produced several hits on the fuselage. On climbing to rejoin the squadron he was able to look briefly in the direction of his victim which was seen to be pouring black smoke and descending in a manner which suggested that its pilot had little control.

After the Blenheims had deposited their loads on St Omer, a further pair of 109s appeared on Kingaby's starboard side and launched a quarter attack. He turned towards them, their tracer passing uncomfortably close, but they were not prepared to fight and both aircraft dived inland. Shortly afterwards two more Bf 109s passed in front at a range of 600 yards and Kingaby opened fire with cannon and machine-gun achieving a number of strikes on the leading machine. Rather than dive out of trouble, the German was stung into retaliation and turned to carry out a head-on attack. Kingaby could see the muzzle flashes as the 109 fired at him, and with a closing speed in excess of 600 mph, each pilot's nerve was tested to the full. The two aircraft avoided collision by only a few feet as the 109 broke away at the very last moment and was not seen again. Although Kingaby did fire at another 109 near Gravelines on the way out, it quickly dived away, apparently undamaged.

A second operation was mounted in the late afternoon (Circus 62) and the Biggin Hill Wing was airborne again at 1650 hrs. The objective on this occasion was meant to be Lille but increasing amounts of cloud meant that the bombers were not seen at the rendezvous point. Although 72 Squadron was to have a relatively quiet trip, both 92 and 609 Squadrons were engaged. The French coast was crossed at the scheduled time and the Wing flew towards St Omer where it came across large numbers of Bf 109Fs. Jamie Rankin informed Michael Robinson (at the head of 72 Squadron) of a section of 109s below and then led 92 towards another group. Even with height advantage he had great difficulty in closing but was eventually able to open fire on the No.5 in a vic of seven from about 300 yards. His first burst had slight deflection but a second was delivered from dead astern and resulted in several HE strikes. The pilot of the 109 obviously still had full control as he put his aircraft into a vertical dive and it was soon lost to view. By this time the rest of the squadron had become split up into sections of four and were attacked from above. A number of ineffectual engagements took place before Rankin ordered the withdrawal at the appointed time.

The bombers were picked up on their return journey but when Rankin was re-crossing the coast near Gravelines he noticed a single 109F which was making attacks in a 'polished manner' on Spitfires of the Escort Cover Wing. He chased after it but could not get closer than 300 yards. Even from this distance his fire was deadly accurate and a three second burst of cannon and machine-gun blew off the port radiator and knocked large pieces off the fuselage. Due to the severe damage to its coolant system, the 109's glycol expired in just a few seconds and flames soon appeared from the engine. It went into a dive and as he circled above, Rankin saw the flames spread along the fuselage. The pilot did not bale out. All of this was witnessed by his wingman and the 109 was later claimed as destroyed.

Paul Richey had an eventful trip, one from which he was lucky to return. He later described his experiences in a report to Fighter Command which was eventually issued by 11 Group as a Tactical Memorandum:

I was Yellow 1 of 609 Squadron taking part in Circus 62, 7 August 1941. Having failed to rendezvous with the main formation of the Biggin Hill Wing, I proceeded to carry out a 'Sphere' entry at Dunkirk and flying over St Omer with the intention of leaving France at Cap Gris Nez. 609 Squadron was top squadron, 92 middle and 72 bottom, and heights were originally from 25–28,000 ft.

Over St Omer many 109s were sighted far below against the cloud and 72, led by Wing Commander Robinson, attacked. 92 lost height by diving and then circled for some time, followed by 609 Squadron. If I may suggest it, I think 92's tactics were mistaken, for both height and speed were lost and nothing gained. In addition the stepped-up formation of 92 and 609 were messed up and generally confused, while the Huns were able to gain height and time and get up-sun with a good view of what was going on.

I was troubled with ice on my hood and windscreen. I was also very bored and cold and was flying sloppily. While my attention was concentrated on a formation above me, I was shot-up in no uncertain manner by a gaily coloured Me 109 diving from behind. My glycol tank was pierced and all my glycol lost. I throttled back and went into an involuntary spin. I could see nothing but smoke, glycol etc and could not recover from the spin which became very flat. I opened the hood to bale out but had great difficulty in removing my harness pin, I think because a) I did not look what I was doing, and b) I was experiencing a lot of 'g'. When I got the pin out I was slowly deciding which side of the cockpit to get out. The smoke abated and I decided to stay in and try to recover, by winding the tail wheel fully forward and using considerable strength on the stick, I did so (the tail was damaged). I dived for cloud and the French coast, weaving, and was attacked by another 109 which I evaded by turning violently and entering cloud. My 'Maiz-dez' was answered immediately over the sea on Button 'D' and I was given a vector.

I was unable to use the vector because of having to weave and control the aircraft. Half way across the Straits at 1,000 ft I tried my engine and was able to use it to the English coast by cutting down boost and revs to a minimum. I had great difficulty in doing up the straps again because of instability of the aircraft which necessitated strong forward pressure on the stick, but succeeded after five minutes. I was comforted by the sight of many rescue launches and buoys and by the Hurricane low cover off the Goodwins. On a fast belly landing at Manston with a still smoking aircraft I found the fire tender very prompt. I would like to stress the following points for the benefit of young pilots :

1) Slackness in the vicinity of the Huns is easy but usually fatal.
2) A Spitfire will last long enough without glycol and even practically without oil, if revs and boost are reduced to an absolute minimum.
3) The sea is much more hospitable than German occupied territory. It is well worth risking attempting reaching it. The chances of rescue are excellent.
4) Do not try a slow forced landing, with damaged control surfaces.

Paul Richey had been the pilots' choice to take over from Michael Robinson as the C.O. of 609 Squadron so there was a fair amount of incredulity in evidence when it was announced that 'Sheep' Gilroy had been given the role instead. Very few people realised the degree of fatigue from which Richey was suffering, perhaps not even the man himself, although the admission above that he had been flying 'sloppily' would seem to indicate that he had an idea that something was wrong. The relentless routine of constant operations imposed an enormous mental strain on the pilots but it was insidious in nature and was not immediately apparent to an untrained eye. Richey's combat experience was highly valued and Fighter Command could ill afford to lose its senior commanders. In the event Richey flew just two more operations with 609 Squadron before being posted to command 74 Squadron which was still recuperating at Acklington in Northumberland.

After a day of bad weather the next major confrontation took place during an evening sweep on 9 August which produced excellent results for 92 Squadron. The number of claims for the Wing as a whole might have been even higher if 72 Squadron had entered the fray but radio interference caused some confusion and they did not engage. The Wing was being led by Jamie Rankin whose combat report describes a hectic few minutes,

I was Garrick leader (also leading the Wing). Rendezvous was made with 609 Squadron over Gravesend at 1735 hrs and the Wing climbed through 10/10 cloud over Kent. I flew south to establish position and managed to identify Dungeness through a small gap in the cloud. Height was then gained over land and the Wing arrived over Rye at 1759 hrs with squadrons at 24/25/30,000 ft. The Kenley Wing could not be seen so one orbit was made and I set off at 1803 hrs without them. Another Wing was seen over the Channel ahead which I assumed to be Kenley at a greater height than they should have been, but it transpired that this was not them. The Wing crossed the French coast between Boulogne and Hardelot at 1812 hrs. One squadron of the Wing in front dived down almost immediately and at the same time I saw 8–12 109s coming from inland and turning round behind us from Le Touquet. I tried to get Knockout (72) squadron to attack and then my own Yellow section, but neither could spot them. I therefore attacked with Red section. The squadron split up into fours and was continuously engaged from then to 1825 hrs. Enemy aircraft were very numerous above, below and at the same height and there was no difficulty in finding targets.

Two formations of seven which I chased with Red section were caught and in both cases I hit 109Fs with cannon, HE strikes being visible. Later at Gris Nez when dogfighting with three 109s, I saw 10–12 more coming up and I ordered the section to dive out and the squadron to return to base. One 109F followed us down at more than 450 mph to 1,000 ft where he opened fire. I swung hard right and he overshot. Turning back on him I fired from 10 degrees deflection with machine-gun only as my cannons were finished. This enemy aircraft, by now at 500 ft, tried to turn right whilst pulling out and crashed into the sea sending up a splash about 100 ft high. I then returned to base. Me 109s were much more inclined to stay and fight and the engagement in the Boulogne – St Omer area was one general dogfight. We could outturn the 109F easily but had not enough speed to close range when in a good position. R/T interference was experienced all the time over France and prevented me from bringing in Knockout squadron who were not engaged into the melee.

Sgt Stan Harrison was flying as Jamie Rankin's No.2 but experienced engine trouble over Boulogne and lost contact with his leader. He then saw three 109Fs and was able to fire a two-second burst at one of them which emitted black smoke. He was then attacked by one of the other 109s which damaged his starboard aileron but he was able to escape by making spiral turns into a cloud layer at 6,000 ft and landed at Hawkinge. The intensity of the battle over Boulogne was such that all aircraft were engaged individually. Sgt Jerrold Le Cheminant (Red 4) dived after a 109 but found that he was not able to make much progress. By this time he was down to around 13,000 ft and there was no sign of the rest of his section so he made for a layer of cloud below. Before he could reach it he was attacked by four 109s. He immediately did a quick aileron turn to starboard, at the end of which he found himself pointing directly at one of the 109s which had broken away from the other three. It was showing practically all its belly and a short burst of cannon and machine-gun fire caused it to break in two near the cockpit. Le Cheminant followed it down and saw it crash in the middle of Boulogne.

P/O Neville Duke was also in combat in the same area but at a much lower height. He was attacked from astern by two Bf 109Fs at 2,000 ft over Boulogne and avoided the first by turning sharply to the left until it was on the opposite side of the circle. He then reversed his turn, pulling as hard as he could so that the 109 went past him on the starboard beam. Tracer then flashed past his cockpit and another 109 went by on his right-hand side. Duke fired a long burst with some deflection, initially from 50 yards but the higher speed that the 109 was carrying meant that it rapidly pulled away. Even so his fire had the desired effect and the 109 went over on its back and did a slow spin into cloud at about 800 ft. Although Duke did not see it crash he was of the opinion that it could not have pulled out before hitting the sea. Shortly afterwards he was jumped by two more 109s and had to dive into a nearby layer of cloud. Instead of giving up, the 109s hung around and were able to latch onto Duke once again when he came out of the cloud to make his escape and chased him to within 2–3 miles of Dover.

Blue section had initially stayed up to cover Red and Yellow sections in their attacks but when further groups of 109s began to join the fray, they too engaged. F/L Tommy Lund (Blue 1) saw four 109s diving onto Red section and closed to 400 yards firing three two-second bursts at the left-hand machine of the upper pair. A stream of black smoke appeared from the 109 as his shells struck but he was unable to press home his attack due to a gun stoppage. The 109 was last seen diving vertically still streaming black smoke. Don Kingaby (Blue 3) covered Lund during his attack but was soon attacked himself from out of the sun. He was forced to break sharply and in doing so lost contact with the rest of his section. He was then set upon by four 109s at 15,000 ft over Boulogne but managed to lose them by selecting maximum boost and climbing into the glare of the sun. With the tactical situation in his favour once more he was able to turn the tables and attack the 109s, but they saw him coming and dived away towards the safety of a layer of altostratus at around 10,000 ft. Kingaby followed them down but was not able to get within firing range before they disappeared from view.

Breaking cloud a few miles inland near Hardelot, there was no sign of the 109s he had been chasing but he decided to hang around for a while to see if anything turned up. Positioning his Spitfire just below the layer of cloud, Kingaby kept a sharp lookout and soon spotted two more 109s climbing out of Le Touquet. He proceeded to stalk them until he was in an attacking position by which time the pair had climbed to about 7,000 ft. The 109s were oblivious to his presence and he was able to close to within 150 yards before opening fire with cannon and machine-gun, the left-hand 109 shuddering violently under the impact of the shells and half rolling into a vertical descent, streaming glycol and black smoke.

A less experienced pilot may have been tempted to follow but Kingaby immediately climbed towards the cloud, thereby restoring his height advantage over the pilot of the remaining 109 who was going round in a steep turn looking for his partner's assailant. When he felt that the time was right, he launched his attack from the port quarter firing a two-second burst. The pilot of the 109 quickly realised his predicament and in an attempt to take the initiative, slammed his throttle shut hoping that this would make his opponent overshoot. Kingaby was not about to fall for this particular ploy and by pulling up the nose of his Spitfire and applying coarse rudder, he was able to decrease his speed and tuck in behind. Utilising his aircraft's famed turning performance to the full it was not long before he was in a firing position. A two-second burst at less than 100 yards slammed into the Messerschmitt which rolled over lazily and dived into the ground about five miles south of Le Touquet. Having used up all of his 20 mm ammunition Kingaby sought the sanctuary of the cloud once more and flew back to Biggin Hill, landing at 1850 hrs.

Several 609 Squadron pilots were also in action including Lt Maurice Choron who chased after three 109s which were seen below in an elongated line astern formation. These aircraft remained out of range as they dived away but on turning to the left at about 22,000 ft Choron saw two more and was able to approach one of these from the port rear quarter. He fired a one-second burst with cannon only which caused a number of pieces of debris to break away from the fuselage near the cockpit. The 109 spiralled down almost vertically but could only be claimed as a probable as it disappeared into the haze at lower levels. P/O Alex Nitelet was credited with having shot down a Bf 109F although he failed to return. It was later to emerge that he had been shot down (possibly by Lt Karl Borris of 6/JG 26) and suffered severe head injuries when his Spitfire turned over on landing. He was spirited away before the Germans arrived and was tended by a French doctor but was to lose his right eye. After recovering he was helped by an escape organisation and finally got back to Britain on Christmas Day 1941 (for the full story of Nitelet's evasion, see Appendix 4)

On 10 August a wing sweep was flown in the early afternoon over the route Ambleteuse – St Omer – Gravelines and on this occasion 72 Squadron bore the brunt of the attacks. F/O R.B. Newton claimed a Bf 109 as damaged over St Omer, however it was P/O Eric Bocock who had the most eventful time as his Spitfire was attacked from out of the sun and hit by cannon shells and machine-gun bullets. In taking violent evasive action he lost contact with the rest of the squadron but he also managed to lose his attacker. As he was now on his own he immediately sought cloud cover at 3,500 ft and headed for the French coast. Once over the Channel he saw a small ship (estimated at 3–500 tons) and as his aircraft still felt normal he dived onto it opening fire with cannon and machine-guns. Members of the crew scattered in all directions but although the vessel was hit, it did not appear to be badly damaged. There was no return fire but the anti-aircraft batteries on the shore more than made up for this and Bocock's Spitfire was bracketed by a barrage of flak of all calibres.

Having pulled up into cloud once more Bocock headed for home but his attack on the ship had also been seen by two Bf 109Fs which followed him. As he briefly came out cloud he saw them in his mirror and ducked back into cloud once more before changing course. When he re-emerged into clear air one of the 109s was crossing about 300 yards in front of him and he fired a deflection shot which hit the 109 towards the rear of the fuselage. Both aircraft were then enshrouded in cloud again but in his confusion following this attack Bocock set his compass wrongly and flew on a reciprocal course. When he emerged from cloud he found himself back over Calais where, once again, he was targeted by heavy flak. Fortunately his aircraft did not suffer any more hits and he was able to regain cloud cover and return without further incident. On landing it was found that his Spitfire had been hit by two explosive cannon shells and several machine-gun bullets.

After a day of rain on the 11th another Circus operation was mounted on 12 August, the objective being Gosnay power station with the alternative (and actual) target of St Omer/Longuenesse. This raid was intended as a decoy to draw fighters away from a deep penetration by 2 Group Blenheims which were carrying out an audacious daylight attack on power stations around Cologne. The Biggin Hill Wing acted as the Escort Cover Wing to six Hampdens with 609 Squadron as top cover. Paul Richey was attacked by a trio of very bright, new-looking Bf 109Fs and then by a singleton, but no harm was done to either side. In the late afternoon a second Circus was flown in the same area and although some 109s were seen they mainly kept their distance. They threatened on just one occasion during which Sgt Carpenter of 92 Squadron was shot up but he managed to return safely to base and was not injured in the attack. P/O Francois de Spirlet of 609 Squadron was fortunate to get home unscathed, however, as he descended out of cloud directly in front of two Bf 109Es. Luckily for him there was further cloud nearby in which he was able to hide and he did not see the two Messerschmitts again.

A regular supply of Atlantic low pressure systems meant that it was virtually one day on and one day off and another bout of bad weather on the 13th resulted in the Biggin Hill squadrons being released at noon. The day after saw a slight improvement in the weather that allowed an early afternoon Roadstead against Boulogne docks. The Biggin Hill Wing acted as the Escort Cover Wing to twelve Blenheims but no enemy aircraft were encountered and cloud conditions prevented the results of the attack from being seen. Later in the day another Circus operation took place when six Blenheims raided the shell factory at Marquise. The Wing fulfilled its function by sweeping about fifteen miles inland from Dunkirk to Calais where accurate flak was encountered. Although various formations of Bf 109s were seen, these stayed well clear and no combats took place.

After yet another day of heavy rain which prevented another visit to Biggin Hill by Lord Trenchard, the Wing had one of its busiest days on 16 August, an early morning sweep with take-off at 0725 hrs being the first of three offensive missions over France. The day was to end with one 609 Squadron pilot being shot down and killed but it took the Grim Reaper three attempts to get his man. The first sweep was flown from Dunkirk – St Omer – Gravelines and there was a brief exchange involving 609's Yellow section led by P/O Baudouin de Hemptinne. The Spitfire flown by P/O D.L. Cropper was hit the hardest and it returned full of holes. Swapping his damaged machine for another, Cropper was airborne again at 1215 hrs for Circus 73 which was a repeat of the raid on Marquise attempted two days previously. He did not get far as his canopy blew out at 30,000 ft leaving him flying an open-cockpit Spitfire in an icy blast of around –40 degrees C. Quickly dropping down to a lower level, he was able to return to Biggin without further incident. Back over France Sgt Nash also had to make a rapid descent due to a heavily frosted windscreen and on levelling out at 1,000 ft chanced upon a Bf 109. In a sharp exchange he was able to put a few bullet holes into it before turning for home.

The final operation of the day (Circus 75) saw the Biggin Hill squadrons airborne at 1740 hrs to act as the Escort Cover Wing for six Blenheims attacking the airfield at St Omer/Longuenesse. On this type of mission the position of the sun was crucially important as regards the tactics of the defending *Luftwaffe* fighters and with a late take off the sun was to their advantage in the initial stages as the RAF flew towards the target. The 109s harried individual sections and managed to prise 609 Squadron's Yellow section away from the protection of the others. P/O Cropper's luck finally ran out and he was last seen with his Spitfire going down in a spin and on fire. P/O Baudouin de Hemptinne (Yellow 1) was at least able to fire at one of the 109s, a combat that was witnessed by Jamie Rankin who saw it eventually dive into the ground. It is highly likely that Cropper was shot down by Hptm Walter Adolph who was the commander of JG 26's II Gruppe. Adolph was the holder of the Knight's Cross but Cropper was to be his twenty-fifth and last victim as he was shot down and killed himself on 18 September.

Several pilots from 72 Squadron were also in action including Sgt Cedric Stone who had become separated from the rest of the squadron when it turned towards the sun inland from Boulogne. On descending to 15,000 ft he was attacked by a pair of Bf 109s, with another pair soon joining in. Although Stone was seemingly hopelessly outnumbered, numerical superiority was not always what it seemed, especially if the attacks were not well co-ordinated. In evading the first attack with a steep turn he was presented with a relatively easy shot as one of the 109s was approaching him from the left at a range of about 100 yards. All he had to do was open fire and let the Messerschmitt fly through his burst. It then went into a steep dive leaving behind a long stream of smoke which gradually thickened so that the aircraft was completely enveloped as it approached the ground. Stone then had his hands full with the other three 109s but was able to hit one of them in the fuselage before finally breaking free and heading for home. On his way back P/O Jimmy Rosser shot up a 'sound detector' at Cap Gris Nez and P/O Eric Bocock attacked a gun emplacement near Hardelot.

Further bad weather on the 17th meant that no large-scale operations could be contemplated however 72 Squadron still managed a squadron patrol over the Channel with the intention of intercepting a number of Bf 109s which were providing cover over a convoy between Cap Gris Nez and Calais. Numerous combats took place in which S/L Desmond Sheen damaged one of the 109s but the most successful pilot once again was Sgt Cedric Stone. The tactics he used were virtually identical to the previous day as another 109 conveniently flew right past him from left to right, straight through his line of fire. It immediately flicked over onto its back and Stone last saw it diving vertically towards the sea. It was claimed as destroyed after another pilot gave evidence that he had seen it dive straight in.

Two more Circus operations were flown on 18 August, the first (No.78) was an attack by nine Blenheims on an engineering works at Lille with Biggin Hill acting as Target Support Wing. The trip passed off uneventfully although the absence of the Close Escort Wing meant that 609 Squadron had to fill in on the way home. During the return journey a mysterious Spitfire with old type camouflage and seemingly no squadron lettering was seen which caused some anxiety among the pilots. The day before Biggin's aircraft had been repainted in a green/grey scheme in place of the former green/brown camouflage paint. Many pilots were suspicious of the aircraft, especially as reports had been received of aircraft coming under attack from what was thought to be a friendly machine. Neville Duke refers to this incident in his book *Test Pilot* (Allan Wingate, 1953) and claims on another occasion to have seen a lone Spitfire patrolling in a manner which made him wary of its intentions. No evidence has ever come to light of a Spitfire being operated by the Germans as described and it seems more likely that it was, in fact, an RAF aircraft, but the reactions of the pilots serve to highlight the strain that they were under and the level of 'twitch' that they were suffering.

The operation to Lille was also notable for the use of a new tactical formation with each section of four aircraft flying in line abreast. This had been decreed by Jamie Rankin who was leading the Wing on this occasion and reflected the disparate views on tactics held by various fighter leaders within the Command. This formation had already been adopted by the Tangmere Wing and was virtually identical to that flown by the *Luftwaffe*. As already related, 'Sailor' Malan had favoured a system based on sections of four aircraft in line astern and this lack of consistency continued into 1942 with some squadrons still employing sections of three with 'weavers' operating to the rear.

The second operation on the 18th was Circus 80, another attack on the shell factory at Marquise. The Wing was given the freedom to patrol at 25–27,000 ft and encountered 109s near Hardelot. No.609 Squadron's Red and Blue sections dived on four Bf 109s that were seen below. Yellow section attempted to follow but had to climb up to 20,000 ft again as the Spitfires were getting in each other's way as they tried to line up to attack. With Yellow section now on its own, it was not the best time to encounter a group of twenty 109s which were seen cruising serenely along at 35,000 ft. Six of these decided to come down and start a fight and P/O Vicki Ortmans (Yellow 2) turned sharply to the left to come round behind two 109s which were threatening other members of the section. These saw him coming and sheered off, but Ortmans then saw another diving away to the south-east. Rather than continue its dive to safety this aircraft began to climb again which allowed the Belgian the opportunity to close in rapidly. Realising his error the German pilot pushed the nose of his aircraft down again and turned to the right but by this time Ortmans was in a firing position and opened up with a four-second burst at 300 yards range. As he stopped firing he saw a bright flash and what appeared to be flames coming from the 109 which was left at about 10,000 ft still going down in a steep dive about five miles inland from Calais.

P/O Du Monceau (Red 2) was among the Spitfires that dived on the first 109s to be seen but in attempting to transfer his attention from one to another, in order not to interfere with the attack being made by Michael Robinson, he blacked out completely when he pulled a little too hard. When he regained consciousness he found that he was alone and looking up saw a formation of five aircraft, all weaving gently. The first was a Spitfire about 1.000 yards ahead of the rest and at first he thought that the others were Spitfires as well until he got closer and saw their yellow markings. The first 109 had yellow under the nose but the rest had yellow under-sides all the way from the engine to the tail unit. As the 109s did not appear to be making much progress Du Monceau was able to climb above them as they chased the lone Spitfire back to the English coast.

Selecting full boost he began to overhaul them but then the first 109 in the line moved into an attacking position on the other Spitfire, the pilot of which seemed to be blissfully unaware that he had four German aircraft behind him. By now Du Monceau was in an attacking position himself but the three rearmost 109s knew he was there and pulled into a climbing turn to the left. He then turned his attention to the leader of the 109s but as they were by now within six miles of the south coast the German pilot decided to give up the chase and return home. Du Monceau followed him back and closed in during a dive from 20,000 ft down to 10,000 ft firing a long burst from 500 yards down to 150 yards, continuing with machine-guns when his cannons ran out of ammunition. The 109 began to pour black smoke which turned red at one point but thinking that his comrades might still be around, Du Monceau broke away in a steep turn and managed to black himself out for a second time. He came to again at 8,000 ft and returned without further incident [this aircraft was later claimed as destroyed on the basis of a report from Sgt Nash who saw black smoke issuing from the sea about 2–3 miles off Calais at the time of this combat].

On the following day Circus 81 took place which was otherwise known as 'Operation Leg', the dropping of an artificial leg for W/C Douglas Bader the leader of the Tangmere Wing who had been shot down on 9 August. Weather conditions were far from ideal with towering cumulus clouds over the Channel which at times grew into storm cells. The Biggin squadrons were to act as the Rear Support Wing by patrolling Dunkirk at 28–32,000 ft which everyone thought would be a 'stooge' but was far from it. Various groups of 109s were seen in twos and fours down to 13,000 ft and sections of 609 Squadron were ordered to attack whenever the opportunity arose. Yellow section was involved the most with P/O de Hemptinne and Sgt E.W. Pollard to the fore, but it was Vicki Ortmans who was to have the most eventful day.

On seeing Yellow 1 and 2 roll over into a dive after a 109, Ortmans decided to follow, together with his wingman, but was left in an unenviable position when the former pair abandoned their attack after only a few seconds and pulled up again. He decided to continue after the 109 but did not achieve any hits before it shot into a layer of cloud. On descending into clear air he saw the same aircraft only 100 yards ahead and fired a three-second burst which produced a stream of glycol. He was not able to take any further action as he was attacked from behind, tracer hitting his starboard wing and aileron. On turning to port two 109s were seen but they did not make any attempt to follow and merely turned away into the clouds. Ortmans crossed the French coast near Dunkirk but as he was not able to weave properly as a result of the damage to his aircraft, another 109 came in behind unseen and opened fire. This time his glycol tank was hit and coolant poured out, some of it coming into the cockpit. Again the 109 did not press home its attack and Ortmans was left to try and coax his damaged machine a little further towards the English coast. He did not get much further as around mid-Channel his Spitfire burst into flames and he was left with no alternative but to invert it and bale out. He was fortunate in that Michael Robinson, 'Pyker' Offenberg and P/O Denis Barnham were on hand to mark his position and put out distress calls. After two hours in his dinghy he was picked up by a rescue launch and was back with the squadron in the evening.

After a day of bad weather a Wing sweep was scheduled for noon on 21 August but this got off to an inauspicious start as Sgt Walter 'Johnnie' Johnston of 92 Squadron recalls,

We were taxiing round the perimeter track at Biggin Hill to get into position for take-off and even taxiing was planned after a fashion. The squadrons joined up into a Wing through a patterned take off which wasted no time and thus no petrol. Not only did we take off in squadron order, but individual aircraft taxied in a set pattern so that we all immediately went into our correct formation positions. We were second off that day with 72 leading and 609 following. Sgt Stan Harrison was immediately in front of me and we were approaching the infamous 'blind' bend in the track with 72 lined up for take-off and pointing towards us. They opened up and as Stan reached the bend he was hit by the outside man in 72. The prop caught his starboard wing root, then chewed into the cockpit. I and the others just had to taxi past – as in the theatre, 'the show must go on!'

Harrison was severely injured in the collision and was taken to Orpington hospital barely alive. Johnston, who was a good friend, concludes the story which has a certain macabre humour.

I went to see him that evening but was told on arrival that he had died. The Ward Sister gave me his watch together with the few contents of his pockets, saying that the watch was still going, and had been on the arm 'when handed in!'

As far as 92 Squadron was concerned the day did not get any better as Sgt J. Aherne failed to return during a sweep carried out later in the day and P/O Philip Archer returned with slight wounds to his legs after being attacked by 109s. P/O Gordon Brettell made it back but crash-landed owing to lack of fuel. No.609

Squadron also lost one pilot over France when Sgt E.W. Pollard was shot down and killed near Dunkirk

The next few days were mainly dull with occasional rain which restricted the number of operations that could be flown. An evening sweep on the 24th was uneventful and although a similar sweep which took place two days later was equally unproductive, P/O E.W.H. Phillips of 92 Squadron failed to return. It is likely that he was shot down by a pilot from JG 2 which put in claims for four Spitfires, although only two were lost, that flown by Phillips and one from 611 Squadron.

On 27 August an early morning escort mission was laid on which turned out to be another visit to St Omer for Circus 85. This was not the best of news for Walter Johnston of 92 Squadron,

I had been promised a forty-eight hour pass from noon on the 27th to get home to Newcastle as the following day was my 21st birthday. The Sergeants in 92 Squadron used to sleep out at a lovely farm down Brasted Hill for safety reasons and as I was the lightest sleeper, I was 'Joe Soap' with the telephone. Very early, somewhere around 0500 hrs as far as I can recall, the phone rang and it was the C.O. stating that a show was on with take-off around 0630 hrs. He then gave me the names of those required and for whom the wagon was on its way. I was dismayed to find that my name was included and so I reminded him that I was due on leave and that he had previously agreed that I would not do a show before noon. His reply was quite simple, along the lines of "Hard luck Johnnie, we need you on this, but don't worry you'll be back in time."

Over France there were quite a lot of 109s and they seemed to be all over the place. If you followed one with your eyes, you suddenly found another getting into position. We broke up into sections then I got a bit adrift in a manoeuvre and, with great surprise and a lot of 'twitch', I heard a rattle in the tail and a 109 flashed past. I knew I had been hit but it didn't seem too bad. Sometimes when you were hit, depending on the angle it went in, it would go round and round and rattle like a nail in a tin can. By then I was completely alone and so I turned for the coast and pointed for home. As I approached the coast I saw a lone Spitfire ahead and to starboard so went to join up for some company. It was Sgt Roff who was clearly in a much worse state than me. His prop was stopped and it seemed to me that he had not seen me coming so I moved in quite close on his starboard side but it was obvious that things were not good. By a few signals (his R/T was dead) I found that he had been wounded although I saw no holes in the aircraft, never mind near the 'office' but he was in a bad way.

I thought I would try to escort him back and got him to about twelve miles off Dunkirk. I tried to get him to bale out but he initially waved away the suggestion until it became imperative that he jumped before he lost any more height. He jettisoned the hood and slowly turned on his back but in doing so he lost even more height. By the time he jumped for it he was fairly low, the 'chute opened O.K. but he was in the water pretty well at once. He released himself from his parachute very close to the surface but I saw in horror that his dinghy was still attached and unopened. I tried to get my own dinghy out to throw to him but it was impossible and as he floated there I climbed up to continue giving Maydays to which I received no acknowledgements. By now

115

I was extremely short of petrol so I went down and waved at him for one last time. He was still alive but that was it, there wasn't anything else I could do for him. I found out afterwards that he hadn't been picked up.

No.72 Squadron also took part in this operation and were repeatedly engaged over France. After being attacked by a Bf 109E Sgt J. Rutherford pulled up and saw two Spitfires being chased by another 109. As he pulled his aircraft round he was able to set up a head-on attack on this machine securing tracer hits on the wing leading edges. He was then chased all the way back to the French coast losing height from 20,000 ft to 500 ft in the process. Just when it appeared that he had finally got away Rutherford saw tracer rounds flashing past on his port side and he was forced to pull the stick hard back and to the left to make a climbing turn into the sun. He escaped further shots but this was the least of his troubles as he had been flying for the last fifteen minutes at full boost and was down to his last six gallons of petrol. He steered for the North Foreland but when he got to within three miles of Ramsgate his engine stopped and he had no choice but to invert his aircraft and take to his parachute. Unlike the unfortunate Sgt Roff, he was picked up by a rescue launch and brought safely ashore. During this operation F/O H. Skalski, also of 72 Squadron, was shot down over France and taken prisoner.

There was another early start for the Biggin Hill Wing on 29 August. Take-off was scheduled for 0630 hrs for an operation in connection with Circus 88, an attack by six Blenheims of 139 Squadron on the railway marshalling yards at Hazebrouck. As the target was approached S/L Desmond Sheen in the lead of 72 Squadron noticed a number of condensation trails up-sun and very soon one German formation assumed a threatening position. Not long after the 109s rolled into their attacking dives and a shouted warning prompted the Spitfires to break sharply towards them. A section of four Bf 109Es passed in front of Sheen's aircraft and he fired at the fourth in line with three quarters deflection. It emitted white smoke from under its starboard wing and turned slowly to the left away from the others, but unfortunately he was unable to take further action as he was coming under attack. On finding that he was completely alone, he dived steeply for the ground carrying out aileron turns whenever his adversaries were in a firing position and although he was able to lose this particular bunch of 109s, he encountered two more near Dunkirk. He found that he was able to out-turn them quite easily and fired a fleeting shot at the leader as he dived away. This was not the last of his problems however, as he was subject to heavy and accurate flak at 1,500 ft as he crossed the coast on his way home but finally managed to find cloud cover over the Channel. During his post flight inspection he found that his aircraft had been hit by a total of four bullet holes in the starboard wing and tailplane.

In the initial exchanges P/O Eric Bocock was attacked by at least three Bf 109Fs at 23,000 ft just to the east of Hazebrouck. He also managed to out-turn them and fired a burst of cannon and machine-gun at the leading aircraft which prompted them to break away. Shortly afterwards he was attacked by another mixed group of 109s (both Es and Fs) but he turned in towards them and fired as two passed in front of him at a range of around 100 yards. Various pieces flew off the lead aircraft and he continued to fire as the second machine appeared in his gunsight. White smoke began to pour from its engine and it went into a spin which soon became flat, at which point it appeared to be completely out of control. Bocock was unable to follow it down as he was attacked yet again but he was able to return home without further incident.

In the meantime P/O Jimmy Rosser was attacked from astern and slightly to port at a height of 18,000 ft. Closing his throttle, he pulled round tightly to the left and the enemy aircraft overshot before turning to the right. Rosser went after it and closed up quite easily firing a two-second burst with slight deflection. Unfortunately he experienced cannon stoppage after just one round had been fired but continued to fire with his machine-guns. Two pieces of debris flew off the 109 and it pulled up and did a climbing turn to the left. Rosser had no difficulty in following this manoeuvre and fired a further burst of three seconds during which more bits were seen to detach. The 109 then began to emit thick black smoke and it skidded away to the right before descending vertically. It was last seen just before it entered cloud by which time it was covered in flames. The 109s that had attacked 72 Squadron were from 4/JG 26 led by Lt Wolfgang Kosse and Oblt Seegatz was credited with shooting down Sgt P.T. Grisdale in P8713. He was last heard of saying that he was coming down over France [news was eventually received that he had been killed]. On the German side Uffz Werner Hetzel died when his Bf 109E-7 Werke Nr 6463 crash-landed to the east of Hazebrouck.

By now the dogfight had spilled out from France and involved JG 26's III Gruppe led by Oblt Joachim Muncheberg, with combats taking place up to half way across the Channel. When approximately ten miles north-east of Dover and at 15,000 ft F/L K. Kosinski saw two Bf 109s and broke away from his section to attack. He fired a short burst at one of them from above and to port and saw his bullets enter the fuselage near the cockpit. A second attack from the rear produced black smoke and he fired again as he followed the 109 in a near vertical dive. Kosinski was unable to close the gap any further and commenced his recovery at 4,000 ft at which point the 109 was still going straight down. On levelling out he was seen by a gaggle of around six 109s but he managed to keep them out of firing range as he fled for the coast and they eventually gave up the chase and turned for home. Not long after he saw another 109 about 400 yards in front and a little to port and he was able to close to 100 yards without being seen. A long burst of machine-gun fire struck home and the German aircraft wobbled badly for a few seconds before falling into cloud. Kosinski immediately dived below the cloud layer in search but did not see it again. As his fuel was running low he then made for the English coast and landed at Manston.

Kazimierz Kosinski was an interesting character who had just celebrated his thirty-fifth birthday. He had been posted to 72 Squadron on 24 July 1941, the culmination of an extremely long journey which had seen him commence his military service as an observer in the Polish Air Force in 1929. After retraining as a pilot he joined 122 Eskadra where he flew the PZL P.11c and was selected to be a member of that unit's aerobatic display team. Following the German occupation of Poland in September 1939 he fled to France, via Rumania. Here he led a special Flight of Curtiss H-75A fighter aircraft which were tasked with the defence of the SNCAC aircraft factory at Bourges that was being used to assemble these aircraft after their arrival from the USA. During this period he was credited with the shared destruction of three German aircraft, all Heinkel He 111s. One of the pilots under his command at this time was Adolf Pietrasiak. With the fall of France he escaped again to the UK and flew with 307 (Polish) Squadron on Boulton Paul Defiants before being transferred to 32 Squadron where he flew Hurricanes. Towards the end of December 1940 he moved to 308 (Polish) Squadron, again on Hurricanes, although the unit converted to Spitfires three months later. During his time with 308 Squadron he was awarded the Polish Cross of Valour.

The final combats in August took place on the 31st and involved 92 Squadron. An early sweep produced no encounters but a second that was flown just before lunch led to several exchanges. This was in connection with Circus 91, the target of which was intended to be the power station at Lille but when the twelve Blenheims from 18 and 114 Squadrons got there they found it covered by cloud and bombed a nearby railway instead. No.92 Squadron had an uneventful passage from Ambleteuse – St Omer – Gravelines and followed the bombers out as far as mid-Channel. Jamie Rankin then led the squadron back towards France and circled about five miles off Gravelines to see if any enemy aircraft were willing to have a fight. After about five minutes various small groups of 109s were seen above and below, 92 Squadron by then being at 18,000 ft. Together with the rest of Red section, Rankin dived on a pair of 109s that were seen below and opened fire with cannon and machine-gun from a range of around 350 yards. He saw two cannon strikes which produced a steady stream of black smoke from the forward fuselage but this aircraft was not pursued as Blue and Yellow sections which had been ordered to remain as top cover were, by this time, engaged with other 109s. The 109 that Rankin had fired at was last seen in a steep dive about three miles off the coast between Calais and Gravelines having left its No.1 which continued in a shallow dive towards France. Sgt Cox later stated that he had seen the first machine crash one mile east of Calais docks.

The patrol was continued with Red section and as flak was seen between Calais and Cap Gris Nez it was thought that friendly aircraft might be in trouble. When the flak area was reached at about 14–15,000 ft many more pairs of 109s were seen which led to a general dogfight. On four occasions Rankin got to within about 400 yards unseen on Bf 109Fs but on each occasion he was spotted at the last moment and they began evasive action. There were no further combats and he returned to base without further incident.

P/O B. Bartholomew, another member of Rankin's section, was also engaged. Flying as Red 3 he followed his leader during the latter's first attack but broke away on seeing another Spitfire being chased by a Bf 109F. Diving down onto the tail of this aircraft he opened fire with a three-second burst closing from 250 to 150 yards seeing various small pieces break off the port wing. Bartholomew then fired another burst from closer still and more debris emerged from the area around the engine and cockpit, including one large piece. He then had to break sharply to avoid a collision with the 109 by which time his altitude was around 6,000 ft. On turning round there was no sign of the German aircraft so it could only be claimed as a probable.

The day was rounded off with a convoy patrol in the evening which passed off uneventfully for most of those taking part however Sgt Kenwood of 92 Squadron became lost in the gathering gloom and had to bale out near Brighton when his Spitfire (W3120) ran out of fuel. He landed safely and was returned to his squadron.

CHAPTER TWELVE

A New Adversary

S eptember got off to a slow start with 92 Squadron carrying out convoy patrols on the 1st and a sweep the following day which produced no encounters. Another sweep on the 3rd was rather more dramatic, especially for P/O Tony Bruce whose Spitfire was shot up during a brief exchange with a Bf 109. He was able to get back across the Channel but had to put his aircraft down at Manston with a glycol leak.

The first major operation occurred on 4 September when twelve Blenheims of 18 Squadron bombed the ammonia plant at Mazingarbe during Circus 93. P/O Gordon Brettell of 92 Squadron had been forced to jump into a spare aircraft when his own Spitfire began leaking coolant shortly before take-off. This enforced change meant that everyone else had gone by the time he finally got into the air and he did not catch up until the Wing was over the Channel. Even then he judged that he would not be able to move into his allotted place with 92 Squadron before the French coast was crossed and instead filled a vacant position in 609 Squadron. As the Wing crossed into France east of Gravelines large numbers of enemy aircraft were seen and attacks were to continue all the way to the target and back. Having just flown over the coast 609 Squadron was on the receiving end of 'nibbling' attacks by several 109s and in turning to avoid one of these Brettell got down-sun of the squadron and lost contact with it.

As he was now alone he decided to return to Biggin but it was not long before he attracted the attention of a pair of Bf 109Fs which appeared behind and to his left, about 1,000 ft above. As they swung in to attack he turned sharply towards them and was able to keep them at bay by using this basic tactic, together with steep climbing turns into the sun. As a result their fire always seemed to be behind, leading him to question the ability of their shooting. After a few minutes Brettell found himself in a better tactical position, being above and up-sun of the 109s and he attacked the No.2. This prompted both to disengage and turn for home and he chased them back towards France. Gradually the range reduced to 300 yards and Brettell fired a long burst from dead astern which produced a trail of black smoke from the 109 which dipped sharply towards a low-lying layer of heat haze. It disappeared at this point still diving at high speed and was later claimed as a probable on doubts that it could have pulled out in time. The rest of the Wing fared little better with P/O D. Clive of 72 Squadron and Sgt 'Goldie' Palmer of 609 Squadron also claiming 109s as probably destroyed for the loss of P/O J.E.T. Asselin of 92 Squadron who was shot down to become a prisoner.

The type of operations that were carried out by Fighter Command depended greatly on the prevailing weather conditions and September was to prove to be one of the driest on record thanks to anticyclonic conditions which persisted for much of the month. Unfortunately for a two week period commencing on the 5th it also brought mist and fog which meant that very little operational flying was possible. This enforced interruption in the so-called non-stop offensive (dubbed by the Germans the nonsense offensive) at least gave the pilots a well-earned break as they had been operating flat out for the best part of two months. As well as offering the pilots the chance to consume more alcohol, the lay-off also gave them the opportunity to reflect on some of their experiences over the preceding weeks.

Flying a high performance aircraft in combat at high altitudes was physically very tiring and pilots needed to be in peak condition to be able to wring the maximum performance from their machines. When in the combat zone it was imperative to fly at high speed to lessen the risk of being attacked unseen and to retain the maximum amount of energy which could be utilised in evasive manoeuvres. Although the Spitfire handled pleasantly at low and medium speeds, its aileron control became progressively heavier at the top end of the speed range. This resulted in a significant increase in the control loads that had to be made to obtain a given rate of roll and this task was made even more difficult by the 'g' loads that were generated during extreme manoeuvring. As combats often took place at heights of 25,000 ft and more pilots also had to overcome extremes of temperature and despite the wearing of silk inner gloves and outer gauntlets, numb hands were a particular problem. Although the formation of ice on the outside of the windscreen could be cleared by a de-icing glycol spray, of greater concern was misting or icing up of the internal face of the bulletproof screen (Neville Duke made sure that he took along a rag that had been soaked in glycol to clear any internal ice).

Walter Johnston of 92 Squadron recalls some of these aspects from his point of view,

> In a steep turn you were pulling an awful lot of 'g' but you became adept at seeing a little bit of grey come across your eyes and you knew that you were about on the verge of blacking out. Then you either kept it where it was, or eased off a little bit. You could hear all right, but you just couldn't see properly. I think everyone blacked out a number of times; hauling it around you actually went before the aircraft shuddered, but with experience you were able to keep it just on the verge. We used to get up to 25/26,000 ft quite regularly, but 30,000 ft and above was really stretching it. On those occasions it was bitterly cold. We used to wear straightforward uniform and we all had our big white sweaters and seaboot stockings. Our wives, sweethearts or mothers used to knit big thick tubes that you could pull up so that they came from the top of your stockings up to your thighs, but it was still mighty cold. Our canopies used to ice up on the inside and you had to loosen your straps, lean forward and try to scratch the ice off, but it didn't really disappear until you got lower down.

For a fighter pilot even seemingly innocuous habits could have serious consequences as Johnston discovered one day during an offensive sweep over France.

> Due to the pure oxygen feed your mouth tended to get very dry so it became a habit to keep some chewing gum inside your boot and in 1941, of course, gum only came in smooth sugar-coated sweets, not in strips like today. If rations allowed, a Mars bar or some such would also find its way into the boot. I once had an extremely unfortunate time in the air due to gum which resulted in a certain amount of embarrassment. At this point I should point

out that I had one false front tooth on a very small palette. On the day in question we had turned on our home leg while escorting quite a large Circus and got jumped just before crossing the French coast. It was everyman for himself for a very short time; then we were suddenly on our own and were able to reform. It was at this stage that I found that I was in rather peculiar trouble.

It is no disgrace to say that when we got jumped my heart started to beat a lot faster, my neck was constantly swivelling and my mouth started to get very dry. Unfortunately this made my gum literally solidify sticking my small false tooth hard onto my bottom teeth and, try as I might, I could not open my mouth to get the false one out. As I was unable to talk, R/T was out of the question. We flew back to Manston and came in to land in our usual, almost formation landing on the huge, wide runway and turned off onto the grass to vacate it for the next gaggle. I just kept going, parked, switched off and ran to the toilet in the rear of the Tower where I swiftly used some hot water to make my mouth normal again. While this had been going on 'upstairs' and after landing, I was receiving radio calls checking on my condition but could not answer, so the others thought that I must have been hit. Once on the ground they ran to the Tower to find me, expecting the worst, and could not believe it when I told them what had happened. Never again did I use chewing gum when flying!

Due to the intense nature of air combat it was important that pilots were medically fit as even a slight head cold could have serious consequences. Neville Duke had reason to reflect on the above advice following an operation over France towards the end of June. Beforehand he had been aware of having a slightly sore throat but as he was needed, and he wanted to go, he did not mention his condition. During the operation 92 Squadron was engaged and Duke was attacked by two Bf 109Fs. In his attempts to escape he put his Spitfire in a steep dive but during the descent he began to experience excruciating pain in his ears. On levelling out he took off his helmet to try to clear his ears only to discover that he was unable to hear the noise of the engine. When he landed at Hawkinge to refuel he could not hear what was being said to him and he feared that the pressure changes during the dive had resulted in serious damage. On examination it was discovered that he had cracked both ear drums and he was sent to Orpington Hospital to recover. Over the next three weeks his hearing gradually returned but it was another lesson learned.

Although offensive operations were mostly out of the question during the early part of September, 'fighter nights' were back on the agenda again where aircraft would be despatched to West Malling for possible night fighting duties. Pilots had to be reminded of 'the form' for this type of flying and 'Sheep' Gilroy thought it a good idea if his pilots had a look at the base from which they would be flying. Unfortunately on their return to Gravesend the mist was so thick that they had to land at Biggin Hill and stay the night. As there was no let up the following day they were marooned at Biggin for the whole of the 6th as well. They finally made it back to Gravesend at 1430 hrs on 7 September but seven pilots were then required to return to West Malling where they carried out some practice night flying. As they did so a sudden (and temporary) improvement in the visibility allowed them to witness a flak barrage that was being put up over Boulogne. The pilots were somewhat 'browned off' to learn that they would be required at attend a pre-Circus conference at Biggin at 0800 hrs on the 8th and the mood did not improve when the operation was promptly postponed. The only flying possible during the rest of the day was some air-to-sea firing during which a mine was set off.

The period of inactivity during the early part of September at least gave the ideal opportunity for further personnel changes to take place. Michael Robinson's time as Wing Leader was to be extremely short as he too was tour expired and he left Biggin Hill in the early part of the month to become the station commander at Manston. His position was filled by Jamie Rankin who was promoted to Wing Commander and the command of 92 Squadron was given to S/L R.M. 'Dickie' Milne DFC who had been posted in as a flight commander on 8 August. Like his predecessor, Milne also hailed from Edinburgh having been born there on 8 July 1919. He joined the RAF on a short service commission in July 1937 and excelled during training, achieving first place on his course in flying, air gunnery and ground subjects. His first taste of squadron life was with 151 Squadron which saw action in France and Milne's first combat victory was a Junkers Ju 87 shot down on 17 May 1940 to the east of Valenciennes. He continued to fly with 151 during the first half of the Battle of Britain and by the time that the squadron was pulled back to Digby in 12 Group on 1 September his score stood at seven confirmed plus one shared. Before joining 92 Squadron he also served at the Central Flying School at Upavon as an instructor and flight commander.

In the space of six months Jamie Rankin had risen from a virtual novice in the fighter world to arguably the most prestigious appointment as leader of the Biggin Hill Wing. He brought his own style of leadership which was rather different from that of 'Sailor' Malan as Walter Johnston of 92 Squadron explains,

> When Jamie took over as Wing Leader things did change a little bit. Malan was a very hard taskmaster. He expected that everybody who he picked to put into a job could do it, and if they couldn't, he got rid of him. He was an excellent tactician, but he was ruthless and had a bit of a reputation for losing his No.2s. Quite often he would take evasive action without any warning and the No.2 was left high and dry, miles behind, which was why some of us used to find ourselves stuck on our own at times.
>
> Jamie was different. He had been a good C.O., but he freely admitted that he was learning, the same as everybody else, because 92 was his first operational trip after a time as an instructor. As far as gunnery was concerned he was damn good, but the thing that impressed me the most was his flying which was absolutely immaculate. If you were supposed to be going into a turn of 110 degrees, you did 110, not 105 or 115, but 110 exactly, so personally I found life easier with him as Wing Leader.

From a social point of view the lack of operations due to the weather could not have been better timed as 92 Squadron celebrated a year in residence at Biggin Hill on 8 September by throwing a big party with cabaret. Such was the standing of the top pilots of the day that Biggin often played host to stars of stage and screen including Laurence Olivier, Vivien Leigh and Jack Warner. The special guest of 92 on its anniversary bash was Noel Coward. Virtually as soon as the celebrations were over, however, the squadron was given notice that within a matter of days it would be moving to Gravesend with 609 Squadron heading back to Biggin. This news dampened the mood considerably and the pilots' frame of mind was summed up by Don Kingaby,

A portrait of F/L John Bisdee of 609 Squadron by C. Orde.

F/L Paul Richey of 609 Squadron (via Norman Franks).

Sgt J.A. 'David' Hughes-Rees of 609 Squadron (via Norman Franks).

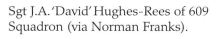

Adj Xavier de Montbron of 92 Squadron.

Sgt David Lloyd of 92 Squadron.

Sgt Hugh Bowen-Morris of 92 Squadron
was shot down and badly injured during
a Circus operation on 23 June 1941.

609 Squadron pilots. L to R Ogilvie, de
Grunne, Bisdee, Van Lierde, Robinson, de
Spirlet, Wilmet (via Norman Franks).

P/O Jean 'Pyker' Offenberg
of 609 Squadron
(via Norman Franks).

Lord Trenchard visits Biggin Hill
and is accompanied by 'Dickie'
Barwell and Michael Robinson
(via Norman Franks).

A Spitfire Vb of 609 Squadron taxies out at Biggin Hill prior to take off.

609 Squadron pilots. Standing – Boyd, de Hemptinne, MacKenzie, Richey, Bisdee, Offenberg. Front – Ortmans, Rigler, Ogilvie, Wilmet. In the foreground are William de Goat and Spit ('Sailor' Malan's dog).

Another Orde portrait showing F/O Keith Ogilvie of 609 Squadron.

Sgt Adolf Pietrasiak of 92 Squadron otherwise known as 'Meaty Pete'.

F/Sgt Don Kingaby in the cockpit of his regular Spitfire W3320 which has an impressive array of victory symbols and a lion motif.

Sgt Walter 'Johnnie' Johnston of 92 Squadron with a member of his groundcrew.

S/L Michael Robinson with some of his Sergeant pilots, l to r Rigler, Palmer, Hughes-Rees and Boyd (via Norman Franks).

S/L Jamie Rankin seen shortly before he took over as leader of the Biggin Hill Wing (via Norman Franks).

Jamie Rankin doing what fighter pilots do best, Noel Coward looks on approvingly (to Rankin's right are Miss Hambro and Beatrice Lillie).

An Orde portrait of P/O J.A. 'Joe' Atkinson of 609 Squadron.

Sgt Walter Johnston of 92 Squadron.

A Spitfire Vb of 92 Squadron displays its classic wing profile.

Spitfire Vb W3320 'The Darlington Spitfire' was Don Kingaby's regular aircraft during the summer of 1941. From 21 July he flew a total of 37 operations in this machine.

P/O Percy Beake of 92 Squadron in Spitfire Vb W3459 'Cape Town V'. This was the aircraft in which F/L Tommy Lund was shot down and killed on 2 October 1941.

The advent of the Focke-Wulf Fw 190 in the late summer of 1941 came as a considerable shock to Fighter Command. This JG 2 machine landed in error at Pembrey on 23 June 1942.

Another view of R6923 QJ-S of 92 Squadron.

P/O Denis Barnham in the cockpit of a 609 Squadron Spitfire discusses a point with P/O Francois de Spirlet.

Sgt Omer Levesque of 401 Squadron.

Don Blakeslee of 401 Squadron seen later in the war when he commanded the 4th Fighter Group USAAF.

Don Morrison (centre) chats with F/L E.L. Neal of 401 Squadron as P/O Don Dougall (ex 92 Squadron) looks on.

Sgt F.E. Jones of 72 Squadron poses in the cockpit of Don Kingaby's former Spitfire W3320.

A portrait of Don Kingaby taken at the end of the war by which time he was a Wing Commander.

We were very brassed off about leaving Biggin Hill – it had provided the squadron with the chance to prove itself and from my own personal point of view it is definitely the luckiest station I have ever flown from. Apart from the operational side, I can also say that I enjoyed life there more than anywhere else in the RAF and I think that all those who were there in those days will agree with me.

Before the move to Gravesend took place 92 Squadron had one last chance to add to its tally from Biggin during a sweep in the afternoon of 17 September. The return of better weather allowed two Circus operations to be flown, the first (No.95) involving Blenheims of 82 and 114 Squadrons attacking the power station at Mazingarbe. On crossing the French coast between Dunkirk and Calais two Bf 109Fs were seen below and Jamie Rankin ordered 92's Yellow section to go down and engage. One of the 109s disappeared smartly inland, but the other circled underneath the section which took it towards the Spitfire flown by Sgt H. Cox who fired a long burst with his cannons down to a range of 100 yards. The 109 was badly hit and he followed it down in a steep dive. As the section had become split up Cox zoomed back up to rejoin his leader and so did not see what happened to the 109, although he felt certain that it would have dived straight in. On the way out Cox went to the assistance of a Spitfire that was under attack and although he succeeded in driving the 109s off, the RAF machine was in obvious trouble and soon disappeared from view.

Blue section had also been under attack and its leader, F/L Tommy Lund, was forced to join up with two other aircraft. When he was near Le Touquet he saw a Bf 109F coming down at him away to his left. As he turned steeply to port the 109 half-rolled and dived, but not quickly enough as Lund had enough time to fire a three-second burst at about 400 yards. The 109, which was following another, streamed black smoke as well as a trail of glycol and did not pull out of its dive, even when its leader did so. From what he had seen Lund later put in a claim for a probable which was accepted. Following this operation the Biggin Hill Wing left France with something of a bloody nose. The Spitfire which Sgt Cox had attempted to help was probably that flown by P/O B. Bartholomew of 92 Squadron who baled out over the Channel but was drowned. During the exchanges over France P/O Gordon Brettell's Spitfire was also badly shot up. He managed to return, albeit wounded. No.609 Squadron also had a far from easy day:

A change in the weather produces no less than three shows. The first is a Roadstead directed against alleged shipping variously reported as off Gravelines and Ostend with 609 Squadron and 615 (cannon Hurricanes) protecting three Blenheims. No shipping is seen and the trip is uneventful.

Flying to Biggin Hill for lunch the Wing takes off as Escort Cover to twenty-four Blenheims raiding Mazingarbe (Circus 95). They have to dive to catch up with the bombers and owing to this haste have no time to wait and engage some twenty Bf 109s which appear immediately on crossing the French coast, except that is for F/O V. Ortmans and Sgt Palmer. These two are mightily assailed, Ortmans' aircraft is hit and Sgt Palmer has to lose altitude owing to trouble with his oxygen equipment. One of F/O Ortmans assailants is what he describes as a 109 with a radial engine and this turns out to be one of the first times the new German fighter, the Fw 190, has been encountered.

The chief impression of Vicki was its ability to change from the horizontal to the vertical without the engine cutting.

The rest of the squadron accompanies the bombers to the target and we are not molested until they recross the coast. F/L Offenberg then hears the Controller say – "Your friends are in trouble over Boulogne" He investigates, and sees two splashes in the sea. F/O Malengreau calls Mayday and immediately afterwards the section contacts four 109s approaching the coast below. One of these separates itself from the others and is immediately shot down by Lt Choron. F/L Offenberg, separated from the others, is attacked four times by two other 109s, the last time within ten miles of Dungeness and his aircraft is holed.

The pilots are not long back at Gravesend before they are ordered off again on Circus 96, Biggin Hill this time acting as Target Support Wing to six Hampdens raiding Mazingarbe. No.609 Squadron flies about in the St Omer area and although many 109s are seen in formations of up to twelve, none are contacted except by P/O Atkinson leading Yellow section. After diving on some 109s, he is turning to rejoin his section when two aircraft which he takes to be Spitfires are seen behind. One begins firing at him but as the deflection is not nearly enough, Atkinson merely tightens his turn. Suddenly his ASI blows out and it seems another aircraft has been firing from above. Half rolling and diving, he crosses Boulogne beach at 2,000 ft and his engine begins to fail. Flames then appear beneath the engine cowling. Calling Mayday, he struggles up to 2,000 ft and bales out in the middle of the Channel. After about an hour he is picked up by a naval launch and none too soon as it is getting late, with visibility reduced by haze. The Officers who pick him up at Dover in the evening find him in excellent form, thanks partly to having consumed a Benzedrine tablet in his dinghy.

Atkinson was extremely lucky to be picked up as he had not been high enough when he transmitted his Mayday call for it to be received. By chance he had been seen by a Spitfire pilot of the Kenley Wing who continued to orbit over his position until he was forced to return to base due to a shortage of fuel, although by this time a rescue launch was on its way. News was received late in the evening that Atkinson was alive and well and was being entertained by the Royal Navy at a hotel in Dover. Four officers set off in the 'Belgian Barouche' (a big Ford estate car that had been presented to 609 by the Belgian government) with Roger Malengreau driving, however he had to ask directions on arriving in Dover. Atkinson was soon found and everyone joined in the party but shortly afterwards the hotel was raided by a large number of policemen looking for the crew of a German bomber which had apparently come down nearby. After successfully crash-landing their aircraft, they had then stolen a large car, dressed up as RAF officers and, in heavily-accented English, had asked the way to a hotel in the centre of Dover. It took some time for the authorities to be convinced that there was no German bomber and that the foreign accent had in fact been Belgian.

Two co-ordinated Circus operations were planned for the afternoon of the 18th but there was considerable confusion when the bombers for one of these missions failed to turn up. In the event the Biggin Hill Wing flew to France and linked up with Circus 99 which was an attack by Blenheims of 139 Squadron on Grand Quevilly power station near Rouen. A number of combats took place but these involved other squadrons and all of Biggin's aircraft returned safely having seen very little of the enemy.

A general overcast the next day tempted 72 Squadron to carry out some Rhubarb sorties with P/O Eric Bocock and Sgt F. Falkiner shooting up a lorry and a gun emplacement near the coast. The pairing of F/L D Stewart-Clark and Sgt J.G. Merrett had mixed fortunes and as they swept inland from Gravelines to Calais they became separated in conditions of poor visibility. On his way back Merrett saw two Bf 109Es in mid-Channel. The German aircraft were about 500 yards ahead, passing from left to right and as he turned to chase after them they descended to sea level and headed back towards France. Merrett opened fire on the No.2 of the pair which did not take any evasive action, however the leader began a turn to port with the obvious intention of getting onto his tail. Keeping an eye on this aircraft, Merrett fired several long bursts at the other Messerschmitt which produced a trail of black smoke but he eventually had to pull up into cloud to avoid the attentions of the lead 109 which was almost in a firing position. Although he got back safely there was no sign of Stewart-Clark and news was received that he had been shot down over the Channel [he had previously been shot down twice when flying with 603 Squadron but it was later confirmed that he had been killed].

Poor weather in the morning of the 20th cleared by the afternoon which allowed Circus 100B to go ahead, one of three co-ordinated Circuses taking place. The Biggin Hill Wing flew as close escort to six Hampdens attacking the marshalling yards at Abbeville [the objectives of the other elements of Circus 100 were Hazebrouck and Rouen]. The number of escort fighters allocated to each raid was much reduced from a normal Circus operation but it was felt that the *Luftwaffe* fighters would not be able to take advantage as they would be stretched over a wide area. The only combats to involve the Wing centred on 92 Squadron and during these engagements Sgt G.P. Hickman was shot down and killed in W3179.

No flying took place in the morning of 21 September due to thick fog but this gradually cleared to permit the Wing to take off at 1520 hrs as escort cover to six Hampdens raiding the railway repair shops at Lille. Apart from flak experienced as high as 28,000 ft, no opposition was encountered until the return journey and then only by 109s in relatively small numbers. 'Sheep' Gilroy at the head of 609 Squadron attacked one of these aircraft, the pilot of which was so incensed by Gilroy's audacity that he chased him back across the Channel but was not able to close sufficiently to get into an attacking position.

All the Spitfires had returned by the time that P/O W.B. Sanders of 609 Squadron appeared over Gravesend. As everyone watched he lowered his undercarriage but as he did so his engine spluttered to a halt. The Spitfire (W3315) was then seen to turn to port and struck an anti-invasion cable on the edge of the aerodrome. This had the effect of swinging it into a gunpost and it came to rest a short distance away with its engine torn off. Sanders was taken to Gravesend hospital from where it was reported that he had sustained a fractured skull and had also broken his leg and collar bone. For two days his life hung in the balance but his condition gradually improved and he was moved to Halton to complete his recovery. No fault was found with his aircraft and it was concluded that he had run out of fuel.

The return of mist and fog over the next few days ruled out operational flying for a time but the bad weather did at least allow the squadron reorganisation to be carried out in a more civilised manner. On 23 September 609 Squadron held a party to celebrate its welcome return to Biggin Hill, and on the following day sixteen aircraft left Gravesend. Back at Biggin Hill they inherited 92 Squadron's dispersal

125

as 609's previous dispersal was now in the hands of 72 Squadron. No.92 Squadron's move in the opposite direction did not quite go as planned as only six aircraft made it to Gravesend on the 24th before the fog closed in once again. The remaining Spitfires were forced to spend an extra night at Biggin before joining up with the others at lunch-time the next day.

On 27 September the RAF attempted another two-part Circus operation (No.103A/B) with twelve Blenheims of 110 and 226 Squadrons raiding the marshalling yards at Amiens while the same number from 114 Squadron headed for Mazingarbe. The Biggin Hill Wing acted as high cover for the second objective and all squadrons were engaged. As far as 609 Squadron was concerned it was obvious that the Germans were going to resist on this occasion, even when crossing the coast at Mardyck at 27,000 ft. A large gaggle of 109s was seen passing under the Wing some 5,000 ft below and the order was given to attack. The fight was so intense that 609 soon became split up into pairs and individuals. Sgt John Van Schaick was attacked by four different aircraft in as many minutes and F/O Giovanni Dieu became involved in a turning competition with a 109. It then made the mistake of turning in the opposite direction which presented Dieu with a beam shot at close range. The 109 was last seen in a vertical dive trailing white, then black smoke.

The squadron was being led by Jamie Rankin who had Vicki Ortmans as his wingman. On the way back from the target the latter saw two 109s coming in to attack and informed his leader who unfortunately did not hear his call and thereby left him to deal with them on his own. During the desperate struggle that followed Ortman's Spitfire was hit in the fuselage but of equal concern was the enforced use of high power settings which rapidly drained his fuel reserves. He was eventually relieved by two other Spitfires but as he crossed over the French coast near Le Touquet his Spitfire was down to its last few gallons of fuel. When his engine finally stopped he was able to glide to within five miles of Dover but then had no choice but to take to his parachute for his second ducking in the Channel in six weeks. Within fifteen minutes of entering the water he was picked up by a fishing boat and later transferred to a rescue launch.

One interesting aspect of the actions over France was that 609 Squadron's Yellow section led by 'Sheep' Gilroy again came into contact with the new German fighter, the Focke-Wulf Fw 190A, which was being introduced to active service by JG 26. This aircraft was about to place the initiative decisively in the *Luftwaffe's* favour, but on this occasion at least, the honours were even and each side lived to fight another day. 'Pyker' Offenberg and P/O du Monceau of Blue section were also in action and the latter claimed a Bf 109F which was left in a vertical dive over the sea, a 72 Squadron pilot later confirming that it had gone straight in.

No.92 Squadron were also busy fending off various groups of 109s. Following the initial order to attack, S/L Dickie Milne led Red section down but the first 109 he went after saw him coming and rapidly accelerated away out of trouble. Milne then tried another but could not catch this one either, so he pulled up again to join the escort cover squadrons. It was not long before they were attacked and the section became split up just to the north of the target. With so many 109s in the area the order was given to withdraw and fortunately Milne was able to join up with his Nos. 3 and 4 (P/O Percy Beake and Sgt Walter Johnston). As the section made its way out it encountered small numbers of enemy aircraft on a regular basis. Near St Omer Milne dived onto one of three 109Fs and fired a no deflection shot which hit the tailplane, a large piece being seen to fly off. The aircraft then flicked over and dived vertically and was last seen still going straight down at about 2,000 ft. As the section continued to be nibbled at on the way out Milne led the section towards some cloud cover but just before they flew into it he saw three 109s on the far side. He was able to launch a surprise attack on one of them which succeeded in damaging the aircraft's glycol system.

One of the most crucial positions in a section was the No.4 and this station was often given to pilots with the best vision. Walter Johnston was renowned for his excellent eyesight and was in his customary position as Red 4 when he became aware of a number of 109s dropping down to attack from astern. Having warned the rest of the section he turned into the attack but ended up in the middle of a Messerschmitt sandwich as the three aircraft all turned in a circle. He opened fire with his cannons but they jammed after only nineteen rounds had been fired. Even so it appeared that he had caused some damage to the leading 109 as two large holes appeared in the fuselage just aft of the cockpit. This 109 left the fight in a steep dive leaving Johnston to out-manoeuvre the other. When he had the chance to look down he saw a parachute below and thought that it was from the 109 he had fired at. Having rejoined his section the withdrawal continued but on the way back Johnston had to warn of yet another attack. He was set upon by a yellow-tailed 109 while two others went for the rest of the section. Once again he was able to get behind it with ease and fired a burst of machine-gun which damaged its tail. By now the section was down to 10,000 ft and when he was attacked for one last time Johnston finally took advantage of cloud cover to make good his escape.

On hearing Johnston's shouted warning P/O Percy Beake had just enough time to take evasive action and missed all but a couple of bullets fired by a 109F which broke away upwards and to port after its attack. Pulling the nose of his aircraft up, Beake was able to get it in his sights and opened up with his cannons. As he looked on the 109 appeared to stagger in the air as though hit and immediately lost height. Although by now the range had extended to around 350 yards he fired a further burst which appeared not to have any effect and the 109 was last seen diving inland towards St Omer. It was later claimed as damaged.

The advent of the Fw 190 in the skies over northern France was to come as a considerable blow to Fighter Command whose pilots were having a difficult enough time dealing with the Bf 109F. The Fw 190 was the outcome of a contract that was placed with Focke-Wulf in the autumn of 1937 for a single-seat fighter. It was designed by a team under the supervision of Dipl Ing Kurt Tank and the prototype was flown for the first time on 1 June 1939. The original BMW 139 radial engine was soon replaced by the more powerful BMW 801 and very soon speeds approaching 400 mph were being achieved. As with any advanced new aircraft there were a number of teething troubles and some of these had still not been eradicated by the time that it was due to enter service. Trials with a captured Spitfire had already shown that although the latter was still better as regards turning performance, in all other respects the Fw 190 was superior, in many cases significantly so. Its higher top speed in particular, allied to its excellent climb and dive performance, gave it the ability to dictate the terms of combat at all times.

The first Fw 190As arrived in France in early August 1941 when the *Erprobungsstaffel* (Operational Test Squadron) moved from the *Luftwaffe's* test facility at Rechlin to Le Bourget to begin the conversion of II Gruppe of JG 26. The pilots were enthusiastic about their new mounts and could not wait to take them into combat but unfortunately the 190 was still plagued by engine reliability problems, in particular overheating and continual failures of the connecting rod of the lower cylinder in the second bank. These difficulties took some time to overcome which meant that the Fw 190 made something of a faltering start to its operational career and at times was not flown to anywhere near its true potential as pilots were wary of something going wrong. This is reflected in the wide variety of opinions as to the aircraft's performance as expressed in the combat reports submitted by RAF pilots. By the time that the technical issues had been solved, however, no one would be left in any doubt as to how good the Fw 190 was.

The weather during the last few days of September deteriorated once again and the only operational flying was a convoy patrol by 72 Squadron on the 29th. A few Rhubarb sorties were attempted by 609 Squadron on the 30th but, ironically, clear conditions over the continent resulted in early returns.

CHAPTER THIRTEEN

A Change of Guard

The start of a new month brought no respite for the Biggin Hill squadrons and on 1 October the Wing was airborne at 1130 hrs. The intention was to sweep east of Dunkirk to St Omer before coming out of France over Gravelines, but cloud conditions were such that the Wing flew down the Channel instead below cloud. The weather was ideal for small formations of German fighters to launch sharp thrusting attacks out of cloud and the first of these was aimed at 92 Squadron. Don Kingaby was leading Blue section when, without warning, he was attacked by four Bf 109s which suddenly appeared from a layer of cloud at around 13,000 ft, forcing him to seek the sanctuary of the overcast above. After an appropriate amount of time, he descended out of the cloud and immediately saw another section of four 109s about half a mile to port and slightly below. Climbing back into the cloud again to conceal his presence, he manoeuvred towards them and timed his descent perfectly to position himself behind the gaggle which was then intent on attacking another group of Spitfires. Closing to a range of 50 yards behind the last 109 in the group, Kingaby fire a one-second burst with both cannon and machine-gun into its belly and it fell away, glycol streaming from its punctured radiators.

Hugging the layer of cloud so that he could not be attacked from above, Kingaby flew about ten miles inland on the lookout for more enemy aircraft. He did not have long to wait as another bunch of 109s appeared away to his left, heading in his direction. Using the same successful tactics as before he was able to come up behind the group unseen and again picked the last one giving it a four-second burst coming round from the starboard quarter to astern at around 100 yards range. As his fire slammed into the 109 it began to stream glycol and Kingaby was forced to manoeuvre sharply to avoid being hit by debris. The 109 fell away in a dive shedding various pieces and eventually the tail was seen to break away as it plunged to earth. Kingaby fired at another of the Germans, but by now they were fully aware of his proximity and he was forced to use the cloud cover once more to escape back to Gravesend.

It is interesting to note that during this operation Kingaby was quite prepared to go hunting for enemy aircraft, even though his wingman had long since disappeared. Normally such an act would have been folly but on this particular occasion with the amount of cloud cover that was available a single Spitfire stood a good chance of not being seen and the cloud also offered a convenient escape route should it be needed. The fact that Kingaby's No.2 had not been able to follow him was not particularly surprising as he had a reputation for being an extremely difficult pilot to follow. Neville Duke occasionally flew as his wingman and he recalls that when in the combat zone he flew his aircraft to the very limit of its performance which meant that it was not easy for his No.2 to stay in touch. In this respect he was similar to 'Sailor' Malan and many of the other top pilots. As one of the 'Experten' of 92

Squadron he was supremely confident in his own ability to fight and survive, and Duke also recalls that on one sweep over France, Kingaby came onto the radio to request assistance as he had, as he put it. . . '12-plus 109s cornered!'

On 2 October the Biggin Hill Wing took off at 1200 hrs to carry out a diversionary sweep routing Berck sur Mer – Abbeville – Le Treport in connection with Circus 104. Weather conditions were perfect with unlimited visibility, and as the Wing proceeded north-east towards Abbeville a number of enemy aircraft could be seen manoeuvring high above. Of the three squadrons involved, 72 and 609 were at full strength, but 92 Squadron which was flying at the lowest level had only been able to put up a total of eight aircraft. As the wing swept over France 92 Squadron's Blue section became detached from the rest of the formation and were considerably lower than they should have been. This was enough to prompt an attack and within a matter of seconds the section leader F/L Tommy Lund (W3459) had been shot down, together with Sgt K.G. Port (W3762) and Sgt N.H. Edge (W3137). None survived.

The remaining member of the section, P/O Tony Bruce, was badly shot up and was injured when a cannon shell exploded on top of the armour plating behind his head, sending splinters of metal into his neck and scalp. There was no follow up attack, however, and he was able to return to crash-land near Ashford. Several pilots from 609 later reported that a 92 Squadron Spitfire had been seen trailing glycol prior to the attack which might account for Blue section becoming detached from the rest of the squadron. Some accounts have stated that the three aircraft of Blue section fell to the guns of Fw 190As of JG 26 but it seems more likely that they were shot down by Bf 109Fs of JG 2. By early October 1941 only a handful of Fw 190As were in service with II/JG 26, whose pilots did not put in any claims on this particular day. In contrast pilots of JG 2 claimed a total of eight Spitfires. The confusion over what type of aircraft had been responsible for the attack did not stop a number of RAF Officers visiting Tony Bruce in hospital. He was of the opinion that they were concerned not so much with his health, more so with information on the new German fighter. Bruce also got the distinct impression that the group had rushed down with somewhat indecent haste to extract the 'gen' while they still could.

The situation became even worse for 92 Squadron the following day. The Biggin Hill Wing, led by Jamie Rankin, formed part of the Escort Cover Wing for Circus 105, but once again 92 could only contribute two sections of four aircraft. Together with 72 and 609 Squadrons, they took off from Biggin Hill at 1338 hrs to link up with six Blenheims of 88 Squadron over Clacton before setting course for the target, the harbour installations at Ostend. On this occasion Don Kingaby was flying as Yellow 3 but he soon had more to contend with than the attentions of German fighters. Having been subjected to some flak over the Channel his problems really began when an electrical fault caused his R/T and reflector gunsight to fail completely. This would normally have been a valid reason to return to base, but as the squadron was already under strength, he chose to stay with them. Because he was now out of touch with his comrades, it was even more imperative for Kingaby to keep a sharp lookout for enemy aircraft as there was a good chance that the 109s would be a few thousand feet above and hidden by the glare of the sun. Flying as Red 4 on the other side of the formation was Walter Johnston in W3895. He recalls subsequent events which he now acknowledges as having been the most frightening experience of his two fighters tours:

We flew along the Channel coast with the Blenheims on our landward (starboard) side, so we were looking over them and over the land from where enemy aircraft would have come. To our left, and above, were 609 Squadron who were covering us, the close escort, and the Blenheims. After the first run, we turned for a second run and remained on the seaward side of the Blenheims. I was on the outside section with Don, number 3, in the other and I had been conscious all the time that he had been looking at me rather a lot. I saw a gaggle up above us, to the rear and side and naturally assumed it to be 609 – after all, that was where they should have been [this was a false assumption as 609 Squadron had already turned away from the target and the aircraft he could see were in fact Bf 109s].

Then once again as I watched, they dropped down onto our formation at a hell of a rate of knots and I shouted out to the C.O. We broke to starboard but they had anticipated our move only too well. As I hauled round, I saw Don doing the same – but almost at the same time the 109s came into his section. Sgt Cox (Yellow 4) had his tail broken off and an explosion up front – Yellow 3 (Don) was out of the way, so they went straight into Sgt Woods-Scawen (Yellow 2) who received a terrible amount of firepower. He rolled over and went straight down.

I had not seen Don since he had actually gone over the top of me. I felt I'd been hit, but could not find anything wrong with my aircraft to account for the 'clang' and sort of 'twitch' it had given. But even so I did not want to be too violent with it. I was quite suddenly in a large empty space of sky and set course gently and merrily for England. At that point I found myself being steadily overhauled by three 109s. I stuffed the nose down to get more speed, but they caught me up and went into line abreast so that whichever way I turned, I was covered. Two more joined them and it was like a lot of cats after one mouse. I got the impression that they were indeed playing with me. The leader kept having a squirt, but was generally out of range and a lousy shot. I wondered if he was the leader that had to 'make' his name safely.

I had no place to go except downwards and I began to think that I would be safer if I jumped, hoping that they would not attack me in the drink. But things then change rapidly. I saw another Spitfire to starboard and behind, coming down and lining up on the 109s. They had got careless and had become engrossed with me. It came down more or less along the line, firing like hell all the way. It went over the top in a flash, climbed, then came back again. As it flew alongside I realised it was Don Kingaby who was making signs that his R/T was u/s and was also pointing his finger ahead and stabbing it, as if to say "Go, you so and so!", and so I did!'

As Johnston made good his escape, Kingaby turned back into the 109s who, by now, had recovered from the shock that he had given them. He now takes up the story,

For a couple of minutes I twisted and turned and evaded their attack, but then they started to come in on me from each quarter. If I broke away to the left or right I knew that one of them would have a sitting shot, so I rammed the stick forward and went down in a spiral dive from 22,000 ft to 4,000 ft. As I went down I looked over my shoulder and saw two Me 109s firing at me and thought for a moment that they would collide. Then a shower of coolant mixture flew up over the instrument panel and into my face and I instantly thought that my engine had been badly hit. My only chance now was to get the hell out of it as fast as I could and hope that I would shake them off in the dive.

By now Kingaby was being followed by seven 109s which were strung out in a line behind him. Although safety was only 5–6 minutes away, every second seemed like an eternity and there was the constant nagging doubt that the Merlin engine of his Spitfire might expire at any time. His only chance was to continue his dive in an attempt to shake off his pursuers. Thankfully his engine held out and, one by one, the 109s turned for home, all that is except his nearest adversary who proved to be particularly persistent and appeared determined to finish him off. After a long chase the German eventually managed to overhaul the Spitfire and Kingaby had little choice but to turn and fight. With his gunsight out of action he was at a distinct disadvantage and the only way of sighting his guns was through an old bead sight which was still fitted to his aircraft. Gradually the Spitfire's superior turning performance began to tell and after two complete turns the situations began to be reversed.

We were fighting just above the sea and when I began to throw him off my tail, he climbed above me and tried to half roll down onto me again. At the last moment he realised that he was too low down to do this, and to avoid going into the drink, he had to roll out again in the same direction as myself. I saw this happening and yanked the throttle back to slow down as quickly as possible. The 109 came out about 150 yards ahead of me and I let him have it from dead astern. Bits flew off him, there was a great cloud of smoke and he went straight in. It was ironic that a few moments before he and his pals had had me 'on ice' so to speak.

Still expecting his engine to quit at any time, Kingaby was anxious to get down as soon as possible and made for the nearest airfield. There were to be no more dramas, however, and within a few minutes the large expanse of grass that was Manston appeared ahead, and a very relieved pilot slipped over the boundary fence to land. After shutting down his engine Kingaby's post-flight inspection revealed the final twist as it became evident that his aircraft had survived the duelling unscathed, and had not suffered any hits at all. It transpired that the glycol that had flooded into his cockpit had not in fact come from the engine, but from a leak in the reservoir that contained de-icer fluid for the windscreen. The only damage to be found consisted of a few popped rivets on the upper surfaces of the wings caused by the extreme loads that had been imposed during the combat.

Kingaby did not hang around long at Manston and soon flew back to base where the others were relating the day's events to S/L de la Torre (92 Squadron's Intelligence Officer). Walter Johnston made it back and remains convinced to this day that, but for Kingaby's timely intervention, he too would have gone the same way as Cox and Woods-Scawen. He also feels sure that Kingaby downed a couple of 109s in the melee, although there is no mention of this in his combat report. Once again 92 Squadron had come up against JG 26, the successful German pilots being *Gruppenkommandeur* Hptm Johannes Seifert and Lt Paul Schauder of the 3rd Staffel.

On 4 October there was a return of mist and fog and no operations were possible for the next week although some Spitfires of 609 Squadron were required to stand by for 'fighter nights'. Practice flying became the order of the day but following one such sortie Sgt W. Greenfield of 609 put up a 'black' by landing wheels up. During a brief interlude when the visibility allowed a little more freedom Vicki Ortmans found time to have a dogfight with a Blenheim and with a wry grin on his return claimed a probable. On the 12th 92 Squadron flew a sweep in the morning which was uneventful except for Sgt Gauthier having to land at Friston with engine failure.

A general improvement in the weather allowed another Circus operation to be laid on in the early afternoon of 13 October (No.108B) but for 609 Squadron the drama started a little earlier:

An adventurous day for a number of pilots. It begins with P/O Van Arenberg ramming P/O de Selys during a practice flight. The former lands successfully at Biggin with a dead engine, the latter spins down from 6,000 ft and finds his ailerons have jammed. Instead of baling out, he is directed by the Controller to West Malling where after several attempts he makes a perfect landing and saves his aircraft. Unfortunately 609 have now had four accidents in 80 hours flying in place of the former average of 1 in 90 – and there has been a blitz about accidents.

About 1330 hours the Wing takes off again as High Cover for a raid on Mazingarbe by eighteen Blenheims. Other bombers have been at work already and only three Wings are in action, the theory being that the 109s will by this time have exhausted their petrol. A few are however encountered by the squadron on the way back, notably a single 109E which Sgt Nash sets on fire and a single 109F which is damaged by P/O Atkinson. F/L Offenberg's section meets another pair over the Channel and one of them is credited as damaged by Offenburg weeks later on the evidence of Sgt Laing, although at the time the former refuses to claim anything. P/O du Monceau joins another squadron and fires at one of six 109s encountered over Le Touquet. Altogether seven pilots have shots. Petrol shortage is then caused by the bombers proceeding to Manston instead of Dungeness. F/O Dieu's engine cuts in mid Channel but he succeeds in making a good landing, wheels down, at Hawkinge. Lt Choron with no air pressure (which means no flaps and no brakes) is directed by the Controller to West Malling but he finds too much congestion of aircraft there and successfully lands at Biggin.

The most eventful trip of the day, however, was had by Dickie Milne who was forced to hand over command of 92 Squadron early in the operation.

We were acting as high cover to a bombing raid on Mazingarbe. I developed a very bad oxygen leak and it was obvious I would be unable to maintain height for long. I signalled to my 'A' Flight commander that I was going down. Breaking away I joined a squadron lower down in the beehive and continued into France. I saw the odd 109 make the occasional dart at our Spitfires but no large formations appeared. We were now just south-east of St Omer and I decided to get down even lower as I still had a long trip ahead without oxygen. It was as I turned slightly and dived that a single 109 came in at me and forced me to take evasive action. I turned hard to port and watched him. I expected him to break off as soon as he saw me turn, but he didn't and so forced me to turn completely round in defence. The pilot of this enemy aircraft was quite determined and broke away hard down with his throttle wide open when he saw I was getting round onto his tail. I was not going to attempt catching him as he was in a 109F and in a hurry.

After this short episode I found myself completely alone and couldn't see a single aeroplane anywhere. I suddenly realised the seriousness of the position and set off hard for home. I was now at 9,000 ft and had been flying in a zigzag course to keep my tail vision clear when I sighted two Me 109s well above and behind me. These I thought had sighted me, but as they came closer I saw that I was in the blind spot beneath their noses so remained undetected. They passed over me and I, below and slightly behind, closed on the No.2 and opened fire. I hit him very hard and he rolled slowly over emitting a lot of smoke and then burst into flames as he went down. I turned onto the leader who had now seen me and I just had time to fire a short burst before he accelerated away with his nose stuffed well down. I saw I had hit his radiator when a lot of glycol came out. Beneath me I saw the first aircraft explode as it hit the ground. Both of these were 109Es.

It was very relieving to find that I was getting near the coast and hadn't run into any large formation of enemy aircraft. I continued to work my way home and was beginning to feel quite safe when two 109Fs appeared from nowhere in my mirror. I hadn't seen them approaching so possibly they may have climbed up. I just had time to skid wildly to the left and slam my throttle shut. The leading 109 went past me and his No.2 pulled slightly up and to the right, overshooting also. They obviously expected to take me by surprise for they certainly were not ready for my sudden action. I swung in quickly behind the leader just as he was about to make off by accelerating and diving and I opened fire at about 70 yards, my shells hitting him all the way up the fuselage. A lot of grey smoke puffed out as he pulled up sharply and to the right, immediately into the position his No.2 had just got into by overshooting. The leader crashed into the bottom of the other aircraft and pieces flew everywhere, I have never seen such a mess. They fell together and I saw the pilot of the uppermost aircraft bale out. I didn't hang about to see him land but headed north, losing my last 1,500 ft just before reaching the coast. I crossed west of Gravelines without receiving any flak and flew on at zero feet landing, rearming and refuelling at Manston.

On the 14 October two sections of 609 Squadron carried out a convoy patrol and although a large sweep was planned for the 16th with an early morning conference taking place, this was postponed due to the weather. This did not prevent F/L Francois de Spirlet and F/O Giovanni Dieu from being scrambled shortly before noon on reports of an enemy aircraft over Mayfield, however, it was not seen and both returned without having fired their guns. Jamie Rankin, who was also airborne at the time, had slightly better luck and attacked some ships in the Channel but this attracted the attention of some Bf 109s which he managed to evade by flying into cloud. When he considered that the danger had passed, he attacked another ship 'out of pique'.

Having been in the front line since its arrival at Biggin Hill in September 1940, 92 Squadron was withdrawn to Digby for a well earned break on 20 October. The announcement was greeted with stunned disbelief by the pilots who even though they were extremely tired, preferred to be in the front line rather than kicking their heels at some operational backwater where nothing happened. In truth they were probably the least qualified to comment on the decision as very few would have been able to recognise the degree of fatigue from which they were suffering. Walter Johnston recalls one occasion when he landed drenched in sweat having been locked in a desperate struggle with two Bf 109s. On leaving his Spitfire he then had difficulty in lighting a cigarette as his hands were trembling so much. He also recalls an incident shortly after the loss of Cox and Woods-Scawen which provides a succinct commentary on the pilots' mood at that time.

> Our nerves were just a wee bit 'shot' and the CO turned to Don and I saying, "Right you two, enough's enough, get off the 'drome. I don't want to see you until tomorrow afternoon." So off we went, pictures in Gravesend and finished up at 'Daniel's Den' where we drank. For the only time in our lives we did something ridiculous and bought three drinks in a round – one for each of us, and the third for Cocky (Sgt Cox),which we shared.

Moving in the opposite direction to replace 92 Squadron was 401 (RCAF) Squadron which could trace its UK deployment back to 21 June 1940. At this time it still had its original peacetime number of 1 Squadron Royal Canadian Air Force and the setting up process was smoothed with the assistance of personnel from 115 Squadron. It initially flew Hurricanes at Middle Wallop and passed through a number of airfields including Croydon, Northolt, Prestwick, Castletown and Driffield, before arriving at Digby in February 1941. It was here that it was re-numbered 401 Squadron on 1 March. Although the squadron had been active during the latter stages of the Battle of Britain and had also taken part in a number of sweeps out of West Malling in July/August 1941, at the time of its move to Biggin Hill it was still relatively inexperienced [to allow for the arrival of 401 Squadron, 72 Squadron moved back to Gravesend].

During its time at Biggin Hill 401 Squadron was led by S/L Norman Johnstone and one of its junior pilots was twenty-four year old P/O Don Blakeslee from Ohio who had joined the RCAF in late 1940. Blakeslee had been fascinated by aircraft from an early age and, together with a friend, had acquired a Piper Cub in 1939. Unfortunately he did not get much experience on it as his friend promply crashed it. Having decided to join the RCAF he calmed his mother's fears by telling her that he would become an instructor and managed to keep this story up even after he had shot down his first German aircraft. He was later to fly with the USAAF and was to command the 4th Fighter Group. P/O Hugh Godefroy from Ontario was twenty-one years old and had been with 401 since April 1941. Like most other tyro pilots at this stage of the war, his training had not taught him how to shoot properly and he would not learn the art of deflection shooting until a rest period at AFDU in 1942. He would end the war as a Wing Commander having shot down seven German aircraft. Another pilot who was just starting his operational career but was to have a bright future was Sgt Geoff Northcote who was born in Rapid City, Manitoba. After serving with 401 Squadron he was to complete a tour in Malta before commanding 402 Squadron in 1943. In the final months of the war he led 126 Wing, a position he retained until August 1945 [Northcote secured six of his eight victories on Spitfire Vb EP120 which is still in airworthy condition and currently flies out of Duxford]

There were a number of other pilots for whom 401 Squadron was to provide their first real experience of the air war over Europe including Sgt Don Morrison from Toronto. He had enlisted in the RCAF in October 1940 and had only arrived in the UK in the summer. After taking the course at 58 OTU at Grangemouth, he was initially sent to 122 Squadron but was transferred to 401 a few weeks later. It was a similar story with Sgt Omer Levesque from Mart Joll in Quebec who had commenced flight training in early 1941, although he had previously served in the RCAF as an AC2. Another recent arrival was twenty year old P/O Ian Ormston who had trained with 2 SFTS at Uplands, Ottawa.

All serviceable aircraft were flown down from Digby and arrived at Biggin Hill in the afternoon of the 20th, the ground personnel taking rather longer as they came by road convoy. The following day 401 Squadron flew its first operation over northern France during a sweep with 72 and 609 Squadrons and one of its sections was engaged. F/O C.A.B. Wallace claimed a Bf 109F with another as a probable but Sgt B.F. Whitson was shot down and taken prisoner. Having had the best gain/loss ratio of any of the Biggin Hill squadrons in 1941, the West Riding Squadron had its worst day for some time with the loss of two pilots. Frank Ziegler recorded the day's events in the squadron ORB.

At 1116 hrs Biggin takes off to act as Rear Support Wing off Boulogne in connection with a mammoth sweep (now known as a Rodeo). Everyone expects this to be a 'stooge' job and no one dreams it is to end sadly with the loss of two of the squadron's best pilots, F/O Vicki Ortmans and Sgt Palmer – the only time this year that more than one has been lost in a day. W/C Rankin is leading the squadron, with S/L Gilroy in charge of Blue section in which P/O Christian Ortmans [brother of Vicki] is flying as his No.2 on his first operational flight, with Vicki Ortmans and Sgt Palmer as a strong 3 and 4. Suddenly the C.O. sees 15–20 109s coming down and calls that he is going down too as there are too many to deal with. The order is either not heard or misunderstood, for the rest of the section does not follow and by the time the C.O. has climbed back to rejoin them, Blue 3 and 4 are already in the thick of it. Sgt Palmer, hit with a deflection shot, is seen to spin down, recover, then make a good landing on the water. But he does not get out and his aircraft sinks upside down. No one sees at all what happens to Vicki.

After lunch the squadron (fifteen aircraft, including W/C Rankin leading an extra section) sets off with four aircraft of 91 Squadron to search the Channel. The search is fruitless but leads to a number of tragic-comedies which help to dispel the gloom. F/O Malengreau instead of taking ops vector home, flies off on a reciprocal, leading his section straight towards France. After much anxious R/T conversation, his followers decide to desert. The flight has, however, led to petrol shortage and mist makes ground visibility practically nil. All pilots need a homing and the R/T log contains priceless examples of excited French. Lt Choron force lands in a field near Rye, F/O Malengreau lands with seven other pilots at Hawkinge (smugly referring to the amount of flak he experienced over Boulogne), Sgt Rigler lands at Lympne, others at Manston and only four at Biggin. These include Sgt Evans with six gallons of petrol after 2 hours 20 minutes in the air.

This was the third time that Vicki Ortmans had failed to return and the circumstances of his disappearance were by far the most worrying. After the last of the aircraft on ASR patrol returned without having seen anything, his brother Christian had to be physically restrained from taking off on his own to look for him. Although the search had been unsuccessful Vicki was still alive and lay in his dinghy where he would remain for the next 1½ days. He was eventually picked up unconscious by the Germans but news of his survival was slow to come through and was confused even more by his use of an alias ('Vicki Ogilvie'). This was an attempt to protect his family in occupied Belgium by claiming to be French Canadian, a piece of subterfuge that appeared to succeed, even though he was eventually sent to the same prisoner of war camp as the inspiration for his new name, his former comrade Keith Ogilvie!

The next real opportunity for 401 Squadron to test itself came on 27 October during a Wing sweep over northern France. The scale of the task was brought home to the newcomers in uncompromising fashion as only half of the aircraft that took off were to return. The prime requirement that the Wing retain its cohesion at all times was lacking on this occasion and, as ever, the resident *Luftwaffe* fighters were ever present to seize upon any opportunity. By the time that Gravelines was reached a number of 401 Squadron Spitfires had fallen behind and the Wing had to make four orbits to allow stragglers to catch up. The Biggin Hill Wing was doubly unfortunate in that the German fighters that could be seen up-sun were the cream of JG 26 led by its *Kommodore*, Obstlt Adolf Galland.

During the last orbit over Gravelines the Wing was attacked and split up with 401 Squadron being the hardest hit. Sgt B.G. Hodgkinson (W3955) became Galland's ninety-third victim but was to survive to become a prisoner of war. Less fortunate were F/O C.A.B. Wallace (AB991) and P/O J.A. Small (AB983) who were both shot down and killed. Soon after P/O C.W. Floody was shot down in W3964 but was able to bale out and was later captured. Two other aircraft were badly shot up including W3452 flown by Sgt G.B. Whitney, but by a superb piece of flying he was able to coax it back over the Channel before baling out from 600 ft. As his parachute opened within 100 ft of the ground he landed heavily but was uninjured. Sgt S.L. Thompson in W3601 found himself in a similar predicament but when he baled out of his damaged machine his parachute failed to open and his body was found close to the mangled remains of his Spitfire which crashed near Deal. In addition to Galland's victory, claims were also submitted by Hptm 'Pips' Priller, Lt Gottfried Helmholz, Lt Johannes Schmidt and Uffz Hans Dirksen.

F/L E.L. 'Jeep' Neal (Red 3) did at least manage to hit back but only after his Spitfire had had its starboard wing damaged by cannon fire. Turning sharply to port he got on the tail of the Bf 109F that had attacked him and fired a three-second deflection burst which produced two explosions near the cockpit. The 109 pulled up and flicked into a spin but Neal was unable to follow as he was attacked once more and was forced to break away in the direction of another group of aircraft which he assumed were Spitfires. Unfortunately these turned out to be more 109s and although he managed to damage one of them, the others turned on him and hit his aircraft in the fuselage. After breaking free he dived for the English coast and crash-landed near Rye [as Neal reported seeing two aircraft going down in flames near where F/O Wallace and P/O Small had been engaged, one of which was an enemy machine, a claim was put in on their behalf, however as no German aircraft were lost it appears that both of these aircraft were Spitfires]. To complete a disastrous day for the Biggin Hill Wing, P/O F. Falkiner of 72 Squadron was shot down in W3704 and was posted as missing.

No.609 Squadron fared slightly better but had to fight for its life to get out of France without suffering similar losses.

It is thought that a Sweep by the Biggin Wing from Nieuport to Gravelines will encounter the usual lack of opposition and be good practice for 401 Squadron. It turns out far otherwise. S/L Gilroy is leading the Wing and as it is orbiting behind Gravelines to allow stragglers to catch up, he reports up to

137

fifty enemy aircraft building up behind them. The suggested reason is that the Wing is on the route of Circus operations against Lille. Though 401 Squadron bears the brunt of the attack, 609's Red section does well to get back intact, two of them being hit, Sgt Galloway (Canadian) by a cannon shell which puts his compressor out of action. Half rolling, he sees a 109 and two Fw 190s and gets on the tail of one of the latter only to find his guns will not work. He eludes them and lands at Manston without brakes or flaps. P/O Smith also suffers a damaged compressor and his guns don't work either.

S/L Gilroy is engaged by three 109s in mid Channel, comes down to sea level and up again in a series of head on attacks. The remaining member of Red section, Lt Choron, sees two Fw 190s proceeding towards Manston at 5,000 ft. He dives on one and after his attack it drops a wheel and dives to 2,000 ft, at which point Choron's attention is directed to four more 190s, one of which is firing at him, with machine-gun only apparently. He causes this one to overshoot and firing at it from the quarter produces a stream of white smoke. The others are not shaken off until five miles off Manston after an engagement lasting ten minutes and Choron lands at Southend. He does not seem to hold the Fw 190s performance in very high regard. The only other 609 pilot to fire is F/L Offenberg at two 109s which came down on Blue section.

Needless to say a post-mortem conference on the above is deemed highly necessary. Before it can be convened 609 are ordered off to protect two rescue boats searching the Channel for missing pilots. This proves to be almost as exciting an affair as the other and Intelligence has its worst day for months as battles accumulate. Group agitates for reports and these become hours overdue. It might, in fact, easily have been the end of 609 'West Riding' Squadron, ops plotting no less than three lots of 15 plus, two of 12 plus, a 9 plus and a 3 plus with 609 and W/C Rankin as the only defence, S/L Gilroy's appeal for help going apparently unheeded until too late. Effective assistance is, however, given by the W/C who appoints himself 'high cover' to 609 and chases fifteen 109s back to France single handed, probably destroying one. He then draws off five Fw 190s and chases then back as well. Meanwhile 609 down below near Dover, have been attacked by another lot of fifteen 109s. S/L Gilroy manages to get within range of the last pair and fires at both, one being seen to turn on its back and go vertically down. The effect of all this is to bring the rest of the enemy formation round into sun to attack and an exciting time is had by all till the enemy eventually decide to go home.

The next few days were characterised by poor weather and very little offensive flying was undertaken. After the debacle of the 27th the Wing practiced formation flying and air firing which was mainly for the benefit of the Canadians and it was impressed on them that strict discipline had to be maintained at all times when in the combat zone. The only operational flying during this period comprised convoy patrols, an uneventful scramble and a Channel patrol which was carried out by two aircraft of 401 Squadron.

CHAPTER FOURTEEN

Stalemate

During the first week in November there was a change of C.O. for 72 Squadron as S/L Desmond Sheen was replaced by S/L Cedric Masterman. He had joined the RAF in 1935 on a short service commission and for a number of years flew in the army co-operation role on the Hawker Audax and Westland Lysander. He took the opportunity to convert to single-engine fighters in 1941 and commanded 232 Squadron on Spitfire IIs at Warmwell before joining 72.

For the Biggin Hill Wing there was a return to offensive operations on the 7th in the shape of a Rodeo that took place in the early afternoon and involved a sweep that took in Dunkirk – St Omer – Berck. Due to a series of early attacks Sgt Peter Nash and Sgt John Van Schaick of 609 Squadron (Red 3 and 4) became separated before the French coast had even been crossed and were forced to join up with Jamie Rankin's section in 72 Squadron. While approaching Le Touquet from the southwest at 26,000 ft three Bf 109Fs in a wide vic formation were seen 1,000 ft above heading in the opposite direction. Having passed overhead they immediately commenced a descending turn to come in from behind and attacked P/O H.J. Birkland who was flying as Yellow 3 of 72 Squadron. As the 109s broke away to the left they were engaged by Van Schaick who fired two short bursts with cannon using slight deflection. As one of the enemy aircraft had disappeared from view he broke away but was relieved to find that there was nothing on his tail. When he returned his gaze to where the 109 had last been seen all that remained was a grey parachute 2,000 ft below. It was later reported that P/O Birkland had been shot down in flames but as he had not been seen to bale out, it was assumed that the parachute seen by Van Schaick was that of the pilot of the 109 he had fired at [news came through later that Birkland was a PoW].

Sgt Nash was also engaged in a dogfight that lasted around ten minutes. He was attacked by six aircraft in all (three Bf 109Fs and three Fw 190As) and during the exchange he fired at one of the 109Fs from the starboard quarter which produced a stream of glycol. This aircraft then went straight down, apparently into the sea. He then fired at an Fw 190A which emitted copious amounts of black smoke before rolling on its back and diving away. When he landed Nash claimed a 109F destroyed and an Fw 190A as a probable but both claims must be questioned. During this fight 609 Squadron had come up against elements of JG 26 who only lost one Bf 109F on this day, the circumstances closely matching that of the claim submitted by Van Schaick. Having disposed of Birkland, it is almost certain that Uffz Heinz Richter of the *Geschwader Stabsschwarm* was shot up by Van Schaick, the German sustaining severe injuries in the process. Although he managed to bale out of his aircraft (Bf 109F-4 Werke Nr 7166) near Desvres he died shortly after reaching the ground.

Despite the message being hammered home that the Wing must maintain its formation over northern France there was yet another example of indiscipline on the 8th and a total of five Spitfires were shot down without loss to the German side. The Biggin Hill Wing was acting as high cover to eight Hurricanes bombers which were to carry out a dive-bombing attack on a distillery at St Pol. These were assisted by four Hurricanes of 615 Squadron for anti-flak work with two Spitfire squadrons of the Tangmere Wing as escort. At the same time as this attack was taking place a diversionary sweep was made by the North Weald Wing which approached the French coast to the east of Dunkirk before returning.

A number of factors conspired against the co-ordination of the various elements of this operation, one of which was high winds at altitude which made it very difficult to achieve accurate timings. With such conditions it was also easy for sections to become displaced in relation to the rest of the Wing formation. From the point of view of the Biggin Hill squadrons the operation started to go wrong at an early stage as the French coast was crossed south of Berck instead of to the south of Le Touquet as had been planned. The Wing then circled Hesdin as the Hurricanes went into the attack but by the time that it reached the coast on the way out a further orbit had to be made to allow stragglers to catch up. On this occasion the German fighters had been scrambled in good time and had been waiting up-sun for any opportunity to pounce. They were helped in their task by low level fog which silhouetted their opponents nicely.

The top squadrons were bounced by many Bf 109Fs of I and III/JG 26 which persisted with their attacks until about eight miles off the French coast. No.72 Squadron was badly hit and P/O N.E. Bishop and Sgt D.R. White were shot down and killed. Sgt Dykes also failed to return as his aircraft suffered engine failure over the Channel and he had to bale out. He was picked up after 1½ hours in the sea and was reunited with his comrades later in the day. No.401 Squadron was also attacked and Sgt R.W. Gardner was killed when his Spitfire dived into the ground. F/O J. Weir was also shot down but survived and was taken prisoner. The pilots who claimed these victories over the Canadians were Lt Friedrich Graf von Uiberacker of the 1st Staffel and Obfw Emil Babenz of the 3rd Staffel.

Although a distillery might, at first, seem to be an odd choice of target, a study carried out earlier in the year had come to the conclusion that distilleries could be used to aid the German war effort. During the early autumn the French and Belgian sugar beet and alcohol industries were in full operation, a situation that usually began in early October, as the sugar beet crop was collected, and lasted for around five months. In other areas of France alcohol was being produced from grape residues during the production of wine and from apples following the manufacture of cider. As the alcohol produced could be mixed with motor spirit to supplement fuel supplies there was an obvious benefit for the Germans, especially as France was the largest producer of pure alcohol in the world, the latest figures available showing a yearly total of around 46 million gallons or 160,000 tons.

As the above figures related to the normal situation in peacetime, there was a good chance that they could now be substantially higher assuming that the production of alcohol had become the primary requirement rather than merely a by-product of the sugar, wine and cider industries. As there were numerous distilleries in northern France not far from the Channel coast there was thus the opportunity for attack by cannon-armed fighters and fighter-bombers. As the distilleries were virtually identical in layout they were easily seen from the air and were particularly vulnerable to cannon fire, especially the distillation plants which consisted of large copper units and a mass of pipes, valves and other apparatus. There was also a good chance that this area of the plant could be set on fire. As distilleries tended to be relatively isolated and had not been hit before there was a good chance that flak (if any) would be light, but this situation would obviously not last if this type of target was to be attacked on a regular basis.

The last of the Circus operations of 1941 (No.110) also took place on 8 November in which twelve Blenheims of 21 and 82 Squadrons were sent to attack railway targets at Lille, although it later transpired that Gosnay had been hit instead. As this attack was co-ordinated to take place shortly after the strike on the distillery at St Pol the Biggin Hill Wing was not actively involved, however, the end result was similar and the tally for these two operations was seventeen Spitfires lost. Only three pilots were able to return to active service, eight were killed and the remainder became prisoners of war. Such high losses were made even worse as they included a Wing Commander and three Squadron Leaders. In reality the onset of winter meant that large-scale operations were no longer feasible but loss rates such as these brought into question the whole concept of attempting to win a battle of attrition with the *Luftwaffe* fighter force in northern France.

After an uneventful sweep along the Channel on the 9 November, heavy rain and occasional fog meant that very little flying was possible over the next week with only convoy patrols on the 11th and another uncontested foray over the Channel on the 15th. On 18 November the Biggin Hill Wing, comprising 401 and 609 Squadrons, took off before midday to rendezvous with eight Hurricanes which were to bomb the distillery at Hesdin. After the attack had been successfully carried out Jamie Rankin gave the order to descend through a cloud layer to seek out any enemy aircraft that might be lurking below. This proved to be easier said than done however and P/O Denis Barnham who was flying Red 3 with 609 Squadron was unable to stay in contact with his section leader and his wingman. His own No.2 also became detached with the result that he broke cloud directly over Cap Gris Nez completely alone. The cloud layer stopped at the Channel, which was clear, and as he was weighing up his situation he was attacked by three Fw 190As. This was the beginning of a desperate battle which was to last for the next fifteen minutes.

Although he found that he could easily out-turn the Focke-Wulfs their superior speed meant that they had no difficulty in staying with the Spitfire even though Barnham selected full boost and left it there, conveniently forgetting about the normal five minute restriction. Mile by mile he managed to edge closer to Dover and the English cliffs but as the attacks were incessant he had to turn constantly and pre-empt each thrust as it came. He fired his guns in short bursts to worry the German pilots and thwart their attacks but was worried that he might run out of ammunition before the 190s had finished with him. There was little chance at this stage of achieving any hits and even if he had he would not have known anything about it, as he was forced to break off after each burst to avoid being hit himself. The battle was fought at extremely low level (the combatants did not get above 100 ft at any stage) and many times it took place just above the waves. Having fought an outstanding defensive action for nearly a quarter of an hour Barnham was finally presented with a decent attacking opportunity from the rear quarter on one of the 190s. A four-second burst struck the Focke-Wulf but as he had to evade yet another attack he was not able to see the outcome. By this stage the aircraft were only two miles south of Dover harbour and Barnham made one final dash for home. To his immense relief he was not attacked again and was able to cross the coast, flying low over a gun position one mile west of the Dover balloons [on the basis of reports by land-based witnesses the Fw 190A was credited as destroyed although JG 26 records show that no aircraft were lost].

The day after this operation 609 Squadron left the Biggin Hill Wing and joined up with 92 Squadron at Digby. Throughout the summer Frank Ziegler had written of 609's achievements and he summed up their record as follows

November saw the long-feared departure of 609 Squadron from Biggin Hill and 11 Group – to Digby. It left, not as a tired squadron of declining morale – as other squadrons leave – but with the pilots still at the top of their form, and with an aggressive experience which has seldom, if ever, been exceeded. In fact the reason 609 had at last to go was to allow another squadron to gain experience too . . . and having been in the Biggin sector since February, 609 could not really grumble. It had destroyed 51 German fighters, probably destroyed another 19 and damaged 41 since its arrival and had only lost 15 pilots, a gain/loss ratio which has probably not been equalled in Fighter Command this year.

Compared with the constant action and the kudos that surrounded Biggin Hill, Digby was a depressing place which appeared to have very little going for it. Even William de Goat took an instant dislike to the place and his first action on getting out of the Harrow transport aircraft he had arrived in was to march into the orderly room. By the time that he had finished the room did not quite live up to its name. He then set about eating the station's Christmas cards in the Adjutant's room before sampling the new shoots on the station commander's prized ornamental trees. It was not a good start.

The difficult job of replacing the West Riding Squadron in the Biggin Hill Wing fell to 124 Squadron which was one of Fighter Command's least experienced units. Although it had existed during the First World War, it had only been involved in training and had not seen any action. It had been re-formed on 10 May 1941 at Castletown which was one of the most northerly airfields in the UK and was situated six miles south-east of Thurso. Over the next six months 124 Squadron carried out numerous coastal and convoy patrols as well as acting as a mini Operational Training Unit to give pilots some operational experience before they went south. It was commanded by S/L Myles Duke-Woolley DFC whose uncle was the famous English conductor and impresario Sir Thomas Beecham. He had been educated at Marlborough and had graduated from the RAF College at Cranwell in 1936. His first posting had been to a night fighter squadron (No.23) and his first combat kill was a Heinkel He 111 that was shot down on the night of 18/19 June 1940 in a Blenheim 1f. During the Battle of Britain he pursued every opportunity to get himself posted on to day fighters and in September he joined 253 Squadron on Hurricanes as a flight commander, achieving further success before the end of the year.

Duke-Woolley's senior flight commander was F/L Tony Barton who had originally joined the Royal Navy in 1936. After flying with 823 Squadron in the Fleet Air Arm, Barton was transferred to the RAF as a Pilot Officer and was posted to 32 Squadron to fly Hurricanes. During the Battle of Britain he destroyed five enemy aircraft but was shot down twice himself, the first time being on 12 August when he had to crash land near Dover. The second occasion was rather more serious and occurred after he had begun flying with 253 Squadron. Barton's Hurricane was severely hit during combat with Bf 109Es over Kent on 20 September and he was badly wounded. On recovery he joined 124 Squadron when it was re-formed. Barton's opposite number was F/L Tommy Balmforth who had joined the RAF on a short service commission in October 1938. Prior to joining 124 Squadron Balmforth had been a ferry pilot flying replacement aircraft to the Middle East and thence to Malta. A desperate shortage of pilots on the island led to him being retained on Malta in 1940 and during his stay there he was credited with shooting down a Macchi MC 200.

Shortly after arriving at Biggin Hill 124 Squadron received a large number of pilots as reinforcements and by the end of the month there were thirty-two on strength, of whom twenty-three were operational. The newcomers comprised several Norwegians including Lt Arne Austeen who, in 1943, was to command 331 (Norwegian) Squadron on Spitfire IXs. Also drafted in were three Australians, a Belgian and two Czechs so that 124 Squadron's make up was particularly cosmopolitan. The small Czech contingent included F/L Jaroslav Kulhanek who was an extremely experienced pilot with over 1,000 hours flying time having served with the Czech Air Force before joining the Armee de l'Air. During the Battle of France he flew the Morane Saulnier MS.406 and shared in the destruction of a Do 17Z on 24 May 1940.

On 21 November 401 Squadron was involved in a three hour convoy patrol which passed off uneventfully although Sgt C.R. Golden crash-landed near Maidstone and had to be taken to hospital with a fractured right thigh, lacerations to the knee and face and shock. The following day the squadron was able to exact some retribution for the losses it had suffered during a sweep with 72 Squadron. Take-off was made at 1500 hrs and the intention was to reconnoitre the area around St Omer. For once the Germans were slow to react and the Spitfires were already over France when aircraft of I and III/JG 26 took off to intercept. This was to be one of the rare occasions when the RAF's fighters had a real height advantage as the German aircraft were first seen as they were climbing through 6,000 ft. No.401 Squadron dived to attack III Gruppe which comprised a mixed formation of Bf 109Fs and Fw 190As. Yellow section was heavily involved with P/O Ian Ormston (Yellow 2) latching onto a 109 which appeared straight ahead in a gentle dive. A four-second burst with cannon and machine-gun produced no visible effect but as he broke off he saw another 109 in a left-hand turn and losing altitude. As it turned it presented Ormston with a full plan view and he fired the rest of his ammunition at full deflection. The 109 then went straight down and was seen to crash in a field about ten miles south of Marck.

P/O Don Blakeslee was flying in the No.3 position in Yellow section and as he went into the attack he selected one of two 109s that were leading the German formation. With the extra speed from the dive he was able to close quite easily and manoeuvred into a position directly astern, firing a two-second burst from 150 yards range. At least one cannon shell struck home as there was an explosion and the 109 was enveloped in heavy black smoke, which was followed by fire. Sgt Don Morrison (Yellow 4) followed Blakeslee during this attack and as he turned away their height was around 5,000 ft. Looking round Morrison saw three Fw 190As near Devres at 6–7,000 ft and immediately climbed at full boost to get the behind the rearmost aircraft. A two-second burst of machine-gun (his cannons had already jammed) had no effect but the 190 pilot evaded by going into a steep right-hand turn which presented the opportunity to fire a long burst from inside his turn. Black smoke was seen to pour from the 190 but it was lost to view as Morrison passed below.

The Spitfires of Blue section having initially maintained their height as top cover for the rest of the squadron were gradually drawn into the fight. Sgt Omer Levesque

(Blue 4) was flying at 15,000 ft about ten miles south-west of St Omer when he saw a Spitfire about to come under attack. Diving down, he identified the German aircraft as an Fw 190 but it saw him coming and went into a steep turn to port. It then dived vertically before climbing again and performed this manoeuvre several times with Levesque firing short bursts whenever he could. His fire appeared to have some effect as blue/white smoke appeared from under the cockpit. Height was gradually lost and at 5,000 ft the hood of the 190 flew off and a partially opened parachute appeared. This was the last that he saw of the aircraft and he then climbed to 10,000 ft and headed north for the coast. Near Devres he saw another 190 and fired a three-second burst of cannon and machine-gun from astern at 300 yards range. The German aircraft evaded and accelerated away and Levesque had to use his boost override to close the gap. A two-second burst produced some white smoke and a number of black explosive puffs on the starboard wing. There was no further evasive action and the 190 flew ahead with its starboard wing low for a few seconds before turning onto its back. Levesque was then attacked himself by an Fw 190 but was able to get away quite easily and returned to base.

The dogfight that had started overland tended to spill out over the Channel and the final combats took place as 401 Squadron were on their way home. Don Morrison had crossed the French coast at 100 ft and was nearly half way across the Channel when he saw three Fw 190As attacking the Spitfire flown by F/L 'Jeep' Neal. Having selected the last of the three he fired a long burst of machine-gun at 200 yards closing to 100 yards range from astern and below. The 190 rolled onto its back at 500 ft and dived down in an inverted position but was then lost to view. Don Blakeslee also fired at two 109s that he encountered on the way back about 5–8 miles east of Dover. Attacking the No.2 he saw his fire hit the 109 to the rear of the cockpit and on the starboard wing tip. Various pieces flew off but as he had already been in the air for an hour he did not press home his attack and returned to Biggin Hill. This seemingly successful action still came at a price as F/O H.A. Sprague was shot down in AD516 and taken prisoner. Two JG 26 pilots made claims at this time, Lt Walter Thorn of the 7th Staffel and Fw Gottfried Weber of the 8th Staffel.

No.72 Squadron was also engaged and on the basis of observations by Jamie Rankin and other pilots, an Fw 190A and a Bf 109F were claimed as destroyed, each aircraft being shared by S/L Cedric Masterman, P/O Jimmy Rosser and Sgt Bernard Ingham. Despite the fact that the score for the day stood at six (three Fw 190As and three Bf 109Fs) the reality was rather different. Even though JG 26 had been caught in a poor tactical position in the climb, only two aircraft had in fact been shot down, an Fw 190A which was forced to crash-land at Coquelles and the Bf 109F-4 of Fw Ignaz Schinabeck of the 1st Staffel. Although the latter was able to bale out, he later died of his injuries in hospital.

The rest of the month was a frustrating mixture of groundings due to bad weather interspersed with occasional convoy patrols. The conditions were so bad that even this type of operation caused problems and on the 24 November poor visibility meant that 124 Squadron was unable to find the convoy it was supposed to be protecting. They were then obliged to put down at Shoreham and in the course of landing the Spitfire flown by P/O R.B. Gilman collided with that flown by F/L Kulhanek at a height of about 75 ft. Although the latter managed to land safely, Gilman's aircraft was wrecked as it stalled onto the undershoot area and he had to be treated for minor injuries. To try to relieve the boredom on 401 Squadron a Rhubarb operation was planned for the 30th involving F/L 'Jeep' Neal, P/O Hugh

Godefroy and Sergeants Hagyard and Whitney. Even this laudable attempt to provide some excitement failed miserably, however, and they returned without having found any worthwhile targets.

The weather during December showed little improvement and it was not until the 8th that any offensive operations could be considered. In the late morning the Biggin Hill Wing escorted eight Hurricanes in an attack on the distillery at Hesdin. All three Gruppe of JG 26 were scrambled to intercept and these were able to pick off two Spitfires from 72 Squadron. Sgt C.L.A. Thompson from Rhodesia was last heard of shortly before crossing over the French coast and Sgt E.G. Enright from Australia who had lost touch with his leader, F/L Campbell, also failed to return. Both pilots were killed. In contrast 401 Squadron had a much quieter time and although enemy aircraft were seen, these were not engaged. The only concern for the Canadians was a ground collision involving the Spitfires of Sgt J.R. Patten and P/O Hugh Godefroy. Thankfully, neither pilot was hurt. A further sweep was carried out in the early afternoon and several 401 Squadron pilots fired their guns including Sgt Don Morrison who claimed a Bf 109F destroyed with another damaged. P/O Don Blakeslee, Sgt Hagyard and Sgt Whitney were also in action, each putting in claims for Bf 109Fs as damaged. This proved to be the last major air battle of the year and the rest of the month was taken up with various defensive patrols whenever the weather permitted.

The month of December also saw the departure of Jamie Rankin as Wing Leader after a highly successful tour. His place was taken by another well known pilot, W/C Bob Stanford Tuck who had just returned to England after a lecture tour in the USA. Tuck was another former 92 Squadron pilot, having been a flight commander at the time of Dunkirk and also during the first half of the Battle of Britain. He later commanded 257 Squadron on Hurricanes and by the time that he came to Biggin Hill his combat score stood at twenty-seven enemy aircraft destroyed, plus two shared. Tuck had the look of a warrior as he was tall and slim with slicked black hair and pencil moustache. He was also more in keeping with the public's image of a fighter pilot as he had an extrovert nature and was rather dashing. Those who came into contact with him could not fail to notice a scar on his cheek. Many were to come away believing that this had been caused by a dual, but it was in fact the result of a broken flying wire when Tuck had been forced to bale out of a Gloster Gauntlet following a mid-air collision.

There would be very little opportunity for Tuck to add to his impressive score although he did play a small part in the demise of the last aircraft to be shot down by a Biggin Hill-based aircraft during 1941. On 17 December 124 Squadron carried out two 'Flotsam' patrols on the lookout for German aircraft which were attempting to use the poor weather conditions to carry out sneak attacks. At 1500 hrs S/L Myles Duke-Woolley at the head of Red section was preparing to hand over the task to other members of the squadron when he heard the controller warn of an enemy aircraft approaching from the south. By this time his Nos. 3 and 4 had already turned for home but looking around, Duke-Woolley saw a twin-engined aircraft flying at 1,800 ft which he identified as a Ju 88. Although he was about 1,000 ft below and was relatively low over the sea the pilot of the Junkers saw him immediately and started climbing at full power for some cloud cover. He gave chase and fired two short bursts of cannon at around 450 yards, hoping that this would slow the German aircraft down.

The cloud was not substantial however and as Duke-Woolley came out of the top of it he found that he was closer, but that the Ju 88 was now diving for a rain shower not far off. The rear gunner was firing back and was aided in his task as the pilot was applying full rudder to make his aim easier. This however had the detrimental effect of slowing the aircraft down and Duke-Woolley fired several more bursts of cannon which hit the Junkers on its fuselage. The port engine was also hit and caught fire. The aircraft flew level for a short time at around 1,000 ft but then began to descend during which three of the crew members took to their parachutes. The last one jumped clear at a height of only 200 ft but his canopy failed to open fully before he hit the water. By now the Ju 88 was inverted and it crashed into the sea in that position. Towards the end of the combat it was fired upon by Bob Tuck who had also joined in the pursuit but as it was clearly beyond hope at this point he did not bother to put in any claim.

One final offensive sweep was carried out on the 18th but no incidents were reported. On their return all aircraft had to land at Manston due to thick fog which had formed in their absence. This persisted for the next three days and eventually the pilots' kit was sent over by road as it appeared that they might be there for some time. Of course, as soon as the kit turned up Sod's Law decreed that the fog should lift and all aircraft were able to return to Biggin Hill around noon on the 21st. On landing Sgt J.K. Ferguson of 401 Squadron had his undercarriage buckle on landing but the damage was only slight and he was unhurt. The gradual deterioration of the airfield surface was to lead to further undercarriage mishaps and on the 23rd the Spitfire flown by Sgt C.S. Pope of 401 Squadron suffered a similar problem. On this occasion the damage was rather more severe, although Pope stepped out unhurt.

Christmas Day saw formation flying carried out in the morning with all aircraft returning in good time for festivities in the Mess from noon. As was traditional in the RAF the Officers performed as waiters and the offerings were considered to be excellent despite the restrictions imposed by rationing. The celebrations continued into the evening and all personnel were in high spirits by the end of the day. It was back to business on the 26th and although no operational flying took place Bob Tuck took the opportunity offered by reasonable weather to fly a practice Wing formation. Unfortunately Sgt W. Rowthorn of 401 Squadron overshot on landing and his aircraft hit the boundary fence, being badly damaged in the process. Rowthorn was flung forwards onto the gunsight and suffered lacerations to his face and a broken nose.

Following convoy patrols on the 27th a Channel patrol was flown on the 28th from Manston. The landing surface was equally poor here and one undercarriage leg of the Spitfire flown by Sgt F.A. Duff of 401 Squadron collapsed when it came into contact with a soft patch. This had the effect of pitching him into P/O Hugh Godefroy's aircraft who was thus involved in a ground collision for the second time in less than a month. No injuries were sustained and both pilots returned to Biggin Hill later in the day in a Blenheim. After further convoy patrols on 29 December, the year ended very much as it had begun with two days of fog in which all aircraft were grounded.

CHAPTER FIFTEEN

The Final Reckoning

Throughout the year of 1941 No.11 Group's squadrons had endeavoured to engage the *Luftwaffe* fighter units based in the northern France at every opportunity, but what, if anything had been achieved? There was much criticism of Fighter Command's offensive at the time and the policy adopted by Sholto Douglas and Leigh-Mallory has continued to be controversial to this day. In defence of his strategy the former later penned a brief assessment which outlined the main benefits as he saw them

It was said at the time and after that the sweeps carried out by Fighter Command in 1941 were a waste of effort. I cannot agree with this view, even though Peirse, who was then commanding Bomber Command, and subsequently Bert Harris, were against them. First, the question of morale. I hold that no air force can achieve air superiority by remaining continuously on the defensive and confining their efforts to the defence of their own country. The sweeps, therefore, were an essential preliminary to a switchover to the offensive, and in this sense they were the forerunners of the invasion of the Continent

Secondly, such sweeps produced many tactical lessons which the pilots of Fighter Command were able to learn and adjust in the best possible circumstances. Thirdly, from a purely tactical point of view, the sweeps kept a high proportion of the German fighter force confined to Europe, and if they had not been carried out much of this force would have been sent to the Eastern Front to operate against Russia. While I do not claim that the sweeps caused the Germans to withdraw fighter squadrons from the newly created Eastern Front, I do think, in fact I am sure, that they did discourage them from reinforcing those fighter squadrons at the expense of the west. Therefore, as what I may call a retaining action, those sweeps were well worth while.

At the end of 1941 Sholto Douglas produced a comprehensive revue of the air operations that had been carried out by Fighter Command during the year and it is proposed to take a detailed look at the section dealing with offensive operations. The necessary operational instructions for this type of mission were drawn up as early as the third week of October 1940 and were revised in the first week of December. The plan which was now adopted involved two types of operation, Circuses and Rhubarbs (known initially by the code name Mosquito but later changed to avoid confusion with the aircraft of the same name). The latter were begun on 20 December 1940 and pilots were given encouragement to organise this type of operation themselves with the help of their squadron Intelligence Officers. In his report Sholto Douglas put emphasis on the fact that the primary objective of Rhubarbs was the destruction of enemy aircraft, however he did recognise that there would be many occasions when none would be seen, in which case he authorised the attacking of suitable targets on the ground as an alternative.

Between 20 December 1940 and 13 June 1941 a total of 149 Rhubarb patrols were flown (amounting to 336 sorties) however forty-five were rendered abortive due to unsuitable weather conditions or other such circumstances. German aircraft were only seen on twenty-six occasions and eighteen engagements took place. These resulted in claims for seven enemy aircraft destroyed for the loss of eight RAF pilots. There were 116 attacks against a wide variety of ground targets which included ships, road vehicles, airfield buildings, grounded aircraft, artillery and searchlight posts, German troops and military camps. Operations on a larger scale commenced on 9 January 1941 when five squadrons of fighters carried out a sweep along the coast of France and the first Circus took place the following day. Between then and 13 June there were a total of eleven Circuses, the objectives for the bombers including the docks at Dunkirk, Calais and Boulogne and a number of airfields. In addition to these there were over forty pure fighter sweeps in which bombers were not involved.

After just three Circus operations had taken place, differences of opinion between Fighter and Bomber Command became apparent. The principal aim of Fighter Command was to shoot down enemy aircraft, whereas Bomber Command, naturally enough, attached rather more importance to the bombing. On the instructions of Air Chief Marshal Sir Charles Portal, the Chief of the Air Staff, a meeting was held between Sholto Douglas and his opposite number in Bomber Command, Air Marshal Sir Richard Peirse on 15 February. It was agreed, albeit reluctantly on Peirse's part, that the main object of a Circus was to force the enemy to give battle under conditions that were tactically favourable to the RAF's fighters. It was also stressed by Fighter Command that to compel the Germans to do so the bombers had to do enough damage to make it impossible for the *Luftwaffe* to refuse to fight. Regarding this last statement it is interesting to note that at the same time Portal was of the opinion that the bombing of objectives in France with the resources available could have 'no decisive military effect' at that stage of the war.

The early Circus operations were not successful in placing RAF fighters in a position that was tactically favourable and Sholto Douglas espoused the view that this was due to his forces operating too low down. He felt that the lowest fighter squadron should have been at 18,000 ft or above, with the highest at around 30,000 ft. For this to be achieved the bombers needed to fly at 17,000 ft or more and this was not always practicable owing to the time taken by the Blenheims that were generally used for these operations to reach that height. Up to 13 June no major fighter battles had occurred and the Germans had been content to pick off stragglers or attempt to exploit any favourable tactical situation that might develop. In the absence of such circumstances they had generally avoided combat which was regarded as 'slightly disappointing'. A certain amount of satisfaction was expressed however as sixteen enemy aircraft had been claimed as destroyed with a substantial number probably destroyed. RAF losses amounted to twenty-five pilots. It was also claimed that one of the ultimate objectives of the RAF's offensive policy had been achieved, namely that it had seized the initiative and forced the Germans onto the defensive.

After three weeks of bad weather Circuses were resumed on 14 June and this marked the beginning of an intensive period of operations which lasted throughout the summer. On 17 June the most ambitious Circus yet attempted took place when eighteen Blenheim bombers with an escort of twenty-two fighter squadrons attacked a chemical plant and power station near Bethune. There was a vigorous reaction from the *Luftwaffe* and nine RAF pilots were shot down however those that returned reported much success [the RAF claimed to have destroyed fourteen German aircraft with another seven probably destroyed whereas actual losses were just two, a Bf 109E from JG 26 and a Bf 109F from JG 2]. It was assumed at the time that the long-expected fighter battle had at last arrived.

On 19 June a meeting was held with the Commanders-in-Chief of Fighter, Bomber and Coastal Commands to discuss the most effective means of continuing the war in the west so that German units could not be withdrawn to the east where the invasion of the Soviet Union was imminent. Ideally it was hoped that the reverse situation would actually result in which units would be withdrawn from the east to reinforce those still in the west. To try to achieve this aim the decision was taken to intensify the offensive against northern France and since the enemy had reacted energetically against the Circus that had been flown to Bethune it was decided to concentrate future attacks on industrial targets in this area which also included Lens and Lille. If the Germans could be encouraged to concentrate their fighter forces here it was also thought that unescorted bomber attacks might be possible round the flank of the defences, especially into north-west Germany. However this plan was soon dropped when daylight attacks in this area showed that the Germans still had adequate fighter defence.

Although it had previously been agreed that the destruction of the enemy fighter force in France was the principal aim of Circus operations the C-in-C of Bomber Command was still not happy and on 3 July Sholto Douglas was informed by the Air Ministry that the object must now be 'the destruction of certain important targets by day bombing and the destruction of enemy fighter aircraft.' This increased emphasis on bombing led to the use of Stirling bombers of 3 Group instead of Blenheims of 2 Group. As far as the escort fighters were concerned this changeover worked in their favour as they found it easier to protect a small forma-tion of Stirlings than a larger number of Blenheims. This arrangement was only temporary however and the Stirlings were withdrawn at the end of the month. During operations over France three had been shot down and another had to be written off when its undercarriage collapsed on landing at Wyton.

During the first few weeks of the intensive period RAF fighter pilots reported outstandingly good results in combat, indeed in his report Sholto Douglas went as far as to suggest that 'something like complete ascendancy had been gained over the opposing fighter force.' For a short time in the middle of June there had been determined opposition but now the Germans appeared reluctant to engage unless the circumstances favoured them. Claims for the remaining period up to the end of July were not quite as good but were still in the RAF's favour. At the end of the month the Air Ministry decided to review the results achieved up to that time.

It was conceded in the report that this was an extremely difficult task as it was virtually impossible to come up with figures that were anywhere near accurate. Although large numbers of enemy aircraft had apparently been shot down it was recognised that there was considerable room for honest error. Even if the claims were accepted at face value there was no way of assessing how many German pilots had survived to fight another day. It was also stated that the RAF's knowl-edge of the German capacity to replace losses was 'scanty'. At this early stage it had already become apparent that the RAF had failed to force the Germans to bring units back from the Eastern Front but it was thought that the losses inflicted had led to reserve training units in France being called up as replacements. The effect of the bombing attacks was virtually unknown.

Although the losses to Fighter Command as regards pilots killed and taken prisoner had been considerable, it was thought that these were not so heavy as to cause 'serious embarrassment.' A comparison was made with the fighting at the height of the Battle of Britain and it was pointed out that the 1941 losses were considerably lighter. In terms of the numbers of aircraft lost, replacements were readily available and no significant problems were experienced with production. In the period from 14 June to the end of July, Bomber Command lost fifteen aircraft during Circus operations but lost another sixteen (out of 115 sorties flown) during attacks on the *Scharnhorst* and *Gneisenau* at Brest and La Pallice. This was further evidence that daylight attacks by bombers on the flanks of the German defensive system were still highly risky.

A further conference was held at the Air Ministry on 29 July to decide whether Circus operations should continue. It was generally agreed that the daylight bombing of Germany in particular, no longer looked like being practicable and so for the foreseeable future night operations would take precedence for the medium and heavy bombers of Bomber Command. This left Circus operations as the only means by which attacks could be made in daylight hours so that the German fighter force could be engaged in large set piece battles. Sholto Douglas reiterated that the co-operation of a bomber force was essential if these operations were to be effective. This view was upheld by Portal and it was decided that the Circus offensive should continue.

A further forty-six Circuses were carried out from 14 June to 31 July involving a total of 374 bomber sorties and over 8,000 fighter sorties. During this six week period 123 RAF pilots were killed or taken prisoner. In addition over 1,000 fighter sorties were flown in connection with attacks on shipping and another 800 on sweeps. Rhubarbs, which had been resumed on 16 July after a month's pause, accounted for another 61. Thus over 10,000 offensive sorties were flown but this figure was bettered by the number of defensive sorties that had taken place, in particular the protection of shipping.

The Circus offensive was resumed on 5 August and twenty-six operations were carried out during the month. Blenheims of 2 Group provided the striking force for twenty-four of them and Hampdens of 5 Group for the other two. The opposition appeared to be more effective during August and the 'balance of advantage' started to swing the other way. This was put down to a more efficient use of their forces by the Germans based on experience built up over the previous weeks. This raised further questions as to the effectiveness of the offensive and it was discussed again at the end of the month. It was generally agreed that it should continue although on a reduced scale which would probably have occurred anyway due to a gradual worsening of the weather. Leigh-Mallory suggested that instead of concentrating largely against the Nord and Pas de Calais areas, the attacks should be delivered over a wider front so as to induce the Germans to spread their fighters more thinly along the coasts of France and the Low Countries. This recommendation was accepted.

During September twelve Circus operations were carried out with another two in the first week of October. The objectives attacked by the bombers included two targets at Rouen, plus one each at Amiens, Le Havre and Ostend. Further cutbacks had to be made in October as it became apparent that the demands of other theatres of war were likely to cause a shortage of fighter aircraft at home. For this reason, and also because the weather was growing less favourable and the situation on the Eastern Front was unlikely to be materially effected by the Circus offensive, Sholto Douglas instructed that future Circuses must only be undertaken in specially favourable circumstances, but that a rigorous offensive should be continued against shipping and 'fringe targets'.

At the same time as Circus operations were reduced in scale greater emphasis was placed on Rhubarbs. As German aircraft were still being met fairly infrequently, the usual outcome of these sorties was the shooting up of any ground target that presented itself. Sholto Douglas could have imposed a rigid 'target policy' but did not want to give the impression that attacks on surface objectives were as important as the destruction of enemy aircraft. However in October the instructions were amended in that pilots were to proceed to a selected surface objective and if they met no German aircraft on the way there, that would be their target. If they did meet enemy aircraft, then the destruction of these aircraft would take priority. Surface objectives were selected by Fighter Command in consultation with the Air Ministry and included canal barges, railway tank wagons, electrical transformers and, for a season, factories engaged in distilling alcohol from beet. On 20 October a long-standing ban on the attack of moving goods trains was withdrawn.

On 21 October a further reduction in the scale of the Circus offensive was made with a limit of six operations per month but in practice there was only one more Circus after this date. This occurred on 8 November when relatively heavy losses were experienced. Thereafter Circus operations were further reduced to three per month but this was made irrelevant by the weather and a direction received from the War Cabinet to conserve resources in order to build up strong forces by the spring of 1942. Another factor was the entry of the USA into the war in December which was liable to affect the supply of American aircraft and lead to equipment shortages. As a result of these restrictions Sholto Douglas ordered that no more Circus operations were to be flown without his permission.

In his summing up of the Circus offensive in 1941 Sholto Douglas gave his objectives as follows:

1) To wrest the initiative from the enemy for the sake of the great moral and tactical advantages bestowed by its possession.
2) In co-operation with Bomber and Coastal Commands to prevent the enemy from withdrawing any more flying units from the Western Front after the middle of June.
3) To induce the enemy to return some of the units already withdrawn by that time thus weakening his offensive capacity on the Eastern Front.

It was concluded that objective number one was achieved within a few months of the opening of the offensive. By the spring of 1941 the initiative in major daylight operations had passed from the Germans, who did not subsequently regain it. Objective number two was also achieved, inasmuch as the Germans did in fact retain on the Western Front throughout the second half of 1941 approximately the same first line fighter force as was present in the late spring. It was also noted that the two *Geschwader* that remained in France were of particularly high quality and that these might have been usefully employed elsewhere. It was recognised that the Germans would have retained a substantial defensive force in any case, but it was estimated that JG 2 and JG 26 represented roughly one third of the total establishment of German first line single-engined fighters. Objective number three was not achieved as any movements between East and West that did occur were by way of exchange rather than reinforcement.

The overall conclusion of the Circus offensive was that it had been responsible for a substantial attrition of the German fighter force but at considerable cost to the RAF. However such an effect could not, by its very nature, be other than transitory so long as the enemy's means of replacement remained intact; for any slackening of the offensive, whether caused by bad weather or the RAF's own losses, would enable the Germans to restore the situation relatively quickly. One of the clearest lessons, as far as the RAF was concerned, was that fighters operating from this country over northern France could, at a sufficient cost, inflict such losses on the opposing fighter force as would bring about local and temporary air superiority. It was also felt that the events of 1941, although they had inevitably been indecisive, had provided valuable experience which would be useful for future operations.

When considering the report that Sholto Douglas produced one cannot help but think that several of his statements were rather disingenuous. The basic tenet of 'Big Wing' theory was that the opposing enemy force would suffer defeat in the face of a numerically superior foe. Even by mid June 1941 Fighter Command could put well in excess of twenty squadrons of fighters in the air over northern France, a force which amounted to over 300 aircraft, considerably more than the strength of JG 2 and JG 26 put together. There can be little doubt that the main aim of Fighter Command was to inflict a significant defeat on the *Luftwaffe* in a battle of attrition but during the course of the year they were consistently out-scored by a ratio of four to one, a fact that Sholto Douglas would have known about at the time due to Ultra decrypts of German requests for replacement aircraft.

It is interesting to note that the main aim of Fighter Command was to 'seize the initiative' from the Germans. After the Battle of Britain this was a laudable objective in that there was no reason to believe that the Germans would not launch another offensive against Britain in 1941. Once it became apparent that attention was being switched to the Soviet Union and forces were being transferred to the Eastern Front however there was little chance of the Germans seizing anything in Western Europe. The fact that Sholto Douglas sought recognition for having 'seized' the initiative merely shows his political skills as he attempted to take credit for something that would have happened anyway!

It was also claimed that Fighter Command, by its actions during 1941, had prevented further reinforcing of the Eastern Front at the expense of the west. It is difficult to accept this as the combined total of fighters available to JG 2 and JG 26 probably amounted to no more than 250 aircraft of which a significant proportion at any one time would not be available due to unserviceability. With these they had to protect the coastline of the whole of northern France from Dunkirk to Brest, a distance of over 400 miles. JG 2 in particular had a huge area to cover from the Seine to the Atlantic coast and individual *Gruppen* had to operate from whichever airfield was nearest to a potential target. It seems highly unlikely therefore that the western defences could have been denuded any further whatever the eventuality and so Fighter Command's assertion that it helped the Soviets in this respect seems unfounded. In its final aim of forcing units to withdraw from the east, Fighter Command recognised that it had failed.

In order to give a clearer insight into the RAF's operations over Northern France in 1941 it is proposed to take a detailed look at the last major operation to be flown before the end of the year (Circus 110 on 8 November). This will offer a further indication as to how the Circus operation had evolved throughout the year. It will also serve to highlight the difficulties of mounting this type of mission in which large numbers of aircraft were required to fit in to the overall plan with a high degree of precision, so that there were no weak areas that could be exploited by *Luftwaffe* fighters.

The objective for the main attack was the locomotive works at Lille but this was preceded by a co-ordinated strike by eight Hurricane bombers against a distillery at St Pol. It will be recalled that the Biggin Hill Wing took part in this phase of the operation and returned having lost five aircraft and four pilots [a Spitfire of the Tangmere Wing was also shot down at this time]. In addition a diversionary sweep was carried out by the North Weald Wing which approached the French coast to the east of Dunkirk before turning for home. The combined actions of these first two phases of the operation had the effect of getting about sixty German fighters into the air ahead of the attack on Lille which was timed to arrive thirty minutes later. This was exactly the kind of reaction that had been hoped for when the operation was put together.

The bombing force consisted of twelve Blenheims and was made up of six aircraft from 21 Squadron based at Watton and six of 82 Squadron from Bodney. The bombers and their escorts were supposed to rendezvous over Manston at 1130 hrs however the first of several miscalculations occurred when the Polish Northolt Wing, which had been designated as close escort, arrived ten minutes early. The Blenheims turned up five minutes later and even though they were five minutes early themselves, set course for France. They were also accompanied by the Polish Wing from 10 Group which provided escort cover. By the time that the Kenley Wing arrived over Manston (one minute early) to perform the duty of high cover, there was no sign of the bombers or their escorts and so wasted three minutes circling as they waited for them to arrive. Having used up precious fuel they headed out over the Channel in the hope that they might be able to catch up.

In the meantime the flight commander of one section of Blenheims experienced engine trouble over the Channel and turned back but was unfortunately followed by the other five aircraft that he was leading. This caused further confusion in that one of the Northolt squadrons turned back as well to provide cover and by the time it was realised what was happening had lost sight of the rest of the Wing. They then returned to their original heading but only saw their colleagues again when they were on their way back. By the time that the remaining Blenheims crossed the coast of France they were protected by only two escort squadrons and the Wing from 10 Group as the Kenley Wing was still not in contact.

The course flown by the bombers also gave cause for concern. They should have crossed the French coast five miles east of Dunkirk but actually made landfall between Calais and Gravelines. Then instead of heading towards Lille, they made for Arras and ended up bombing Gosnay in error. This was despite the fact that the Kenley Wing Leader later reported the weather to be fairly good and although there was some haze, he had been able to pick out St Omer from the coast and had no difficulty in finding his way to Lille. As the Blenheims turned over Arras the 10 Group Wing inexplicably turned inside them which put the Spitfires ahead of the aircraft they were supposed to be protecting and caused further bewilderment for the close escort squadrons. The Poles made no attempt to adjust their position and continued to fly ahead of the bombers for the remainder of the journey home. From this point in the operation the close escort squadrons of the Northolt Wing were constantly engaged.

Having been unable to join up with the Blenheims and their close escorts the Kenley Wing had made straight for the target area and had then wheeled westwards on seeing anti-aircraft bursts some way to the south-west of their position. They eventually picked up the bombers in the Bethune area and from that time onwards fulfilled their role as high cover. The top squadron of the Wing (No.452) suffered frequent attacks and owing to this and the delay at the beginning of the operation some of their aircraft began to run short of fuel. Two pilots were later forced to bale out over the Channel but were picked up.

During the withdrawal phase further support was to have been provided by the Hornchurch Wing plus another Wing of Spitfires which was to fly down from 12 Group. In the event fog at Hornchurch prevented their aircraft from getting airborne at the scheduled time so that the 12 Group squadrons were left with no alternative but to set out alone. They had originally been ordered to patrol at 20–23,000 ft but with the non-appearance of the Hornchurch Wing which was to have provided top cover this had been amended to 24–27,000 ft. Despite this they continued to fly at the lower height as they made for Dunkirk which had the effect of surrendering the tactical advantage to the German side. Worse was to follow as the Wing then flew within range of the Dunkirk flak batteries and although none of the Spitfires were hit, the formation was broken up which gave the opportunity to the 109s and 190s above to use their height advantage to dive down to pick off stragglers.

Following a slight improvement in the weather at Hornchurch one of its squadrons was able to take off and climbed over the Channel to an altitude of 28–30,000 ft from where it was able to provide protection for the 12 Group Wing. It was also in position to escort the bombers on their way home and later reported seeing attacks on the rear of the formation. Sections were dispatched to drive off these enemy aircraft but no claims were made.

In his report on Circus 110 AVM Leigh-Mallory concluded that on the main penetration the casualties inflicted on his squadrons were 'not high'. He also expressed the opinion that the German casualties were lower than normal as on this occasion the higher wings had not been in position 'to exploit the tactical advantage which the high escorting Wings normally have.' He stated that this operation could not be regarded as one of the more successful as the RAF had lost four aircraft for only three enemy aircraft destroyed but this conveniently ignores losses elsewhere. He was highly critical of both the Biggin Hill Wing and the Spitfires provided by 12 Group. In the case of the former he questioned the judgement of the leader (Jamie Rankin did not fly on this occasion) and as regards the 12 Group squadrons he emphasized the fact that they flew lower than they should have done and also flew over the Dunkirk flak area which was not necessary.

On reading this report one does not get the slightest impression that Leigh-Mallory was concerned that the strategy he had championed throughout the year was not working, even though the 'numbers game' for this particular operation showed that sixteen Spitfires had been lost for just two Fw 190s shot down [actual claims were five destroyed plus three probably destroyed and five damaged but the true picture would have been known from *Luftwaffe* replacement requests obtained via Ultra]. Of the RAF losses, eight pilots had been killed, five had been taken as prisoners of war and only three were safe. More worryingly, among the casualties were a Wing Commander and three Squadron Leaders, experienced pilots that Fighter Command could ill afford to lose.

This operation highlighted the fact that each element of a Circus operation was dependent on the other and a missed rendezvous or a fogbound airfield was liable to have serious consequences for the other squadrons. It also showed that recent operational experience was vital as the 12 Group squadrons were led by thirty-three year old W/C D.R. Scott AFC who was flying on his first offensive sortie. Not only did he fly at the wrong height, his handling of the Wing was poor in that his turns were made too tightly so that aircraft on the outside of the formation were unable to maintain their position. This situation was then exacerbated by getting too close to the flak defences at Dunkirk. As they orbited above, the Fw 190As of II/JG 26 led by Hptm Joachim Muncheberg could not believe what they were seeing and immediately dived onto 412 Squadron which was acting as top cover for the rest of the Wing. In a matter of seconds three Spitfires were shot down including S/L C. Bushell who was killed. W/C Scott went the same way and it has been reported that his last radio message was 'I guess I'm too old for this boys'.

The Poles of the escort squadrons lost four aircraft shot down and amongst this number were the aircraft flown by S/L W. Szczesniewski, the C.O. of 315 Squadron and S/L W. Wilczewski of 316 Squadron both of whom became PoWs. As already stated the German losses amounted to two Fw 190As, Uffz Karlheinz Kern of JG 26's 4th Staffel was killed while attempting a crash-landing near Dunkirk and Oblt Theo Lindemann, the Adjutant of II/JG 26, was badly injured when he tried to land his burning aircraft not far from where Kern had crashed. Three other aircraft suffered damage in force-landings although it is not certain if these incidents were combat related. The Bf 109Fs of JG 2 also took part in the battle but no losses were reported.

The assertion made by Leigh-Mallory that his high escort Wings usually had tactical advantage over the defending fighters is not borne out in pilots' combat reports, nor is there any sign of this supposed superiority in the profit and loss account because, as already stated, the *Luftwaffe* consistently outscored the RAF by around four to one throughout 1941. This was exactly the opposite of what Leigh-Mallory had hoped for when he embarked on his offensive against the German fighter force in northern France at the beginning of the year. In some respects the roles that had been apparent during the Battle of Britain were reversed, the obvious one being that the Germans were now fighting over territory that they held themselves. One big difference however was that during the battles over southern England the RAF had been forced to engage each raid as it appeared as the destructive power of the bomber formations gave them no choice. As the offensive element of a typical Circus operation consisted of a dozen or so Blenheims, each dropping four 250 lb bombs from around 17,000 ft, the Germans knew that the damage that could be caused by these aircraft would not be extensive and thus they had the luxury of being able to decide when they engaged, if at all. The defending German formations were also led by experienced leaders who even if they did not have height advantage were extremely adept at staying out of trouble.

One of the decisive factors in the RAF's victory of the previous year had been the use of radar and by 1941 the Germans had an equivalent system operating in northern France. This had been developed in the late 1930s in parallel with the British system however each country tended to be complacent about the achievements of the other. In Britain it was thought that the Germans knew very little about radar but the arrival of the Oslo Report in 1939 suggested that development of an early warning system might be rather more advanced than had been envisaged. This document was compiled by Hans Ferdinand Mayer, a telecommunications director at Siemens who was opposed to the Nazi regime. Its contents included details of the radar systems that had been developed by the Germans and although it was initially treated with considerable suspicion by the British the document was eventually proved to be genuine.

During 1940 a new German code name 'Freya' began to appear in decoded messages sent by the Enigma encrypting device in connection with German intercepts of British aircraft. Over the next few months further evidence was compiled and eventualy the tell-tale pulse signals were picked up. The Freya system operated on 120MHz (around 2½ metres) which was relatively long and provided range and bearing. A second radar known as Wurzburg was also developed and this operated on a much shorter wavelength of around 553MHz (54 centimetres). This was a very advanced system for the time and provided height information for use by flak batteries and at night by searchlights and night-fighters. With the setting up of a command and control system to process the information received from the radar stations and direct fighters onto their targets, the Germans were well equipped to deal with the RAF's incursions into northern France in 1941.

They were also well equipped when it came to the airborne assets at their disposal. The principal adversary of RAF Fighter Command throughout 1941 was the Messerschmitt Bf 109, initially the E or Emil variant, however during the first half of the year this was gradually replaced by the F or Friedrich. In the last four months of the year the second-generation Focke-Wulf Fw 190A was also encountered in small numbers. Although the Spitfire II/V possessed similar or superior performance to the Bf 109E/F in several respects it lost out in terms of altitude performance and vertical penetration which was of crucial importance in the dogfights that took place over northern France. From the very early days of air fighting it had been recognised that he who had the advantage of height controlled the battle and the combination of an early warning radar system, together with the excellent climb performance and superior service ceiling of the 109 meant that even the RAF's high cover Wings rarely had height advantage over their adversaries. Even if they did it was often a ploy on the part of the Germans as a section would be used as bait while a larger formation waited up-sun for an opportunity to strike. The 109 was also blessed with better dive performance than the Spitfire V and a frequent *Luftwaffe* tactic was to carry out a single pass attack in a steep dive before either continuing the dive to low level or zoom climbing back to altitude.

On one occasion high over northern France Sgt Walter 'Johnnie' Johnston of 92 Squadron witnessed a potentially demoralising demonstration of the Bf 109F's superiority at altitude. On this particular day Jamie Rankin was leading the squadron as the twelve Spitfires flew at an altitude in excess of 30,000 ft. At this sort of height the Mark V was well outside its comfort zone and all the squadron's aircraft were hanging on their props with the pilots casting anxious glances at their airspeed indicators as the pointer wound backwards close to the stalling speed. Out of the corner of his eye he sensed movement and looking to his right was amazed to see a Bf 109F moving in to join up with the RAF fighters. The German pilot held his position for some time and appeared almost to be mocking his opponents. He knew that he was perfectly safe as if any of the Spitfires had attempted to attack him they would immediately have stalled and would have lost considerable height before regaining control. After satisfying his curiosity the German pilot accelerated away in a climb leaving Johnston thinking just what he would give to be able to fly an aircraft that could perform like that.

If this was not bad enough the advent of the Fw 190A made the RAF's job even more difficult. Although it did not posses the altitude performance of the Messerschmitt it more than made up for this in superior speed and rate of roll which put the Spitfire V at a serious disadvantage. Due to technical difficulties, in particular cooling of its fourteen cylinder two-row BMW 801 radial engine, its introduction to service with JG 26 was protracted and it did not play a significant part in the air war in 1941.

As well as operating aircraft that were superior in several key aspects of performance and under a very efficient early warning system, JG 2 and JG 26 possessed some of the *Luftwaffe's* most experienced fighter pilots. Following the death of Hptm Wilhelm Balthasar on 3 July 1941 the command of JG 2 went to Hptm Walter Oesau who returned from the Eastern Front. Oesau was one of the first fighter pilots to be sent to fight in the Spanish Civil War and had also taken part in the French campaign and the Battle of Britian. On joining JG 2 he was only six victories away from his century. Other pilots included Hptm Hans 'Assi' Hahn who led III Gruppe. During the course of 1941 he was to account for twenty-eight RAF aircraft, all of which were single-engined fighters. He was to survive the war with a score of 108. Lt Erich Rudorffer began his career with JG 2 on 1 November 1939 and was to remain with the unit until mid-1943. He was also very successful in 1941 and shot down twenty-one RAF aircraft, although by the end of the war his victory tally stood at 224 making him the seventh highest scoring ace. Another top scoring pilot in 1941 was Oblt Egon Mayer who shot down twenty-five which, apart from one Blenheim and one Hurricane, were all Spitfires. Also of note are Oblt Rudolf 'Rudi' Pflanz who accounted for eighteen RAF fighters in 1941 and Hptm Karl-Heinz Greisert who shot down ten.

It was a similar situation at JG 26 which was led by Oberstlt Adolf Galland. Like Oesau, Galland had gained valuable experience in Spain before taking part in the Battle of France. He was particularly successful during the Battle of Britain where he was credited with having shot down thirty-six RAF fighters and during 1941 he accounted for a further thirty-eight. Galland remained with JG 26 until 22 November 1941 when he was named General der Jagdflieger. By coincidence his total for the year was matched by Hptm Josef 'Pips' Priller the leader of JG 26's 1st Staffel. Priller had previously flown with JG 51 and whilst flying with this unit he shot down twenty aircraft commencing with a Spitfire over Dunkirk. He was posted to 1/JG 26 on 20 November 1940 and by the end of the following year his score stood at fifty-eight (Priller was another high-scoring German ace to survive the war with 101 victories). Other notables on JG 26 included Oblt Johannes Seifert with sixteen kills in 1941 and Oblt Gustav 'Micky' Sprick with eight. The latter was killed on 28 June 1941 in similar circumstances to Wilhelm Balthasar of JG 2 when the wing of his Bf 109F broke during an evasive manoeuvre. Although he only spent the last four months of the year flying in northern France, Oblt Joachim Muncheberg brought valuable combat experience to the theatre having recently fought over Malta with JG 26's 7th Staffel which had been based in Sicily. On his arrival his score stood at forty-eight and by the end of the year it had risen to sixty-two.

From the above it can be seen that the *Luftwaffe* made no attempt to transfer their top pilots away from the west to fight in the east. Indeed in some cases, notably that of Walter Oseau who was moved from JG 3 to JG 2, the reverse was the case. This was taken by Fighter Command as a positive outcome of their actions during 1941 however this might be overstating the case somewhat. Even Sholto Douglas had to admit that by early October the situation on the Eastern Front had reached a stage at which it was 'unlikely to be materially affected by the Circus offensive'.

So what indeed had been achieved during the hard fought air battles over northern France in 1941? Clearly there was no strategic change as the locally-based *Luftwaffe* units were not defeated and the losses inflicted on the RAF, although heavy, were readily sustainable as replacement pilots and aircraft were available. Any benefits were thus of a secondary nature but even here it is difficult to credit Fighter Command with having achieved anything significant. The RAF justified its offensive by stating that it had taken the initiative from the Germans in the west but this ignores the fact that as soon as the decision was made to attack the Soviet Union this was surrendered in any case. It was also hoped to prevent further fighter units being withdrawn to the east and the fact that they were not was also seen by Fighter Command as a positive outcome of its strategy. However the Germans had to leave sufficient forces in the west to defend the Channel coast and the Brest peninsula, in particular its naval bases which were bound to come under periodic attack. As already stated they could not contemplate reducing their forces in the west any further considering the length of coastline that needed to be protected.

Fighter Command also claimed to have won air superiority over northern France and in the strict definition of the term this was true as they could conduct operations at times of their choosing without prohibitive interference by the opposition. However the benefits of this situation were not decisive as the offensive element of Circus operations could only inflict minimal damage. Because of this the *Luftwaffe* was not obliged to commit its forces to stopping these attacks as had been the case with the RAF during the Battle of Britain. Instead they were content to attack on the fringes or take advantage of any indiscipline to pick off stragglers. By doing so large scale air battles were not a regular occurrence which had the effect of denying the RAF the opportunity to inflict a significant defeat on the German side by taking advantage of its numerical superiority.

Although it was generally recognised that the claims contained in pilots' combat reports would not be an accurate figure of actual German losses this did not prevent Leigh-Mallory from producing statistical reviews based on this data. In early September he estimated that from the start of the year 11 Group squadrons had shot down 444 German aircraft with another 192 probably destroyed and 240 damaged. In fact *Luftwaffe* losses for the whole year were less than 200 and in the period from the beginning of June to the end of December, which included the most intensive fighting, were actually 128 from all causes. Over this same timescale RAF Fighter Command as a whole lost 572 single-engined day fighters with 314 pilots being killed and 121 taken prisoner. Losses of this magnitude were extremely serious, the most worrying aspect being the number of senior pilots (flight commander and above) who were being shot down. From June 1941 the RAF lost thirty Flight Lieutenants either killed or taken prisoner, plus twenty Squadron Leaders, six Wing Commanders and one Group Captain.

Despite these setbacks it has to be said that Fighter Command was stronger at the end of 1941 than it had been at the start of the year which showed how successful the expansion of the pilot training organisation had been. At the end of the Battle of Britain there were fifty-two operational squadrons in the day fighter role however only about half could be considered as first-line squadrons. As it was thought likely that the Germans would attempt another aerial assault on Britain in 1941 Sholto Douglas requested that his forces be increased to eighty squadrons but due to the needs of other commands, this figure was reduced to sixty-four. In the event of course Hitler sent his forces into the Soviet Union in June 1941 and although this meant that there would not be large scale attacks on Britain in the immediate future, the strength of the Soviet resistance could not be foreseen. To Sholto Douglas it seemed likely that the Germans might well bring the Eastern campaign to a successful conclusion within a measureable time, in which case there would probably be a renewal of the daylight offensive in the west. Accordingly further additions were made to the day fighter force so that by the end of 1941 Fighter Command had seventy-five squadrons at its disposal [by way of comparison there were only thirty-four fighter squadrons available for the defence of the Middle and Far East].

Given the decision to retain a large force of day fighters in the UK these had to be used in such a way as to uphold pilots' morale and to quench their desire for action. The question was could some of these squadrons have been put to better use in other theatres, notably Malta and North Africa. The main concern for Sholto Douglas was that the Germans would wrap up the Soviet campaign relatively quickly in which case they would be able to turn their attention to Britain once again. For this to happen the Soviet Union would have had to be defeated before the onset of winter otherwise the war on the eastern front would probably drag on into the following year. Even if the Germans had been successful it is unlikely that they would have attempted to attack Britain again until the summer of 1942. However the war could have been effectively lost before this if the island of Malta had fallen.

Malta was strategically significant in that it was Britain's only base in the Mediterranean from which to attack German supply lines to North Africa. Without Malta it would only have been a matter of time before the Axis forces were victorious in North Africa which would have led to the removal of British influence in Egypt and the prospect of the Germans controlling the supply of oil from the Middle East. In 1941 the island came under attack from German forces as well as Italian and, ironically, this did lead to forces being withdrawn from the eastern front as *Luftlotte* 2 moved to Sicily from the Moscow sector in November. Malta was to remain under British control but it was a close run thing and the term 'narrow margin' which became synonymous with victory in the Battle of Britain could equally be applied to the heroic struggle to save this vital base. There are many more parallels, not least that the man who finally oversaw the island's survival was Air Vice-Marshal Sir Keith Park who used the same successful tactics that he had employed in 1940 to save Britain with the minimal forces at his disposal.

While Sholto Douglas and Leigh-Mallory were engrossed in their offensive over northern France the crucial air battles were being fought in the Mediterranean. The fact that units were transferred to Sicily from the eastern front shows that the Germans fully appreciated the significance of Malta which was in marked contrast to the piecemeal reinforcements made by the RAF in 1941 for the island's air defence. The AOC-in-C of Fighter Command and his deputy could attempt to justify their policy by playing the 'numbers game' and by claiming several key advantages, but in doing so they ensured that the RAF maintained considerable strength where it was not needed and thereby risked the loss of a vital asset. The facts are that the RAF was out-scored by four to one in the air battles over northern France. At the same time it did not wrest the initiative from the *Luftwaffe* as this was willingly given up and the strategy adopted did not have the slightest effect on the eastern front. Even the assertion that the Circuses of 1941 paved the way for the air operations after D-Day is wide of the mark as the use of tactical air power in 1944 had its origins in the deserts of North Africa. Given all of this it seems that the Germans were not far from the truth when they referred to the non-stop offensive as the nonsense offensive.

Envoi

The following section looks at pilots' careers after they left the Biggin Hill Wing.

'Dizzy' Allen – Left 66 Squadron at the end of 1941 and was posted to 286 Squadron on anti-aircraft co-operation duties for a rest. After the war he commanded 1 and 43 Squadrons and undertook various staff appointments until retiring from the service in January 1965 as a Wing Commander. He wrote several books and died on 31 May 1987.

Philip Archer – After serving with 92 Squadron he flew with 416 Squadron in 1942 and was awarded a DFC in September of that year. He was designated to take over command of 402 Squadron but was killed on 17 June 1943 when attached to 421 Squadron. His Spitfire IX (LZ996) was shot down by Fw 190s of JG 26 near St Omer.

Denis Barnham – At the end of 1941 he was posted to 154 Squadron and joined 601 Squadron in April 1942 as a flight commander. He flew with this unit from Malta and claimed four enemy aircraft destroyed before being flown back to the UK in June due to ill health. He later instructed at 57 OTU but was invalided out of the service in April 1945 after suffering a duodenal ulcer. An accomplished artist he became Art Master at Epsom College and died on 16 April 1981.

Tony Barton – After receiving a DFC in early 1942 he was sent to Malta and flew with 126 Squadron becoming its C.O. in April 1942. He returned to the UK in August 1942 having been awarded a bar to his DFC. He then flew with 53 OTU at Llandow but was killed in a flying accident on 4 April 1943.

Eric Barwell – Was posted to 125 Squadron in July 1941 and took over command six months later but reverted to flight commander when the unit received Beaufighters in February 1942. Apart from a spell with HQ, 10 Group he remained with this unit until August 1944 by which time it was flying Mosquito XVIIs. Towards the end of the war he took over as the leader of 148 Wing and also commanded 264 Squadron for a short time before leaving the RAF in September 1945. He died on 12 December 2007.

Philip 'Dickie' Barwell – Was badly injured in early 1942 when the engine of his Spitfire cut on take-off and he broke his back in the subsequent crash landing. Although his back was encased in plaster he continued to fly. On 1 July 1942 he was flying with Bobby Oxspring when they were jumped by Spitfires of the Tangmere Wing. Barwell was shot down in error and was killed.

Percy Beake – Later flew Bell Airacobras for a short time with 601 Squadron before instructing at 58 OTU. He returned to operations in December 1942 with 193 Squadron on Typhoons and later commanded 164 Squadron, shooting down an Fw 190 shortly after D-Day. On completion of his tour he was posted to the Fighter Leaders' School at Milfield as an instructor. He left the RAF in 1946 with the rank of Squadron Leader having been awarded a DFC.

Don Blakeslee – Later flew with the USAAF and commanded the 335th Fighter Squadron on P-47 Thunderbolts. Promoted to Lieutenant-Colonel in May 1943 he commanded the 4th Fighter Group and eventually returned to the USA in October 1944 having flown nearly 500 missions. He continued to serve in the

USAAF/USAF after the war and led the 31st Fighter Group and the 27th Fighter Wing, flying F-84 Thunderjets with the latter unit in Korea. He retired from the service in April 1965.

'Bogle' Bodie – Was posted to 310 (Czech) Squadron in March 1941 as a flight commander before taking over a flight on 152 Squadron three months later. He was killed on 24 February 1942 when he crashed during low level aerobatics.

Eric Bocock – Stayed with 72 Squadron until March 1942 when he was posted to 602 Squadron as a flight commander. He secured five combat victories with this squadron and was awarded a DFC. He continued to serve after the war but was killed on 13 September 1946 when his Meteor III broke up during a slow roll.

Roger Boulding – On release from PoW camp in 1945 he converted onto Lancaster bombers and took over the command of 35 Squadron in June 1947. In the 1950s he returned to fighters and commanded 249 Squadron in Egypt. He retired from the RAF in November 1966 to run a hotel and died on 2 March 1993.

Bob Boyd – At the end of his tour with 609 Squadron he was commissioned and later joined 41 Squadron to fly the Spitfire XII. He was shot down and killed on 6 September 1943 when his aircraft was hit by flak during a Ramrod operation to the area around Rouen.

Donald Carlson – After service with 58 OTU, he commanded 154 Squadron in March 1942 and was awarded a DFC. He then continued to lead 154 after it was transferred to the Middle East. Subsequently he became C.O. of 32 Squadron and also commanded Bone airfield in Algeria. He continued to serve in the RAF post-war and retired as a Squadron Leader in 1958. He died on 17 August 1983.

Baudouin de Hemptinne – Was killed on 5 May 1942 when serving with 122 Squadron. He was shot down by an Fw 190 of JG 26 near Ypres during Circus 157.

Francois de Spirlet – Remained with 609 Squadron when the unit converted to the Hawker Typhoon. He was killed on 26 June 1942 when a tyre burst on take-off and he collided with another aircraft.

Neville Duke – Was posted to 112 Squadron in the Middle East in November 1941 and was to become one of the RAF's top scoring pilots with twenty-six confirmed victories. He flew with 92 Squadron once again in the desert and later commanded 145 Squadron. On return to the UK in early 1945 he became a production test pilot with Hawker Aircraft and in 1951 was promoted as Chief Test Pilot. He was to be particularly associated with the Hawker Hunter and in 1953 captured the World Air Speed Record. A back injury forced his retirement from testing but he continued to fly and retained interests in aviation. He died on 7 April 2007 after becoming unwell when flying his Grumman AA-5B.

Myles Duke-Woolley – Continued to lead 124 Squadron until June 1942 by which time he had received a bar to his DFC. He then took over the Debden Wing and later spent time at HQ, 8th US Bomber Command before moving to 84 Group, 2 TAF. After the war he took several staff appointments and also commanded Acklington and Debden before retiring from the service with the rank of Group Captain. He died on 16 October 1991.

Yvan Du Monceau – Became a flight commander with 350 Squadron in March 1942. After a rest period as an instructor at 61 OTU, Rednal, he joined 349 Squadron in May 1943 as its C.O. and remained with this unit until July 1944. He was awarded a bar to his DFC. After the war he helped form the new Belgian Air Force and remained in the service until his retirement in January 1973 when

162

his rank was Major General. His last post was as Commander of the Belgian Tactical Air Force. He died in 1984 from cancer.

Ronnie Fokes – Became tour expired in May 1941 and joined 53 OTU at Heston as an instructor. Following a short spell at CFS he returned to Heston but to 61 OTU. His second tour commenced with 154 Squadron but was transferred to 56 Squadron in March 1942 where he flew Hawker Typhoons. After a time as a test pilot at Gloster Aircraft he returned to operations with 193 Squadron and was then given the command of 257 Squadron. On 12 June 1944 he was killed when he attempted to bale out of his Typhoon after being hit by flak near Caen.

Athol Forbes – Remained with 66 Squadron until October 1941 before taking a staff post at 10 Group HQ. As a Wing Commander he was sent to India in July 1943 and served with 165 Wing. After the war he became SASO at HQ 221 Group and left the service in 1948 as a Group Captain. He received a bar to his DFC and was also awarded an OBE. He died in 1981.

Johnnie Freeborn – Was posted to 57 OTU as an instructor in June 1941 before commencing a second tour as a flight commander with 602 Squadron. He took over as C.O. of 118 Squadron at Coltishall in June 1943 and remained with this unit for the next twelve months. Promoted to Wing Commander, his last posting was as leader of 286 Wing in Italy. He retired from the service in 1946 and is currently living in retirement in Southport.

George 'Sheep' Gilroy – Left 609 Squadron in May 1942 having been awarded a bar to his DFC. Was posted as leader of 324 Wing in Tunisia in November 1942 and survived a mid-air collison on 28 January 1943 that led to the death of F/L E.B. Mortimer-Rose. He returned to the UK in late 1943 having received a DSO. On promotion to Group Captain he commanded Wittering and Blakelow before becoming the C.O. of 603 Squadron RAuxAF in the immediate post war years. He later returned to sheep farming in Scotland and died on 25 March 1995.

Ralph 'Tich' Havercroft – Left 92 Squadron in July 1941 but did not return to operations after suffering from a nervous breakdown. Instead he became a test pilot at Duxford before attending the course at ETPS and flying with Supermarines and at Boscombe Down. After a trip to the USA he became an instructor at ETPS and was awarded an AFC. He later commanded the Handling Squadron at Manby and left the RAF in June 1963. He died on 7 May 1995.

Bob Holland – After leaving Biggin Hill he remained with 91 Squadron until November 1941 when he was sent to 61 OTU. His second tour was as a flight commander with 615 Squadron commencing in February 1942 and he served with this unit in the Far East. He went on to command 607 Squadron before returning to 615 as its C.O. He stayed in the RAF post war and died on 17 November 1954.

Desmond Hughes – Later flew as a flight commander with 125 Squadron on Beaufighters before being sent to the Middle East to join 600 Squadron. He went on to command 604 Squadron and by the end of the war his score stood at eighteen confirmed destroyed plus one shared. He stayed in the RAF after the war and rose to high rank becoming an Air Vice-Marshal in 1967. His final post before retirement in 1974 was as SASO, Near East Air Force. He died on 11 January 1992.

'David' Hughes-Rees – After being shot down he returned to 609 Squadron in November 1941 and was commissioned the following month. He left 609 in March 1942 and became an instructor at 73 OTU, Abu Sueir in Egypt. He contracted poliomylitis and died on 30 April 1943 at the age of twenty-two.

Walter 'Johnnie' Johnston – Became an instructor at 61 OTU in December 1941 before moving to the Central Gunnery School at Sutton Bridge. He returned to operations with 234 Squadron in 1943 and flew with this unit over the D-Day period when he survived being shot down by flak. His final post in the RAF was as Chief Flying Instructor with No.1330 Conversion Unit at Bilbeis in Egypt. He left the service as a Squadron Leader but continued to fly with the Volunteer Reserve until 1959. At the time of writing he lives in Cornwall.

Johnny Kent – In 1941 he was Wing Leader at Northolt and then Kenley but returned to 53 OTU as CFI at the end of the year. He went on to command Church Fenton and held a number of staff posts including planning the air operations for the recovery of the Greek islands. After the war he was Chief Test Pilot at Farnborough for a time and also commanded Odiham and Tangmere. He left the service in December 1956 and died on 7 October 1985.

Don Kingaby – Ended the war as a Wing Commander having also served with 111, 64 and 122 Squadrons. The only RAF pilot to be awarded three DFMs, he also received the DSO, the American DFC and a Belgian *Croix de Guerre*. He remained in the RAF after the war and commanded 72 Squadron on de Havilland Vampires. He left the service in 1958 and eventually emigrated to the USA where he died in 1990 after a long illness.

Brian Kingcome – Posted initially as an instructor at 61 OTU, he later commanded 72 Squadron before becoming Wing Leader at Kenley. He also commanded the Fighters Leaders' School and 244 Wing in the Mediterranean theatre. After the war he took up several staff appointments but contracted tuberculosis in 1950 and had to leave the RAF in 1954. At the time of his retirement he was a Group Captain and had been awarded the DFC and bar and DSO. He died in February 1994.

Kazimierz Kosinski – Was posted to 302 Squadron in November 1941 as a flight commander. On 26 January 1942 he was shot down and killed by Oblt Erich Leie of JG 2 during a shipping reconnaissance south of Rame Head.

Jaroslav Kulhanek – Continued to serve with 124 Squadron but was shot down and killed by an Fw 190A of II/JG 26 on 13 March 1942 during Circus 114.

Jerrold Le Cheminant – Remained with 92 Squadron until September 1941 when he became an instructor at 53 OTU, Llandow. He was commissioned in May 1942 and joined 72 Squadron in North Africa. On 2 December 1942 he was shot down by German 'ace' Oblt Kurt Buhligen of II/JG 2 but was unhurt. During his time with 72 Squadron he destroyed three Bf 109s before being posted to 232 Squadron as a flight commander in April 1943. He was awarded a DFC the following month. After the war he continued to serve in the RAF and retired in 1972 as a Wing Commander having also received an OBE.

Omer Levesque – Was commissioned in early 1942 but was shot down and taken prisoner on 12 February during the air operations over the Channel in connection with the breakout by the *Scharnhorst* and *Gneisenau*. He spent the rest of the war in Stalag Luft III but rejoined the RCAF after the war and flew in Korea on attachment to the USAF where he shot down a MiG-15. He retired from the RCAF in 1965.

'Sailer' Malan – After his time as Wing Leader at Biggin Hill, Malan was CFI at 58 OTU at Grangemouth before undertaking a lecture tour of the USA. On his return he took over command of the Central Gunnery School at Sutton Bridge and then returned to Biggin in 1943 for a ten month tour as station commander. His posts for the remainder of the war were as C.O. of 19 Fighter Wing of 2 TAF,

145 (Free French) Wing and the Advanced Gunnery School at Catfoss. He was released from the RAF in 1946 and returned to South Africa but was diagnosed with Parkinson's disease in the 1950s and died in 1963.

Stanley Meares – Was awarded a DFC on 22 July 1941 and a month later he was posted to 71 'Eagle' Squadron as C.O. On 15 November 1941 his Spitfire was in collision with that flown by P/O R.O. Scarborough and both pilots were killed.

Dickie Milne – Was also to command 222 Squadron and in January 1943 returned to Biggin Hill as Wing Leader. He was shot down on 14 March by Fw 190s of JG 26 and spent the rest of the war as a prisoner. On his release he became Wing Leader at North Weald but left the RAF in 1946 to work for English Electric. He continued to work in the aircraft industry in military aircraft sales and was also involved in several licence-building agreements.

Don Morrison – Continued to fly with 401 Squadron and was shot down during the Dieppe Raid on 19 August 1942, however he was picked up and returned to his unit. He became a flight commander the following month only to be shot down and badly wounded on 8 November. Whilst in hospital he had a leg amputated. He was repatriated in October 1943 (along with **Don Dougall** ex 92 Squadron) and returned to Canada, becoming an instructor at 20 EFTS, Oshawa. After the war he worked for Trans Canada Airways. He died on 28 January 1994.

Roy Mottram – Was posted to 54 Squadron as a flight commander in June 1941 but was shot down and killed by a Bf 109 of JG 2 on 31 August of that year during a sweep over northern France.

Tony Mould – Was commissioned in May 1941 and after leaving 74 Squadron re-trained as a night-fighter pilot. He was killed on 20 January 1943 (along with his navigator P/O W. Fisher) when his Mosquito II crashed during an interception patrol near Bradwell Bay.

Peter Nash – Left 609 Squadron in January 1942 having been commissioned and joined 249 Squadron in Malta two months later. He had considerable combat success and by 16 May his score was ten confirmed destroyed plus one shared. On the following day he claimed a Bf 109F of 5/JG 53 but was shot down and killed near Dingli on Malta'a west coast.

Jean 'Pyker' Offenberg – Remained with 609 Squadron throughout the rest of 1941. On 22 January 1942 a 92 Squadron pilot carried out a practice attack on Offenberg's Spitfire but in doing so collided with it and removed its tail section. Offenberg was unable to get out and was killed when his aircraft dived into the ground.

Peter Olver – Was posted to the Middle East in mid-1942 to join 213 Squadron. He then became a flight commander on 238 Squadron before being posted back to 213 as a supernumery Squadron Leader. He went on to lead No.1 (SAAF) Squadron and took over 244 Wing following the death of W/C Ian Gleed. He was shot down over Sicily and taken prisoner on 11 July 1943. In the post-war years he lived for a time in Kenya before returning to the UK to farm in Wiltshire.

Vicki Ortmans – After being shot down over the Channel on 21 October 1941 he spent thirty-six hours in a dinghy before being rescued by the Germans and taken prisoner. After the war he flew once again for the Belgian Air Force before joining Sabena. He was killed on 12 August 1950 when flying a Tiger Moth.

Bobby Oxspring – Commanded 91 Squadron in early 1942 and then led 72 Squadron with whom he had considerable combat success in the Middle East.

Before the end of the war he was leader of 24 Wing, 141 Wing and the Detling Wing. Post war he was C.O. of 54 Squadron on Vampires and led this unit's goodwill tour of Canada and the USA in 1948 which marked the first crossing of the Atlantic by jet fighters. He retired from the RAF in 1968, his last post being as the commander of Gatow airfield in Berlin. He died on 8 August 1989.

William Payne – Left 92 Squadron on 4 July 1941 to instruct at 53 OTU. He was promoted to Warrant Officer in August 1942 and the following month joined the Photographic Reconnaissance Unit as a supernumery. He was posted to 540 (PR) Squadron in November 1942 and to 541 Squadron at the end of the year. On 13 January 1943 he did not return from a mission to Norway when flying Spitfire PR.IV R7044.

John Pickering – Left 66 Squadron in April 1941 to be an instructor but returned to the unit in September having been promoted to Flight Leutenant. He was posted out again on 25 October 1941 and went to 53 OTU, Llandow. He was killed on 15 February 1942 when his Spitfire was in collision with that flown by **Bob Poulton** (see below).

Adolf Pietrasiak – Transferred to 308 Squadron in late July 1941 but was shot down over northern France on 19 August after claiming his seventh Bf 109. He was able to evade and returned to the UK via Spain and Gibralter. He went on to fly with 317 Squadron before returning to 308 Squadron in September 1943. He was killed on 29 November 1943 when he collided with his wingman over the Channel during Ramrod 339.

Bob Poulton – Became an instructor at 53 OTU, Llandow where he survived a mid-air collision on 15 February 1942 that killed F/L John Pickering (ex 66 Squadron). In March 1942 he joined 611 Squadron but was involved in a car accident and on recovery was posted to 64 Squadron, becoming a flight commander. He was also awarded a DFC. On 14 January 1944 he had to bale out of his Spitfire IX near Dieppe after engine failure and spent the rest of the war as a PoW. Although released from the RAF in 1946, he rejoined in 1951 and continued to serve until 1968.

Jamie Rankin – Returned to Biggin Hill in April 1942 for a second tour as Wing Leader. He commanded 15 Fighter Wing in 2 TAF in 1943 and then 125 Wing during the D-Day landings. He was awarded a DFC and bar and a DSO and bar. After the war he served in Dublin as Air Attache and as a Group Captain he commanded Duxford in the mid 1950s before retiring from the service in 1958. He died in Edinburgh many years ago.

Paul Richey – After commanding 74 Squadron for a short time he was given command of 609 Squadron in June 1942 flying Typhoons. He was promoted to Wing Commander in October 1942 and posted to the Far East but suffered a period of ill health and subsequently returned to the UK, serving with SHAEF until March 1945. After the war he commanded 601 Squadron RAuxAF. He died on 23 February 1989.

Tommy Rigler – Remained with 609 Squadron until May 1942 but was wounded when hit by a flak ship on 15 January 1942 during a Rhubarb operation. On recovery he flew with 610, 504, 229 and 603 Squadrons and ended the war with the rank of Squadron Leader. He was awarded a DFC in May 1945 and died in 1986.

Michael Robinson – After commanding RAF Manston, he returned to operations on 1 January 1942 as Wing Leader at Tangmere. At this time his victory tally stood at sixteen enemy aircraft destroyed plus four probables but before he could add to his score he was shot down and killed on 10 April 1942 (together with his wingman Maurice Choron) by Fw 190s of II/JG 26.

Jan Rogowski – Was posted to 308 Squadron in August 1941 before joining 1489 Flight in June 1942 for target towing duties. He returned to operations with 302 Squadron in June 1943 and then took an instructors course at 16 FTS at Newton. His third tour was with 306 Squadron commencing in June 1944 and flying Mustang IIIs he claimed three V-1 flying bombs with another two shared. He ended the war as a Warrant Officer with the Virtuti Militari (5th Class) and the Silver Cross of Merit. After the war he stayed in Britain and died on 17 August 1997.

Arthur Sanders – Continued to lead 264 Squadron until June 1941 when he was awarded a DFC. He was then promoted to Wing Commander as C.O. of 85 Squadron but was killed on 31 October 1941 when flying a Havoc on a night interception sortie over the Channel near Deal.

Eugene 'Strop' Seghers – Was killed on 26 July 1944 when flying with 91 Squadron. His Spitfire XIV (RM743) was in collision with a V-1 flying bomb north of Dungeness. At the time of his death he was a Flight Lieutenant and had been awarded a DFC.

Desmond Sheen – After leading 72 Squadron he commanded Manston, Skeabrae and Drem airfields. He left the RAF in 1946 but rejoined in 1950 and became Wing Leader at Leuchars in 1955. Subsequently he served in Transport Command and was later Air Advisor to the UK High Commissioner in New Delhi, India. On retiring from the RAF he worked for BAC/BAe. He died in April 2001.

Jaroslav Sika – Joined 310 Squadron in March 1942 and remained with this unit until July 1944. After the war he stayed in the RAF and flew Mosquito night-fighters with 25 Squadron.

Bob Spurdle – After leaving 74 Squadron in April 1941 he flew with 91 Squadron and also trained to fly Hurricanes from CAM ships. Transferring to the RNZAF he became a flight commander with 16 Squadron in the Pacific but returned to the European theatre in 1944 where he was to command 80 Squadron on Tempests. He ended the war as a Squadron Leader having been awarded the DSO, DFC and bar and returned to New Zealand where he began an engineering business. He was also a keen sailor. He died at Whitianga on 5 March 1994.

Cedric Stone – Was commissioned in October 1941 and awarded a DFM. He was posted to 73 Squadron in the Middle East in April 1942 but was shot down on 17 June by Oblt Hans-Joachim Marseille of I/JG 27 and injured his neck when baling out. Because of this he was not cleared to return to operations and was to spend the rest of the war as a ferry pilot.

Ted Thorn – Was promoted to Warrant Officer in October 1941 and posted to 32 Squadron. He was commissioned and commanded the unit from April-September 1942. He later flew with 169 Squadron as a flight commander and ended the war with DFM and bar, DFC and bar. He was killed on 12 February 1946 when the Meteor III he was flying dived into the ground out of cloud. Fred Barker, his former gunner, stayed with 264 Squadron until 1943 when he was sent to the Middle East as an air gunnery instructor. He was commissioned and left the RAF in 1946 with the rank of Flying Officer.

John Van Schaick – Was commissioned at the end of 1941 and was awarded a DFM. He joined 137 Squadron on Westland Whirlwinds as a flight commander and continued to fly with this unit until December 1942. He then instructed at 59 OTU, Milfield but was killed on 20 February 1943 during a low flying exercise in a Miles Master.

Trevor 'Wimpy' Wade – Was posted to 123 Squadron in June 1941 where he was awarded a DFC and later flew with 602 Squadron. In 1943 he became OC Flying at AFDU and for this work he received an AFC. He left the service as a Squadron Leader and in 1947 joined Hawker Aircraft as a test pilot. He was killed on 3 April 1951 when flying the Hawker P.1081.

Geoff Wellum – Flew with 52 OTU and 65 Squadron (as a flight commander) before joining 1435 Flight in Malta in August 1942. Here he suffered severe sinusitis and was flown back to the UK where he eventually joined Gloster Aircraft as a test pilot. He remained in the RAF after the war and retired in June 1961 to work in the City of London. He has since written a best-selling autobiography (First Light – Viking, 2002) and at the time of writing is living in Cornwall

Allan Wright – Another member of the Biggin Hill Wing to serve at the Central Gunnery School at Sutton Bridge, he later flew Beaufighters with 29 Squadron and achieved a night 'kill' on 3 April 1943 when he shot down a Ju 88. He went on to command the AFDU at Wittering and ended the war as a Wing Commander. Post war he stayed in the RAF and his last command was the Ballistic Missile Early Warning Station at RAF Fylingdales. He lives in retirement in Devon.

Air Combat Claims of the Biggin Hill Wing – 1941

Combat claims of squadrons operating from the satellite at Gravesend and the forward airfield at Manston are also included in the table.

Date	Pilot	Sqn	Type	Location	Dest	Prob	Dam
23/1/41	P/O R.H. Fokes	92	Bf 110	Nr Manston			½
23/1/41	Sgt D. Lloyd	92	Bf 110	Nr Manston			½
2/2/41	S/L A.G. Malan	74	Bf 109E	Boulogne	1		
2/2/41	Sgt A.D. Payne	74	Bf 109E	Nr Boulogne	1		
2/2/41	Sgt A.H. Smith	74	Bf 109E	Nr Boulogne		1	
3/2/41	P/O A.C. Bartley	92	He 111	Thames estuary	1		
5/2/41	S/L A.G. Malan	74	Do 215	Nr Dover	¼		
5/2/41	F/L J.C. Freeborn	74	Do 215	Nr Dover	¼		
5/2/41	P/O W. Armstrong	74	Do 215	Nr Dover	¼		
5/2/41	P/O P. Chesters	74	Do 215	Nr Dover	¼		
5/2/41	P/O R.H. Fokes	92	Ju 87	Manston	¼		
5/2/41	P/O C.H. Saunders	92	Ju 87	Manston	¼		
5/2/41	Sgt H. Bowen-Morris	92	Ju 87	Manston	¼		
5/2/41	Sgt Ream	92	Ju 87	Manston	¼		
14/2/41	P/O J.H. Pickering	66	Bf 109E	Nr Dover		1	
14/2/41	Sgt D.E. Kingaby	92	Bf 109E	Nr Cap Gris Nez	1		
22/2/41	P/O E.W.G. Churches	74	Bf 109E	30m E of Margate	½		
22/2/41	Sgt N. Morrison	74	Bf 109E	30m E of Margate	½		
1/3/41	P/O R.L Spurdle	74	Bf 109E	Cap Gris Nez	1		1
1/3/41	P/O R.L Spurdle	74	Bf 109E	Nr Ramsgate	1		
1/3/41	Sgt J.N. Glendinning	74	Bf 109E	Cap Gris Nez	1		
4/3/41	F/L J.C. Freeborn	74	Do 215	Nr Dunkirk			½
4/3/41	P/O H.R.G. Poulton	74	Do 215	Nr Dunkirk			½
13/3/41	F/L A.R. Wright	92	Bf 109E	South coast			2
18/3/41	P/O E.W.G. Churches	74	Bf 109E	SW of Folkstone	1		
19/3/41	P/O A.K. Ogilvie	609	Bf 109E	S of Dungeness			1
24/3/41	P/O R.L. Spurdle	74	Ju 88	Nr Ramagate		½	
24/3/41	Sgt W.P. Dales	74	Ju 88	Nr Ramsgate		½	
25/3/41	P/O R.L. Spurdle	74	Do 215	Nr Ramsgate			½
25/3/41	Sgt W.P. Dales	74	Do 215	Nr Ramsgate			½
27/3/41	S/L P.A. Wood	74	Bf 109E	Nr Dungeness	1		
6/4/41	F/L A.C. Bartley	74	Bf 109	St Omer area (on grd)			1

Date	Pilot	Sqn	Type	Location	Dest	Prob	Dam
6/4/41	P/O R.L. Spurdle	74	Bf 110	Nr St Omer	1		
7/4/41	Sgt J. Rogowski	74	Bf 109E	Cap Gris Nez	1		
7/4/41	P/O J. Howard	74	Bf 109E	Nr St Inglevert			1
7/4/41	P/O P. Chesters	74	Bf 109F	St Nicholas-at-Wade	1		
10/4/41	S/L J. Rankin	92	He 59	Nr Boulogne	1		
11/4/41	Sgt A.D. Payne	74	Bf 109	Nr Dover			1
19/4/41	S/L J. Rankin	92	Bf 109	Dungeness	½		
24/4/41	F/L J.B.H. Brunier	92	Bf 109	Dungeness	½		
24/4/41	P/O R.H. Fokes	92	Bf 109F	Off Cap Gris Nez	1		
26/4/41	Sgt E.A. Mould	74	Bf 109E	Nr Calais			1
28/4/41	P/O R.J.E. Boulding	74	Bf 109	Margate		1	1
7/5/41	P/O H.R.G. Poulton	74	Bf 109	North Foreland	1		
7/5/41	P/O W.J. Sandman	74	Bf 109	Broadstairs			1
7/5/41	S/L M.L. Robinson	609	Bf 109E	Channel, off Calais			1
8/5/41	P/O W. Armstrong	74	Bf 109	Nr Dungeness	1		
8/5/41	S/L M.L. Robinson	609	Bf 109E	Off Dungeness	2		
8/5/41	F/L J. Curchin	609	Bf 109	Off Dungeness	1½		
8/5/41	Sgt J.A. Hughes-Rees	609	Bf 109	Off Dungeness	½		
8/5/41	Sgt R.T.D. Mercer	609	Bf 109	Off Dungeness		1	
8/5/41	Sgt A.G. Palmer	609	Bf 109	Off Dungeness		1	
8/5/41	Sgt T.C. Rigler	609	Bf 109	Off Dungeness	2		
9/5/41	P/O T.S. Wade	92	Bf 109	Dungeness – Ashford	1		
9/5/41	Sgt H. Bowen-Morris	92	Bf 109	Dungeness – Ashford	1		
9/5/41	P/O S.J. Hill	609	Bf 109	Dungeness			1
10/5/41	P/O R.J.E. Boulding	74	He 111	Ashford	1		
16/5/41	Sgt D.E. Kingaby	92	Bf 109	Off Hawkinge			1
16/5/41	Sgt D.E. Kingaby	92	Bf 109	Nr Calais	1		
16/5/41	S/L J. Rankin	92	Bf 109	15m S of Dover	¼		
16/5/41	F/L A.R. Wright	92	Bf 109	15m S of Dover	¼		
16/5/41	P/O T.S. Wade	92	Bf 109	15m S of Dover	¼		
16/5/41	Unknown	92	Bf 109	15m S of Dover	¼		
16/5/41	P/O A.K. Ogilvie	609	Bf 109	Nr Dover	1		
16/5/41	P/O S.J. Hill	609	Bf 109	Nr Dover	1		1
17/5/41	W/C A.G. Malan	BH Wg	Bf 109	Channel off Dover			1
21/5/41	W/C A.G. Malan	BH Wg	Bf 109F	North Foreland			
21/5/41	P/O J.D. Bisdee	609	Bf 109	Channel, off Deal	½		
21/5/41	P/O V. Ortmans	609	Bf 109	Channel, off Deal	½		
21/5/41	Sgt J.A. Hughes-Rees	609	Bf 109	Channel, off Deal			1
26/5/41	F/O H.C. Baker	74	Bf 109	Dover Straits	1		
4/6/41	Sgt W.J. Payne	92	Bf 109	S of Dungeness			1
4/6/41	P/O V. Ortmans	609	Bf 109F	Nr Dover	1		
4/6/41	Sgt T.C. Rigler	609	Bf 109F	Nr Dover	1		½
4/6/41	S/L M.L. Robinson	609	Bf 109F	Nr Dover			½
9/6/41	P/O W.J. Sandman	74	Bf 109	Dover Straits		1	1
11/6/41	F/O D.C. Carlson	74	Bf 109	Nr Dunkirk		1	
11/6/41	P/O J.D. Bisdee	609	Bf 109	Dunkirk – Gravelines			1
12/6/41	S/L J. Rankin	92	Bf 109F	Channel, off Dover	1		
14/6/41	S/L J. Rankin	92	Bf 109E	S of Marquise	1		

Date	Pilot	Sqn	Type	Location	Dest	Prob	Dam
14/6/41	Adj X. De Montbron	92	Bf 109	S of Marquise			1
16/6/41	S/L J.C. Mungo-Park	74	Bf 109F	Nr Cap Gris Nez	2		
16/6/41	P/O W.J. Sandman	74	Bf 109	Nr Cap Gris Nez		1	
16/6/41	Sgt G.J. Stuart	74	Bf 109	Nr Boulogne	1		
16/6/41	Sgt R.L. York	74	Bf 109	Hardelot		1	
16/6/41	S/L J. Rankin	92	Bf 109F	Le Touquet		1	
16/6/41	F/L C.B.F. Kingcome	92	Bf 109F	Le Touquet		1	
16/6/41	P/O T.S. Wade	92	Bf 109F	Le Touquet	1		
16/6/41	Sgt H. Bowen-Morris	92	Bf 109E	Le Touquet	1		
17/6/41	W/C A.G. Malan	BH Wg	Bf 109F	NW of Bethune	1		
17/6/41	F/L A.R.Wright	92	Bf 109	Bethune		1	
17/6/41	Sgt W.J. Payne	92	Bf 109	Nr Boulogne	2		
17/6/41	F/O A.K. Ogilvie	609	Bf 109	Le Touquet	1		
17/6/41	P/O J.D. Bisdee	609	Bf 109E	Nr Le Touquet	1		
17/6/41	P/O F.X.E. De Spirlet	609	Bf 109	Nr Le Touquet	1		
18/6/41	S/L J. Rankin	92	Bf 109E	Nr Cap Gris Nez	1		
18/6/41	P/O S.J Hill	609	Bf 109	Nr Dover		1	
21/6/41	W/C A.G. Malan	BH Wg	Bf 109F	Boulogne	1		
21/6/41	W/C A.G. Malan	BH Wg	Bf 109F	Le Touquet	1		
21/6/41	F/L D.C. Carlson	74	Bf 109	Channel	1		
21/6/41	F/L D.C. Carlson	74	Bf 109	Off Boulogne		1	
21/6/41	Sgt J. Cole	74	Bf 109	Channel	1		
21/6/41	Sgt E.A. Mould	74	Bf 109	Off Ramsgate		1	
21/6/41	S/L J. Rankin	92	Bf 109E	Channel	1½		
21/6/41	P/O T.S. Wade	92	Bf 109E	Channel	½		
21/6/41	Sgt G.W. Aston	92	Bf 109	Nr Boulogne	1		
21/6/41	F/Sgt R.E. Havercroft	92	Bf 109	Nr Boulogne			1
21/6/41	F/O A.K. Ogilvie	609	Bf 109	Le Touquet	1		
21/6/41	Sgt R.J. Boyd	609	Bf 109F	Le Touquet	1		
21/6/41	P/O V. Ortmans	609	Bf 109	W of Le Touquet			1
22/6/41	W/C A.G. Malan	BH Wg	Bf 109F	Dunkirk	1		
22/6/41	P/O E.A. Mould	74	Bf 109	SW of Dunkirk			1
22/6/41	P/O W.J. Sandman	74	Bf 109	Bergues	2		
22/6/41	Sgt W.J. Payne	92	Bf 109	Dunkirk			1
22/6/41	F/O J.D. Bisdee	609	Bf 109F	Nr Gravelines	1		
22/6/41	P/O J.H.M. Offenberg	609	Bf 109E	Nr Gravelines			1
22/6/41	Sgt T.C. Rigler	609	Bf 109	Dunkirk area	3		
23/6/41	W/C A.G. Malan	BH Wg	Bf 109F	SE of Boulogne	2		
23/6/41	S/L J. Rankin	92	Bf 109E	SE of Boulogne	2		
23/6/41	F/O T.S. Wade	92	Bf 109	Hardelot area		1	
23/6/41	P/O P.L.I. Archer	92	Bf 109E	SE of Boulogne	1		
23/6/41	P/O D.C. Dougall	92	Bf 109	Hardelot area	1		
23/6/41	P/O N.F. Duke	92	Bf 109F	SE of Boulogne			1
23/6/41	Sgt D.E. Kingaby	92	Bf 109	SE of Boulogne	1		
23/6/41	Sgt J. Le Cheminant	92	Bf 109	SE of Boulogne			1
24/6/41	W/C A.G. Malan	BH Wg	Bf 109F	Nr Gravelines	1		
24/6/41	P/O H.R.G. Poulton	74	Bf 109	Gravelines		1	
24/6/41	Sgt W.J. Payne	92	Bf 109E	Gravelines	2		

171

Date	Pilot	Sqn	Type	Location	Dest	Prob	Dam
24/6/41	F/O J.D. Bisdee	609	Bf 109F	Dunkirk area		1	
24/6/41	Sgt R.J. Boyd	609	Bf 109F	Dunkirk area		1	
24/6/41	Sgt T.C. Rigler	609	Bf 109F	Dunkirk area		1	1
25/6/41	W/C A.G. Malan	BH Wg	Bf 109F	St Omer	1		
25/6/41	F/L A.R. Wright	92	Bf 109F	Gravelines	1		
25/6/41	P/O N.F. Duke	92	Bf 109F	Nr Dunkirk	1		
25/6/41	Sgt W.J. Payne	92	Bf 109E	Off Gravelines	1		
26/6/41	W/C A.G. Malan	BH Wg	Bf 109F	Gravelines		1	
26/6/41	S/L J. Rankin	92	Bf 109E	S of Gravelines	1		
26/6/41	F/L A.R. Wright	92	Bf 109E	Dunkirk	1		
26/6/41	P/O G.H.A. Wellum	92	Bf 109	Gravelines			1
26/6/41	Sgt R.E. Havercroft	92	Bf 109E	Gravelines	1		
26/6/41	Sgt W.J. Payne	92	Bf 109	Gravelines			1
27/6/41	F/L C.H. Saunders	74	Bf 109E	Nr Lille		1	
27/6/41	F/L P.H.M. Richey	609	Bf 109F	S of Dunkirk			1
28/6/41	W/C A.G. Malan	BH Wg	Bf 109E	Nr Calais	1		
30/6/41	W/C A.G. Malan	BH Wg	Bf 109E	Nr Lille	1		
30/6/41	S/L M.L. Robinson	609	Bf 109E	S of Dunkirk			1
30/6/41	F/L P.H.M. Richey	609	Bf 109F	Foret de Nieppe	1		
30/6/41	F/L P.H.M. Richey	609	Bf 109F	Nr St Omer		½	
30/6/41	F/O R.F.G. Malengreau	609	Bf 109F	Nr St Omer		½	
30/6/41	P/O V. Ortmans	609	Bf 109E	Lille	1		
30/6/41	Sgt J.A. Hughes-Rees	609	Bf 109	NW of St Omer	1		
2/7/41	W/C A.G. Malan	BH Wg	Bf 109E	Lille	½		
2/7/41	Sgt W.G. Lockhart	74	Bf 109E	Lille	½		
2/7/41	F/Sgt D.E. Kingaby	92	Bf 109F	Nr Gravelines	2		
2/7/41	Sgt D.E. Lloyd	92	Bf 109	Northern France	1		
2/7/41	Sgt A Pietrasiak	92	Bf 109E	Off Dunkirk	1		
3/7/41	W/C A.G. Malan	BH Wg	Bf 109E	Nr St Omer			2
3/7/41	P/O H.R.G. Poulton	74	Bf 109	Hazebrouck	1		
3/7/41	F/L D.C. Carlson	74	Bf 109	Hazebrouck	1		
3/7/41	F/Sgt D.E. Kingaby	92	Bf 109E	Nr St Omer		1	
3/7/41	S/L M.L. Robinson	609	Bf 109F	Hazebrouck	2		
3/7/41	P/O Y.G. Du Monceau	609	Bf 109F	N of St Omer			1
3/7/41	P/O V. Ortmans	609	Bf 109	Hazebrouck			1
4/7/41	W/C A.G. Malan	BH Wg	Bf 109E	St Omer area	1½		2
4/7/41	S/L S.T. Meares	74	Bf 109	Gravelines			1
4/7/41	Sgt A. Pietrasiak	92	Bf 109E	St Omer area	½		
4/7/41	Sgt A. Pietrasiak	92	Bf 109F	St Omer area	1		
4/7/41	S/L M.L. Robinson	609	Bf 109F	Bethune			1
4/7/41	F/L P.H.M. Richey	609	Bf 109F	St Omer area			2
5/7/41	W/C A.G. Malan	BH Wg	Bf 109E	Nr Lille			1
5/7/41	S/L S.T. Meares	74	Bf 109	Lille			1
6/7/41	W/C A.G. Malan	BH Wg	Bf 109F	Nr Gravelines	1		
6/7/41	Sgt W.G. Lockhart	74	Bf 109	NE France	2		
7/7/41	F/L D.C. Carlson	74	Bf 109	Nr Candas			1
7/7/41	Sgt G.F. Trott	74	Bf 109	Nr Lille	1		1
7/7/41	P/O P.L.I. Archer	92	Bf 109F	Nr Lille	1		1

Date	Pilot	Sqn	Type	Location	Dest	Prob	Dam
7/7/41	F/O J.H.M. Offenberg	609	Bf 109F	Nr Le Touquet	1		
8/7/41	S/L J. Rankin	92	Bf 109F	St Omer area		1	
8/7/41	P/O G.H.A. Wellum	92	Bf 109F	St Omer area		1	
8/7/41	Sgt A. Pietrasiak	92	Bf 109F	Off Gravelines	1		
8/7/41	S/L M.L. Robinson	609	Bf 109F	S of Gravelines			1
8/7/41	Sgt J.A. Hughes-Rees	609	Bf 109	W of Lens	1	1	
9/7/41	S/L J. Rankin	92	Bf 109F	Bethune – Hardelot	1	1	
9/7/41	P/O P.L.I. Archer	92	Bf 109F	Bethune area	1		
9/7/41	P/O G.H.A. Wellum	92	Bf 109F	Bethune area	1		
9/7/41	Sgt A. Pietrasiak	92	Bf 109F	Bethune area	2		
9/7/41	Sgt G.C. Waldern	92	Bf 109	Bethune area			1
9/7/41	F/L J.D. Bisdee	609	Bf 109F	Nr Le Touquet	1		
10/7/41	S/L M.L. Robinson	609	Bf 109F	Hardelot	1		
10/7/41	F/L P.H.M. Richey	609	Bf 109F	S of St Omer			1
11/7/41	G/C P.R. Barwell	BH Wg	Bf 109	Nr Cassel	1		1
11/7/41	F/O J.W. Lund	92	Bf 109	Nr Calais	1		
11/7/41	Sgt A. Pietrasiak	92	Bf 109F	Nr Calais	1		
11/7/41	S/L M.L. Robinson	609	Bf 109F	Cassel – St Omer	1		
11/7/41	F/L P.H.M. Richey	609	Bf 109F	St Omer – Dunkirk		1	2
11/7/41	P/O Y.G. Du Monceau	609	Bf 109F	E of Dunkirk		1	
11/7/41	P/O E. Seghers	609	Bf 109	Nr Cassel	1		
11/7/41	Sgt R.J. Boyd	609	Bf 109F	36m SE of Dunkirk	1		1
11/7/41	Sgt K.W. Bramble	609	Bf 109	Nr Cassel			1
12/7/41	S/L M.L. Robinson	609	Bf 109F	S of Cap Gris Nez	1		
14/7/41	S/L M.L. Robinson	609	Bf 109F	Nr Le Touquet	1		
19/7/41	Sgt J.C. Carpenter	92	Bf 109	Dunkirk		1	
19/7/41	F/O J.H.M. Offenberg	609	Bf 109	Dunkirk			1
21/7/41	Sgt J.E. Van Schaick	609	Bf 109	N of Calais			2
22/7/41	P/O C. Gosling	72	Bf 109	Nr St Omer			1
23/7/41	W/C A.G. Malan	BH Wg	Bf 109F	St Omer – Bethune			1
23/7/41	Sgt J. Sika	72	Bf 109	Mazingarbe	1		
23/7/41	F/L P.H.M. Richey	609	Bf 109E	Foret de Nieppe	1		
23/7/41	Sgt A.G. Palmer	609	Bf 109	Mazingarbe			1
24/7/41	W/C A.G. Malan	BH Wg	Bf 109	Hazebrouck			1
24/7/41	F/L C.B.F. Kingcome	92	Bf 109F	Off Le Havre	1		
24/7/41	P/O J.A. Thomson	92	Bf 109	SW of Dunkirk	1		
24/7/41	Sgt C.H. Howard	92	Bf 109	S of Dunkirk		1	
24/7/41	Sgt W.L.H. Johnston	92	Bf 109F	S and SE of Dunkirk		2	
24/7/41	S/L M.L. Robinson	609	Bf 109F	St Omer area	1		1
24/7/41	Sgt T.C. Rigler	609	Bf 109F	St Omer area	1		
7/8/41	W/C M.L. Robinson	BH Wg	Bf 109F	Mardyck – Gravelines		1	
7/8/41	S/L J. Rankin	92	Bf 109F	Off Gravelines	1		1
7/8/41	F/Sgt D.E. Kingaby	92	Bf 109F	St Omer area		1	1
7/8/41	Lt M.P.C. Choron	609	Bf 109	NE of Calais			1
7/8/41	Sgt P.A. Nash	609	Bf 109F	St Omer			1
7/8/41	Sgt T.C. Rigler	609	Bf 109F	Nr St Omer			1
9/8/41	S/L J. Rankin	92	Bf 109F	Boulogne area	1		2
9/8/41	F/O J.W. Lund	92	Bf 109	E of Boulogne		1	

Date	Pilot	Sqn	Type	Location	Dest	Prob	Dam
9/8/41	P/O N.F. Duke	92	Bf 109F	Boulogne	1		
9/8/41	F/Sgt D.E. Kingaby	92	Bf 109F	Boulogne	1	1	
9/8/41	Sgt H.S. Harrison	92	Bf 109	Nr Boulogne			1
9/8/41	Sgt J. Le Cheminant	92	Bf 109E	Nr Boulogne	1		
9/8/41	Lt M.P.C. Choron	609	Bf 109	NE France		1	
9/8/41	P/O A. Nitelet	609	Bf 109F	NE France	1		
10/8/41	F/O R.B. Newton	72	Bf 109	St Omer			1
10/8/41	P/O E.P.W. Bocock	72	Bf 109F	NE of Calais			1
16/8/41	Sgt C.P. Stone	72	Bf 109F	St Omer	1	1	
16/8/41	F/O J. Thompson	92	Bf 109F	E of Dunkirk		1	
16/8/41	F/O B. De Hemptinne	609	Bf 109	Ambleteuse	1		
16/8/41	Sgt P.A. Nash	609	Bf 109F	Gravelines area			1
18/8/41	F/O V. Ortmans	609	Bf 109F	Nr Calais	1		
18/8/41	P/O Y.G. Du Monceau	609	Bf 109E	S of Dover	1		
19/8/41	F/O B. De Hemptinne	609	Bf 109	Nr Gravelines			1
19/8/41	P/O Y.G. Du Monceau	609	Bf 109E	Off Boulogne			1
19/8/41	F/O V. Ortmans	609	Bf 109F	Calais area			1
19/8/41	Sgt E.W. Pollard	609	Bf 109	Nr Gravelines			1
21/8/41	F/O B. De Hemptinne	609	Bf 109	NE France			1
21/8/41	Sgt J.E. Van Schaick	609	Bf 109	NE France		1	
27/8/41	W/C M.L. Robinson	BH Wg	Bf 109F	Gravelines area	1		
27/8/41	Sgt J. Rutherford	72	Bf 109	Nr St Omer			1
27/8/41	Lt M.C.P. Choron	609	Bf 109F	Nr St Omer	1		
27/8/41	F/O J.H.M. Offenberg	609	Bf 109	Nr St Omer		1	
29/8/41	S/L D.F.B. Sheen	72	Bf 109E	E of Hazebrouck			1
29/8/41	F/L K. Kosinski	72	Bf 109	E of Hazebrouck	1	1	
29/8/41	P/O E.P.W. Bocock	72	Bf 109	E of Hazebrouck		1	1
29/8/41	P/O W.J. Rosser	72	Bf 109	E of Hazebrouck	1		
29/8/41	F/O F.X.E. De Spirlet	609	Bf 109	Nr Gravelines	1		
29/8/41	F/O J.H.M. Offenberg	609	Bf 109	Hazebrouck		1	
29/8/41	F/O V. Ortmans	609	Bf 109	NW of Dunkirk			½
29/8/41	Sgt A.G. Palmer	609	Bf 109	NW of Dunkirk			½
31/8/41	S/L J. Rankin	92	Bf 109F	Calais – Gravelines	1		
31/8/41	P/O B. Bartholomew	92	Bf 109F	Calais – Gravelines		1	
31/8/41	P/O N.F. Duke	92	Bf 109	Calais – Gravelines			1
31/8/41	P/O P.H. Humphreys	92	Bf 109	Calais – Gravelines			1
4/9/41	P/O D. Clive	72	Bf 109F	Nr Mazingarbe		1	
4/9/41	P/O E.G. Brettell	92	Bf 109	Nr Mazingarbe		1	
4/9/41	Sgt A.G. Palmer	609	Bf 109F	Nr Mazingarbe		1	
17/9/41	W/C J. Rankin	BH Wg	Bf 109F	Nr Hardelot			1
17/9/41	Sgt H. Cox	92	Bf 109F	Hazebrouck – Calais	1		
17/9/41	F/O J.W. Lund	92	Bf 109	Hazebrouck – Calais		1	
17/9/41	Lt M.C.P. Choron	609	Bf 109	NE France	1		
19/9/41	Sgt J.G. Merrett	72	Bf 109E	Off Gravelines		1	
20/9/41	F/L J.H. Sanderson	92	Bf 109	Nr Abbeville		1	
27/9/41	W/C J. Rankin	BH Wg	Bf 109F	Le Touquet area	1		2
27/9/41	F/L R.M.D. Hall	72	Bf 109	Nr Mazingarbe		1	
27/9/41	Sgt F. Falkiner	72	Bf 109	Nr Mazingarbe	1		

Date	Pilot	Sqn	Type	Location	Dest	Prob	Dam
27/9/41	S/L R.M. Milne	92	Bf 109	SW of St Omer		1	
27/9/41	S/L R.M. Milne	92	Bf 109	Guines – Calais			1
27/9/41	P/O P.H. Beake	92	Bf 109	Nr Guines			1
27/9/41	Sgt W.L.H. Johnston	92	Bf 109F	Foret de Nieppe		1	
27/9/41	Sgt W.L.H. Johnston	92	Bf 109F	S of Calais			1
27/9/41	F/L J.H.M. Offenberg	609	Bf 109F	N of St Omer			1
27/9/41	F/O G.E. Dieu	609	Bf 109F	Nr Mardyck		1	
27/9/41	P/O Y.G. Du Monceau	609	Bf 109F	St Omer area	1		
1/10/41	F/L K. Kosinski	72	Bf 109F	Over Channel	1	1	
1/10/41	F/Sgt D.E. Kingaby	92	Bf 109F	Off Cap Gris Nez	1	1	
2/10/41	S/L D.F.B. Sheen	72	Bf 109E	Abbeville		1	
3/10/41	F/Sgt D.E. Kingaby	92	Bf 109F	Off Ostend	1		
13/10/41	S/L R.M. Milne	92	Bf 109E	S of St Omer	1		1
13/10/41	S/L R.M. Milne	92	Bf 109F	S of St Omer	2		
13/10/41	F/L J.H.M. Offenberg	609	Bf 109F	NW of Le Touquet			1
13/10/41	P/O J.A. Atkinson	609	Bf 109F	NW of Le Touquet			1
13/10/41	Sgt P.A. Nash	609	Bf 109E	W of Bethune	1		
21/10/41	W/C J. Rankin	BH Wg	Bf 109F	Nr Le Touquet	1		
27/10/41	W/C J. Rankin	BH Wg	Fw 190	Off French coast	1		
27/10/41	W/C J. Rankin	BH Wg	Bf 109F	W of Folkstone	1		
27/10/41	F/L E.L. Neal	401	Bf 109	S of Mardyck		1	1
27/10/41	F/O C.A.B. Wallace	401	Bf 109	N of Poperinghe	½		
27/10/41	P/O A.E. Harley	401	Bf 109	N of Poperinghe			1
27/10/41	P/O J.A. Small	401	Bf 109	N of Poperinghe	½		
27/10/41	S/L G.K. Gilroy	609	Bf 109	Off French coast	2		
27/10/41	Lt M.C.P. Choron	609	Fw 190	Nr Mardyck		1	1
7/11/41	P/O W.J. Rosser	72	Fw 190	Berck			1
7/11/41	Sgt P.A. Nash	609	Bf 109F	Nr Le Touquet	1		
7/11/41	Sgt P.A. Nash	609	Fw 190	Nr Le Touquet		1	
7/11/41	Sgt J.E. Van Schaick	609	Bf 109F	NE of Le Touquet	1		
8/11/41	P/O F. De Naeyer	72	Bf 109	Nr St Pol		1	
8/11/41	S/L G.K. Gilroy	609	Bf 109	Nr St Pol	1		
8/11/41	Sgt C. Ortmans	609	Bf 109	Nr St Pol		1	
18/11/41	F/L E.L. Neal	401	Bf 109F	Le Touquet – Berck		1	
18/11/41	F/O H.A. Sprague	401	Bf 109F	NW of Le Touquet		1	
18/11/41	P/O D.J.M. Blakeslee	401	Bf 109F	Berck			1
18/11/41	P/O I. Gilbert	401	Bf 109F	Berck		1	
18/11/41	Sgt D.R. Morrison	401	Bf 109F	N of Le Touquet		½	
18/11/41	P/O D. Barnham	609	Fw 190	Cap Gris Nez – Dover	1		
22/11/41	S/L C.A. Masterman	72	Fw 190	Boulogne area	1/3		
22/11/41	P/O W.J. Rosser	72	Fw 190	Boulogne area	1/3		
22/11/41	Sgt B. Ingham	72	Fw 190	Boulogne area	1/3		
22/11/41	S/L C.A.Masterman	72	Bf 109E	Boulogne area	1/3		
22/11/41	P/O W.J. Rosser	72	Bf 109E	Boulogne area	1/3		
22/11/41	Sgt B. Ingham	72	Bf 109E	Boulogne area	1/3		
22/11/41	Sgt E.G. Enright	72	Fw 190	Boulogne area		1	
22/11/41	Sgt C.L.A. Thompson	72	Fw 190	Boulogne area		1	
22/11/41	P/O D.J.M. Blakeslee	401	Bf 109E	S of Calais Marck	1		

Date	Pilot	Sqn	Type	Location	Dest	Prob	Dam
22/11/41	P/O D.J.M. Blakeslee	401	Bf 109E	E of Dover			1
22/11/41	P/O I.C. Ormston	401	Bf 109E	S of Calais Marck	1		
22/11/41	Sgt J.A.O. Levesque	401	Fw 190	St Omer – Boulogne	1	1	
22/11/41	Sgt D.R. Morrison	401	Fw 190	Desvres	1		
22/11/41	Sgt D.R. Morrison	401	Fw 190	Mid Channel			1
22/11/41	Sgt G.W Northcott	401	Bf 109E	S of Calais Marck			1
8/12/41	P/O D.J.M. Blakeslee	401	Bf 109F	Off Cap Gris Nez			1
8/12/41	Sgt W.D. Hagyard	401	Bf 109F	Off Cap Gris Nez			½
8/12/41	Sgt D.B.Whitney	401	Bf 109F	Off Cap Gris Nez			½
8/12 41	Sgt D.R. Morrison	401	Bf 109F	Off Cap Gris Nez	1		1
17/12/41	S/L M. Duke-Woolley	124	Ju 88	Off North Foreland	1		

Night Air Combat Claims – 264 Squadron – Boulton Paul Defiant

Date	Crew	Type	Location	Dest	Prob	Dam
9/1/41	Sgt P. Endersby – Sgt Chandler	Ju 88	Beachy Head			1
12/3/41	P/O F.D. Hughes – Sgt F. Gash	He 111 – (a)	Dorking	1		
12/3/41	P/O T. D. Welsh – Sgt L.H. Hayden	He 111	Nr Hastings	1		
13/3/41	Sgt Wilkin – Sgt V.W.J. Crook	He 111	Beachy Head		1	
8/4/41	S/L A.T.D. Sanders – P/O Sutton	He 111 – (b)	Nr Hitchin	1		
8/4/41	P/O F.D. Hughes – Sgt F. Gash	He 111	Nr Biggin Hill		1	
9/4/41	F/S E.R. Thorn – F/S F.J. Barker	He 111 – (c)	Godalming	1		
10/4/41	F/O E.G Barwell – Sgt A. Martin	He 111 – (d)	Beachy Head	1		
10/4/41	P/O F.D. Hughes – Sgt F. Gash	He 111 – (e)	Nr IoW	1		
11/4/41	F/O E.G Barwell – Sgt A. Martin	He 111 – (f)	Beachy Head		1	

a) He 111 G1+GN of 2/KG 55

b) He 111 W/Nr 3628 1H+ET of 9/KG 26

c) He 111 G1+DN of 5/KG 55

d) He 111 1H+1D of III/KG 26

e) He 111 6N+HL of KGr 100 (claimed as a Ju 88)

f) Probably He 111 of I/KG 55 also attacked by an aircraft of 604 Squadron

Operational Aircraft Losses of Biggin Hill Squadrons – 1941

Date	Pilot	A/c	Sqn	Remarks
10/1/41	Sgt L.E. Freese	P7561	74	Ran out of fuel and crash-landed at Detling; pilot died later
2/2/41	S/L E.J.C. Michelmore	P7741	74	Shot down near Boulogne during fighter sweep, pilot killed
11/2/41	P/O S. Baker	P7568	66	Shot down by Bf 109s near Boulogne, pilot killed
11/2/41	P/O P.R. Mildren	P7520	66	Shot down by Bf 109s near Boulogne, pilot killed
14/2/41	P/O P. Olver	P7602	66	Damaged in combat by Bf 109s, a/c returned to service, pilot safe
14/2/41	P/O D.A. Maxwell	P7541	66	Shot down by Bf 109 over the Channel during patrol, pilot killed
14/2/41	Sgt C.A. Parsons	P7522	66	Damaged in combat by Bf 109s, a/c returned to service, pilot safe
14/2/41	F/L H.R. Allen	P7504	66	Damaged in combat by Bf 109s, a/c returned to service, pilot wounded
15/2/41	Sgt C.A. Parsons	P7670	66	Damaged during combat, a/c returned to service, pilot wounded
24/2/41	Sgt N. Morrison	P7778	74	Failed to return from patrol, pilot killed
24/2/41	Sgt J. Rogowski	P7559	74	Crash landed at Eastbourne after patrol, pilot injured
1/3/41	S/L P. Wood	?	74	Shot up during defensive patrol, pilot wounded
12/3/41	Sgt J.N. Glendinning	P7506	74	Shot down by Bf 109s of JG 51 near Dungeness, pilot killed
27/3/41	P/O A.H. Smith	P7328	74	Shot down off Dungeness during patrol, pilot killed
27/3/41	Sgt P.M.A. MacSherry	P7785	609	Shot down off Dungeness during patrol by Bf 109 of I/LG 2, pilot killed
10/4/41	P/O P. Chesters	P7854	74	Crashed at Manston when attempting low level roll, pilot killed
11/4/41	Sgt Gaskell	X4062	92	Shot down over the Channel by Bf 109 of JG 51, pilot killed
19/4/41	P/O E.W.G. Churches	P7381	74	Shot down over Channel by Bf 109 of JG 53, pilot killed
21/4/41	Sgt C.G. Hilken	P7614	74	Attacked by Bf 109 of JG 51 during patrol, pilot wounded
29/4/41	Sgt G.C. Bennett	P7669	609	Shot down by Bf 109 of JG 51 off Dunkirk during Roadstead, pilot killed

Date	Pilot	A/c	Sqn	Remarks
6/5/41	P/O J. Howard	P8364	74	Shot down by Bf 109 of JG 51 during Roadstead, pilot killed
6/5/41	Sgt A.D. Arnott	P7537	74	Shot down by Bf 109 of JG 51 during Roadstead, pilot PoW
6/5/41	Sgt A.F. Wilson	P7928	74	Shot up during Roadstead, pilot baled out over England, safe
8/5/41	P/O Maitland-Thompson	?	92	Shot up during defensive patrol, pilot baled out, wounded
9/5/41	Sgt R.T.D. Mercer	P7305	609	Shot up during combat with JG 53, crashed on landing, pilot killed
21/5/41	P/O R. de Grunne	P7436	609	Shot down over the Channel during Circus operation, pilot killed
4/6/41	F/L J. Curchin	P7292	609	Shot down over the Channel during an ASR search, pilot killed
9/6/41	P/O W.K. Burgon	W3186	74	Shot down by Bf 109s of JG 26 over the Channel, pilot killed
11/6/41	Sgt G.A. Chestnut	P8654	609	Crashed into Ramsgate cliffs after combat with Bf 109s of JG 26
17/6/41	P/O H.F. Parkes	R7278	74	Shot down during Circus operation, pilot PoW
17/6/41	P/O R.J.E. Boulding	W3251	74	Shot down during Circus operation, pilot PoW
18/6/41	P/O S.J. Hill	W3211	609	Shot down by Bf 109 over Channel, pilot killed
21/6/41	Sgt G.W. Aston	R6923	92	Shot down during Circus operation, pilot baled out, rescued
22/6/41	P/O F.X.E. de Spirlet	W3116	609	Shot down over the Channel, pilot baled out, rescued
23/6/41	Sgt H. Bowen-Morris	R6761	92	Shot down during Circus operation, pilot badly wounded, PoW
25/6/41	P/O T.S. Wade	W3264	92	Shot up during sweep, a/c returned to service, pilot wounded
26/6/41	Sgt G.W. Aston	P8532	92	Failed to return from escort patrol, pilot PoW
27/6/41	S/L J.C. Mungo-Park	X4668	74	Shot down during sweep by Bf 109s of JG 26, pilot killed
27/6/41	P/O W.J. Sandman	W3210	74	Shot down during sweep by Bf 109s of JG 26, pilot PoW
27/6/41	Sgt C.G. Hilken	W3252	74	Shot down during sweep by Bf 109s of JG 26, pilot PoW
2/7/41	P/O S.Z. Krol	W3263	74	Failed to return from sweep, pilot PoW
2/7/41	Sgt Evans	W3259	74	Failed to return from sweep, pilot PoW
3/7/41	Sgt Cochrane	W3232	74	Failed to return from sweep, pilot missing
3/7/41	F/L X. De Montbron	X4476	92	Shot down during escort patrol, pilot PoW
4/7/41	Sgt W.G. Henderson	W3258	74	Failed to return from sweep, pilot killed
4/7/41	F/O A.K. Ogilvie	X4664	609	Shot down during Circus operation, pilot PoW
6/7/41	P/O W.M. Skinner	W3208	74	Shot down during Circus operation, pilot PoW
6/7/41	Sgt L.R. Carter	W3176	74	Shot down during Circus operation, pilot killed
6/7/41	Sgt W.G. Lockhart	W3317	74	Shot down during Circus operation, pilot evaded
6/7/41	Sgt C.G. Todd	W3331	92	Failed to return from escort patrol, pilot killed
7/7/41	Sgt C. Stuart	W3172	74	Shot down into the sea during sweep, pilot wounded, rescued
7/7/41	Sgt G. Evans	W3115	609	Shot down by Bf 109, pilot baled out over Channel and rescued
8/7/41	P/O P.H. Beake	W3265	92	Shot down over Channel during escort patrol, pilot baled out and rescued

Date	Pilot	A/c	Sqn	Remarks
8/7/41	Sgt J.A. Hughes-Rees	W3239	609	Ditched near Goodwin Sands after escort patrol, pilot rescued
10/7/41	F/O J.M. Godlewski	W3411	72	Shot down during sweep, pilot killed
10/7/41	Sgt A.J. Casey	P8600	72	Shot down during sweep, pilot killed
10/7/41	Sgt C.L. Harrison	P8604	72	Shot down during sweep, pilot killed
10/7/41	Sgt C.G. Waldern	W3403	92	Shot down over the Channel during escort, pilot baled out and rescued
11/7/41	P/O D.C. Dougall	W3183	92	Shot down during escort operation, pilot badly wounded and PoW
14/7/41	Sgt W. Lamberton	R7219	72	Shot down during Circus operation, pilot wounded and PoW
17/7/41	P/O L.B. Fordham	P8544	72	Shot down by flak during patrol, pilot baled out over Channel but drowned
19/7/41	Sgt R.F. Lewis	W3181	72	Shot down during Circus operation, pilot killed
19/7/41	Sgt C.G. Waldern	W3326	92	Shot down during Circus operation, pilot killed
21/7/41	Sgt K.W. Bramble	W3307	609	Shot down during Circus operation, pilot killed
23/7/41	Sgt J.W. Perkins	W3256	72	Shot down during Circus operation, pilot PoW
24/7/41	Sgt G.F. Brecken	W3316	72	Shot down during Circus operation, pilot PoW
24/7/41	Sgt S.H. Vinter	W3381	92	Shot down over the Channel during sweep, pilot killed
31/7/41	Sgt R. Boyd	W3187	609	Shot down by flak off Calais, pilot baled out and rescued
3/8/41	P/O E.A.G.C. Bruce	W3245	92	Damaged by flak during Rhubarb, a/c returned to service, pilot wounded
7/8/41	Sgt C.H. Howard	W3568	92	Failed to return from sweep, pilot missing
7/8/41	Sgt G.P. Hickman	R7161	92	Shot up during sweep, crash-landed, a/c returned to service, pilot injured
9/8/41	P/O A Nitelet	W3254	609	Shot down during Circus operation, pilot wounded but evaded
16/8/41	P/O D/L Cropper	P8745	609	Shot down during sweep, pilot killed
18/8/41	Sgt G.E. Hann	R7346	92	Failed to return from sweep, pilot killed
19/8/41	P/O V.M. Ortmans	W3241	609	Shot down and baled out into Channel, pilot rescued
21/8/41	Sgt H.S. Harrison	?	92	Hit by a/c of 72 Squadron when taxiing at Biggin Hill, pilot died later
21/8/41	Sgt J. Aherne	W3409	92	Shot down during sweep, pilot killed
21/8/41	P/O P.L.I. Archer	W3330	92	Shot up during sweep, pilot wounded
21/8/41	Sgt E.W. Pollard	W3651	609	Shot down during Circus operation, pilot killed
26/8/41	P/O E.W.H. Phillips	W3576	92	Failed to return from sweep, pilot killed
27/8/41	F/O H. Skalski	?	72	Shot down during Circus operation, pilot PoW
27/8/41	Sgt Rutherford	P8609	72	Shot down during Circus operation, pilot baled out over Channel, rescued
27/8/41	Sgt E.H. Roff	W3319	92	Shot up during sweep, pilot baled out over Channel but not picked up
29/8/41	Sgt P.T. Grisdale	P8713	72	Shot down during Circus operation, pilot killed
31/8/41	Sgt Kenwood	W3120	92	Pilot baled out on becoming lost when returning from convoy patrol, safe
4/9/41	P/O J.E.T. Asselin	W3182	92	Failed to return from sweep, pilot PoW
17/9/41	P/O B. Bartholomew	AB915	92	Shot up during sweep, pilot baled out into Channel but drowned
17/9/41	P/O E.G. Brettell	W3709	92	Shot up during sweep, a/c returned to service, pilot wounded

Date	Pilot	A/c	Sqn	Remarks
17/9/41	P/O J.A. Atkinson	W3767	609	Shot down during sweep, pilot baled out over Channel, rescued
19/9/41	F/L D. Stewart-Clark	W3516	72	Failed to return from Rhubarb, pilot killed
20/9/41	Sgt G.P. Hickman	W3179	92	Shot down during sweep, pilot PoW
21/9/41	P/O W.B. Sanders	W3315	609	Crash-landed after Circus operation, a/c w/o, pilot injured
27/9/41	Sgt A.F. Binns	AB843	72	Shot down during Circus operation, pilot killed
27/9/41	Sgt J.G. Merrett	P8560	72	Shot down during Circus operation, pilot killed
27/9/41	P/O V. Ortmans	W3625	609	Shot up during Circus operation, pilot baled out into Channel and rescued
2/10/41	F/L J.W. Lund	W3459	92	Shot down during sweep, pilot killed
2/10/41	Sgt N.H. Edge	W3137	92	Shot down during sweep, pilot killed
2/10/41	Sgt K.G. Port	W3762	92	Shot down during sweep, pilot kiled
2/10/41	P/O E.A.G.C. Bruce	W3657	92	Shot up during sweep, crash-landed on return, pilot wounded
3/10/41	Sgt H. Cox	W3710	92	Shot down during Circus operation, pilot killed
3/10/41	Sgt G.E. Woods-Scawen	AB779	92	Shot down during Circus operation, pilot killed
21/10/41	Sgt B.F. Whitson	AB863	401	Shot down during sweep, pilot wounded and PoW
21/10/41	F/O V. Ortmans	W3850	609	Shot down during sweep, pilot PoW
21/10/41	Sgt A.G. Palmer	AD136	609	Shot down during sweep, pilot killed
26/10/41	Sgt L. Stock	AB822	72	Shot down during sweep, pilot killed
26/10/41	P/O F. Falkiner	W3704	72	Failed to return from sweep, pilot missing
27/10/41	F/O C.A.B. Wallace	AB991	401	Shot down during sweep by Bf 109s of JG 26, pilot killed
27/10/41	P/O C.W. Floody	W3964	401	Shot down during sweep by Bf 109s of JG 26, pilot PoW
27/10/41	P/O J.A. Small	AB983	401	Shot down during sweep by Bf 109s of JG 26, pilot killed
27/10/41	Sgt B.G. Hodgkinson	W3955	401	Shot down during sweep by Bf 109s of JG 26, pilot PoW
27/10/41	Sgt S.L. Thompson	W3601	401	Shot up during sweep by Bf 109s of JG 26, crashed on return, pilot killed
27/10/41	Sgt G.B. Whitney	W3452	401	Shot up during sweep by Bf 109s of JG 26, pilot baled out on return, safe
7/11/41	P/O H.J. Birkland	W3367	72	Failed to return from sweep, pilot PoW
8/11/41	P/O N.E. Bishop	W3511	72	Shot down during Ramrod operation, pilot killed
8/11/41	Sgt Dykes	AB893	72	Engine failed on return from Ramrod, pilot baled out into Channel, rescued
8/11/41	Sgt D.R. White	AB855	72	Shot down during Ramrod operation, pilot killed
8/11/41	F/O J. Weir	AB922	401	Shot down during escort operation, pilot wounded and PoW
8/11/41	Sgt R.W. Gardner	AA925	401	Shot down during escort operation, pilot killed
15/11/41	Sgt K. Laing	AD507	609	Shot down by flak near Calais, pilot PoW
21/11/41	Sgt C.R. Golden	AD255	401	Crash-landed after convoy patrol, pilot injured
22/11/41	F/O H.A. Sprague	AD516	401	Shot down during sweep, pilot PoW
8/12/41	Sgt E.G. Enright	AA749	72	Failed to return from Ramrod operation, pilot killed
8/12/41	Sgt C.L.A. Thompson	AA864	72	Failed to return from Ramrod operation, pilot killed

APPENDIX THREE

Details of selected operations carried out by Biggin Hill squadrons

Pilots and aircraft (details as recorded in Squadron Operations Record Books)

Circus 2 – Boulogne – 2 February 1941

66 Squadron		74 Squadron		92 Squadron	
S/L A. Forbes	P7541	S/L A.G. Malan	P7542	S/L J.A. Kent	X4272
P/O J.H. Pickering	P7625	F/L J.C. Freeborn	P7623	F/L C.B.F. Kingcome	R6908
P/O Mildren	P7521	P/O W. Armstrong	P7353	Sgt D.E. Lloyd	X4779
Sgt Hunt	P7671	P/O R.L. Spurdle	P7740	P/O S. M-Thompson	X4561
P/O D.A. Maxwell	P7538	P/O P. Chesters	P7591	P/O T.S. Wade	X4419
F/L H.R. Allen	P7669	S/L E.J.C. Michelmore	P7741	Sgt D.E Kingaby	R6833
P/O S. Baker	P7504	F/L J.C. Mungo-Park	P7537	F/O A.R. Wright	R6904
P/O P. Olver	P7602	P/O E.W.G. Churches	P7316	P/O Watling	R6924
Sgt Cook	P7440	P/O Smith	P7352	Sgt J. Le Cheminant	X4616
Sgt C.A. Parsons	P7522	P/O H.R.G. Poulton	P7559	Sgt De Montbron	X4484
Sgt Maithew	P7600	Sgt N. Morrison	P7506	Sgt H. Bowen-Morris	X4618
Sgt Wylde	P7668	Sgt Payne	P7667		

Battle of the Dinghy – 8 May 1941 – 609 Squadron

S/L M.L. Robinson	P7881	Sgt T.C. Rigler	P8422	F/L P.H.M. Richey	P8266
F/L J. Curchin	P8264	Sgt A.G. Palmer	P7625	F/O R. Malengreau	P8241
F/O W. Van Lierde	P7305	Sgt R.T.D. Mercer	P7734	P/O Y.G Du Monceau	P7834
P/O E.G.A. Seghers	P8270	Sgt R.J. Boyd	P8098	Sgt J.A. Hughes-Rees	P8271

Circus 13 – Chocques Chemical Works – 17 June 1941

74 Squadron		92 Squadron		609 Squadron	
F/L D.C. Carlson	W3171	S/L J. Rankin	R7161	S/L M.L. Robinson	W3238
F/O R.J.E. Boulding	W3251	Sgt R.E. Havercroft	X4476	P/O S.J. Hill	W3211
F/O W. Armstrong	W3170	Sgt W.J. Payne	W3120	Sgt A.G. Palmer	W3207
P/O E.A. Mould	W3127	F/O R. Mottram	R6904	P/O V. Ortmans	W3240
Sgt A.F. Wilson	-	F/L A.R. Wright	R6923	P/O R.F. Malengreau	W3187
Sgt Dykes	W3367	Sgt J. Le Cheminant	R7346	P/O J.A. Atkinson	W3209

181

74 Squadron		92 Squadron		609 Squadron	
P/O S.Z. Krol	W3210	Sgt D.E. Lloyd	W3181	P/O R.E.J. Wilmet	W3241
Sgt R.W. York	X4668	F/O C.H. Saunders	R7195	P/O E.G.A. Seghers	W3180
P/O H.F. Parkes	R7278	F/O G.H.A. Wellum	W3128	F/L J.D. Bisdee	W3115
Sgt C. Stuart	W3177	P/O T.S. Wade	R6761	Sgt J. Hughes-Rees	W3239
Sgt Mallett	W3178	Sgt G.W. Aston	-	P/O F.X.E de Spirlet	W3179
				F/O A.K. Ogilvie	W3117

Circus 103B – Mazingarbe – 27 September 1941

72 Squadron		92 Squadron		609 Squadron	
S/L D.F.B. Sheen	W3380	S/L R.M. Milne	W3817	S/L G.K. Gilroy	P8699
Sgt Pocock	W3440	P/O P.H. Beake	W3444	F/O J.A. Atkinson	W3850
Sgt Dykes	AB822	F/L J.W. Lund	W3459	F/O V. Ortmans	W3625
F/L K. Kosinski	W3511	P/O P. Humphreys	W3375	F/O G.E. Dieu	AB975
P/O N.E. Bishop	W3441	Sgt Atkins	W3599	P/O D.A. Barnham	W3621
Sgt J. Rutherford	AB818	P/O Cocker	W3762	F/O R.E.J. Wilmet	X4666
F/L R.M.D. Hall	W3704	Sgt Carpenter	R8640	F/L J. Offenberg	W3574
Sgt A.F. Binns	AB843	P/O E.A.G.C. Bruce	AB779	Lt M. Choron	AB901
Sgt Falkiner	AB922	Sgt G. E. Woods-Scawen	W3710	P/O I.G. Du Monceau	P8585
Sgt J.G. Merrett	P8560	Sgt W.L.H. Johnston	AB395	Sgt T.C. Rigler	AB802
P/O E.P.W. Bocock	W3429	P/O P.L.I. Archer	AB847	Sgt J.E. Van Schaick	R6882
Sgt B. Ingham	AB893				

Wing Sweep – 21 October 1941

72 Squadron		401 Squadron		609 Squadron	
F/L Campbell	W3511	S/L Johnstone	AB974	S/L G.K Gilroy	P8699
Sgt B. Ingham	W3430	P/O A.E. Harley	W3131	Sgt A.G. Palmer	AD136
F/Sgt Pocock	AA749	F/O McColl	W3127	P/O D.A. Barnham	AD202
Sgt J. Rutherford	AB818	Sgt G.W. Northcott	W3178	Sgt G. Evans	P8585
Sgt D.R. White	AB822	F/O Weir	AD228	F/O V. Ortmans	W3850
F/L K. Kosinski	R7265	P/O H.C. Godefroy	AD254	F/L F.X.E. de Spirlet	AD137
F/L R.M.D. Hall	AB817	F/O C.A.B. Wallace	AB991	F/O G.E.F. Dieu	AB975
P/O C. Gosling	AB893	P/O J.A. Small	W3601	Sgt R.A. Lallemant	X4666
Sgt Watson	W3321	F/O E.L. Neal	AD253	W/C J. Rankin	W3312
Sgt Dykes	W3367	Sgt G.B. Whitney	W3452	P/O MacKenzie	W3173
		Sgt B.F. Whitson	AB863	Sgt J.E. Van Schaick	R6882
		Sgt Thompson	AD249	Lt M. Choron	W3236
				P/O I.G. Du Monceau	AD352
				F/O R.F. Malengreau	AD348

'Flotsam' Patrol – 24 November 1941 – 124 Squadron

S/L M. Duke-Woolley	BL321	F/L A.R.H. Barton	W3632	F/L T. Balmforth	W3332
Sgt W.J. Hibbert	R7343	Sgt M.P. Kilburn	W3799	Sgt A.R. Reid	AA761
Sgt Larcher	P8797	F/L J.F. Kulhanek	BL336	P/O F.H.J. Ashton	AB819
Sgt Hull	AB845	P/O R.B. Gilman	R6722	Sgt Moore	R7302

APPENDIX FOUR

Escape and Evasion

D uring 1941 two pilots who were shot down over northern France when flying with the Biggin Hill Wing managed to evade capture and eventually returned to Britain to fight again.

The first was Sgt W.G. Lockhart of 74 Squadron who failed to return from a Circus operation (No.35) on 6 July. Guy Lockhart was born at Mortlake in south London in 1916 and was educated at St Vincent's School, Eastbourne and Sevenoaks School. At the age of nineteen he joined the RAF on a short service commission in 1935 and after training at No.2 FTS was posted to 65 Squadron at Hornchurch where he flew the Gloster Gauntlet II. In 1937 he served with No.2 Air Armament School at North Coates but was the subject of a court martial for a low flying offence, one in which the AOC, who was on an inspection, was forced to throw himself to the ground. He was found guilty and as a result was thrown out of the service.

By 1939 the likelihood of war meant that the RAF needed all the pilots it could get and Lockhart was able to join the Volunteer Reserve as a Sergeant following his call-up up in September. After training he was posted to 602 Squadron before joining 74 Squadron on 29 June 1941. On 6 July the *Luftwaffe* was particularly aggressive and all RAF aircraft on operations were soon split up. Lockhart was later to claim the destruction of two Bf 109s during the dogfight but was then attacked from his rear port quarter from out of the sun. There was no warning and the first he knew of it was when the magazine in his port wing was hit by a cannon shell. This caused his cannon shells to explode and around two-thirds of the wing was blown off as a result.

His Spitfire flicked into a stable left-hand spin but the elevator controls were useless. Lockhart attempted to get out of the cockpit but was unable to do so by the slipstream, however he was eventually thrown clear when the aircraft suddenly lurched at a height of around 16,000 ft. His subsequent recollection was that he pulled the ripcord almost immediately and although the parachute opened, he found that the shroud lines were entangled around his neck. On looking up he saw that the parachute was slashed and twisted forming, in effect, two small parachutes with a twist between. This meant that he was unable to control the parachute and he was falling very much faster than he should have been. As he descended the Bf 109F that had shot him down circled around him but the pilot did not shoot.

Lockhart came down near the village of Erguy about eighteen miles east of Boulogne and was fortunate to land in the top of a tree which broke his fall, but he was knocked unconscious in the process. When he came to he found that he was on the ground still wearing his parachute harness and with the canopy caught in the tree above. He was in considerable pain as he had dislocated a knee and had a broken arm, but was able to twist his knee back into place so that he could walk

183

and was then helped by two boys who took him to a farm on the edge of the village. Shortly after arriving the farmer appeared but did not stay long and the boys warned him that he had left to try to contact the Germans.

Lockhart recalled a lecture that he had attended at Grangemouth where various recommendations were made for pilots who found themselves on their own in northern France. One of these was that they should contact the local priest but when he turned up he was drunk and merely tried to persuade Lockhart to give himself up. Despite his broken arm and injured knee he took his dinghy and set off alone with the intention of making for the coast where he hoped to be picked up by a Lysander. As he was only able to hobble along at a very slow pace he was soon overtaken by the two youngsters who had already helped him, together with another man. They eventually persuaded Lockhart to trust them and convinced him that he would be better off in the hands of the French resistance.

Although he had not seen his aircraft crash, he discovered that it had come down not too far away at Avesnes. He was concerned that it should not fall into the hands of the Germans (in particular the IFF set) so sent the boys to discover its whereabouts. They reported back later that it appeared to have hit the ground at high speed and was completely destroyed, the engine being buried several feet in the ground.

Lockhart was taken to a safe house and spent the next four weeks there during which his arm and knee healed. In that time he collected as much information as he could and was able to observe some aerodromes personally. At one point he even considered stealing a Bf 109 to get away, but some French friends told him that all aircraft on the ground were placed under an armed guard. As he also had no idea how to start one up he eventually gave up on the scheme.

When he had fully recovered from his injuries Lockhart began to make preparations for his eventual escape via Gibralter. He had been helped by Norbert Fillerin and his family who were well known within the resistance organisation and helped a large number of airmen to escape. Lockhart was eventually sent to Lille with false papers and as he spoke excellent French was able to get into conversation with a number of German pilots at the Café Belle Vue. He got the impression that they were an experienced bunch and indeed some of them wore the Iron Cross. All of the group that Lockhart conversed with were fighter pilots and they appeared to be very pleased with their Bf 109Fs, considering the latest version of the Messerschmitt to be much better than the Spitfire V.

It was in Lille that Lockhart met up with F/O D.N. Forde of 145 Squadron in whose company he was to make the long journey south. Forde had baled out after being shot down on 23 July during an offensive sweep from Tangmere and had been initially concealed in a farmhouse near Rousseauville in the Pas de Calais. On 8 August the two pilots, together with a guide, proceeded to Abbeville where they were able to use their false documentation to pass through a checkpoint and board a train for Paris. From here they travelled to Chalons and crossed the demarcation line into Vichy controlled territory on 9 August. The boundary was crossed by train with the connivance of the driver and guard who were bribed but shortly afterwards Lockhart was apprehended as they were walking over a bridge.

As the others made good their escape Lockhart was taken away for questioning which lasted for around four hours. His grasp of the French language helped once again but despite the fact that he was able to persuade his interrogators that he was Belgian, they were not entirely convinced of his story and informed him that he would be taken to Paris under armed guard for further investigation. His only

184

chance now was to get away again before he boarded the train back to Paris and by good fortune he was able to slip his guard at the railway station, eventually making his way to Marseille where he met up once again with Forde.

On 14 August Lockhart and Forde left Marseille by train for Perpignan and were met there by a Spanish guide who conducted them across the Pyrenees. By now the party had grown somewhat and included among their number was Sgt J. Mensik of 312 Squadron who had been shot down on 8 July. A week later they were stopped by police when walking along a road and arrested. Imprisonment followed in various jails before they arrived at Miranda del Ebro on 7 September. Lockhart was released for repatriation the following month and was flown back to the UK from Gibralter (together with Mensik) on 21 October, Forde having been flown home nine days before.

Shortly after his return Lockhart was posted to 138 (Special Duties) Squadron where he flew Whitleys but as a result of his experiences in France he put his name forward to be transferred to the unit's Lysander flight which involved making nocturnal flights into occupied Europe. He was commissioned in December 1941 and was then transferred to the newly formed 161 Squadron which was also tasked with flights into France. In June 1942 he was awarded a DFC and by the following month had been promoted to the rank of acting Squadron Leader (substantive Flying Officer).

On the night of 31 August/1 September he was flying a Lysander in connection with SIS Operation Boreas II when it crashed on a temporary strip near Macon in France. He was carrying two French agents at the time and the three had no alternative but to make their way to the south coast. Four days later they were evacuated from Narbonne Plage to Gibralter by a Polish-crewed felucca and although stopped by coastguards who took the Frenchmen, Lockhart made it safely to the British base where he was returned to Britain once again, this time in an aircraft of his former squadron, No.138.

Two weeks after his return Lockhart was awarded the DSO and was promoted to the substantive rank of Flight Lieutenant. His meteoric rise continued in 1943 when he was made a substantive Squadron Leader in April, however by this time he was already an acting Wing Commander and was serving in the Deputy Directorate of Intelligence which was in charge of special duty operations. Towards the end of 1943 his RAF career took another change of direction as he became a flight commander on 627 Squadron which flew Mosquito IVs as part of the Light Night Striking Force. On 1 January 1944 Lockhart took over the command of 692 Squadron, also equipped with the Mosquito, but on 24 March he was posted to 7 Squadron which was equipped with four-engined Lancaster heavy bombers.

On 27 April 1944 Guy Lockhart took off from Oakington at 2226 hrs in Lancaster III JB676 for an operation to Friedrichshafen but was shot down by a night fighter, his aircraft crashing at Reichenbach, two kilometres south-east of Lahr/Schwarzwald. Lockhart was killed together with all the other six members of his crew and they are buried at the Durnbach War Cemetary. He was awarded a bar to his DFC which was gazetted after his death on 6 June 1944.

The other pilot to make it back successfully to Britain after being shot down was twenty-six year old P/O Alex Nitelet, another of the substantial Belgian contingent in 609 Squadron having been posted in on 21 July 1941. Nitelet was taking part in his very first offensive sortie on 9 August (Circus 68), an operation which also saw the loss of W/C Douglas Bader, the Tangmere Wing Leader.

As he was new to operations Nitelet was flying as Red 2 behind his C.O. but as the squadron began weaving over France he lost contact with his colleagues whilst flying directly into the sun and ended up completely on his own. On looking around he saw another squadron of Spitfires flying slightly above him and proceeded to join up with them flying as 'Red 5'. After flying in this position for a few minutes Nitelet saw another formation of Spitfires below and noticed that there were only three aircraft in the right-hand section. He decided to join this other squadron and thus descended to take up the No.4 position.

Shortly after joining up with these aircraft a warning was issued that six Bf 109s were heading towards them and this was immediately followed by a further message that another six 109s were moving in to attack from their 2 o'clock position. These aircraft were spotted about 200 ft above and the leader of the Spitfires ordered his aircraft to turn to the right in an attempt to foil their attack. Once again Nitelet was unable to keep up with the rest of the squadron and soon found himself on his own again about 500 yards behind. Realising the danger he was now in he decided to dive away out of trouble and hope that none of the German aircraft milling around had seen him.

During the dive he noticed that his indicated airspeed was over 500 mph and only began to pull out when between 6,000 and 8,000 ft. Unfortunately no less than six Bf 109s had followed him down and during the chase these split up into two sections of three, positioning themselves to his right and left so that whichever way he turned he was covered. By the time he levelled out at 3,000 ft the 109s were very close and he was forced to turn to his left, but in doing so left himself open to attack by one of the other 109s away to his right. Although the 109 opened fire, the attack was ineffectual and his Spitfire was not hit.

By now Nitelet was flying in a left-hand turn with the six 109s circling around him in a right-hand turn. He was attacked twice more and again received no hits but his position was virtually hopeless as he was completely surrounded and unable to break free. One of the 109s then made a head-on attack which also failed in its objective but at least it allowed Nitelet to open fire as the German aircraft passed in front of him. His fire struck home and the 109 wavered in the air before diving away trailing glycol. As he was engrossed with this aircraft he was attacked from the rear and this time the fire was deadly accurate. His Spitfire was badly damaged and he was wounded in the leg, arm and face. As he was now at a very low level he had no alternative but to crash land and after side-slipping he put down in a field at Lumbres, about eighteen miles south-west of St Omer. It was a very heavy landing during which the left wing was torn off and the aircraft turned onto its back. Although he had opened the hood, it closed again during the landing and Nitelet was thrown forward to hit his head on the gunsight, briefly losing consciousness as his aircraft slid to a halt. He recovered almost immediately however and was able to climb out. As he did so he was heartened to hear from some French people who rushed to his aid that the 109 he had shot at had crashed and caught fire about two kilometres away.

The head injury that Nitelet had sustained was sufficiently serious for him to lose an eye but he was fortunate that the first people to attend the scene were able to spirit him away into the care of the French resistance. As he had not destroyed the IFF set in his aircraft he ordered one of the Frenchmen who had helped him to return to his machine but when the man did, nothing happened when he pressed the appropriate button. He then tried to set fire to the aircraft but was unsuccessful and the Spitfire was removed by the Germans the following day. By this time Nitelet was resting at the home of Vincent Ansel who was a member of Norbert Fillerin's escape organisation. He was subsequently looked after by the Fillerin family at Renty where his wounds were tended by doctors who were sympathetic to the Allied cause.

During his enforced rest period a number of other pilots passed through the house he was staying in including F/L Denis Crowley-Milling of 610 Squadron who had been shot down on 21 August when participating in Circus 84. His stay was only a brief one as he was quickly passed down the line but Nitelet got to know Sgt P.V. Bell of 602 Squadron rather better. Pat Bell had been shot down on 21 September and had suffered minor injuries as a result. When he had recovered Bell and Nitelet were moved on to join other evaders but prior to heading to Marseille the latter found that he had enough time to travel to Brussels to visit his parents.

On his return he found that the party had grown further with the inclusion of an American, P/O Oscar Coen of 71 'Eagle' Squadron. Coen had been attacking a train on 20 October during a Rhubarb operation when one of the trucks blew up with such force that the coolant system in his Spitfire was punctured by debris and he was forced to bale out. Another addition was F/L R.G.A. Barclay DFC a former Battle of Britain 'ace' with 249 Squadron. Barclay had been taking part in Circus 100B on 20 September when his 611 Squadron Spitfire was damaged during combat with Bf 109s and he had to carry out a forced landing.

The party eventually comprised thirteen evaders (four fighter pilots, three bomber aircrew and six soldiers) together with three guides who travelled by different routes, before meeting on a train to Abbeville. Their journey then took them to Paris and Tours before crossing into Vichy France and continuing to Toulouse and Marseilles. Nitelet had further treatment for his injured eye whilst in Marseilles and as a result he was taken across the Pyrenees on his own before being deposited at the British consulate in Barcelona where he met up with the other RAF evaders who had already arrived. They then travelled to Gibralter via the British embassy in Madrid and Nitelet and Coen were flown back to the UK on 25 December 1941. After his return, Nitelet paid a visit to his old squadron whereupon Frank Ziegler attempted to take some credit for his evasion. The Belgian cut him short saying 'But you didn't give me a purse that day, I had to go to Brussels to borrow from my mother' [foreign currency was supposed to be issued to pilots in the form of a purse before a sortie over occupied Europe, but many of these went missing and some, like Nitelet, claimed never to have received it in the first place. Over the course of the war it is likely that a considerable sum was lost in the general confusion of fighter operations, more often than not to the benefit of pilots!]

With the injury that he had sustained there was no chance of a return to flying but, like Lockhart before him, he was determined to return to France and use his experience as an evader, together with his continental upbringing, to help the war effort in general and others who had also suffered the misfortune of being shot down. Nitelet flew to France in a Lysander of 161 Special Duties Squadron on 28 May 1942 to become a radio operator for the Pat O'Leary (or PAO) escape line, the same organisation that had extricated him from occupied Europe the previous year.

Patrick Albert O'Leary was the assumed name of a Belgian army doctor by the name of Albert-Marie Guerisse. He had served with the Belgian army in May 1940 but had got away to the UK and later secured a naval commission as a Lieutenant-Commander. On the night of 25 April 1941 he was aboard HMS Fidelity, a 1,500 ton heavily-armed merchantman which was involved in an SOE operation to land agents on the coast of France near Perpignan. The agents were put ashore by a small landing craft but a sudden squall capsized the vessel and O'Leary was arrested when he waded ashore and was sent to St Hippolyte du Fort near Nimes.

While he was incarcerated he was introduced to Captain Ian Garrow, a Seaforth Highlander, who had been active in helping British servicemen to escape from his base at Marseilles. O'Leary managed to escape in June 1941 and began to work with Garrow and took over command of the line when the Scot was arrested by the French police in October 1941. The escape line that he organised was one of the most successful of the war and was responsible for returning around 600 personnel to the Allied cause so that they could carry on the fight. Among this number was Guy Lockhart who was one of the first to proceed down the line.

By April 1942 O'Leary was in desperate need of a radio operator who was motivated and knew what he was doing. His initial choice proved unsuitable and he was replaced by Alex Nitelet whose arrival highlighted the dangers of clandestine missions into France by night. The Lysander that was used was flown by F/L John Mott but it became bogged down in soft ground after landing and Mott was captured as he tried to set fire to it [after being imprisoned in France he managed to escape the following year when he jumped from a train as he was being moved to Germany]. Nitelet in the meantime had managed to get away without being seen and took up his duties as a radio operator in an apartment in Marseilles owned by Dr Georges Rodocanachi who had treated him the previous year. By coincidence on the night that Nitelet landed in France, Guy Lockhart was carrying out another operation which had the aim of returning Edouard Daladier, the former French Prime Minister, to the UK. In the event, Daladier did not wish to leave France and as the SOE officer who had been sent to contact him had been arrested, Lockhart had to return empty handed when he did not receive any light signals from the landing strip he had been sent to.

In addition to his radio duties Nitelet also acted as a guide during Operation Bluebottle, the evacuation of evaders by sea from St Pierre Plage near Narbonne. One of the evaders he assisted was S/L Whitney Straight of 242 Squadron who had been shot down by a flak ship during a Roadstead operation on 31 July 1941. A pre-war racing driver, he was to become the managing director of BOAC in 1947. Nitelet was also involved in the breakout of British servicemen from a French prison and their subsequent pick up by sea. Not long afterwards during a parachute drop near Nimes he was arrested with three others and imprisoned in Lyons before being moved to Chambaran. Although not in immediate danger the situation changed suddenly with the German occupation of southern France on 11 November 1942. The French commandant at Chambaran was persuaded that the Germans were likely shoot a number of the prisoners and this led to several releases including Nitelet who made his way back to Marseilles. He later spent time at Toulouse where he met up again with Ian Garrow who had been rescued from captivity, and in early 1943 the two men were taken by one of O'Leary's guides into Spain. After visiting the British consulate in Barcelona, Nitelet was flown back to Britain from Gibralter on 7 February 1943.

After the Second World War Alex Nitelet served in the Belgian Air Force and eventually retired in April 1969 with the rank of Colonel. He died on 6 January 1981.

The Great Escape

The story of the Great Escape from the PoW camp known as Stalag Luft III in 1944 is widely known thanks mainly to the feature film which was produced and directed by John Sturges and released by United Artists in 1963. It tells the true story of the audacious breakout of Allied prisoners of war by tunnel and the measures taken by the Germans for their recapture. By chance a number of pilots who had flown with the Biggin Hill Wing in 1941 were to take part in the mass escape and some were to die as a result of the decision to murder fifty of those who took part when they were apprehended.

The camp was situated 100 miles to the south-east of Berlin at Sagan in Silesia, but after the Second World War this area became part of western Poland and the town is now known as Zagan. The first prisoners of war arrived in April 1942 and over the next two years the camp grew enormously and eventually accommodated 10,000 officers. The location for the camp was chosen very carefully. Not only was it situated deep within Germany, it was built on sandy subsoil which would make tunnelling extremely hazardous as there was a high probability of excavations collapsing. In addition the yellow nature of the sandy soil meant that it would not be easy to dispose of the spoil without the guards noticing. The accommodation was also designed to make life for any would-be tunneller as difficult as possible as the floor of each nut was raised off the ground so that the underneath area could be easily inspected. Further defences included a series of microphones which were connected to a listening station to monitor for any obvious signs of underground digging.

Although the Germans went to great lengths to prevent any escapes they underestimated the ingenuity of their captives and the first breakout at Stalag Luft III occurred in October 1943 from the East compound. The escape by three British officers was also portrayed in a film, The Wooden Horse, which was released in 1950. This involved the digging of a relatively shallow tunnel, the entrance of which was hidden under a wooden vaulting horse which was big enough to house the tunneler and the excavated material. At the end of each session a cover was placed over the entrance to the tunnel and covered with dirt. Even though the apparatus was placed in exactly the same position every day the Germans never suspected that anything was amiss and the noise made by the 'gymnasts' masked that of the digging taking place below. The escape was completely successful and all three escapees made it back home.

Even while the Wooden Horse escape was being planned and implemented, others were considering a much bigger mass breakout. Three much deeper tunnels were proposed which were to extend about 30 feet below the surface of the ground so that no sound would be picked up via the microphones. These tunnels were known as 'Tom', 'Dick' and 'Harry', the construction of which was an incredible feat of engineering and improvisation. Virtually every prisoner within the camp had a skill of some sort, including a number who had mining experience. One of these was P/O (subsequently promoted to F/L) Wally Floody formerly of 401 Squadron who had been shot down on 27 October 1941 on his very first operational flight from Biggin Hill.

Floody was born at Chatham in Ontario on 28 April 1918 and grew to be tall at 6 ft 3 in with dark hair and hazel eyes. He left school early to try to get a job but this was at the time of the Great Depression and he had to travel to find work which included a spell as a cowboy in Alberta and a hard rock gold miner in northern Ontario. It was this latter occupation that was to give him the expertise to become the 'tunnel king' at Stalag Luft III. Although his mining experience would obviously be of great value it appears as though the Escape Committee were somehow led to believe that he was in fact a mining engineer, a misconception that Floody either initiated himself, or at the very least made no effort to correct, as he was desperate to escape. Even though his qualifications may not have been quite as impressive as he made out, his abilities could not be questioned and he was tireless in his efforts, both in the design and construction of the tunnels.

Although the huts were built above ground, there was the opportunity to sink a vertical shaft that could not be seen from the outside as each building had a heating stove which was placed on a base with brick and concrete foundations. The entrances to tunnels 'Tom' and 'Harry' passed through the middle of these whilst that for 'Dick' was concealed in a drain in a shower room. Unfortunately the entrance for 'Tom' was discovered by the Germans and despite the fact that 'Dick' was never found it had to be abandoned when its intended exit point was cleared of trees and used for further expansion of the camp. This left 'Harry' as the only viable alternative and its construction continued throughout 1943. The horizontal shaft was only 2 ft square although there were several larger chambers along the length of 336 ft which were used as staging posts. Wooden shoring was used to support the tunnel and every bed in the camp lost around 50–60 per cent of its boards as the tunnel progressed.

Wally Floody was concerned not only with the design of the tunnels, he also played a big part in their construction, however the sandy soil meant that digging was a highly dangerous task and on two occasions he was buried when the roof collapsed onto him. The second time he was crawling naked through a tunnel when a section caved in and trapped him. He was fortunate in that his head was close to a trap door leading to a secret shaft which meant that he was able to breath. A rescue operation was immediately set in motion and after an hour he was finally pulled to safety. The physical and psychological strains of constant tunnelling had a cumulative effect on Floody's health and towards the end he became gaunt and hollow-eyed. He was destined not to take part in the escape as the Germans knew that something was being planned and moved eighteen 'suspects', including Floody, to another camp. He was to survive the war and returned to his native Canada where he became an entrepreneur and helped to found the Royal Canadian Air Forces Prisoners of War Association. Floody acted as a technical advisor for the film The Great Escape and it is generally recognised that the character played by Charles Bronson is based on his experiences. He died in 1987.

'Harry' was eventually completed in early 1944 and it was decided that the breakout would take place on the night of 24/25 March. It was hoped that over 200 prisoners would be able to escape via the tunnel before daylight. The decision as to who would go depended to a large extent on a prisoner's ability to make it back and priority was given to officers with previous experience of escaping and those who were able to speak German or other European languages. Next in line were the prisoners who had played a significant role in the construction of the tunnel. These two groups stood the best chance of success as they were issued with false papers and clothes so that they could travel by train and hope to blend in with the mass of foreign workers that frequently travelled throughout Germany at that time. The other places on the escape were allocated by the drawing of lots. The men who filled these positions possessed false documentation that was very basic and was unlikely to pass a thorough inspection. It was understood that this group would escape entirely on foot, only travelling at night to avoid detection.

Of those chosen to take part in the escape, four were pilots who had flown with the Biggin Hill Wing in 1941 including Gordon Brettell, the former racing driver who had joined 92 Squadron in April 1941 along with Neville Duke. Following his time with the East India Squadron, Brettell was promoted to Flight Lieutenant and was posted as a flight commander to 133 Squadron, one of the three 'Eagle' squadrons made up of US volunteers. This involved a return to Biggin Hill but the unit soon moved to Great Sampford in Essex where it converted to the brand new Spitfire IX. On 26 September 1942 Brettell led the squadron as escort to B-17 Flying Fortresses of the 97th Bombardment Group who were to attack the Focke-Wulf aircraft plant at Morlaix, near Brest. With a round trip of just under 250 miles the operation should have been straightforward, but the Spitfires flew over a dense overcast and the pilots were unaware that they were being blown too far to the south by a northerly jetstream of over 100 mph.

When the rendezvous with the bombers was reached there was no sign of the B-17s who had in fact arrived twenty minutes early and had already set course for their objective. The Spitfires flew south in pursuit and eventually met up with their charges heading back towards them, having given up any hope of finding the target. Fuel was then wasted as they were forced to zigzag to stay with the bombers and after more than two hours in the air, Brettell led the squadron down through the cloud as by now they should have been approaching the south coast of England. Having descended below the overcast, a coastline was seen with a large town off to the left which was assumed to be Plymouth, but in actual fact was the well defended naval base at Brest. The German anti-aircraft crews opened up with a formidable barrage and Brettell's aircraft received a direct hit in its starboard wing, causing it to flick into a spin and giving its pilot no chance of baling out. Amazingly he survived the subsequent crash and crawled out of the wreckage with relatively minor injuries. All of 133 Squadron's other Spitfires (except one which had returned early with engine trouble) were either shot down or crash-landed, out of fuel [shortly before this incident Brettell had been awarded a DFC which was gazetted on 29 September].

After interrogation at Dulag Luft, Brettell spent time at a PoW camp at Hartmannsdorf in Saxony where he was required to spend a period in the 'cooler' following an escape attempt. While he was there the solitude inspired him to write a poem which he called 'Escape',

> If you can quit the compound undetected
> And clear your tracks nor leave the smallest trace
> And follow out the programme you've selected
> Nor lose your grasp at distance, time and place
> If you can walk at night by compass bearing

Or ride the railways by day and night
And temper your elusiveness with daring
Trusting that sometimes bluff will find a way
If you can swallow sudden sour frustration
And gaze unmoved at failure's ugly shape
Remembering as further inspiration
It was, and is, your duty to escape
If you can keep the great Gestapo guessing
With explanations only partly true
And leave them in their heart of hearts confessing
They didn't get the whole truth out of you
If you can use your 'Cooler' fortnight clearly
For planning methods wiser than before
And treat your miscalculations merely
As hints let fall by fate to teach you more
If you scheme on with patience and precision
It wasn't in a day they builded Rome
And make escape your sole ambition
The next time you attempt it – YOU'LL GET HOME

Brettell was then sent to Stalag Luft III where he became heavily involved in the camp's escape organisation, contributing to the intricate work that went into producing forged documentation. By the early summer of 1943 a new compound was nearing completion to the north of the existing accommodation and volunteer prisoners were required to grub up tree roots to clear what would become the parade ground. Recognising the possibilities for escape, Brettell decided to go along. Together with a friend, he hid in the roof of one of the huts at the end of the day's work while the others in the work party rigged the head count so that their absence went unnoticed. After dark the two got away and in three days made it as far as Stettin on the Baltic coast, only to be recaptured and sent back to endure twenty-one days in solitary confinement.

Having failed in his first attempts to escape Brettell was determined that he would take part in the mass breakout that was being planned and his valuable work as a forger, together with the experience gained on the run, led to him being one of the first to be selected. He was joined by three other Biggin Hill pilots, F/O S.Z. Krol of 74 Squadron who had been shot down on 2 July 1941, F/L H.J. Birkland of 72 Squadron who had failed to return from a sweep over northern France on 7 November 1941 and F/L Keith Ogilvie of 609 Squadron. 'Skeets' Ogilvie had been shot down and badly wounded on 4 July 1941 and was to spend the next nine months in hospital before he was fit enough to be sent to Stalag Luft III.

On the night of the escape those who had been chosen plus the others who had secured a place via the drawing of lots gathered in Hut 104 and the first prisoner to emerge from the tunnel exit was F/L Johnny Bull at 2215 hrs. To his horror he discovered that the exit was only thirty yards from the fence and was well short of the tree line. This was to slow up the numbers who could be put through the tunnel as every escaper had to wait until it was clear for him to make his way to the refuge of the forest. It had been hoped to put one man out every minute but the actual rate achieved was more like one every five minutes. There was further disruption when power was switched off due to an air raid and other problems were experienced. Several escapers took too much equipment with them and became stuck in the tunnel, while some officers who should have remained to haul others through the tunnel on the wheeled trolley that had been made, left their posts without being relieved. By 0455 hrs only eighty-seven escapers had descended into the tunnel of which seventy-six had made good their getaway. It was at this time that a sentry patrolling outside the fence discovered the exit and the next man out was arrested at gunpoint. While all this was going on Keith Ogilvie was hiding in the woods but on hearing the sound of gunfire he immediately made off and headed south.

By this time Gordon Brettell, Stanislaw Krol and Henry Birkland had already escaped and were fleeing the area as quickly as they could. Krol who was No.19 on the list of escapers, had teamed up with F/L Sydney Dowse (No.3), a former PRU Spitfire pilot. The latter had intended to go to Berlin alone where he was to stay with a contact for two weeks before moving on to Danzig, but owing to the position of the tunnel exit he came to the conclusion that the escape would be quickly discovered and changed his plans. Due to the delays in the tunnel he felt that he did not have enough time to get to the station at Sagan to catch the train to Breslau, however this train was running late and he would easily have made it had he tried. Instead Dowse and Krol went off through the woods together and spent the next twelve days walking along a route which took them from Liegnitz to Breslau and then Oels. On 5 April they were caught near Kempo which was just over the border in Poland. They were seen by a member of the Hitler Youth who alerted the Landwacht and they were taken to the local police station. At the time of their capture Dowse was wearing civilian clothes and Krol was dressed in an air force greatcoat and trousers. From the police station they were taken to a civil prison where they were put in separate cells.

Whilst in prison Krol and Dowse were interrogated separately by someone purporting to be a *Luftwaffe* officer and afterwards they were interviewed on more than one occasion by the prison governor. During one of these Dowse asked what was to happen to both of them. He was informed that Krol would be returned to Sagan but that he would be taken by the Gestapo to Berlin as he had already made four attempts to escape. On 12 April two members of the Gestapo arrived to take Dowse away, both men carrying revolvers under the left armpit. Dowse repeated the question concerning his friend and asked them if he was about to be shot, to which they replied 'Good gracious no, he is being sent back to Sagan – we can promise that'. Before he left the prison Dowse ran to Krol's cell to say goodbye and had a brief conversation with him before he was taken away.

After being interrogated in Berlin, Dowse was taken to Sachsenhausen concentration camp near Oranienberg. It was while he was being held in the Sonderlager (special camp) that he managed to escape once again (together with G/C Harry 'Wings' Day who had been one of the leading figures in the Escape Committee at Stalag Luft III) but their freedom lasted only eight hours before they were recaptured. He then spent many weeks alone in a cell and had to endure further interrogations but he was not physically abused. Along with others Dowse was moved once again to the Sonderlager on 15 February 1945 in order to prepare them for a proposed transfer to Dachau. With the end of the war he was flown back to Britain and along with other survivors of the Great Escape was debriefed fully in order that the perpetrators of the crimes associated with the breakout could be brought to justice. Despite what had been said at the prison in Breslau, Stanislaw Krol was not taken back to Sagan and was shot on 14 April. It is thought that his executioner was a Gestapo officer by the name of Lux and his body was cremated at Breslau. As far as Lux was concerned justice was to come a little earlier than for some of his compatriots as he was killed during fighting with the Russians in 1945.

Of the other escapers, those who did not have the necessary false documents to be able to travel by train stood little chance of getting very far. These included Henry Birkland, a tough, twenty-six year old Canadian who was soon recaptured near Sagan. Like many others who were apprehended he was placed in the custody of the Breslau Gestapo and was last seen alive on 31 March. He was another to be murdered by Lux, together with his immediate superior Dr Wilhelm Scharpwinkel, and his body was cremated at Liegnitz.

After emerging from the tunnel and crawling into the cover provided by the trees that surrounded the camp, Gordon Brettell met up with three RAF Flight Lieutenants, Romas Marcinkus, Henri Picard and Gilbert W. 'Tim' Walenn. These four were able to travel by train and made it as far as Danzig without arousing too much suspicion. Their luck soon ran out however and they were recaptured at Scheidemuhl and handed over to the local Gestapo. All four men were shot on 29 March probably by Hauptmann Reinholt Bruchardt who worked under Dr Venediger, the Gestapo Chief who ordered the killings. The bodies were disposed of in the crematorium at Danzig.

Having scurried away on hearing the gunfire when the tunnel was discovered, Keith Ogilvie was completely on his own as he attempted to find his way through the forest in the dark and in sub zero temperatures. He was dressed in a khaki battle dress with rank markings, khaki trousers and greatcoat (with service buttons) and a brown balaclava. He carried the usual escape equipment including maps and a PoW identity disk. Like most of the later escapers who intended to get away on foot he carried basic rations in his coat pockets. Unfortunately he did not get very far as he was spotted in the early hours of the 26th by the Landwacht who handed him over to uniformed men which he took to be the autobahn police. At first he was taken to a rest house nearby but was then driven by car to an inn at Holbau. It was here that he was joined by five more escapers and all were then transferred to the civilian jail at Sagan.

After being stripped and searched and left with nothing but their clothes they were put in a communal cell which contained around nineteen men. At about 0100 hrs on 27 March they were wakened and put into a van with SS guards and driven for about 2½ hours to another jail. Although Ogilvie had no idea where he had been taken, others informed him that they were in Gorlitz. The prisoners were held three to a cell but other than being constantly moved from one cell to another very little happened over the next two days.

On 29 March Ogilvie was taken to the Gestapo headquarters where he was questioned by an interpreter in an army uniform in the presence of a civilian and a female typist. He was asked for a number of personal details but most of the questions were in connection with the breakout, his interrogator being particularly interested in who it was that had given the order to get out. The main line of questioning concerned the tunnel itself, the length of time it had taken to complete, tools used, the number who had escaped and how the forged documents had been made. He was also asked why everyone appeared to be heading to the south (the Germans seemed to think that the escapees might be heading towards a common rendezvous). To most of these questions Ogilvie gave no reply.

At the end of the interrogation a statement was produced and translated so that Ogilvie was made aware of its contents. Although he had given little away it seemed to him to be a fair assessment of what he had said. At this point the typist spoke to the interpreter who turned to Ogilvie and informed him "The young lady says you are lucky." When asked why, he replied "You have escaped in a soldier's uniform, therefore you will be tried before a military court – the others will not be so lucky." He was then returned to his cell but once again was moved on a regular basis. Because of this he came into contact with many other escapers who had been recaptured and Ogilvie later estimated that the numbers had grown to thirty-five. Henry Birkland was among these prisoners and Ogilvie was one of the last people to see him alive.

On 30 March Ogilvie saw a small group of escapers leave the jail in handcuffs under the control of civilians. This happened on other occasions (usually at night) and involved up to six men who had been collected in one cell beforehand. At the time those that were left were told that these men were being taken away for a second interrogation. On the night of the 31st Ogilvie and three other men were moved to another cell where they were told that they would be returning to Sagan. On this occasion at least the Germans were telling the truth and two days later they left the jail under the guard of three *Luftwaffe* soldiers from Stalag Luft III. On arrival back at the camp they were put in the North compound Arrest Block and after a period of confinement were returned to the main detention area where they remained until release in May 1945.

Of those who managed to escape only three were successful. Per Bergsland and Jens Muller (both Norwegian) made it to Sweden and the Dutchman, Bram van der Stok travelled through Germany, Holland, Belgium and France before crossing the border into Spain and returning to the UK via Gibralter. The breakout enraged Hitler who initially wanted all of those recaptured to be shot, but under the guidance of his closest advisors, including Goering and Keitel, his demands were modified. Even so the order went out from Himmler that fifty of the escapers were to be shot. Under normal circumstances escaped prisoners were dealt with by the civilian police, but those involved in the Great Escape were put under the control of the Gestapo. Prisoners were usually removed from their cells in groups, supposedly for further questioning, but during transit they were given the opportunity to 'stretch their legs' at a stopping off point. They were then shot 'whilst trying to escape'. As none of the fifty had been wounded during their supposed attempt to get away it was a clear sign that they had all been murdered.

When he returned to Canada in 1945 Keith Ogilvie told the story of his escape to the Canadian press and put his survival down to 'sheer luck'. The choice of who was to be murdered appears to have been carried out in a largely random fashion. It has been suggested that those of central European origin were singled out and although the list of those that were to be executed contained six Poles, two Czech pilots were among the survivors. In all, six Canadians were among the dead so Keith Ogilvie was very lucky indeed. After the war he transferred to the RCAF and flew many different types of aircraft from a B-25 Mitchell which was used to fly high-ranking officers around the country, to the Canadair Sabre jet fighter. He retired from the air force as a Squadron Leader in 1963 and died in Ottawa on 26 May 1998.

Index

Names *(Ranks as contemporary)*

Aherne, Sgt J. 114
Allen, F/O H.R. 15, 19, 26–9, 161
Archer, P/O Philip 77, 91, 94, 114, 161
Armstrong, P/O Bill 26, 36
Arnott, Sgt A.D. 53
Asselin, P/O J.E.T. 119
Aston, Sgt G.W. 74
Atkinson, P/O J.A. 58, 60–1, 71, 124, 133
Auret, Lt N.H. 2
Austeen, Lt Arne 143

Bader, W/C Douglas 9–10, 59, 113, 185
Baker, F/O Henry 62
Baker, P/O Stanley 16, 23–4, 26–7
Balfour, Harold 10
Balmforth, F/L Tommy 142
Baraldi, P/O Jimmy 39, 61
Barclay, F/L R.G.A. 187
Barker, Sgt Fred 42, 44–5
Barnham, P/O D.A. 98, 103, 114, 141, 161
Bartholomew, P/O B. 118, 123
Bartley, F/O Tony 20, 25, 36, 39, 47
Barton, F/L Tony 142, 161
Barwell, P/O Eric 42, 44–5, 64, 161
Barwell, G/C 'Dickie' 64, 86–7, 95–6, 98, 100, 161
Barwise, Lt H.B. 2–3
Beake, P/O P.H. 126–7, 161
Beecham, Sir Thomas 142
Bell, Sgt P.V. 187
Bennett, Sgt G.C. 52
Bergsland, F/L Per 195
Birkland, P/O H.J. 139, 192–4
Bisdee, F/L John 31, 52, 56, 60–2, 67, 71, 75, 83, 93, 98, 104
Bishop, P/O N.E. 140
Blakeslee, P/O Don 135, 143–4, 145, 161–2
Bocock, P/O Eric 92, 110, 112, 116, 125, 162
Bodie, P/O C.A.W. 15, 21, 23, 26, 29, 162
Boulding, P/O Roger 18, 53, 57, 72, 162
Bowen-Morris, Sgt Hugh 21, 26, 56, 70, 77
Boyd, Sgt R.J. 66, 74, 96, 104, 162
Bramble, Sgt K.W. 100
Brand, AVM Sir C.J.Q. 3, 9

Breckon, Sgt G.F. 99
Brettell, P/O Gordon 46, 114, 119, 123, 191–4
Brown, F/Sgt F.S. 3
Bruce, P/O Tony 119, 130
Brunier, F/L 50
Bull, F/L Johnny 192
Burgon, P/O W.K. 69
Bushell, S/L C. 155
Byrne, P/O V.G. 17

Campbell, F/L 145
Carlson, F/L Don 73–4, 86, 90, 162
Carpenter, Sgt J.C. 85, 99, 110
Carter, Sgt L.R. 89
Casey, Sgt A.J. 94
Chadwick, Air Mechanic 2
Chandler, Sgt 42
Chesters, P/O Peter 25–6, 47
Chestnut, Sgt Guy 67, 72
Choron, Lt Maurice 98, 105, 109, 124, 133, 136, 138, 167
Churches, P/O Wally 18, 33, 36, 49
Churchill, Winston 91
Clive, P/O D. 119
Coen, P/O Oscar 187
Cole, Sgt J.E. 73
Cook, Sgt Harry 16, 23
Corbin, Sgt Jimmy 17
Coward, Noel 52, 122
Cox, Sgt H 118, 123, 131–2, 135
Crook, Sgt 43
Cropper, P/O D.L. 98, 111
Crowley-Milling, F/L D. 187
Curchin, F/L Johnnie 31, 39, 51, 54–5, 65–6, 72, 104

Dales, Sgt W.P. 38–9
Davies, F/O J.W.E. 3
Day, G/C Harry 193
de Goat, F/O William 78–9, 91, 142
de Grunne, P/O Rodolphe 60, 62
de Hemptinne, P/O Baudouin 72, 98, 103, 111, 113, 162
de la Torre, S/L 132
de Montbron, Adj Xavier 37, 39, 68
de Selys, P/O J. 133
de Spirlet, P/O Francois 49, 64–5, 67, 71, 76, 111, 134, 162
Dickie, Lt 1

Dieu, F/O G.E.F. 126, 133–4
Dougall, P/O Don 77, 96, 165
Dowding, ACM Sir Hugh 7–11
Dowse, F/L Sydney 193
Duff, Sgt F.A. 146
Duke, P/O Neville 46, 51, 59, 79, 108–9,
   112, 129, 162, 191
Duke-Woolley, S/L Myles 142, 145–6, 162
Du Monceau, P/O Yvan 49, 52, 96, 105,
   113, 126, 133, 162–3
Dykes, Sgt 140

Edge, Sgt N.H. 130
Endersby, Sgt P. 42–3
Enright, Sgt E.G. 145
Evans, Sgt G. 91, 136

Falkiner, Sgt F. 125, 137
Ferguson, Sgt J.K. 146
Fisher, P/O W. 165
Floody, P/O C.W. 137
Fokes, P/O Ronnie 20, 24, 26, 39–40, 50,
   163, 190
Folkard, Sgt M.C. 98
Forbes, S/L Athol 15, 18, 163
Forde, F/O D.N. 184–5
Fordham P/O L.B. 98
Fraser, Rt Hon Peter 95
Freeborn, F/L Johnnie 17, 22, 26, 36, 48,
   57, 163
Freese, Sgt L.E. 24
Furnival, Lt J.M. 2

Galloway, Sgt 138
Gardner, Sgt R.W. 140
Garrow, Capt Ian 188
Gash, Sgt Fred 42–5
Gaskell, Sgt 49
Gauthier, Sgt 133
Gibbons, Caroll 52
Gilman, P/O R.B. 144
Gilroy, S/L G.K. 103, 105, 107, 121,
   125–6, 136–8, 163
Gleed, W/C Ian 165
Glendinning, Sgt John 18, 35–6
Godefroy, P/O Hugh 135, 145–6
Godlewski, F/O J.M. 94
Golden, Sgt C.R. 143
Greenfield, Sgt W. 132
Gribble, F/L George 65
Grice, G/C Richard 3–5
Grisdale, Sgt P.T. 117

Hagyard, Sgt 145
Halahan, P/O 37
Harris, AM Sir Arthur 147
Harrison, Sgt C.L. 94,

Harrison, Sgt Stan 89, 108, 114
Havercroft, Sgt Ralph 21, 80–1, 163
Hayden, Sgt L.H. 42–3, 45
Henderson, Cpl Elspeth 5
Henderson, Sgt W.G. 87
Hickman, Sgt G.P. 125
Hilken, Sgt Clive 82
Hill, P/O Sydney 32, 49, 51–2, 55, 57–8,
   64–6, 72
Hodgkinson, Sgt B.G. 137
Holland, F/O Bob 19, 39, 163
Howard, Sgt C.H. 101–2
Howard, P/O John 48, 53
Howell, F/L F.J. 32
Hughes, P/O Desmond 41–5, 163
Hughes-Rees, Sgt J.A. 32, 54–5, 71, 84,
   93, 163
Hulton-Harrop, P/O M.L. 17
Humphreys, P/O P.H. 89
Hunt, Sgt Douglas 16

Ingham, Sgt Bernard 144
Ingham, AC2 37

Johnson, G/C J.E. 11
Johnston, Sgt Walter 89, 102, 114–6,
   120–2, 126–7, 130–2, 135, 156, 164
Johnstone, S/L Norman 135

Kendal, P/O John 16
Kent, S/L Johnny 18–19, 24, 29, 34, 164
Kenwood, Sgt 118
Kerr, Deborah 20
Kershaw, P/O Tony 37
Kingaby, Sgt Don 21–2, 29, 58–9, 76–7,
   85, 89, 92, 94–5, 105–6, 109, 122–3,
   129–132, 135, 164
Kingcome, F/L Brian 19, 34, 48–9, 68,
   70–1, 101–2, 164
Kosinski, F/L K. 117, 164
Krol, F/O S.Z. 192–3
Kulhanek, F/L Jaroslav 143–4, 164

Lacey, Sgt J.H. 102
Laing, Sgt K. 133
Lamberton, Sgt W. 97
Levesque, Sgt Omer 135, 143–4, 164
Lewis, Sgt R.F. 99
Le Cheminant, Sgt Jerrold 37, 78, 108, 164
Leigh, Vivien 122
Leigh-Mallory, AVM Trafford 7, 9–11, 30,
   55, 88, 147, 150, 154–5, 159
Lillie, Beatrice 52
Lloyd, Sgt David 24, 48–9, 85, 96
Lockhart, Sgt W.G. 89, 183–5, 188
Lund, F/L Tommy 109, 123, 130
Lyle, F/L 58

Macdonald, F/L Peter 10
Macneal, Moira 19
Macneal, Sheila 19
MacKenzie, P/O P. 66, 104
MacSherry, Sgt P.M.A. 39
Maithew, Sgt 23
Maitland-Thompson, P/O Sebastian 27, 51, 56
Malan, W/C Adolph 17, 24, 26, 29–30, 36, 46, 58–60, 67, 73–4, 76–80, 82–3, 86–9, 100–1, 103, 122, 129, 164–5
Malengreau, P/O Roger 49, 84, 97, 124, 136
Marcinkus, F/L Romas 194
Martin, Sgt 44–5
Masterman, S/L Cedric 139, 144
Maxwell, P/O D.A. 29
Meares, S/L Stanley 82, 88, 165
Mensik, Sgt J. 185
Mercer, Sgt Bob 39, 54–5
Merrett, Sgt J.G. 125
Michelmore, S/L E.J.C. 25
Mildren, P/O P.R. 27
Milne, S/L R.M. 122, 126, 133–4, 165
Morrison, Sgt Don 135, 143–5, 165
Morrison, Sgt Neil 33
Mortimer, Sgt Elizabeth 4
Mortimer-Rose, F/L E.B. 163
Mott, F/L John 188
Mottram, P/O Roy 20–21, 49, 53, 165
Mould, P/O Tony 18, 73, 165
Muller, P/O J. 105
Muller, F/L Jens 195
Mungo-Park, S/L John 18, 30, 36, 65, 69, 81–2

Nash, Sgt P. 98, 111, 113, 133, 139, 165
Neal, F/L E.L. 137, 144
Newton, F/O R.B. 110
Nitelet, P/O Alex 110, 185–8
Northcott, Sgt Geoff 135

Offenberg, F/L 'Pyker' 72, 74, 81, 90, 98–9, 104–5, 114, 124, 126, 133, 138, 165
Ogilvie, F/O Keith 31, 37, 49, 52, 58, 61, 63, 67, 71, 74–5, 81, 83, 87–8, 137, 192–5
Olivier, Lawrence 122
Olver, P/O Peter 16, 23, 29, 165
Ormston, P/O Ian 136, 143
Ortmans, P/O Christian 136
Ortmans, F/O Vicki 49, 51, 58, 60, 62, 65–6, 71, 76, 78, 81, 84, 98, 113–4, 123, 126, 133, 136, 165
Overton, F/L Charles 31–2

Oxspring, F/L Bobby 15, 26, 29, 161, 165–6
Palmer, Sgt A.G. 54–5, 58, 71, 97, 101, 119, 123, 136
Park, AVM Keith 7, 9–11
Parkes, P/O H.F. 72
Parsons, Sgt Claude 16, 29
Patten, Sgt J.R. 145
Payne, Sgt A.D. 25
Payne, Sgt William 68, 71, 78–80, 166
Peirse, AM Sir Richard 104, 147–8
Phillips, P/O E.W.H. 115
Picard, F/L Henri 194
Pickering, P/O John 15, 29, 166
Pietrasiak, Sgt Adolf 66, 86–7, 93–4, 117, 166
Pollard, Sgt E.W. 98, 113, 115
Pope, Sgt C.S. 146
Port, Sgt K.G. 130
Portal, ACM Sir Charles 10, 148
Poulton, P/O Bob 36, 86, 166
Preston, Kath 19
Preston, Teddy 19

Rankin, W/C Jamie 29, 34, 37, 39, 48–50, 67–70, 73–4, 77, 80, 91, 93, 106–8, 111–2, 118, 122–3, 126, 130, 134, 136, 138–9, 141, 144–5, 154, 156, 166
Ream, Sgt 26
Richey, F/L Paul 31, 55–8, 60, 65, 81, 83–4, 91, 93, 95–6, 100–1, 106–7, 110, 166
Rigler, Sgt Tommy 32, 54–5, 66, 75, 79, 101, 136, 166
Robinson, W/C Michael 30, 32, 49, 54–5, 60–1, 63–5, 67, 71–2, 83–4, 93, 95–9, 101, 103, 106–7, 113–4, 122, 166–7
Roff, Sgt E.H. 115–6
Rogowski, Sgt Jan 33, 48, 167
Rose, P/O F.C. 17
Rosser, Sgt Jimmy 92, 117, 144
Rowthorn, Sgt W. 146
Rutherford, Sgt J. 116

Sanders, S/L Arthur 41, 44, 167
Sanders, P/O W.B. 125
Sandman, P/O W.J. 62, 69, 76, 81
Saunders, P/O Cecil 20, 26, 49
Scarborough, P/O R.O. 165
Scott, W/C D.R. 155
Seghers, P/O Eugene 49, 51, 95, 167
Sheen, S/L Desmond 91, 100, 112, 116, 139, 167
Sholto Douglas, ACM Sir William 7, 10–11, 91, 104, 147–152, 159
Shute, S/L Freddie 19

Sika, Sgt Jaroslav 100, 167
Sinclair, Sir Archibald 47
Skalski, F/O H. 116
Skalski, F/O M. 98
Skinner, Sgt Bill 18, 49, 89
Small, P/O J.A. 137
Smigielski, Sgt Jan 98
Smith, Sgt A.H. 25, 39
Smith, P/O 36
Soden, G/C Frank 22, 30, 32, 46–7
Sowrey, Major Fred 2
Sprague, F/O H.A. 144
Spurdle, P/O Bob 18, 25, 35–6, 38–9, 47, 167
Squire, Sgt H. 34
Stephen, F/L Harbourne 18, 36
Stewart, Sgt 69
Stewart-Clark, F/L D. 125
Stockman, Lt Edgar 2
Stone, Sgt Cedric 92, 111–2, 167
Straight, S/L Whitney 188
Stuart, Sgt C. 91
Sutton, P/O F.C. 44
Szczesniewski, S/L W. 155

Thomas, F/L Sam 45
Thomson, F/L J.A. 102
Thompson, Sgt C.L.A. 145
Thompson, Sgt S.L. 137
Thorn, Sgt Ted 42, 44–5, 167
Todd, Sgt C.G. 89
Trenchard, Lord 96, 111
Trott, Sgt G.F. 90
Tuck, W/C R.S. 145–6
Turner, Lt E.E. 2–3
Turner, Sgt Helen 5

Van Arenberg, P/O L. 133
Van der Stok, F/L Bram 195
Van Lierde, P/O Willi 49–50, 58, 66
Van Ryneveld, Pierre 9
Van Schaick, Sgt J.E. 98, 100, 126, 139, 167–8

Wade, P/O Trevor 20, 39–40, 49, 55, 70, 74, 78, 168
Waldern, Sgt C.G. 94–5, 99
Walenn, F/L G.W. 'Tim' 194
Wallace, F/O C.A.B. 136–7
Warner, Jack 122
Watling, P/O Bill 27
Watson-Watt, Robert 8
Weir, F/O J. 140
Wellum, P/O Geoff 20, 40, 79, 94, 168
Welsh, P/O Terry 42–3
White, Sgt D.R. 140
Whitney, Sgt G.B. 137, 145

Whitson, Sgt B.F. 136
Wilczewski, S/L W. 155
Wilkin, Sgt 43
Wilkins, Arnold 8
Willcocks, Sgt P.H. 15
Williams, P/O 42
Wilmet, P/O Bob 49, 58
Wilson, Sgt A.F. 53
Wimperis, H.E. 7
Wood, S/L P.A. 35, 39
Woods-Scawen, Sgt G.E. 131–2, 135
Wright, F/L Allan 19, 23, 49, 68, 79–81, 168
Wylde, Sgt 23, 26

Yorke, Sgt R.W. 70

Ziegler, F/O Frank 32, 51, 54–5, 57, 60, 72, 75, 136, 142, 187

German/Luftwaffe

Adolph, Hptm Walter 111

Babenz, Obfw Emil 140
Balthasar, Hptm Wilhelm 86, 157
Borris, Lt Karl 110
Bruchardt, Hptm Reinholt 194
Buhligen, Oblt Kurt 164

Dirksen, Uffz Hans 137

Ebersberger, Oblt Kurt 67
Ewald, Uffz Otto 73

Falkinger, Fw Wolfgang 80
Frohner, Uffz Erich 97

Galland, Obstlt Adolf 137, 157
Gottschlich, Fw Walter 26
Greisert, Hptm Karl-Heinz 157
Grundmann, Fw Gerhardt 55

Hahn, Hptm Hans 'Assi' 157
Heger, Lt Julius 55
Helmholz, Lt Gottfried 137
Hess, Rudolf 60
Hetzel, Uffz Werner 117
Hufenreuther, Hptm Albert 57

Kern, Uffz Karlheinz 155
Kosse, Lt Wolfgang 117

Leie, Oblt Erich 164
Lindemann, Oblt Otto 155

Marseille, Oblt Hans-Joachim 167
Mayer, Oblt Egon 157
Mayer, Hans Ferdinand 156
Menge, Lt Robert 69
Molders, Major Werner 16, 36, 54–5
Moller, Fw Friedrich 48
Muncheberg, Oblt Joachim 117, 155, 157

Neumann, Lt Erdmann 72

Oesau, Hptm Walter 157

Pflanz, Oblt Rudolf 157
Pingel, Hptm Rolf 98
Poopel, Lt Gunther 55
Pones, Lt Karl 55
Priller, Oblt Josef 88, 97, 99, 137, 157

Richter, Uffz Heinz 139
Rudorffer, Lt Erich 157

Scharpwinkel, Dr Wilhelm 194
Schauder, Lt Paul 132
Schinabeck, Fw Ignaz 144
Schmidt, Lt Johannes 137
Seegatz, Oblt 117
Seifert, Hptm Johanes 132, 157

Sprick, Oblt Gustav 'Micky' 157
Struck, Fw Gunther 50

Tank, Kurt 127
Thorn, Lt Walter 144
Tilly, Ofw Hans 90

Venediger, Dr 194
von Uiberacker, Lt Friedrich Graf 140

Weber, Fw Gottfried 144
Westphal, Oblt Hans-Jurgon 72

Zimmer, Uffz Werner 51

French/Belgian

Ansel, Vincent 187

Daladier, Edouard 188

Fillerin, Norbert 184, 187

Guerisse, Albert-Marie 187–8

Rodocanachi, Dr Georges 188